Great Treatise on the Stages of Mantra

(sngags rim chen mo)

(Critical Elucidation of the Key Instructions in All the Secret Stages of the Path of the Victorious Universal Lord, Great Vajradhara)

Chapters XI–XII

The Creation Stage

By Tsong Khapa Losang Drakpa

TREASURY OF THE BUDDHIST SCIENCES series

The American Institute of Buddhist Studies (AIBS), in affiliation with the Columbia University Center for Buddhist Studies and Tibet House US, has established the Treasury of the Buddhist Sciences series to provide authoritative English translations, studies, and editions of the texts of the Tibetan Tengyur (*bstan 'gyur*) and its associated literature. The Tibetan Tengyur is a vast collection of over 3,600 classical Indian Buddhist scientific treatises (*śāstra*) written in Sanskrit by over 700 authors from the first millennium CE, now preserved mainly in systematic 7th–12th century Tibetan translation. Its topics span all of India's "outer" arts and sciences, including linguistics, medicine, astronomy, socio-political theory, ethics, art, and so on, as well as all of her "inner" arts and sciences such as philosophy, psychology ("mind science"), meditation, and yoga.

The present work is contained in a related series comprised of the Collected Works of Tsong Khapa Losang Drak pa (bLo bZang Grags pa, 1357–1419) and His Spiritual Sons, Gyaltsap (rGyal Tshab) Darma Rinchen (1364–1432) and Khedrup Gelek Pelsang (mKhas Grub dGelegs dPal bZang, 1385–1438), a collection known in Tibetan as rJey Yab Sras gSung 'Bum. This collection also could be described as a voluminous set of independent treatises and supercommentaries, all based on the thousands of works contained in the Kangyur and Tengyur Collections.

THE DALAI LAMA

Letter of Support

The foremost scholars of the holy land of India were based for many centuries at Nālandā Monastic University. Their deep and vast study and practice explored the creative potential of the human mind with the aim of eliminating suffering and making life truly joyful and worthwhile. They composed numerous excellent and meaningful texts. I regularly recollect the kindness of these immaculate scholars and aspire to follow them with unflinching faith. At the present time, when there is great emphasis on scientific and technological progress, it is extremely important that those of us who follow the Buddha should rely on a sound understanding of his teaching, for which the great works of the renowned Nālandā scholars provide an indispensable basis.

In their outward conduct the great scholars of Nālandā observed ethical discipline that followed the Pāli tradition, in their internal practice they emphasized the awakening mind of *bodhichitta*, enlightened altruism, and in secret they practised Tantra. The Buddhist culture that flourished in Tibet can rightly be seen to derive from the pure tradition of Nālandā, which comprises the most complete presentation of the Buddhist teachings. As for me personally, I consider myself a practitioner of the Nālandā tradition of wisdom. Masters of Nālandā such as Nāgārjuna, Āryadeva, Āryāsaṅga, Dharmakīrti, Candrakīrti, and Śāntideva wrote the scriptures that we Tibetan Buddhists study and practice. They are all my gurus. When I read their books and reflect upon their names, I feel a connection with them.

The works of these Nālandā masters are presently preserved in the collection of their writings that in Tibetan translation we call the Tengyur (*bstan 'gyur*). It took teams of Indian masters and great Tibetan translators over four centuries to accomplish the historic task of translating them into Tibetan. Most of these books were later lost in their Sanskrit originals, and relatively few were translated into Chinese. Therefore, the Tengyur is truly one of Tibet's most precious treasures, a mine of understanding that we have preserved in Tibet for the benefit of the whole world.

Keeping all this in mind I am very happy to encourage a long-term project of the American Institute of Buddhist Studies, originally established by the late Venerable Mongolian Geshe Wangyal and now at the Columbia University Center for Buddhist Studies, and Tibet House US, to translate the Tengyur into English and other modern languages, and to publish the many works in a collection called *The Treasury of the Buddhist Sciences*. When I recently visited Columbia University, I joked that it would take those currently working at the Institute at least three "reincarnations" to complete the task; it surely will require the intelligent and creative efforts of generations of translators from every tradition of Tibetan Buddhism, in the spirit of the scholars of Nālandā, although we may hope that using computers may help complete the work more quickly. As it grows, the *Treasury* series will serve as an invaluable reference library of the Buddhist Sciences and Arts. This collection of literature has been of immeasurable benefit to us Tibetans over the centuries, so we are very happy to share it with all the people of the world. As someone who has been personally inspired by the works it contains, I firmly believe that the methods for cultivating wisdom and compassion originally developed in India and described in these books preserved in Tibetan translation will be of great benefit to many scholars, philosophers, and scientists, as well as ordinary people.

I wish the American Institute of Buddhist Studies at the Columbia Center for Buddhist Studies and Tibet House US every success and pray that this ambitious and far-reaching project to create *The Treasury of the Buddhist Sciences* will be accomplished according to plan. I also request others, who may be interested, to extend whatever assistance they can, financial or otherwise, to help ensure the success of this historic project.

May 15, 2007

Great Treatise on the Stages of Mantra

(*sngags rim chen mo*)

(Critical Elucidation of the Key Instructions in All the Secret Stages of the Path of the Victorious Universal Lord, Great Vajradhara)

Chapters XI–XII

The Creation Stage

By Tsong Khapa Losang Drakpa

INTRODUCTION AND TRANSLATION
by
Thomas Freeman Yarnall

Edited by Robert A.F. Thurman

Treasury of the Buddhist Sciences series
Tengyur Translation Initiative
Complete Works of Jey Tsong Khapa and Sons collection

Published by
The American Institute of Buddhist Studies
Columbia University Center for Buddhist Studies
Tibet House US

New York
2013

Treasury of the Buddhist Sciences series
Tengyur Translation Initiative
Complete Works of Jey Tsong Khapa and Sons collection
A refereed series published by:

American Institute of Buddhist Studies
Columbia University
80 Claremont Avenue, room 303
New York, NY 10027

http://www.aibs.columbia.edu

Co-published with Columbia University's Center for Buddhist Studies and Tibet House US

Distributed by Columbia University Press

Printed in the United States of America on acid-free paper.

23 22 21 20 19 18 17 16 15 14 13 5 4 3 2 1

ISBN 978-1-935011-01-9 (cloth)

Library of Congress Cataloging-in-Publication Data

Tson-kha-pa Blo-bzan-grags-pa, 1357-1419.
[Snags rim chen po. Chapter 11-12. English]
Great treatise on the stages of mantra (Sngags rim chen mo) : (critical elucidation of the key instructions in all the secret stages of the path of the victorious universal lord, Great Vajradhara) : chapters XI-XII, the creation stage / by Tsong Khapa Losang Drakpa ; introduction and translation by Thomas Freeman Yarnall ; edited by Robert A.F. Thurman.
pages cm. -- (Treasury of the Buddhist sciences)
Includes translation into English from Tibetan.
Includes bibliographical references and index.
ISBN 978-1-935011-01-9 (cloth : alk. paper)
1. Tantric Buddhism--Early works to 1800. 2. Spiritual life--Dge-lugs-pa (Sect)--Early works to 1800. I. Yarnall, Thomas F. II. Thurman, Robert A. F. III. Title.
BQ7950.T754S5713 2013
294.3'923--dc23

2013002079

This book is dedicated to
H.H. the Dalai Lama and the people of Tibet

and to the fond and inspirational memory of
Ven. Pema Losang Chögyen
(1957–1996)

Contents

Part Two: Annotated English Translation

Appendixes

Glossary

Selected Bibliographies

Indexes

Series Editor's/Editor's Preface

Homage to Vajrasattva!
Homage to Jey Tsong Khapa Losang Drakpa!

I am delighted to welcome to the *Complete Works of Jey Tsong Khapa and Sons* sub-series of our *Treasury of the Buddhist Sciences* series Thomas Yarnall's excellent study of the creation stage chapters of Tsong Khapa's master *Great Treatise on the Stages of Mantra* (to refer to it by its nickname, *sngags rim chen mo*), soon to be followed by the perfection stage chapters.

In 1970–1971, I spent a year in India with the American Institute of Indian Studies, working on a translation and study of Tsong Khapa's *Essence of True Eloquence, Differentiating the Interpretable and Definitive Meanings of the Buddha's Discourses*. During that year I had the privilege and pleasure of working closely on the Tibetan edition of that text in frequent meetings with His Holiness the Dalai Lama. I was given excellent instruction in the difficult points and deeper meanings of Buddhist Central Way hermeneutical thought. When I had to leave India, His Holiness charged me to take up the responsibility to see to the translation of the *Complete Works of Jey Tsong Khapa and Sons*. He specially requested me to follow my *Essence of True Eloquence* translation by working with the Abbot of the Gyuto Tantric University, the late Venerable Tara Tulku, to translate the *Great Treatise on the Stages of Mantra*. I earnestly resolved to do so, in spite of the fact that His Holiness' senior teacher, the Ganden Throne-holder Kyabjey Lingtsang Rinpochey, transmitter to me of various *Esoteric Community* teachings, was strongly opposed to the general publication of such works, once mentioning specifically this *Great Treatise on the Stages of Mantra* as not to be widely disseminated, though he allowed that if His Holiness, wanted it done, he had to approve, in spite of his misgivings!

Though I enthusiastically committed to undertake the immense task, still, as fate would have it, for year and years, too many other responsibilities and duties prevented me from fulfilling His Holiness' request. Most fortunately, my friend and colleague Professor Jeffrey Hopkins stepped into the breach and did fine translations of the first fifth of the work, covering in three volumes Tsong Khapa's treatments of the keys of the practices of the Action, Performance, and Yoga Tantra classes. Then again, after I moved to Columbia University, Dr. Thomas Yarnall, our present author and translator, undertook the chapters on the creation and perfection stages of the Unexcelled Yoga Tantra class, initially as his doctoral dissertation project and now with the publications at hand. I am therefore very much relieved that Dr. Yarnall's meticulous and sustained effort has come to such a beneficial fruition, bringing the original request for the entire work that much closer to fulfillment.

I will leave the detailed introduction of the creation stage text below to Dr. Yarnall. I would like, however, to point out what I consider a remarkable thing about Tsong Khapa's treatment of the creation stage of the Unexcelled Yoga Tantra, an insight which I was very much pleased to learn from reading Dr. Yarnall's dissertation, *The Emptiness that is Form* (which will emerge further developed as an independent treatise in the following year). From Tsong Khapa's biography, we learn that his inspiring angel, the wisdom bodhisattva Mañjushrī, instructed him during his time of deep study that his special mission as a practitioner and teacher would be to pay special attention to the subtleties of the relative, conventional reality, balancing the profound insights of his important predecessor, the seventh CE century Indian master sage, Chandrakīrti, focusing on the critical exploration of ultimate reality. In the exoteric philosophical literature, Tsong Khapa carried out that inspiration by bringing the sophisticated logical and epistemological sciences developed by the Indian sages Dignāga and Dharmakīrti into coordination with the critical philosophy focused on voidness or emptiness of the most advanced Centrist (Madhyamaka) cultivation of transcendent wisdom. He further expressed the nonduality of the transcendent wisdom of voidness through his deeply compassionate engagement with the relativities of ethics, education, social development, spiritual art, and scientific progress, thereby initiating the powerful social movement—which I call the "Ganden Renaissance"—that transformed Tibet.

Dr. Yarnall took this perspective on Tsong Khapa's core contribution in the exoteric sphere and applied it, quite originally, in a brilliant new direction, showing how it affected Tsong Khapa's personal practice of and public instruction in the esoteric teachings of the Tantra. At the highest level of the Unexcelled Yoga Tantras, the perfection stage yogas represent the most spectacular practices of Tantric practitioners seeking ultimate attainment, the great adepts (I like to call them "psychonauts") of India and Tibet who tended to hurl themselves into the vast spaces of ultimate reality, meeting there the indivisible enlightened minds of all enlightened beings. But foundational for them are the creation stage yogas, which are essential for growing the body of each individual buddha, involving compassionate concern about the arrangements of relative, conventional reality, as they mandate sustained, detailed, careful, imaginative, artistic creation of the intricately detailed divine identities, embodiments, and environments of the exquisite mandalas deployed in the Tantras. Since Tsong Khapa noticed that in both India and Tibet there was a tendency to rush toward the ultimate, he fulfilled his mandate from Mañjushrī by insisting on understanding, implementing, and facilitating others to implement, a flawless and comprehensive practice of the creation stage, without which the embarking on the perfection stage yogas would be premature, reckless, and even dangerous. So just as Tsong Khapa's exoteric philosophical achievement was to refine his contemporaries' and successors' understanding of the ordinary relativity of conventional reality of logic, epistemology, ethics, and other arts and sciences, his technological achievement was to refine their understanding of the extraordinary relativity of the extraordinary conventions of the esoteric mandalas, visionary yogas, and profound psychic adventures into the deepest zones of death, between state, and birth, through terror and bliss.

So now this second aspect of Tsong Khapa's central mandate has been elucidated by our present author with great originality and solid scholarship. Its root in Tsong Khapa's major esoteric work is presented in this volume, and the detailed implications of this insight are very well laid out in Dr. Yarnall's forthcoming companion volume, *The Emptiness that is Form*.

A related important historical point worth mention is how this should improve modern scholarship's understanding of the life contribution of Tsong Khapa. There is a stereotype still out there that he was mainly a scholastic master, a kind of Buddhist "academic," as well as a monastic reformer, a kind of puritanical monkish sort, and not a great practitioner or yogī saint, such as Milarepa or any of the other more colorful luminaries in the Tibetan firmament. To the contrary, one of his major innovations in Tibetan history was his founding of Tantric monasteries devoted to Unexcelled Yoga Tantra practice and performance, beginning with the Gyumay Tantric monastic college in Lhasa and the Tantric college in his Ganden monastery on Nomad mountain. His *Great*

Treatise on the Stages of Mantra was written precisely to provide the keys for the training curriculum of those specialized monasteries; as he himself states in a passage below, he gives in it all the key vital instructions for practical implementation of the most important steps on the path of development taught in the ocean of Tantric literature, filled with profound root texts and complex systematic technical treatises. Seen in the light of this work, therefore, Tsong Khapa can be clearly perceived to have been a master teacher of advanced meditational practice; since he made the successful performance of the unexcelled yogas of the most far-reaching Tantras accessible to a much larger cohort of practitioners than had ever enjoyed such access previously in Indian or Tibetan history. This then explains the phenomenal success of his movement over the next several centuries, without significant political backing, as witnessed by the explosion of monastic university building throughout the Tibetan world, satisfying the expanding demand of Tibetans of all walks of life for facilities for ethical, philosophical, and spiritual learning and training.

Finally, in regard to the ever-looming issue of publishing anything at all about the esoteric Tantras, held for millennia in strict secrecy in many societies, as I have said before, our venture follows the authorization and reasoning of His Holiness the Dalai Lama; that misunderstanding of Tantra already abounds widely among both Buddhists and non-Buddhists, and so it is necessary to be fully transparent about the authentic teachings. Some esoteric secrets keep themselves: they are incredible to some, incomprehensible to others, and often are approached as the romantic fantasy or science fiction of a far away ancient culture. Further, a determined researcher will find almost anything nowadays, if they look hard enough. Thus, it is our hope and intention in publishing this book (and other books giving authentic information about the highest Tantras) that people should find accurate clarification about the amazing "mental" or "inner" sciences and technologies of the Indian and Tibetan masters, the scientists and yogī/nīs of the Unexcelled Yoga Tantras of Universal Vehicle Buddhism!

We have many people to thank—First of all the Tibetan and Mongolian scholar lamas who opened the treasury of the Tantras and their literature: the late Venerable Geshe Ngawang Wangyal; the late Kyabjey Lingtsang Rinpochey; His Holiness the Dalai Lama; the late Venerable Tara Tulku Rinpochey; the late Eminence, Serkhong Tsenshab Rinpochey;

the late Professor Masatoshi Nagatomi; Dr. Lozang Jamspal. I proudly and heartily thank the present author, Dr. Thomas Yarnall, for his sustained and insightful labor of love in researching, introducing, translating, and annotating this amazing and extremely important text.

Lastly, among the many generous benefactors of the American Institute of Buddhist Studies over forty years, I must especially thank the anonymous benefactor of the Jey Tsong Khapa Endowment of the Columbia University Department of Religion's Center for Buddhist Studies; Mr. Joel McCleary for his generous hclp and steady encouragement; Ms. Lavinia Currier of the Sacharuna Foundation, whose generous donations and grants enabled the work at a crucial time to advance to the penultimate stage; to Mr. Marc Benioff and Mrs. Lynne Benioff for their generous, world-changing support; and Mr. William T. Kistler, Mrs. Eileen Kistler, and Mr. Brian Kistler of the Kistler Foundation for their visionary recognition that amid the many crises and catastrophes afflicting the multitudes of suffering beings around the world, the recovery and translation needed to open the door for the modern mind to the inner or spiritual science of the Buddhist tradition remains a high priority for the awakening of humanity; perhaps essential to empower us to rise to the challenges we all face together at this critical planetary moment.

Robert A.F. Thurman (Ari Genyen Tenzin Choetrak)

Jey Tsong Khapa Professor of Indo-Tibetan Buddhist Studies,
Columbia University;
President, American Institute of Buddhist Studies;
Director, Columbia Center for Buddhist Studies;
President, Tibet House US.

Ganden Dekyi Ling
Woodstock, New York
November 10, 2012 CE
Tibetan Royal Year 2139, Year of the Iron Tiger

Author's Acknowledgements

This translation truly has been a collaborative one, and could never have been completed without the generous assistance of more individuals and institutions than I possibly can mention here; I express my deepest, heartfelt thanks to all of them. While they all share in the credit for the production of this work, any and all remaining errors are solely my own.

First and foremost, I must make a special mention of my mentor (and now colleague and collaborator), Robert Thurman. It was he who first introduced me to the wonders of Buddhist thought and culture and to the Tibetan language over three decades ago at Amherst College. Inspiring, wise, and patient, he has been my primary guide in these studies ever since, and now has provided indispensible insight and editorial assistance in preparing the present translation.

I am very grateful to my long-time friend and colleague Christian Wedemeyer for kindly consenting to read and critique a penultimate draft of this book under a tight deadline. With impecable care and scholarly expertise he offered many invaluable suggestions; those which I had time to implement greatly improved the book. Likewise, I am grateful to Annie Bien and to Jensine Andresen for attentive copy-editing of penultimate drafts of the book.

I also would like to give a special acknowledgement to all the other superb professors with whom I was fortunate to study while in the graduate program in Religion at Columbia University, including Prof. Ryuichi Abe, Losang Jamspal, Matthew Kapstein, Wayne Proudfoot, Thomas Tanselle, Gary Tubb, Angela Zito, and many others. Also important were my first year Sanskrit teachers at the University of Washington, Prof. Collet Cox and Richard Salomon. The late Gene Smith of the Tibetan Buddhist Resource Center, Bob Chilton and Robert Taylor of the Asian Classics Input Project, and Paul Hackett of Columbia University provided me with invaluable bibliographical and technical assistance.

I also have benefited immensely from conversations and debates with many friends over the years. Special mention goes to my life-long friend Steffan Soule who always helps to "keep it real," centering all conversation and action in the moment and always moving from the heart. I have also been fortunate to engage with many gifted colleagues in recent years, including Christian Wedemeyer, David Gray, Laura Harrington, Albion Moonlight Butters, John Campbell, Paul Hackett, David Kittay, Yael Bentor, and many others. I would especially like to acknowledge the inspiration and assistance of the late Ven. Pema Losang Chögyen, the Namgyal monk in our Columbia University graduate program who tragically passed away in 1996. It was he who encouraged me to work with chapters eleven and twelve of Tsong Khapa's *sngags rim chen mo*, and he offered invaluable assistance with this work in its earlier stages. He was a dear friend and is sorely missed. This book is dedicated to his fond memory.

Special mention must also be made of the many Tibetan scholars and lamas with whom I have had the great fortune to study for over three decades, including H.H. the Dalai Lama, H.H. Dagchen Rinpoche, Trinley Rinpoche, Ven. Dezhung Rinpoche, and many others. They have all been inspirational living examples of the buddhas' penetrating wisdom and deep compassion.

A special thanks is due to my dear mother, Barbara Rona, and to her husband and my long-time friend, Tom Rona, for their invaluable, heart-felt, and freely given spiritual, emotional, intellectual, and financial support over countless years. Likewise, I thank my beloved late father, Stephen R. Yarnall, and his wife Lynn Yarnall, for their generous love, support, and encouragement in as many ways over as many years. And finally, I owe a great debt of gratitude to my wife Mary Yarnall, my "goddess of appreciation" from Nepal, who has selflessly and patiently supported me in this project for over a decade, and to our beautiful son Mati, who has patiently endured the many years of his dad's academic and professional ordeals, inspiring me with his open-hearted love, shining intelligence, and enthusiasm for life, his radiant presence serving as a constant reminder of the importance and joy of living for others.

Thomas Freeman Yarnall
White Plains, NY
November 10, 2012

Abbreviations & Sigla

{###a}	A three-digit number (followed by "a" or "b") enclosed in curly brackets is a reference to the folio number and side of the TL edition of the *NRC*
[...]	Material added by translator
ACIP	Asian Classics Input Project
AIBS	American Institute of Buddhist Studies (at Columbia University, New York)
BA	*The Blue Annals (deb ther sngon po)*, by gZhon nu dpal (translated by Roerich, 1976)
Das	Sarat Chandra Das' *Tibetan-English Dictionary*
Dharma Index	The Nyingma Edition of the sDe-dge bKa'-'gyur/bsTan-'gyur Research Catalogue and Bibliography
Gold	Melvyn Goldstein's *Tibetan-English Dictionary*
LC	Lokesh Chandra's *Tibetan-Sanskrit Dictionary*
Lhasa	Lhasa edition of the Tibetan canon
LRC	*Lam Rim Chen mo—The Great Treatise on the Stages of the Path*, by Tsong Khapa
MS	Manuscript edition of the *NRC* (see p. 344)
MW	Monier-Williams' *Sanskrit-English Dictionary*
NRC	*sNgags Rim Chen mo—The Great Treatise on the Stages of Mantra*, by Tsong Khapa
RY	Rangjung Yeshe Dictionary of Tibetan
Skt.	Sanskrit (language)
**saṃskṛta*	Sanskrit terms reconstructed from Tibetan

Tengyur chart	Appendix III herein
THL	Tibetan and Himalayan Library Translation Tool
Tib.	Tibetan (language)
TL	Tahsi Lhunpo editon of the *NRC* (see p. 344)
Tōh.	Tōhoku catalogue of the Derge edition of the Tibetan canon
TT	*Tantra in Tibet*—Hopkins' translation of ch. 1 of Tsong Khapa's *NRC*, with an introduction by the Dalai Lama
YGST	*Yoga of the Guhyasamāja Tantra*, by Alex Wayman
YT	*Yoga of Tibet*—Hopkins' translation of chs. 2–3 of Tsong Khapa's *NRC*, with an introduction by the Dalai Lama
ZH	The Zhol edition of the *NRC* (see p. 344)

Typographical Conventions

We have strived generally to present Tibetan and Sanskrit names and terms in a phonetic form to facilitate pronunciation. For most Sanskrit terms this has meant that—while we generally have kept conventional diacritics—we have added an *h* to convey certain sounds (so *ś*, *ṣ*, and *c* are rendered as *sh*, *ṣh*, and *ch* respectively). For Sanskrit terms that have entered the English lexicon (such as "nirvana"), we use no diacritical marks. In more technical contexts (notes, bibliographies, appendixes, and so on) we use full standard diacritical conventions for Sanskrit, and Wylie transliterations for Tibetan.

Tools & Resources

Tsong Khapa's *NRC* is a superlative guide for entering and navigating the vast ocean of the Indo-Tibetan Buddhist Tantric traditions and practices. Still, as noted in the introduction below, this guide is itself very complex, often requiring its own meta-guide to be of optimal benefit to the modern reader. It is toward this end that the various apparatuses in this volume are offered. These various tools and resources (discussed below) will function as maps, charts, and compasses to further orient and locate the reader in his/her journey through these amazing waters.

Appendixes I & II: Topical Outlines (sa bcad) of NRC Chapters XI–XII

The topical outlines (*sa bcad*) of *NRC* chapters XI–XII found in the tables in Appendixes I and II (in English and Tibetan) were constructed by extracting and arranging the topic headings and numbers embedded in the Tibetan prose of the *NRC* itself (e.g., "The first topic, ___, has three sub-topics: ___, ___, and ___; the first of these has two sub-topics: ___, and ___; now to discuss the first..." etc.). Once these topics were thus extracted and arranged, then to identify and distinguish the twenty-four different levels of the outline, I imposed upon these extracted components my own system of nested indents and a numbering system using letters, Roman and Arabic numerals, and various punctuation marks. Finally, I then also interpolated these same outline letters/numerals and headings (as grey text within square brackets) back into the translation itself.

In addition to the topic headings themselves, the outline tables in these Appendixes also indicate the folio and side where a given topic is introduced (that is, named), as well as the folio and side where that topic ultimately is discussed (which often may be many folios later, and which usually will begin simply with a phrase such as "Now as for the third [sub-topic]...").

It will be very helpful for the reader to consult this outline at times while reading through the translation, to keep oriented with respect to what broader themes, topics, and sub-topics are being discussed, to maintain a sense of what a given passage is supposed to be addressing, and to have a sense of what sections and topics should be coming up. The broad scope of this outline is discussed in the introduction below.

Bibliographies of Cited Canonical (Kangyur/Tengyur) Texts

The first bibliography of cited canonical Tibetan texts is sorted by English title, and includes the full Tōhoku cataloguing information (including Sanskrit and Tibetan titles, author names, Derge locations, and Tōhoku number), as well as the abbreviated Tibetan title(s) which Tsong Khapa uses to refer to these texts. Thus, when the reader encounters a reference to a cited text in the translation, this bibliography should be the first place to turn to determine precisely what text it is. The second bibliography of cited canonical Tibetan texts (containing only the Tōhoku number and the English title) is sorted by Tōhoku number, and is intended to be used by specialists who already know the Tōhoku numbers and may want to look up a given text that way.

Appendix III: Tengyur Chart

This chart will be very useful in helping the reader to determine where a given Tengyur Tantric commentarial text fits into the overall Buddhist Tantric system. The Tibetan compilers of the Derge Tengyur (c. 1300s CE) arranged these texts in a very structured, logical order. These texts were then given sequential "Tōhoku numbers" by the cataloguers at the Tōhoku University in Japan in the 1930s. Once the reader knows the Tōhoku number for a given text (for which see the paragraph above), s/he then can look up this text in the Tengyur chart (which is sorted by Tōhoku number). This then will reveal what sub-section of the Tantric section of the Tengyur the text belongs to (e.g., what class of Tantra it is in, what specific Tantra it is commenting upon, and so on).

Glossary

The glossary includes technical terms in Tibetan and Sanskrit, with their English translations as used herein, sorted by the English. This will be useful both to specialists as well as to those interested in learning these terms.

Indexes

The index of cited canonical texts (with English title and Tōhoku number) and the index of cited canonical authors (by Sanskrit name) will provide further means for looking up and cross-referencing these sources, and the general index will be of use for locating other topics.

PART ONE

INTRODUCTION

Introduction

Overview

The present book contains the first ever annotated English translation of the eleventh and twelfth chapters of the fourteen-chapter treatise *Critical Elucidation of the Key Instructions in All the Secret Stages of the Path of the Victorious Universal Lord, Great Vajradhara*[1]—commonly abbreviated as the *Great Treatise on the Stages of Mantra* (*sngags rim chen mo*, hereafter cited as *NRC*)—the magnum opus written by the famous Tibetan polymath Tsong Khapa Losang Drakpa (1357–1419). In this monumental treatise Tsong Khapa provides an in-depth analysis of a sweeping array of topics pertaining to the theory, practice, and exegetical interpretations of all four classes of Indo-Tibetan Buddhist Tantra. In the opening chapter of the full treatise Tsong Khapa provides an overview and a highly original analysis and critique of competing interpretations of the nature of Tantra itself (that is, of what it is that characterizes Tantra and distinguishes it as a unique Vehicle of Buddhist practice), concluding that the distinguishing characteristic of all four classes of Tantra is the general practice of "deity yoga" (*devatāyoga*, *lha'i rnal 'byor*), also known as "buddha yoga." In the next three chapters (two through four) he then gives a presentation and an incisive analysis of each of the first three classes of Tantra: Action, Performance, and Yoga Tantra; and in the remaining ten chapters (five through fourteen, constituting about 77% of the entire treatise) he focuses on the fourth class, that of Unexcelled Yoga Tantra.

Regarding Unexcelled Yoga Tantra, in chapters five through ten Tsong Khapa covers a wide range of topics regarding the rites, procedures, and initiations pertinent to the understanding and practice of this highest class of Tantra. Then from among the two stages of practice unique to this class of Tantra—the creation stage and the perfection stage—chapters eleven and twelve (presented herein) focus on the creation stage, and chapters thirteen and fourteen (to be presented in a forthcoming publication in this series) focus on the perfection stage.

---

[1] *rgyal ba khyab bdag rdo rje 'chang chen po'i lam gyi rim pa gsang ba kun gyi gnad rnam par phye ba.*

Regarding the two chapters presented herein, chapter eleven (entitled "The need to accomplish enlightenment through the integration of the two stages"[2]) investigates the creation stage vis-à-vis its relationship with the perfection stage, clarifying the inter-relationship between the two stages and emphasizing the indispensible function that creation stage practices serve to develop the practitioner's body-mind "bases" for the practice of the more advanced perfection stage practices; and chapter twelve (simply entitled "The creation stage"[3]) investigates a wide range of both theoretical and practical topics relevant to this stage of practice. Together these two chapters constitute about one-fifth (18%) of this monumental esoteric treatise.

* * *

It is evident that Tsong Khapa wrote the *NRC* for a well-educated and experienced audience of Tibetan Buddhist scholar-practitioners. As such, the *NRC* is a very advanced treatise, requiring much of the reader. To gain a deep, informed appreciation of the themes and issues explored in the *NRC*, at a minimum the reader should have a solid grasp of the theory and practice of exoteric Universal Vehicle Buddhism. Indeed, Tsong Khapa himself regularly stresses throughout the *NRC* that the various esoteric issues he is addressing therein presuppose and require that the reader have a clear understanding of (or at least a good familiarity with) the types of correlated exoteric issues that he addresses in his exoteric companion volume, the *Great Treatise on the Stages of the Path* (*lam rim chen mo*, hereafter cited as *LRC*). Without such a minimal (albeit extensive) exoteric background, a reader of the *NRC* almost certainly will misconstrue (or miss altogether) many of Tsong Khapa's intricately argued points.

While meeting this requirement for an exoteric background already places a relatively large burden upon the would-be reader of the *NRC*, meeting this one requirement alone is less than fully sufficient. Since the *NRC* was not intended to be an introduction to Tantra (although today it might serve in part as such), the reader ideally also should have at least a general familiarity with some of the theory and practice of esoteric

---

[2] *rim gnyis zung 'brel gyis byang chub sgrub dgos par bstan pa.*

[3] *bskyed pa'i rim pa bstan pa.*

(Tantric) Buddhism. In addition, it is also immensely helpful for the reader to have some grounding in the historical and textual contexts informing the *NRC*, including the genesis, structure, and contents of the Tibetan Buddhist canonical collections (the Kangyur and Tengyur), as well as the various Indian Buddhist exegetical traditions pertaining to Tantra.

Providing such an extensive background is obviously far beyond the scope of this short introduction. Nevertheless, in an attempt to provide at least some scaffolding for the reader, in the following introductory pages I will cover very briefly a select few of the key topics mentioned above. In particular, from among several important themes that cut across the many topics explored in the chapters presented herein, one particularly persistent theme that we will highlight in this introduction involves various problematic issues pertaining to the reconciliation of an apparent incompatibility in general between the practice of deity yoga and the goal of the "nonconceptual" realization of emptiness (an esoteric correlate of the exoteric problem of reconciling form and emptiness), as well as related issues pertaining to the explanation and justification in particular of the purpose, functioning, and necessity of creation stage yoga. Tsong Khapa directly confronts these issues, examining a variety of perennial Indian and Tibetan objections to the practice of deity yoga that contend that such yoga—with its apparent hyper-conceptual focus on an abundance of analytical, visualized content—runs counter to the goal of achieving the "nonconceptual" state of buddhahood, and so on. In these contexts in the *NRC* Tsong Khapa explicitly typologically aligns such objections (here pertaining to the *esoteric* practice of deity yoga) with analogous *exoteric* objections raised and addressed in India by scholar-adepts such as Kamalashīla (in his *Stages of Meditation*, and elsewhere), and by Tsong Khapa himself in his own exoteric treatises. In both contexts, exoteric and esoteric, Tsong Khapa analyzes and elucidates others' responses to these objections while synthesizing his own comprehensive solution to these matters.

In the esoteric context of the *NRC* Tsong Khapa addresses these complex issues both in theory as well as in practice. In brief, firstly we can note that Tsong Khapa's responses to such objections are aimed at providing reasoned arguments and canonical citations to demonstrate in *theory* both (1) how it should be *possible* to integrate and simultaneously experience constructive perceptions and deconstructive awareness of emptiness, and (2) how it also should be *necessary* to do so. We will see that he argues that it is specifically the "conception and perception of ordinariness" (and not just any conceptuality or perception) that is the manifestation of the "intrinsic reality habit" to be targeted for negation in the Tantric Vehicle, and that it is the development of the "conception and perception of extra-ordinariness" (or what we can call "the mandala-mind")[4] that is seen to be the non-reified alternative that must function as the necessary cause of a buddha's form body.

Secondly, we can note that Tsong Khapa also offers explanations and citations to demonstrate how in *practical* and *yogic* terms deity yoga in general and the creation stage in particular are necessary. We will see that he reveals that (1) conceptual, constructive deity yogas in general (the esoteric "perception side")[5] *can* be integrated with and reconciled with nonconceptual, nonconstructive emptiness (the "empty side"),[6] because that is the nature of the nondual relationship that exists between the perception side and the empty side (emptiness *entails* relativity, it does not deny it, as Tsong Khapa frequently argues in his exoteric texts); and that (2) the conceptual/perceptual yogas in general indeed *must* be practiced, because such psycho-physical practices form the necessary homological basis for the development of the extraordinary perceived body and environment as well as the extraordinary selfless subjectivity and identity. Moreover, in this regard we will see how Tsong Khapa cites canonical passages (representing the cumulative record of centuries of pragmatic, experiential knowledge) to demonstrate that (3) *in practice* it is *necessary* for a yogī first to develop the special "artificial" perceptual/conceptual yogas of the creation stage in particular, in order to prepare and ripen his/her body-mind continuum for the advanced, homologically related "natural" yogas of the perfection stage that can directly engage and develop the subtlest levels of that continuum and thereby lead directly to the achievement of a buddha's integrated body-mind manifest as a nondual form body and truth body.

* * *

---

4 Based on Tsong Khapa's sources such as Shāntarakṣhita. See below, p. 63ff.

5 *snang phyogs*.

6 *stong phyogs*.

Beyond the short introduction presented in the following pages, my forthcoming book, *The Emptiness that is Form* (hereafter cited as *EF*) —which may be viewed as a companion volume to the present text—will explore further some of the historical, canonical, philosophical, and practice-related information required to properly contextualize the investigations in the *NRC*. This will include more in-depth explorations of: the nature and genesis of the Indian Buddhist canon and its transmission to and reception in Tibet; some of the key Indian and Tibetan authors, translators, texts, and exegetical traditions involved in this history; the life and times of Tsong Khapa himself; the history of philosophical ideas (particularly related to emptiness, perception, and conceptuality) leading up to Tsong Khapa's time; Tsong Khapa's own elaboration of Buddhist deconstructive philosophy, and some suggestions for possible comparisons with some deconstructive views and methodologies of contemporary post-structuralist disciplines; the typological relationships between the exoteric issues addressed in the *LRC* and the esoteric issues addressed in the *NRC*; the elaborate, subtle, psycho-physical model of humans and their environment revealed in the Buddhist Unexcelled Yoga Tantras; and the Tantric Buddhist view of human evolution, potential, and enlightenment. Further information, background, and analysis also may be found in some of the books listed in the bibliography herein.[7]

---

[7] For a further background in Unexcelled Yoga Tantra in general, including its subtle body-mind system in particular, see the following (sorted by author, date): Cozort (1986); Geshe Kelsang Gyatso (1982, 1994, 1997a); Lati Rinbochay and Hopkins (1979); Lessing and Wayman (1978); Mullin (1996, 1997); Panchen Sonam Dragpa (1996); Thurman (1988, 1991, 1994); Tsong Khapa (1977, 1981, 2005, 2010); Varela (1997); Wayman (1991, 1993); Wedemeyer (1999, 2007, 2013); Yangchen Gawai Lodoe (1995).

Indian and Tibetan Buddhist Background: Texts and Traditions

The Indian Buddhist Renaissance Culture

The early centuries of the first millennium CE in Northern India witnessed the dawn of a renaissance culture that would soon blossom to profoundly affect civilizations across Asia for the next millennium and a half. A key focal center and engine for this renaissance was Nālandā, the world's first university (c. 430/530–1234 CE). Founded and headed by Buddhists, this renowned institution was truly universal in character, attracting the very best faculty and students from across Asia to participate in a diverse, international educational community of thousands of Buddhists and non-Buddhists, ordained, lay, and secular, engaged in advanced education in all of India's classical "outer" arts and sciences (linguistics, medicine, astronomy, sociopolitical theory, ethics, art, and so on) as well as all of her classical "inner" arts and sciences (philosophy, psychology and mind science, meditation, yoga, and so on).

Soon many other Indian universities such as Odantapura (early 700s–1198 CE) and Vikramashīlā (late 700s–1235 CE) were founded and networked into an unprecedented liberal educational system. Over many centuries the rich diversity of the Indic arts and sciences was distilled into the tens of millions of Sanskrit texts housed in university and private libraries, representing a vast cultural treasury more than one hundred times the classical Greek and Latin holdings of the Library of Alexandria.[8]

In the seventh to ninth centuries hundreds of Tibetans traveled to these Indian universities for advanced education, returning with renowned Indian scholar-adepts to establish scores of similar institutions in Tibet. Over the eighth to fourteenth centuries teams of Indian and Tibetan

---

[8] Richard Gombrich (1978, 24), citing data from the late Sanskritist David Pingree, gives the following estimate for currently extant Sanskrit manuscripts:

> Surviving Sanskrit literature is many times as large as Latin and Greek literature together. There may be as many as two million manuscripts extant, though they are perishing fast. (For comparison, there are perhaps about thirty thousand Greek codices.)

David Pingree himself reported to me the much higher estimate for historically extant Sanskrit manuscripts: "The number of Sanskrit (or 'Indic,' including Prakrits and vernaculars) [texts] was roughly estimated to be 30,000,000 (thirty million) by Kapila Vatsyayan." (Personal correspondence to the author, 2005.)

scholar-adepts edited and translated into Tibetan thousands of key Sanskrit texts from these Indian universities.

By the mid-to-late fourteenth century, generations of Indians and Tibetans had completed the compilation, editing, and organization of these texts that would come to comprise the Tibetan Buddhist canon, including the 1,100+ texts contained in the Kangyur, and the nearly 4,000 texts contained in the Tengyur. The Kangyur is comprised of Tibetan translations of Sanskrit treatises accorded the status of *buddhavachana* (literally "buddha speak," awakened or enlightened statements regarding the nature of reality). Comprised primarily of texts attributed to "the" Buddha (Shākyamuni), such texts also could be attributed to *a* (any) buddha; and (in principle at least) such a text could be attributed to anyone, provided that the content of the text could be shown/interpreted to be in complete accordance with other texts widely validated as *buddhavachana*. These treatises included Sūtras (discourses covering a wide array of topics, including analytic philosophy, epistemology, meditation, the development of compassion, etc.); Tantras (revealing an array of possible enlightened gestalts or world-forms); as well as compiled treatises on Vinaya (ethics and discipline), Abhidharma (scientific analyses), and many other genres. The Tengyur is comprised of almost 4,000 Tibetan translations of key Sanskrit works by over 700 Indian authors. Ostensibly comprised of commentaries on Kangyur texts, the Tengyur also includes many highly original, standalone works, covering the full range of topics included in the classical Indian Buddhist inner and outer arts and sciences. This combined canonical collection (Kangyur-Tengyur) preserved the essential "genetic code" for the life of the remarkable Indian Buddhist renaissance culture, and its translation and transmission to Tibet enabled the continued growth and further evolution of this renaissance culture in Tibet.

Tsong Khapa and Fourteenth Century Tibet

Tsong Khapa Losang Drakpa (1357–1419) was born at this unique moment in Buddhist history. He was among the first generations of scholar-practitioners in Tibet to have access to the complete, organized body of knowledge contained in the Kangyur and Tengyur. This put him and his contemporaries in the unprecedented position of being able to survey and compare the various practices, doctrines, arguments, issues, and so forth which developed over the entire fifteen-hundred year history of Indian Buddhist traditions, schools, lineages, and so on. Thus, it was in this unique historical context that Tsong Khapa's equally unique genius was nurtured and flourished, enabling him to craft the masterful analyses and syntheses contained in the "collected works" (*gsung 'bum*) that comprise his immense literary output, which includes over two hundred treatises filling eighteen volumes and spanning all topics of exoteric and esoteric Buddhist theory and praxis.

While browsing through any of Tsong Khapa's encyclopedic works —all of which extensively draw on and cite the texts of Kangyur and Tengyur—it is easy to get the sense that one is being lead by an expert guide on a tour through the great Indian university libraries themselves. In the two chapters alone of the *NRC* translated herein Tsong Khapa quotes extensively from manifold canonical sources, including multiple root Tantras as well as over one hundred commentarial texts by over fifty well-known Indian Buddhist authors (see the bibliography and indexes herein). Moreover, in addition to explicitly referencing and analyzing the texts and issues from this Indian context, Tsong Khapa also references and analyzes (often implicitly, occasionally explicitly) many of the views and interpretations of his Tibetan predecessors (spanning six centuries) and contemporaries.

Tsong Khapa's Principal Writings: The Great Treatise on the Stages of the Path (LRC), and The Great Treatise on the Stages of Mantra (NRC)

Regarding the relative importance of Tsong Khapa's hundreds of writings, the most famous and influential exoteric treatise is no doubt his comprehensive *LRC*, which he completed in 1402 at Rva-sgreng monastery; and his most famous and influential esoteric treatise is no doubt his equally comprehensive sequel, the *NRC*, which he completed in 1405 at 'Ol kha.[9] The present Dalai Lama highlights the unique, superlative status accorded these two particular texts by Tsong Khapa when he succinctly

---

[9] Stein (*Tibetan Civilization*, 80) mistakenly indicates that Tsong Khapa composed both the *LRC* and the *NRC* at Rva-sgreng monastery in 1403. The dates given here for the composition of the *LRC* and *NRC* are from David Ruegg's introduction to the partial translation of the *LRC* contained in *The Great Treatise* (Snow Lion, 2000, vol. I, 27–28). The *LRC* date and location is confirmed by Thurman (*Speech of Gold*, 88), and the date is confirmed and discussed at some length by Napper (*Dependent-Arising*, 6; and especially 644–45n4). The locations for the composition of the *LRC* and *NRC* are from Thurman (*Life & Teachings*, 23–25).

writes, "Among the eighteen volumes of his collected works, the *Great Exposition of the Stages of the Path Common to the Vehicles* [*LRC*] and the *Great Exposition of Secret Mantra* [*NRC*] are the most important" (*TT*: 21). It is a substantial portion of the latter of these "most important" texts, then, that constitutes the translation presented herein.

Given that the *LRC* and *NRC* are the two most important texts written by an author who is almost universally acknowledged to be one of the most important and influential figures of Tibetan Buddhist history, it is rather remarkable how nascent and relatively scarce contemporary scholarship (studies and/or translations) regarding these texts has been. Of these two, the limited scholarship pertaining to the *LRC* has been ahead of the even more limited scholarship pertaining to the *NRC*. In this regard, in 1978 we saw the publication of Alex Wayman's *Calming the Mind and Discerning the Real*, which contained an English translation of the *LRC* sections on serenity and insight meditation (*shamatha* and *vipashyanā*), representing approximately the final third of the *LRC*. Then over a decade later, with the publication of Elizabeth Napper's *Dependent-Arising and Emptiness* in 1989, we received a much improved English translation[10] and an extensive study of just the insight section of the *LRC*. However, it was only after an additional fifteen years (and only in the last decade) that we finally have seen the publication of an authoritative English translation of the entire *LRC* (published by Snow Lion Publications), completed in three volumes through the fine work by the Lamrim Chenmo Translation Committee headed by Joshua Cutler and comprised of fourteen primary translators and a host of other support staff (the size of this committee alone demonstrates the monumental scope of this

---

[10] Napper (*Dependent-Arising*, appendix II, "Alex Wayman's Translation Considered," 441–473) presents a very persuasive and devastating critique of the many types of both incidental and substantive flaws contained in Wayman's *Calming the Mind* translation. Wayman's response in his preface to the revised 1997 edition of his *Calming the Mind* book is trivial and in no way addresses the substance of Napper's critique. My own assessment of Wayman's translations in *Calming the Mind* and in his other works (*YGST*, and so on) is equally critical. Nevertheless, much of Wayman's published research and scholarship still can be of great value to the critical reader aware of more recent buddhological scholarship (especially if the reader is sufficiently skilled to compare and assess the original Sanskrit or Tibetan of any suspect passages). For this reason I feel a sense of gratitude for the pioneering work of this late scholar, and I have found it useful at times to reference and to rely on his work, however provisionally.

endeavor). Volume I (434 pp.) of this translation of the *LRC* was published in 2000, volume III (447 pp.) in 2002, and volume II (295 pp.) in late 2004.

The equally important and almost identically monumental *NRC*[11] has been even less studied or translated. Again, in the 1970s we saw several publications that included studies and English translations of disparate short passages from the *NRC*, such as Stephen Beyer's *The Cult of Tārā* (1973), and various books and articles by Wayman such as *The Yoga of the Guhyasamāja Tantra* (1977, hereafter cited as *YGST*); and over the years we also have seen various other articles and parts of books by a handful of other scholars (including Hopkins, Cozort, Kelsang Gyatso, and a few others) containing translations and/or studies of various limited portions of the *NRC*. Most significantly, we have been fortunate to see the following three publications by Jeffrey Hopkins and H.H. the Dalai Lama: *Tantra in Tibet* (1977, hereafter cited as *TT*); *Yoga of Tibet* (1981, later republished as *Deity Yoga*, hereafter cited as *YT*); and now finally (over two decades later) *Yoga Tantra* (2005). These three books contain the only English translations and studies of complete chapters of the *NRC* to date. *TT* is a translation and study of the first chapter, covering many introductory, theoretical, and methodological issues pertaining to Tantra as a whole; *YT* is a translation and study of the second and third chapters, covering the first two of the three lower classes of Tantra, Action and Performance Tantra; and *Yoga Tantra* is a study and translation of the

---

[11] While accurately assessing the relative extents of Tibetan blockprint and manuscript texts has been difficult in the past, recently created electronic (ASCII) editions of the *LRC* and the *NRC* (courtesy of the Asian Classics Input Project [ACIP]), allow us to make the following precise comparisons:

	LRC	*NRC*	*NRC % of LRC*
syllables	283,207	271,532	= 95.88% of *LRC*
characters	1,017,927	991,229	= 97.38% of *LRC*

Regarding the absolute extent of the *NRC*, the Tashi Lhunpo (TL) blockprint edition used as the primary source herein is 512 folios in length. This is 1024 folio sides, with each side containing Tibetan text equivalent to about one "page" of text in English translation (in a standard 6" x 9" formatted book such as the present volume). Thus a formatted English translation of the complete *NRC* would be over 1,000 pages in extent; and with front and back matter, notes, etc., it could be expected to match the 1,176 pages constituting the three volumes of the *LRC* translation published by Snow Lion Publications.

fourth chapter, covering the third of the three lower classes of Tantra, Yoga Tantra. Together these first four chapters (of fourteen total) comprise the first 23% of the *NRC*.

Tsong Khapa on the Critical Use of Texts

When one first delves into Tsong Khapa's encyclopedic *LRC* or *NRC*, one's encounter with the thousands of passages from hundreds of canonical Buddhist sources that Tsong Khapa cites in support of his arguments can be overwhelming. At first this seemingly heavy reliance on canonical citation may seem oddly inconsistent with the general Buddhist emphasis on the primacy of reliance on rational analysis over scriptural authority. Thus it is important here at the outset to explain and contextualize (1) the Buddhist presentation of the nature of knowledge; (2) the nature and genesis of Buddhist "canonical" texts containing and representing such knowledge; and (3) the way in which Tsong Khapa (and other authors who share this methodology) cite such canonical texts.

Buddhist traditions universally agree that attaining a deep, coherent, precise, accurate understanding of the nature of reality (of "what is true") is the primary key to cutting the root cause of suffering and to reaching the ultimate evolutionary goal of buddhahood. According to general Buddhist theory, ontology and epistemology are thoroughly interdependent: "experiences" are not "given" (*data*) but rather are relativistically constructed, and as such they are fundamentally and profoundly interpretive acts. Deluded conceptions lead to deluded perceptions and experiences, which in turn feed back to reinforce and create more deluded conceptions. Thus, to break through this cycle of interdependent delusory conception (theory/construct) and perception (practice/experienced construction), rational, critical analysis functions as the sole therapeutic tool necessary (even if not sufficient) to determine whether a particular experience (presentation/interpretation) of reality is coherent and ultimately meaningful, useful, and liberative.

It is for these reasons that mainstream Buddhist traditions insist on the necessity of rational, critical analysis to interpret any presentation of "reality." This pertains whether that presentation is said to derive from one's own or someone else's first-hand "direct experience" of reality (whether ordinary or extraordinary, mundane or supramundane, relative or ultimate), or from some second-hand, indirect knowledge distilled in some recorded source—a written text or an oral text/transmission—considered to be authoritative (whether represented as being "scientific," or as "sacred," "revealed," and so on). And so, as the means for attaining such an understanding of the nature of reality, almost all such traditions reject any type of final reliance on scriptural authority. Instead, these traditions emphasize the primary role of developing rational, critical analysis to definitively determine—in spite of any appealing scriptural statements or any compelling perceptions or experiences to the contrary—a coherent presentation of reality (that is, of what could or could not be the case, or what must or must not be true), leading to penetrating insight and ultimately to the direct experience of reality or of "ultimate truth" itself.

Regarding the Buddhist canonical texts themselves that are held to represent a comprehensive record of critical investigations into and valid knowledge concerning reality, we already have noted in our discussion of *buddhavachana* that in its very nature and genesis the Buddhist canon is unique. The texts of the Kangyur and (to an even greater extent) the Tengyur can be seen to have emerged not through reference to "religious" authority but rather through the culmination of centuries of the Buddhist cultures' rigorous conventional, rational, public debate and empirical verification.[12] As such, these collections arguably can be considered more of a "cultural" or "scientific canon" than a "religious" one. Thus, educated references to or citations from such a canon may be fruitfully compared not so much to citations from a religious canon of established, final, dogmatic "Truth" as to a lawyer's citation of legal precedent, or to a scientist's citation of a well-tested (though always provisional) theory, a well-established body of research, or a widely validated record of empirical findings.

Finally, regarding the ways in which Tsong Khapa himself uses these canonical sources, it is important to acknowledge that he consistently and regularly emphasizes the points we have outlined above. Thus,

---

[12] It is granted that—as is the case with all cultural products—the emergence of this canon also was influenced by many other factors, including social, political, and economic forces, and so on. Nevertheless, I am suggesting here that debate, philosophical and/or experiential verification, consensus, etc., played a much more central and formative role in the production of the Indo-Tibetan Buddhist canon than typically would be expected for the production of such a canon. For a recent lucid discussion of some of these issues, see Wedemeyer 2013, ch. 3.

for example, right at the outset of the first chapter of the *NRC* he states the following:[13]

> The two [types of] scripture [Buddhist and non-Buddhist] are the objects to be scrutinized [to determine] which does or does not represent the truth. Therefore, to use them as a means to establish [the truth of] one's contentions would be inappropriate, and thus only reasoning should be used to analyze what does or does not represent the truth.

Given his frequent elaborations of such points, it should be clear that for Tsong Khapa (as for the majority of the Buddhist traditions as a whole), while an author may employ canonical citation to *help make a case* for a particular interpretation of Buddhist theory or practice, such citation alone will never be sufficient to *close* the case. Canonical citation can lend great weight to an argument or interpretation, but it can never lend *irrefutable* weight. Rather, canonical citation must be employed only as a subordinate complement to reasoned analysis. In the end, Tsong Khapa agrees with mainstream Buddhist scholarly practice in arguing that it is only rational, critical analysis—applied in specific, conventionally agreed upon ways and contexts, and subject to discourse, debate, and review among informed participants—that still must be the final arbiter in any specific case.[14]

Furthermore, we can note that when an author such as Tsong Khapa does cite a passage from such a canonical collection in defense of his arguments and interpretations (and in conformity with his own personal experience), this will lend maximum weight and plausibility to his case only when he clearly acknowledges and transparently reveals the overall context of the passage in question (thus avoiding the charge of "quoting out of context"). This in turn will entail that the author be able to demonstrate plausibly that his use and interpretation of the particular cited

---

[13] *lung gnyis ni bden pa'i don can yin min dpyod pa'i gzhi yin pas rtsod gzhi sgrub byed du mi rung ba'i phyir rigs pa nyid kyis bden pa'i don can yin min dbye bar bya'o,* (*NRC*: 4a.2–3). Cf. *TT*: 87.

[14] For more on these issues, see Hopkins (1984; 2008, especially 263–301), Jinpa (2002), and Thurman (1989).

passage accords with the meaning of similar passages on the same topic, by the same author, within the same exegetical tradition, and so forth; and this further will entail that the author be well versed in the variety of topics, techniques, interpretive categories, methodologies, traditions, authors and lineages, and so forth that he cites.

This is of course an extraordinarily high bar for any author to clear. As noted above, certainly the unique historical period in which Tsong Khapa was born provided the circumstances for a scholar-practitioner to have the possibility of meeting such a daunting challenge; but it is a compelling testament to Tsong Khapa's unique genius that he in fact did so with such mastery. Throughout his *LRC*, *NRC*, and his many other works, like a skilled detective investigating a complex case he demonstrates a keen awareness of the importance of the context and intertextuality of cited evidence (often noting variant translations); he carefully investigates and analyzes multiple Indian and Tibetan commentarial traditions, noting both continuities and discontinuities (and/or contestations) in their presentations and interpretations; and having meticulously surveyed and assessed this vast array of commentarial evidence, he renders what he deems to be the most plausible interpretation of the facts based upon reasoning and a preponderance of evidence.

Thus, if we look carefully at the way Tsong Khapa uses the many canonical passages he cites, we will see that he uses them not as the primary means to close a case but rather as supportive pieces of evidence to accomplish the following types of limited objectives: (1) to refute an opponent who claims that the Buddhist tradition (or a certain sub-tradition, school, author, etc.) "never (or always) states such and such"; (2) to interpret and properly contextualize the particular language, categorical structure, etc., employed by a particular author or text, to demonstrate that it should be understood or classified in a particular way and/or that it is (or is not) relevant to a particular context, etc.; (3) to demonstrate the wider context of a particular statement, text, or doctrine (a) in order to qualify it, to show its intended limits or applications, or (b) in order to add credence to his interpretation of it; (4) to amass (through multiple citations from multiple sources) a preponderance of evidence to strengthen his argument that the Buddhist tradition (sub-tradition, school, author, etc.) should be understood in a particular way; and so on.

And so throughout his many writings we see that Tsong Khapa repeatedly stresses what he views to be the urgent need both for educational exposure to the vast breadth of the sources of the Buddhist tradition (as embodied in its textual canons), as well as for the analytical ability to critically penetrate the depths of such sources (and of one's experience of reality itself). And yet, he often laments, unfortunately in his time there was too little of each. Thus, in the very opening verses to his exoteric *LRC* he states:[15]

> These days, those who strive at yoga study very little,
> And those who study a lot are unskilled in the keys of
> experiential cultivation.
> For the most part they look at the scriptures through
> partisan eyes,
> Lacking the ability to analyze the import of the treatises
> with reason.

And likewise in the very opening verses to his esoteric *NRC* he states:[16]

> Those for whom the scriptural traditions do not arise as
> precepts, content with just a part,
> Those unable to analyze the import of the treatises with
> immaculate reason,
> And those who study a lot but do not strive at practice
> Will be unable to please the victors.

In each of these contexts he then indicates his sincere motivation to write these respective books in order to help to remedy these imbalances.

Having completed this preliminary review of the nature of the sources on which Tsong Khapa relies, as well as the nature of his use of and reliance on these sources, we now are ready to begin an exploration of these sources themselves.

---

[15] *deng dus rnal 'byor brtson rnams thos pa nyung, ,mang thos nyams len gnad la mi mkhas shing, , phal cher gsung rab blta la phyogs re'i mig, ,lung don rigs pas 'byed pa'i mthu med pas, ,* (*LRC* ACIP: 2a–b). Cf. *The Great Treatise* (Snow Lion, 2000, vol. I), 33–34.

[16] *gzhung lugs gdams par ma shar phyogs res tshim, ,lung don dri med rigs pas dpyod mi nus, , mang du thos kyang sgrub la mi brtson pa, ,de yis rgyal ba dgyes par mi nus par,* (*NRC*: 2b.1–2). Cf. *TT*: 84–5.

Indian Tantric Exegetical Systems of the Ārya and Jñānapāda Traditions

Of the many Buddhist Tantric treatises, traditions, and classes, the Unexcelled Yoga Tantra known as the *Esoteric Community Tantra*[17]—along with its extensive commentarial literature—is one of the most important sources for Tsong Khapa's analysis of esoteric Buddhist theory and practice. According to traditional accounts, this Tantra was taught by Shākyamuni Buddha himself (c. the sixth century BCE).[18] Modern scholars assign the redaction of the text of this root *Tantra* as it now exists to the fourth to sixth century CE.[19] Regarding the exegetical tradition, all agree that after the Buddha none of the first several individuals in the lineage of transmission composed commentaries on the *Esoteric Community* (or at least none survive).[20] Then about the time of Saraha (late eighth century CE) there appears the first *Esoteric Community* commentary, the *Esoteric Accomplishment*,[21] by a Shrī Mahāsukhanātha (a.k.a. Padmavajra or Devachandra).

It is also at about this time (late eighth century CE) that two distinct *Esoteric Community* exegetical traditions begin to emerge in India. The first is the Ārya (Noble) tradition, a.k.a. the tradition of the Ārya Father and Sons, named after its founder, the Ārya Nāgārjuna, and his spiritual

---

[17] All canonical texts cited herein in the introduction and in the translation are given with an English translation of the title, to facilitate reading for the non-specialist. For specialists, complete bibliographical information (including cross-referenced titles in English, Sanskrit, and Tibetan, Tohoku numbers, Derge volume and folio locations, etc.) can be found in the bibliographies. For the very few texts mentioned in this introduction but not cited by Tsong Khapa, basic bibliographic information is included in the footnotes.

[18] See for example, the *Blue Annals* (*deb ther sngon po*; hereafter cited as *BA*), 359–60. The *Blue Annals* is the authoritative Tibetan historical chronicle by gZhon nu dpal (1392–1481). All citations from the *Blue Annals* herein are from the translation by Roerich (1976).

[19] Wayman constructs a plausible textual/historical argument (*YGST*, 96–102) by which he tentatively assigns the root *Esoteric Community Tantra* itself to the fourth century CE.

[20] This according to Tsong Khapa's *Brilliant Illumination of the Lamp of the Five Stages* (*rim lnga gsal sgron*). See Thurman's translation (2010, 69; Tib. 21b.2–3). See also Wayman, *YGST*, 90.

[21] Tōh. 2217: *Guhyasiddhi*. Note that while the *Guhyasiddhi* was the first *Esoteric Community* commentary to *appear*, traditional accounts maintain that Nāgārjuna and others wrote such commentaries centuries earlier (see note 23 below), even though such earlier commentaries did not appear publically until the time of the *Guhyasiddhi*.

"sons," including especially Āryadeva and Chandrakīrti. The second is the Jñānapāda tradition, named after its founder, Buddhashrījñāna (a.k.a. Jñānapāda). Tsong Khapa distinguishes these quite carefully, and while he generally is known for relying primarily on the Ārya tradition, he makes extensive use of both traditions in the *NRC*. Thus, to properly contextualize and understand the sources upon which Tsong Khapa bases most of his arguments and observations in the *NRC*, it is necessary here to briefly describe the historical genesis and distinguishing exegetical characteristics of thesc two traditions.

The Ārya Exegetical School

Nāgārjuna founded the Ārya school of Tantric exegesis, whose lineage, style and interpretation Tsong Khapa usually (though not at all exclusively) follows.[22] Philosophically, members of this lineage are generally well-known to have adopted a Dialecticist Centrist (**prāsaṅgika mādhyamika*) view. Within the lineage of Tantric exegesis, the *Blue Annals* (hereafter cited as *BA*) indicates that Nāgārjuna "had many disciples, but the chief ones were the four: Śākyamitra (Śākya bśes gñen), Āryadeva, Nāgabodhi (kLu'i byaṅ-čhub) and Candrakīrti"[23] (*BA*, 359–360). Kṛishṇāchārya (Nag po pa) is then listed as another important

---

[22] Nāgārjuna wrote the following key commentaries on the *Esoteric Community Tantra*: 1) *Abbreviated Practice* (Tōh. 1796: *Piṇḍīkṛta-sādhana*), on the creation stage; 2) *The Five Stages* (Tōh. 1802: *Pañcakrama*), on the perfection stage; 3) *Extensive Commentary on the Eighteenth Chapter* (Tōh. 1784A = P2649: *Aṣṭādaśa-paṭala-vistara-vyākhyā*), a commentary on the *Further Tantra of The Esoteric Community* (Tōh. 443: *Guhyasamāja Uttaratantra*), important since Chandrakīrti's *Illumination of the Lamp* (Tōh. 1785: *Pradīpoddyotana*) does not cover this; and 4) *Tantra Commentary* (Tōh. 1784: *Tantraṭīkā*), on the root *Esoteric Community Tantra* (overshadowed by Chandrakīrti's *Illumination of the Lamp*). See *YGST*, 91ff. (Nāgārjuna's authorship of Tōh. 1784A, and perhaps 1784, is considered uncertain by some scholars.)

[23] The traditional Buddhist position is that these Tantric authors are the same authors who wrote the Dialecticist Centrist philosophical texts. Moreover, Tsong Khapa and others present persuasive arguments that the philosophical views expressed in the Dialecticist texts accord with the views and methodologies of the Tantras. While modern Western scholars typically assert that these must be later authors who adopted the same names, I concur with Wedemeyer (PhD dissertation, Columbia University, 1999) that these scholars have not proven their case either with any irrefutable historical data or with any methodologically sound historiography. For these reasons, I see no justification for dismissing or revising the traditional attributions and will accordingly accept and use them (even if provisionally) throughout this introduction.

Indian figure in this lineage two generations later, and Atīsha is included in this lineage in the eleventh century (364). Important Tibetans later in this lineage include 'Gos khug-pa lhas-brtsas and his long line of descendants, including the important translators Pa-tshab and Chag Lotsawa, and then Bu-ston Rinpoche, Khyung-po Lhas-pa, and of course finally Tsong Khapa (360–67).

Of greatest importance to the Ārya school is the Tantric hermeneutic developed in Chandrakīrti's *Illumination of the Lamp*. This text elaborates upon the hermeneutical schema of the "seven ornaments" revealed in the *Intuition Vajra Compendium*, one of the *Esoteric Community* explanatory (*vyākhyā*) Tantras. Among these seven are included, for example, such hermeneutical categories as the "four procedures" and the "six parameters," described as keys designed to unlock different levels and nuances of meaning appropriate to different yogic levels in various Tantric passages within the root *Esoteric Community Tantra*.[24] According to this Ārya tradition, none of the Unexcelled Yoga Tantras can be properly and fully understood without these keys.[25] Indeed, use of this particular hermeneutical system may in fact be said to characterize the Ārya school and to distinguish it from the Jñānapāda school; as Wayman correctly observes: "[While v]arious commentaries on the [*Guhyasamāja*] *mūlatantra* belong to the Jñānapāda school...probably the freedom from Candrakīrti's classifying terms in the later commentaries is the best indication of inclusion in that [Jñānapāda] school" (*YGST*, 95; brackets added).

Besides Chandrakīrti's *Illumination of the Lamp*, other important Ārya texts which follow this hermeneutic and which Tsong Khapa cites more than once in the sections of the *NRC* considered herein include: Nāgārjuna's *The Five Stages* and *Abbreviated Practice*; Āryadeva's *Lamp that Integrates the Practices* (abbrev. *Practice Integration*); and Nāgabodhi's *Graded Presentation of the Esoteric Community Practice*.[26]

---

24 For an elaboration of these complex categories, see Thurman (1988).

25 Tsong Khapa corroborates this, indicating that this Ārya Tantric hermeneutic was essential to his understanding of the theory and method of the Tantras in general. For this reason he is commonly known to have relied primarily on the Ārya tradition's esoteric exegesis of the *Esoteric Community Tantra* for his understanding. See, e.g., Thurman, *Speech of Gold* (76ff.), and "Destiny Fulfilled," in *Life & Teachings of Tsong Khapa*.

26 See Wedemeyer (1999 and 2007) for an excellent study of the Ārya Tantric tradition as a whole and for translations of key Tantric works by Āryadeva.

The Jñānapāda Exegetical School

Buddhashrījñāna (a.k.a. Jñānapāda) founded the Jñānapāda school in the late eighth century. He studied at Nālandā University, focusing particularly on *Prajñāpāramitā* under Haribhadra, and thus he adopted the Idealist Dogmaticist Centrist (**yogācāra-svātantrika-mādhyamika*) philosophical view of that Centrist master.[27] Then, according to the *Blue Annals*, after teaching at Nālandā for a time he left for Oḍḍīyāna in search of Tantric teaching, and there he studied many Action and Yoga Tantras (*BA*, 367). He then traveled and studied with several yoginīs, learning Unexcelled Yoga Tantra from them. He studied "Prajñā Tantra" (that is, Yoginī Tantra) from a man named "Young Child," and "Upāya Tantra" (that is, Yoga Tantra) from Rakṣhitapāda, who was (interestingly) a disciple of Āchārya Nāgārjuna. Finally, failing to "perceive the Ultimate Essence" (*Dharmatā*) under this teacher, he traveled to the Kupaja forest north of Bodhgayā to study under the Āchārya Mañjushrīmitra. At one point Mañjushrīmitra "transformed himself into a mandala of Mañjughoṣa" and, after Jñānapāda made some prayers,

> Then the lord of the Maṇḍala ('Jam-dpal dbyaṅs [Mañjughoṣa]) bestowed on him [Jñānapāda] his oral instructions (Źal-luṅ [*Mukhāgama*], Tg. 1854). The ācārya then understood the Ultimate Essence [*Dharmatā*] and he became a yogin possessed of pure wisdom.[28] Mañjughoṣa in order to benefit future living beings, permitted the ācārya to compose...fourteen treatises[29] in agreement with the Scriptures.... (*BA*, 370; brackets added)

Tsong Khapa frequently refers to and cites the texts of this influential master and of many of his key disciples throughout the creation stage sections of the *NRC* presented herein. Of the fourteen texts that

---

[27] Ruegg, *Literature of the Madhyamaka School of Philosophy in India*: 101–103.

[28] As high a level as this obviously is, the *Blue Annals* later notes: "It is said that the ācārya Buddhaśrījñāna was able to realize the manifestation of the Ultimate Essence on the Higher Stage (lam mthon-po), but could not transform his physical body (gzugs-kyi phuṅ-po, rūpa-skandha) into that of Vajrakāya" (*BA*, 371).

[29] See the *Blue Annals* (370–71) for a list and discussion of the these treatises.

Mañjughoṣha "permitted the ācārya to compose," we can note that Jñānapāda's *The Samantabhadra Sādhana* is of particular importance to Tsong Khapa's analysis of deity yoga and of the creation stage. Indeed, interestingly, in these contexts we will see that Tsong Khapa cites texts from the Jñānapāda exegetical tradition far more frequently than those from the Ārya school. In these sections Tsong Khapa regularly makes statements such as:

> {399a}...In the context of the first stage [that is, the creation stage], regarding the way to indivisibly unite both the perception that has the pattern of the circle of the mandala and the wisdom that realizes the meaning of selflessness, and {399b} the way to thereby stop the self-habit which is the root of the suffering of existence—Jñānapāda's tradition is clear....

Later on in our translation, after abundant citations from and references to texts by Jñānapāda and many others in his lineage, Tsong Khapa concludes with a succinct summary of Jñānapāda's characterization of deity yoga, followed by a clear indication of the vast scope of this master's influence:

> {402b}...Jñānapāda explains the yoga of the nonduality of the profound and the vivid in which one develops certitude about emptiness and [has one's certain subjective mind] arise as the objective aspect, the deity; and [many other] Indian adepts explain [like this] using precisely this [explanation by Jñānapāda] as a source....

Then, as an example of one such Indian adept, Tsong Khapa cites Shrīdhara who says: "...The supreme ones such as Jñānapāda, etc. clearly explain these very things"; and Tsong Khapa concludes simply by indicating that "there are also many others who follow this [great master Jñānapāda]" (*NRC* 402b).

Regarding other important figures within this school, Jñānapāda is said to have had eighteen "excellent disciples," four of whom "attained the degree of Great Vajradharas (...i.e. buddhahood) in this very life" (*BA*, 371). These four are Dīpaṅkarabhadra, Prashāntamitra, Rāhulabhadra, and Mahāsukhatāvajra. Other famous direct disciples include Vitapāda, Buddhaguhya, and Buddhashānta; and later on this school claims Shāntipa (Ratnākarashānti), Thagana, Shraddhākaravarman, Padmākara, Abhayākaragupta, Smṛiti, Shūnyashrī, Balin Āchārya (Kṛiṣhṇapāda the junior), Karṇapa (Ratnavajra), as well as many famous Tibetans (Rinchen Zangpo, Bu-ston, and 'Gos lo-tsā-ba himself are listed within one lineage in the *Blue Annals* [373–74]). Again, we will see that most of these Indian masters from this lineage are cited a great many times by Tsong Khapa in the sections of the *NRC* translated herein, and that their commentaries on Jñānapāda's *The Samantabhadra Sādhana* are of particular importance to Tsong Khapa.

ABHAYĀKARAGUPTA

Of the many Jñānapāda scholar-practitioners Tsong Khapa cites, one late Indian author deserves special mention due to his universally acknowledged authority and his great importance to the presentation in the *NRC*. This is the early-to-mid-twelfth century scholar Abhayākaragupta (often cited by Tsong Khapa and other Tibetans as "Abhaya" or "Abhya"). The *Blue Annals* indicates that Abhaya was a disciple of Nāropa (*BA*, 795), and that "his works belong to the system of...Jñānapāda" because "he mainly followed on the dKyil-'khor-gyi čho-ga bži-brgya lṅa-bču-pa" (371–72). This latter text which Abhaya "mainly followed" —the title of which is translated herein as *The Mandala Rite of the Glorious Esoteric Community*, and which also frequently is referred to as *The Four Hundred and Fifty Verses*—was written by Jñānapāda's direct disciple, Dīpaṅkarabhadra. This text as well as several commentaries on it are cited quite often in the *NRC*.

All traditional as well as contemporary sources are unanimous in according Abhaya the highest praise.[30] The *Blue Annals* says simply of him that he "was endowed with a mind free of illusions in regard to any of the systems of the Prajñāpāramitā or Tantra, from the Lesser sciences (rig-gnas phra-mo) to the Anuttara-yoga-Tantra" (1046). Alex Wayman, who refers often to Abhaya's works in his *YGST*, describes Abhaya

---

[30] Moreover, in Tibetan tradition Abhaya is considered a former incarnation of the Panchen Lamas (oral communication from the late Ven. Pema Losang Chögyen). All of which makes it even more surprising and unfortunate how little has been written in any Western language on this extremely important and influential master, and how very little of his work has been translated.

simply as a "towering tantric commentator of the last period of Indian Buddhism" (95); and the Indian historian Sukumar Dutt reports that the Tibetan historian Tāranātha (b. 1575) said of Abhaya that "All the Indian teachers of the Mahāyāna who came after him openly accepted him as the standard" (1988, 346). Tāranātha himself offers the most informative account of Abhaya's prestige in his famous *History of Buddhism in India* (written in 1608):[31]

> Shortly after...[king Rāmapāla] became king, the great *ācārya* *Abhayākaragupta was invited to act as the *upādhyāya* of Vajrāsana [Mahābodhi Monastery at Bodh Gayā]. After many years he was appointed as the *upādhyāya* of *Vikramaśīla and *Nalendra [= Nālandā]....
>
> Among the Mahāyānīs of the time, the foremost was *ācārya* *Abhayākara.... Even the Śrāvakas had high regard for him as an expert in Vinaya.... Of particular significance was the reformation of the Law [Dharma] by him, and the *śāstra*-s he composed were widely read in the later period....
>
> The two *ācārya*-s, namely this *ācārya* and *ācārya* *Ratnākaraśānti-pa,...who came later, were comparable in qualities to the older *mahā-ācārya*-s like *Vasubandhu and others....
>
> It is remarked that this *mahā-ācārya* Abhayākara was practically the last among the most famous great *ācārya*-s who fully nourished the Law with their scholarship, compassion, power and wealth. And this is true. Hence he is to be viewed as having transmitted the thoughts of the *jina* and his spiritual sons to the later living beings. Therefore, his works should be respected more than those of the *ācārya*-s that came after the Six Jewels. His greatness is obviously proved by his holy words. (1981, 313–14; brackets added)

---

[31] The *rgya gar chos 'byung*. See Tāranātha (1981).

Thus, for Tsong Khapa to back up his arguments in the *NRC* with canonical citations (that is, to persuasively cite the consensus view on Tantric *buddhavacana*), it is clear that he could not have chosen a more respected and authoritative source than Abhayākaragupta.

Regarding Abhaya's works, according to my count of the thorough cataloguing done in the Dharma Publishing Index of the Tibetan canon, Abhaya authored more than thirty Sanskrit texts included in Tibetan translation in the Tengyur,[32] and he collaborated on the translation from Sanskrit into Tibetan of almost 150 texts. According to the *Blue Annals* (*BA*, 1046), Abhaya composed the following three texts in particular in accordance with instructions he received from Vajrayoginī in a dream: *Abhaya's Commentary on the Buddha-Skullbowl Tantra*,[33] the *Clusters of Instructions*, and the *Vajra Rosary*. The latter two (which are included among the texts Abhaya also personally helped to translate into Tibetan)[34] are relied on and cited extensively by Tsong Khapa in the *NRC*. Indeed, the *Vajra Rosary* is considered a kind of "root text" for the *NRC*,[35] and the *Clusters of Instructions* is cited in the *NRC* far more times than any other source.

---

[32] Chattopadhyaya (Tāranātha's *History*, 434) suggests that the Tengyur attributes about fifty works to Abhaya. He does not explain how he made this estimate.

[33] Tōh. 1654: *Abhayapaddhati*.

[34] It is interesting to note that the translations of both of these texts were revised within a few generations after Abhaya. Chag lotsawa (1197–1265, acc. *BA*, p. 1047) revised the *Vajra Rosary*; and dPyal Chos kyi bzang po (1189–1260, acc. *BA*, pp. 518–19) together with the Kashmīri Mahāpaṇḍita Shākyashrībhadra (1127–1225, acc. *BA*, p. 1064) revised the *Clusters of Instructions*. That these revisions were made in spite of the fact that Abhaya himself had personally overseen the original translations of his own texts presumably indicates that these later scholars saw the need to (re)translate them (contra Napper, 1995, 40) "into the current idiom of the culture" of thirteenth century Tibet.

Apparently the *Vajra Rosary* was a favorite text for scholars to (re)translate, again presumably due to enthusiasm to try out different idioms, nuances, evocative connotations, interpretations, etc. (perhaps similar to Nāgārjuna's *Kārikās* or Shāntideva's *Bodhicaryāvatāra* today). As the *Blue Annals* says: "The Vajrāvali having been translated by many lo-tsā-bas, there exist many different versions (of it). Nowadays most people favor the translation by Čhag (lo-tsā-ba)" (*BA*, 1047–48). After all this creative translation activity there did emerge a consensus of "most people"—a preponderance of evidence—that one translation, Chag's, was superior. Chag's is then the only version of the *Vajra Rosary* that ultimately makes it into all of the extant Tengyur editions (in the Dharma Index).

[35] Oral communication from the late Ven. Pema Losang Chögyen.

Differences Between the Ārya and Jñānapāda Exegetical Schools

Regarding the overall style of these two exegetical traditions, in general my experience has been that the writings of Jñānapāda, Abhayākaragupta, and others in the Jñānapāda school tend to be much more readable than those of the Ārya school. As Wayman puts it, "The Jñānapāda school took greater care with literary polish than the Ārya school" (*YGST*, 95). However, whether this greater clarity is due to having taken "greater care," or whether it may be due to some other factors (histories of the promulgation and redaction of the different texts, differing commitments to clarity vs. obscurity,[36] and so on) would seem to be an open question.

Regarding the influence that these authors' exoteric philosophical views exerted on their esoteric writings, while such influences are not always explicitly emphasized, we nonetheless generally can discern that such exoteric views do inform and (often implicitly) underlie these authors' esoteric writings. Thus, the Tantric exegesis of members of the Ārya tradition tend to be infused with a distinct, radically nondualistic Dialecticist Centrist flavor, while the Tantric exegesis of members of the Jñānapāda tradition tend to have a more Idealist Dogmaticist Centrist flavor. So, for example, regarding the latter, Wayman remarks:

> Buddhaśrījñāna studied the Prajñāpāramitā under the celebrated specialist Haribhadra, and this part of his training is quite evident in his tantric works. He adopted an interpretive position in which at each point the explanations of the Guhyasamāja are tied in with Mahāyāna Buddhism, particularly of the Prajñāpāramitā type. (*YGST*, 94)

Regarding Tantric exegesis itself, we already have noted above that the complex "seven ornament" Tantric hermeneutic (with its "four procedures" and "six parameters") was unique to the Ārya school. Wayman highlights yet another Tantric emphasis (connected with this hermeneutic) unique to the Ārya school. This emphasis involves categories pertaining to the subtle and extremely subtle psycho-physical states

---

[36] See Thurman, "Vajra Hermeneutics."

present in all sentient beings at all times throughout life, but which normally are made manifest and are encountered only in the process of ordinary death and in the between state (after death and before rebirth), and which are intentionally accessed and directly transformed only through Unexcelled Yoga perfection stage practice. Here the subtle category includes "the three luminance-intuitions" and "the eighty instincts" (what Wayman translates as "the three lights" and "the eighty *prakṛtis*"), and the extremely subtle category includes "the mind of clear light" (see Table 1 and surrounding discussion, below). Wayman notes that while Ārya Nāgārjuna's works "...stressed the three lights and the Clear Light, the theory of eighty *prakṛtis* or *vikalpas* going with three *vijñānas*, interpreted with Yogācāra-type vocabulary probably adopted from the *Laṅkāvatāra-sūtra*" (*YGST*, 91), this emphasis appears to be one of the distinguishing characteristics of the Ārya school, for (perhaps surprisingly) the Jñānapāda school, "...at least as far as its literary products are concerned, does not bother with the topics of the three lights and the Clear Light so prevalent in the works of the 'Ārya' school" (*YGST*, 94). Wayman elaborates this observation with a hypothetical illustration:

> If the Jñānapāda school comes across a term in the *Guhyasamājatantra* like '*prakṛtiprabhāsvara*', it would be prone to explain it just as in non-tantric Buddhism, to wit 'intrinsically clear' (said of the pure consciousness); while a writer of the Ārya school would be likely to say it means (in what is called the 'pregnant sense') 'the Clear Light along with the (80) *prakṛtis* (of the three lights'). (*YGST*, 94)

"However," he then prudently notes, "...it may well be the case that the Jñānapāda school does not deny that 'pregnant sense' but reserves it for the oral tradition, rigorously kept apart from the written works" (94).

Thus, we may note that while the Ārya hermeneutical analysis may be critical to a deeper understanding of the overall arc of Tantric theory and practice in general, it should be clarified that it is the topics explicitly pertinent to the perfection stage in particular that it illumines in a unique way. Moreover, while the perspective gained from this Ārya hermeneutic does indeed also shed crucial light on particular issues pertaining to the topics of creation stage yoga and deity yoga in general, it seems that for Tsong Khapa many issues pertaining to the creation stage are explained more than adequately (and often much more thoroughly) by Jñānapāda and members of his tradition.

These differences then have a direct and discernible effect on Tsong Khapa's exposition of the topics of deity yoga and the creation stage in the *NRC*. In most cases, when he needs to explicate some general aspect of these topics (such as what steps and procedures there are) or some theoretical issue (such as how birth, death, and the between state *generally* correspond to the three buddha bodies; or the central issue that the conceptual mind of deity yoga is compatible with a mind realizing emptiness), Tsong Khapa will cite texts from the Jñānapāda tradition. Since Tsong Khapa is more often than not engaged with such issues in the context of the chapters of the *NRC* translated herein (and, e.g., in the first chapter), in these contexts he cites texts from the Jñānapāda tradition far more often than those from the Ārya tradition. Furthermore, while the Ārya tradition relied more on the *Esoteric Community Tantra*, the Jñānapāda tradition relied more on the Tantric literature associated with the *Hevajra* and *Supreme Bliss* (*Chakrasaṁvara*) Tantras, and accordingly in the *NRC*'s discussions of creation stage and general deity yoga we see the texts from these latter Tantric systems cited far more frequently than others. However, when Tsong Khapa needs to address issues pertaining to the specific "realities" or "bases" corresponding to the homologous symbolic components of the creation stage (how various symbolic elements *specifically* correspond to the subtle psycho-physical luminance-intuitions manifest at death, and so forth), he will cite texts from the Ārya tradition.[37]

[37] For Tsong Khapa's own statement in the *NRC* regarding this difference in the level of specificity between the Ārya and Jñānapāda traditions, see the passage at 421a in our translation (see also our discussion of this passage in the introduction below, p. 69ff.).

Overview of Esoteric Buddhism

Deity Yoga: The Defining Characteristic of the Mantra Vehicle

It will be useful here at the beginning of our brief overview of esoteric Buddhism (a.k.a. "Tantra," "Mantra," or the "Vajra Vehicle") to clarify what it is that Tsong Khapa argues characterizes this Vehicle. Early in the *NRC* Tsong Khapa addresses this issue through the process of exploring what it is within the Universal Vehicle that distinguishes its two sub-vehicles, the exoteric Transcendence Vchicle and the esoteric Vajra Vehicle. After exploring and rejecting various theses as implausible,[38] and after arguing that no two vehicles to liberation can have a difference in the wisdom (*prajñā*, *shes rab*) pertaining to the ultimate view of emptiness,[39] he concludes that it must be the art aspect (*upāya*, *thabs*) that can provide the only possible basis for differentiating between the esoteric and exoteric Universal Vehicles.

Having then narrowed down the scope of possible distinctions to some *special* aspect of the practical arts, he continues his analysis by examining the nature of the causal relationships that hold between (1) the

---

[38] See *TT*: 110–113.

[39] This is an enormous and complex topic in itself; there is not sufficient space to go into these arguments here. In the *NRC* (see, e.g., *TT*: 93–99) Tsong Khapa briefly recapitulates arguments which he makes at length elsewhere (*Essence of Eloquence*, *LRC*, etc.) to the effect that while the *treatises* and *philosophical systems* (*siddhānta*) associated with the Individual and the Universal Vehicles differ in the subtlety of their articulation of the view of emptiness, successful *practitioners* of these two vehicles (arhats and bodhisattvas, respectively) cannot differ with respect to the wisdom realizing emptiness which they each must develop. This is because liberation from saṁsāra is not possible without direct, intuitive, and complete realization of the selflessness of both persons and things (Tsong Khapa maintains that this is a uniquely Dialecticist Centrist argument, and he supports this argument with numerous passages from the *Transcendent Wisdom* scriptures, Nāgārjuna, Chandrakīrti, and so on). Rather, practitioners of these vehicles must differ only with respect to the arts (*upāya*, *thabs*) they practice, and thus with respect to their physical development (the Individual Vehicle practitioners do not develop a buddha's form bodies whereas the Universal Vehicle practitioners do). Likewise, between the two Universal sub-vehicles, Tsong Khapa argues that the profound view of emptiness was fully articulated in the reasoned arguments and presentations of the exoteric Transcendence Vehicle, and that there can be no higher view somehow articulated in or attainable through the esoteric Vajra Vehicle (this directly countering the position of certain contemporary and previous lamas such as Dol-po-pa).

development of wisdom and the achievement of a buddha's truth body (corresponding roughly to a buddha's "mind" of intuition), and (2) the accumulation of merit (or the practice of art) and the achievement of the fruitional bodies of a buddha (the beatific body and the emanation body). He notes that both Universal sub-vehicles employ meditative techniques involving equipoise on emptiness—the cause of the sixth transcendence, wisdom—that *directly* simulate a buddha's truth body; and that thus, not only is the view of emptiness necessarily the same in both Universal sub-vehicles, but also the homogeneous causality that holds between the development of wisdom and the achievement of a buddha's truth body is essentially the same in both. On the other hand, while both Universal sub-vehicles agree that it is the accumulation of merit—through the art of practicing the other five transcendences, such as generosity, etc.—that serves as the evolutionary cause for the achievement of a buddha's form bodies, he notes that none of these practices *directly* (or homogeneously) simulate such form bodies, and thus he contends that the causality that holds between such practices and the achievement of a buddha's form bodies can be only a *general, supportive, indirect* one. Furthermore, he argues, it is only an explicitly conformative art—a practice involving the direct simulation of a buddha's form bodies—that could serve as the *direct* (or homogeneous) cause for those form bodies. He then notes that "deity yoga" is just such a practice, and that while this practice is lacking in the exoteric Transcendence Vehicle, it is not lacking in the esoteric Vajra Vehicle; and thus he finally determines that it is the presence of this unique art in the Vajra Vehicle that distinguishes it as a separate sub-vehicle within the Universal Vehicle.[40] Thus, after this series of considerations, he concludes:[41]

---

[40] It should be noted that Tsong Khapa's identification of deity yoga as being the defining characteristic of Tantra—although supported by key Indian sources—was highly original, and unprecedented in Tibetan exegesis. See Hopkins 2008 (pp. 205–242) for a discussion and translation of Bu-ston's survey of nine alternate Indian views regarding the distinctiveness of Tantra, which views would have competed for favor in Tibet prior to Tsong Khapa's time.

[41] The following is my translation of this earlier passage of the *NRC* (16a.3–16b.2). See *TT*: 115–16 for Hopkins' translation. See also the Dalai Lama's comments on and summary of these same points at *TT*: 42–43, 55–57. The Tibetan of this passage is as follows: *de'i phyir theg chen gyi lam gyi khyad par gyi gtso bo ni gzugs kyi sku skal ba dang ldan pa'i gdul bya la snang nas 'khor ba ji srid gnas kyi bar du sems can rnams kyi*

(cont'd)

> ...Therefore, it must be said that the primary feature distinguishing the paths of the Universal Vehicle is the art which causes one to appear as a form body to fortunate students, to become a savior and a refuge for sentient beings as long as saṁsāra lasts.... Thus, the [Universal] Vehicle is divided into two [sub-vehicles] due to the great distinction involving a dissimilarity in the body of the paths regarding the art for achieving a form body for the sake of others.
>
> ...Moreover, the primary feature of this [unique Mantra-Vehicle] art is [described] from the perspective of achieving a form body, because the art which is the means for achieving the form body—which [art] is precisely deity yoga, which is a meditation which simulates the form of that [form body]—is superior to the arts of other Vehicles.

Tsong Khapa then completes this argument by citing the following important canonical passage from the first chapter of *The Vajra Pavilion Tantra* (within the *Hevajra Tantra* literature) to support this conclusion that deity yoga serves as the defining characteristic of Tantra:[42]

---

mgon skyabs mdzad pa'i rgyur gyur pa'i thabs la bya dgos so, , ... des na gzhan don gzugs kyi sku sgrub pa'i thabs la lam gyi lus mi 'dra ba'i khyad par chen po yod pas theg pa gnyis su mdzad pa yin te, ... thabs kyi gtso bo yang gzugs sku sgrub pa'i cha nas yin la, gzugs sku'i sgrub byed kyi thabs ni de dang rnam pa 'dra bar sgom pa'i lha'i rnal 'byor nyid theg pa gzhan gyi thabs las mchog yin pa'i phyir ro, ,

42 The following is again my translation of this earlier passage of the *NRC* (16b.3–5). See *TT*: 117 for Hopkins' translation. Cf. also Thurman, "Unexcelled Yoga," pp. 4–5. See *EF* for my detailed discussion of this passage, for notes concerning the translation itself, and for references to alternate translations. The Tibetan of this passage is as follows: *rdo rje gur gyi le'u dang po las, gal te stong pa thabs yin na, ,de tshe sangs rgyas nyid mi 'gyur, ,rgyu las 'bras bu gzhan med phyir, ,thabs ni stong pa nyid ma yin, ,lta ba rnams las log rnams dang, ,bdag tu lta ba 'tshol rnams kyi, ,bdag tu 'dzin pa bzlog pa'i phyir, ,rgyal ba rnams kyis stong pa bstan, ,de phyir dkyil 'khor 'khor lo zhes, ,bde ba'i thabs kyi sdom pa ste, ,sangs rgyas nga rgyal rnal 'byor gyis, ,sangs rgyas nyid yun ring mi 'gyur, ,ston pa sum cu rtsa gnyis mtshan, ,mnga' bdag dpe byad brgyad cur ldan, ,de phyir thabs des bsgrub bya ste, ,thabs ni ston pa'i gzugs can no, ,zhes gsal bar gsungs so, ,*

The first chapter of *The Vajra Pavilion*...clearly states:

> If emptiness were the method,
> Then there could be no buddhahood.
> Since there is no effect which is different from its cause,
> The method is not emptiness.
>
> The victors teach emptiness
> To reverse the self-habit
> Of those who have [nihilistically] turned away from [all] views
> And of those who seek a self-view.
>
> Therefore, it is "the circle of a mandala"—
> The method is a blissful binding.
> Through the yoga of buddha-pride
> Buddhahood will not far away.
>
> A Teacher has the thirty-two signs
> And a ruler's eighty minor marks;
> Therefore, you should practice with that method –
> The method which has the Teacher's form.

Deity Yoga Defined and Further Elaborated

We saw above (p. 22) that Tsong Khapa's succinct definition of deity yoga (paraphrasing Jñānapāda) is as follows: deity yoga is "the yoga of the nonduality of the profound and the vivid in which one develops certitude about emptiness and [has one's certain subjective mind] arise as the objective aspect, the deity." To rephrase and elaborate on this briefly, we may formulate the following definition:

> Deity yoga is an esoteric Buddhist meditation practice involving *a yoga in which the practitioner's (subjective)* ***mind*** *realizing emptiness simultaneously nondually arises or perceives itself in the (objective, perceived)* ***form body*** *of a buddha.*

Moreover, for such deity yoga to effect its intended radical transformation of the practitioner's body-mind systems, the practitioner must repeatedly cultivate this yoga until s/he has thoroughly achieved both of its aims:

1. The development of *divine/buddha pride*—an extraordinary, limitless, awakened, yet empty buddha-identity—which is intentionally cultivated to replace the "pride of ordinariness" (that is, the practitioner's ordinary, limited, saṁsāric, reified identity)
2. The development of *vivid divine perception*—the clear, vivid, stable perception of one's body as a pure buddha body, and of one's environment as a pure, liberative, mandala or buddha-field—which is intentionally cultivated to replace the "perception of ordinariness" (that is, the practitioner's ordinary, limited, saṁsāric, reified perception of the world).[43]

Deity Yoga in the Four Classes of Tantra

In addition to demonstrating that the characterization of deity yoga given above was sufficiently narrow to precisely distinguish Tantra as a unique Vehicle, Tsong Khapa also had to demonstrate that this characterization was sufficiently *broad* to serve to characterize the major types and levels of practice coming under the heading of Buddhist "Tantra." In this regard, while there were many classifications of Tantra evident in the multitude of esoteric Indian Buddhist treatises and commentarial traditions, many Indians came to adopt the fourfold schema of Action (*kriyā*), Performance (*caryā*), Yoga (*yoga*), and Unexcelled Yoga (*anuttara yoga*) Tantra, as presented, for example, in the *Vajra Pavilion Tantra*.[44] Many Tibetans from the early Sakyas (eleventh century) through to the great Bu-ston (early fourteenth century) also adopted this fourfold schema, and in his *NRC* Tsong Khapa likewise follows this mainstream schema.[45]

---

43 The topics of divine pride and vivid perception are discussed extensively in the context of Unexcelled Yoga Tantra in the chapters translated herein.

44 For *NRC* citations from this Tantra and from Shraddhākaravarman regarding the fourfold schema, see *TT*: 151.

45 The only difference being that Tsong Khapa rejected his Tibetan predecessors' notion that Unexcelled Yoga Tantras should be given a threefold subdivision into "Father," "Mother," and "Nondual" Tantras, arguing instead that all such Tantras had to be nondual, and thus advocating a twofold subdivision into only Father and Mother Tantras (the former emphasizing illusion body, the latter emphasizing the clear light, but both nondually integrating both).

Thus, Tsong Khapa had to demonstrate that the characterization of deity yoga given above was broad enough to be the common defining characteristic for all four of these classes of Tantra. Moreover, this characterization of deity yoga also had to be able to encompass the various sub-divisions of deity yoga that exist in the different Tantric classes. In this regard, the basic divisions of yogas that exist in the three lower Tantric classes (Action, Performance, and Yoga, discussed in *NRC* chapters two through four) are distinct from the divisions that exist in the class of Unexcelled Yoga Tantra (discussed in *NRC* chapters five through fourteen). In short, deity yoga in the three lower Tantras is divided into "yogas with signs" (*sanimitta-yoga*, *mtshan bcas kyi rnal 'byor*) and "yogas without signs" (*animitta-yoga*, *mtshan med kyi rnal 'byor*), whereas deity yoga in Unexcelled Yoga Tantras is divided into yogas of the "creation stage" (*utpattikrama*, *bskyed rim*) and those of the "perfection stage" (*niṣpannakrama*, *rdzogs rim*). Furthermore, within each Tantric class the former yogas (yogas with signs and creation stage yoga)—also called "conceptual yogas" (*brtags pa'i rnal 'byor*)—are preliminary yogas which tend to emphasize more the development of concentration and vivid perception; whereas the latter yogas (yogas without signs and perfection stage yogas)—also called "nonconceptual yogas" (*ma brtags pa'i rnal 'byor*)—are more advanced yogas which build upon the earlier yogas to more directly integrate realization of emptiness and vivid perception and to more directly manifest the actual empty bodies of a buddha.[46] Nevertheless, despite these differences in emphasis, Tsong Khapa and his sources clearly do show that all such yogas at all levels in any class of Tantra must always nondually integrate both the realization of emptiness as well as the vivid perception of oneself as a "deity" (variously described or understood); and thus Tsong Khapa succeeds in demonstrating that the characterization of deity yoga given above is indeed both narrow and broad enough to satisfy all of the above requirements.

Tsong Khapa then surveys in the opening chapter of his *NRC* a wide range of Indian and Tibetan opinions regarding what it is (beyond the mere yogic sub-divisions mentioned above) that precisely distinguishes and defines each of the four classes of Tantra. After again using reasoned

---

[46] The precise definitions and characteristics which distinguish these different yogas get quite technical and are discussed further in *EF*.

arguments and scriptural citation to reject various Indian and Tibetan positions regarding this,[47] he sides with Abhayākaragupta and others (such as Vīryavajra) who cite such Unexcelled Yoga Tantras as *The Kiss Tantra* (within the *Supreme Bliss Tantra* literature)[48] to argue that the four Tantra classes were taught for four different types of practitioners who would be able to use and transform four different types and levels of desire on the path. By then citing various passages from Tantras of each of the three lower classes as well, Tsong Khapa suggests that this basis for classifying the four Tantras is common to all Tantras and is not just imposed upon the lower three from an Unexcelled Tantra perspective.[49]

The general Tantric principle here is that different psycho-physical responses triggered by the arousal of different types and levels of desire give rise to successively more refined or subtler types of "(bliss-) consciousnesses" or subjectivities, and that while these normally would bind one more strongly to saṁsāra, if these subtler subjectivities are intentionally aroused in a controlled meditative context and then utilized to meditate on special empty objects (that is, on extraordinary objects nondually perceived/conceived to be empty, rather than on ordinary objects of desire reified as intrinsically real), then there can be effected a liberative realization and a transformation at a subtler and more profound level than otherwise would be possible. Thus, with respect to our basic definition of deity yoga given above, the successive classes of Tantra evoke increasingly subtler states of "mind" (and body) to engage in "realizing emptiness," and it is these increasingly subtler subjectivities that then nondually "arise in the form of a deity."

Subtler Body-Mind Bases, Paths, and Fruits in Unexcelled Yoga Tantra

Regarding these increasingly subtle states of body-mind evoked in the successive classes of Tantra, we have noted above[50] that the class of Unexcelled Yoga Tantra uniquely accesses and utilizes the subtlest of these psycho-physical states (which states are themselves sub-divided into

---

[47] See *TT*: 153–56.

[48] See my note on 356b of the translation.

[49] See *TT*: 156–61 for Tsong Khapa's discussion of the above points.

[50] See esp. pp. 6–7, 26–28.

"subtle" and "extremely subtle" levels). Most sentient beings normally are aware only of their gross body-mind systems during their waking states throughout their lives. The subtler states also are present in all sentient beings at all times; however, these subtler states normally are made manifest and are encountered only somewhat in the experience of sleep (in dream states, and in deep sleep), and only fully in the process of ordinary death and in the between state (after death and before rebirth).

At the gross level the body is comprised of the five physical elements, and the mind is comprised of the six sense-consciousnesses. Together these are subsumed under the well-known Buddhist schema of the five body-mind systems (*skandha*, *phung po*). At the "subtle" level the "body" (or subtle physical state) is described as being comprised of nerve channels (*nāḍī*, *rtsa*), wind-energies (*prāṇa*, *rlung*), and neural drops (*bindu*, *thig le*), and the "mind" is described as being comprised of three luminance-intuitions (*āloka-jñāna*, *snang ba ye shes*) involved with eighty instincts (*prakṛti*, *rang bzhin*). At the "extremely subtle" level the "body" (or the subtlest physical state) is described as being comprised of the wind-energy carrying the clear light (*prabhāsvara*, *'od gsal*) in the "indestructible drop" (*akṣarabindu*, *mi shigs pa'i thig le*), and the "mind" is described as being comprised of the mind of clear light energies in the indestructible drop. These three levels of the body-mind complex are presented below in Table 1 (see p. 38). In addition, the three further subdivisions of the subtle mind (in increasing order of subtlety)—including the subjective experiences and the instincts associated with each of these levels—are presented in Table 2 (see p. 38).

It is this ordinary body-mind complex (especially at the subtle and extremely subtle levels) that is referred to as the "base" or "basis" that is to be purified. Also included under this rubric of the "basis"—in addition to (1) the gross, subtle, and extremely subtle body-mind—are the various states (at three levels of increasing subtlety) that this ordinary body-mind experiences, including (2) waking, dreaming, and deep sleep; as well as (3) life, the between state, and the state of death. These three bases and their three sets of states are presented in the top third of Table 3 (see p. 39).

All of the primary yogas involved in creation stage practices as well as in perfection stage practices reference and explicitly interact with these bases, and they do so in such as way as to function as "paths" (or arts/methods) for the purification of those bases. The alignments between the three levels of bases and (1) three corresponding creation stage yogas, as well as (2) three corresponding perfection stage yogas, are presented in the middle third of Table 3.

When each of these bases is purified by its corresponding (creation stage and perfection stage) paths, it transforms into its purified "fruit" or "result." There are purified results to be accomplished while still on the path to buddhahood, including states of "waking gross body re-entry," "waking illusion body," and "waking deep trance"; and then there are the fully purified results of the three bodies of buddhahood. These various levels and types of results are presented in the bottom third of Table 3.

	Body & Environment	**Mind**
Gross	Five-element body & environment	Six sense-consciousnesses
Subtle	Nerve channels (*nāḍī*, *rtsa*), wind-energies (*prāṇa*, *rlung*), neural drops (*bindu*, *thig le*)	Three luminance-intuitions involved with eighty instincts (*prakṛti*, *rang bzhin*) (*see* Table 2)
Extremely subtle	Wind-energy carrying the clear light (*prabhāsvara*, *'od gsal*) in the indestructible drop	Mind of clear light energies in the indestructible drop

Table 1: The gross, subtle, and extremely subtle body-mind complex[51]

	Subjective Experience	**80 Associated Instinctual Patterns**
Luminance (*āloka, snang ba*)	Empty sky pervaded by white moonlight	33 instincts related to desire
Radiance (*[āloka-]ābhāsa, [snang ba] gsal ba/ mched pa*)	Empty sky pervaded by red sunlight	40 instincts related to anger
Imminence (*[āloka-]upalabdhi, [snang ba] nyer thob*)	Empty sky pervaded by radiant darkness	7 instincts related to misknowledge

⇓ ⇓ ⇓ Increasing Subtlety ⇓ ⇓ ⇓

Table 2: The subtle mind's experiences and instincts[52]

[51] Based on Thurman, *The Tibetan Book of the Dead*, p. 37, Figure 4.

[52] Based on Thurman, *The Tibetan Book of the Dead*, p. 37, Figure 7.

		Increasing subtlety ⇒	⇐ *Sādhana* sequence	
Basis (or basis of purification)	*as ordinary body-mind* (*see* Table 1)	Gross body-mind	Subtle body-mind	Extremely subtle body-mind
	as ordinary life state	Waking	Dreaming	Deep sleep
	as ordinary transmigratory state [life-cycle] (the "three betweens")	Life	Between	Death
Path (or means of purification) (or path conversion)	*of creation stage*	Assuming the full form of the deity(-ies) in the mandala	Arising as the deity's seed syllable or hand implement	Meditation on emptiness/ clear light after 8 dissolutions of death
	of perfection stage	Re-entering one's ordinary gross body as an emanation	Arising as the illusion body	Dissolution of wind-energies in indestructible drop
Result	*on path*	Waking gross body re-entry	Waking illusion body	Waking deep trance
	at buddhahood	Emanation body	Beatific body	Truth body

⇓ ⇓ ⇓ Increasing Purification ⇓ ⇓ ⇓

Table 3: How a person's three ordinary BASES *are transformed by the* PATHS *of the two stages into the three* RESULTANT *buddha bodies on gross, subtle, and extremely subtle levels*[53]

[53] Based on information in the *NRC*, and on charts in Cozort's *Highest Yoga Tantra* and in Thurman's *The Tibetan Book of the Dead*.

The Homological Relationship Between Base, Path, and Fruit

A very important aspect of the schema of base, path, and fruit pertains to the continuity that exists between them. Indeed, the word "Tantra" itself (which literally means "continuum") often is explained to refer to this particular continuity. In contemporary terms, this type of continuous interrelationship can be described as a "homological" relationship. The concept of "homology" is associated most often with its use in biology (and evolution), where it denotes corresponding structures (or structural resonances) which can be attributed to descent from a common ancestor. The Oxford English Dictionary defines the adjective *homologous* as "Having the same relation, proportion, relative position, etc.; corresponding," and it describes its use in biology as follows: "Having the same relation to an original or fundamental type; corresponding in type of structure; ...said of parts or organs in different animals or plants.... Distinguished from *analogous*." This term also has been used in many of the social sciences to denote similarly corresponding structures or relationships. So, for example, in the area of religious studies Gavin Flood explains:[54]

> Identification, or 'cosmical homology', as the historian of religions Mircea Eliade has called it [in 1937],...might be said to be a principle of Indian religion. It is present in the vedic tradition from the *Ṛg Veda* and is found in all later Indian traditions, including Buddhism and Jainism.... [I]dentifications or homologies...become...central in later esoteric traditions....

Thus, in the context of Buddhist Unexcelled Yoga Tantra, when we say that base, path, and fruit are homologically related, this connects to the biological/evolutionary use of this idea, except that, whereas in the biological context homologous structures pertain to similar "parts or organs in *different* animals" (e.g., a bat's wing, a whale's flipper, and a human hand) that are considered to have evolved from a common ancestor, in the Tantric context the homologous structures pertain to related components (base, path, and fruit) within *a single individual's evolutionary continuum*.[55]

---

[54] Gavin Flood, *An Introduction to Hinduism* (Cambridge: Cambridge University Press, 1996), 48.

[55] For more on this topic, see the section on homological relationships below, p. 65ff.

How Vivid Pure Perception is Made Real

Artificial and Non-artificial Development; Interdependent (Homologous) Signifiers and Signified Bases

In the context of deity yoga in general we saw that the creation stage yogas of Unexcelled Yoga Tantra are considered "conceptual yogas" (*brtags pa'i rnal 'byor*), in contrast with the perfection stage yogas, which are considered "nonconceptual yogas" (*ma brtags pa'i rnal 'byor*).[56] In the context of Unexcelled Yoga Tantra itself we sec related terminology that highlights a similar distinction. Here it clearly is acknowledged that creation stage yogas—in spite of their real ability to *represent* and to *ripen* and to *connect to* the underlying realities of the subtler bases—are "just mental creations or mere designation" (*blos bskyed cing brtags pa tsam*), only symbolic, and thus "artificial" (*bcos ma*). It is only the advanced, "non-artificial" (*bcos min*) yogas of the perfection stage that can work directly with the subtle bases, making them "fit for action" (*las su rung ba*) to develop into an actual, non-artificial, "natural" (*rnal ma*) divine illusion body that ultimately will become a buddha's beatific body. Thus, the yogas of the two stages—as well as the "deities" they each create—are different in this essential way. Tsong Khapa explains:

> {370a}... Both of the stages, each relying on its various methodologies within its own context, are indeed similar in causing you to become perfected as a divine body; however, they are dissimilar in the way that they do this.
>
> Thus, in the creation stage you perfect yourself as a divine body through the methods of [visualizing] vowel and consonant letters, with moon and sun coming from those, then seed letters and hand-symbols, etc., [ultimately arising as a divine body]; being mental creation, this is just designation.
>
> In the perfection stage, through the force of making fit for action the [actual] referents of what were [merely]

[56] See above, p. 34.

> symbolized [in the creation stage] by vowel and consonant letters, moon and sun, etc.—[e.g.,] the white and red spirits of enlightenment {370b} and the wind-energies—and through the power of actualizing the three intuitions of luminance, radiance, and imminence, you arise from mere wind-mind as an [actual] illusory divine body; and thus this is perfection as a divine body without designation or fabrication by the mind.

However, despite this essential difference, even though the symbolic elements of the creation stage are "artificial," they are not *arbitrary*. This is because there is a close similarity in form (indeed a homology) between this "mere symbolism" and the "actual referents" of this symbolism—that is, between the designative signifiers and the signified bases of designation. Indeed, such special creation stage signifiers and their signified bases are intimately and *inextricably interconnected*, as Tsong Khapa shows in a subsequent passage (some forty-four folios later):

> {414a}... [Abhaya's] *Clusters of Instructions* states:
>
> > Also, regarding these seed syllables, such as the syllable *A*, etc.: with respect to whether the signified and the signifier are the same or different, they {414b} are analyzed as being not different, and thus that is also how they should be presented; for example: "the syllable *A*, [which is] the realm of space," etc.
>
> So according to this you should understand that the signified and the signifier are not different also in terms of their intent.

Thus, due to this special homological interconnection, the artificial forms of the creation stage have the unique capacity to resonate with, activate, and begin to shape and transform the non-artificial or "natural" processes of the subtle body-mind.

The Need for Creation Stage Yogas: Setting up the Distinctive Relativities for the Perfection Stage Yogas

Thus, according to Tsong Khapa and his sources, this ability to prepare the way for the natural yogas of the perfection stage is unique to the yogas of the creation stage. Connecting with the observation that creation stage deity yoga is distinguished from the deity yogas of the lower Tantras on account of its ability to simulate the subtler bases, the symbols and artificial yogas of the creation stage are likewise distinguished for their ability to prepare the subtle body-mind for the actual yogas of the perfection stage:

> {371b}...[R]egarding deity-creation yoga—although [all classes of Tantra] are similar insofar as they include the creation of a deity body from methods such as letters and hand-symbols and moon, etc., still, from the perspective of those methods, the ability to set up the distinctive relative circumstances that ripen one's continuum for the development of the yogas of psychic heat and the drop —which are the signified meanings of all of those things [letters, hand-symbols, moons, etc.]—[that ability] does not exist in the [Tantras which are] not Unexcelled. Such a thing [which so ripens] is spoken of as the creation stage. Thus, it is the case that the lower Tantras do not have the creation stage....

And as he says in a related passage (some twelve folios later):

> {383a}... In general, the creation stage is necessary not just because through the visualization of oneself as a deity there is a transformation into a distinctive pride and perception. For if it were only that, then even all of the lower classes of Tantra would have the complete essentials of the creation stage, and since [visualization of just] one deity would be sufficient, meditation on the [whole] circle of the mandala would become pointless. Therefore, [the unique necessity of the creation stage is due to thc fact that through it alone,] by meditating the complete set of the habitat and inhabitant mandalas that purify [respectively] the ordinary vessel and contents

> that are the bases of purification—[which complete set is] the import of the Tantra, as elucidated by the great scholar-adepts—one correlates the many distinctive relativities of the bases of purification and the means of purification, and [*thereby*] one thoroughly develops the roots of virtue which [later] produce the superlative realizations of the perfection stage.

Thus, we may say that creation stage vivid perceptions are able to "get a handle on" the perfection stage levels of body-mind in a way that other deity yoga vivid perceptions cannot. They do this because their special signifiers (letters, implements, moons, and so on, visualized in special key locations within the body) directly link to their signified referents (subtle minds, drops, and so on) through a homological relationship involving "distinctive relative circumstances" (*rten 'brel khyad par can*) that activate the ripening of those signified referents.

How the Lower Tantras "Get at" Unexcelled Yoga Tantra

Now many have noted that the symbols used in the three lower Tantras, as well as the ritual sequence engaged in their sādhanas (involving an unfolding from emptiness to moons, letters, implements, and so on) are very similar to those of the Unexcelled Yoga Tantras. For example, after describing the process of evolving through the six deities in an Action Tantra sādhana, Tsong Khapa's student Khedrup Jay says, "Those [deities] are what are asserted to be created by the five manifest enlightenments in the higher Tantras."[57] Likewise, after citing a passage from the *Vairochanābhisaṁbodhi Tantra* (a Performance Tantra) that connects "pure bodies" with the yoga without signs, and connects "impure bodies" with the yoga with signs, Tsong Khapa then notes that: "[Chandrakīrti's]

---

[57] *de rnams ni rgyud sde gong ma'i mngon byang lngas bskyed kyi dod do*. The Tibetan here is based on Khedrup Jay's *Introduction* (Lessing and Wayman, 1978, 162; see p. 163 for their translation; see also their note 16 to those pages for a clear one-to-one comparison between the six deities and the five manifest enlightenments). In short, deity yoga sādhana practice in the three lower Tantras involves a process of development from an "ultimate deity" (emptiness), through four intermediate steps or "deities," culminating in oneself manifesting as the sixth deity, the completed "sign deity." For more on these six deities, see *YT*.

Illumination of the Lamp explains that this passage indicates the deity bodies of the two stages [of Unexcelled Yoga Tantra]."[58]

Given such similarities and such statements, it seems reasonable to wonder why the symbols and ritual sequences employed by the lower Tantras should not be able to activate the subtle body-mind bases as well. The answer given here by the present Dalai Lama is quite interesting. He elaborates on the above cited passage from the *Vairochanābhisaṁbodhi Tantra* as follows:

> [T]he *Vajrapani Initiation* [a Performance Tantra]... [presents a teaching] like the teaching of the union of illusory body and clear light in the *Guhyasamaja*...[a Highest Yoga Tantra].... Though the *Vajrapani Initiation*, being a Performance Tantra, cannot explicitly set forth such a union, which is found only in Highest Yoga Tantra, it can be said that what it is getting at is the union of illusory body and clear light.
>
> ...[I]t can be said that the doctrine of the bodies of the two stages is hidden in the *Vairochanabhisambodhi*, not in the sense of being taught non-manifestly but in the sense of being hidden without in the least being taught. Since from among the two types of hidden meanings it is this latter, the words of the *Vairochanabhisambodhi* do not either explicitly or implicitly indicate these topics, but it still can be said that they are getting at the bodies of the two stages. (HHDL, *YT*: 13)

This notion that the language and yogas of this Performance Tantra are somehow "getting at" the goal of Unexcelled Yoga Tantra in some "hidden" way which cannot even be said to be an "implicit" indication is very intriguing. Somewhat later the Dalai Lama goes further and states that this Performance Tantra even can be "cited as a source for the two bodies in Highest yoga Tantra" (*YT*: 38). Although it is clear that the

[58] *sgron gsal las kyang lung 'dis rim pa gnyis kyi lha'i sku bstan par bshad do / /* (*NRC*: 89a.1–2). Cf. *YT*, 186. See also Lessing and Wayman (1978, 206n6), where the same passage is cited and addressed.

tradition does not maintain that the three lower Tantras teach or can activate the subtle bases, the above answer suggests that practice of the lower Tantras might in a sense "mature" the practitioner for the higher practices of the creation stage, the practice of which in turn will further "mature" the practitioner for the real development of the subtle bases in the perfection stage. This would suggest that there is a high degree of coherence—indeed a homological continuity—manifest across all of the yogas of all four classes of Buddhist Tantra.

* * *

The Structure and Content of the *NRC*

Chapters I–XIV: The Chapter Titles of the NRC

To better understand the context of the two *NRC* chapters translated herein, it will be useful first to consider the titles of all fourteen chapters:

I.	General Teaching on the Doors of Different Stages for Entry to the Teaching (*Tantra in Tibet*)	1a–42a
II.	The Stage of Progressing on the Path of Action Tantra (*Yoga of Tibet* [or *Deity Yoga*])	42a–87b
III.	The Stage of Progressing on the Path of Performance Tantra (*Yoga of Tibet* [or *Deity Yoga*])	87b–95b
IV.	The Stage of Progressing on the Path of Yoga Tantra (*Yoga Tantra*)	95b–117a
V.	The Stage of How to Perform the Earth Rite, After Knowing the Key of the Path and Doing the Preliminary Propitiation	117a–157b
VI.	The Stage of How to Perform the Preparation Rite	157b–219a
VII.	The Stage of the Rites of Drawing and Producing the Mandala and of Offering Worship	219a–247b
VIII.	The Stage of Oneself Entering, Taking Initiation, and Bringing the Disciple into the Mandala	247b–272a
IX.	The Stage of the Vase Initiation Rite	272a–294b
X.	The Stage of the Rite of the Three High Initiations along with the Concluding Rites	294b–348a
XI.	The Need to Accomplish Enlightenment Through the Integration of the Two Stages	348a–375a
XII.	The Creation Stage	375a–442a
XIII.	General Presentation of the Perfection Stage	442a–476b
XIV.	The Perfection Stage that is Meditated in the Beginning, Together with its Practices; and the Result of the Path	476b–512a

Table 4: The Fourteen Chapters of the NRC

Chapters V–XIV (Unexcelled Yoga Tantra Sections): Overview of the Topical Outline

Moreover, it will be useful further to look at an abbreviated form of Tsong Khapa's topical outline (*sa bcad*) for the Unexcelled Yoga Tantra sections of the *NRC*—which span chapters V–XIV (ff. 117a–512a)—to see the macro structure within which all of the sub-sections on Unexcelled Yoga are contained. For this we can begin by looking at Table 5, which reveals how the topics covered in our chapter XI fit into the structure set up in the previous Unexcelled Yoga chapters:[59]

CHAPTER V [Beginning of the Sections on Unexcelled Yoga Tantra]	
C' The three sections on Unexcelled Yoga	117a–512a
1' The general divisions of the path	117a–119b
2' The structure of the path	119b–121b
3' The path itself which has that structure	121b–512a
a' Becoming a suitable vessel for the path	121b–348b
[... **Chapters V–X** ...]	...
CHAPTER XI [The Integration of the Two Stages (Introduction)]	
[... Housekeeping (see below) ...]	348a–b
b' Purifying the commitments and vows	348b–351a
c' How to experientially cultivate the path	351a–504b
i' Learning about and contemplating the path	351a–352b
ii' Experiential cultivation of the path	352b–504b
[... **Chapters XI–XIV** ...]	[...]

Table 5: Topical Outline of Unexcelled Yoga Sections (Overview)

Here we can see that the *NRC* section on Unexcelled Yoga (**C'**, a sixth-level outline heading) constitutes the vast bulk (77%) of the entire

[59] The titles of these sections as given here are very abbreviated. See Appendixes I and II for a complete topical outline including the full titles and the entire structure of all the sections of chapters XI–XII. See the section above on "Tools and Resources" (p. xxii ff) for an explanation of how this topical outline was extracted from the text of the *NRC*.

treatise (395 folios, from 117a to the end at 512a). Within that, the first two of the three macro sections (seventh-level headings **1'–2'**), which discuss the general overall structure of this path, occupy only a few folios (117a–121b). After this, it is the final seventh-level macro section (**3'**), an examination of the path of Unexcelled Yoga Tantra itself, that occupies the real bulk of the text (121b–512a).

Next, within that seventh-level macro section (**3'**), we can note that almost the entirety of chapters V though X is subsumed under an eighth-level sub-topic heading (**a'**) entitled "becoming a suitable vessel for the path" (spanning 121b–348b [there are of course a great many sub-sub headings under this that we are not considering here]). This means that all of the topics we saw above mentioned in the titles of chapters V through X (see Table 4)—including earth rites; preliminary propitiations; preparation rites; drawing and producing the mandala; offering worship; oneself entering, taking initiation, and bringing the disciple into the mandala; the four initiations; and the concluding rites—relate to helping the practitioner become "a suitable vessel for the path."

Our chapter XI—after a folio of "housekeeping" (see below)—then picks up with the next eighth-level sub-topic heading (**b'**), a very brief section covering the topic of "purifying the commitments and vows" (in the few folios spanning 348b–351a), before then moving into the third and final eighth-level sub-topic heading (**c'**), on "how to experientially cultivate the path," which defines the topic of the great majority of the remainder of the text (351a–504b).

Finally, within this eighth-level macro section (**c'**) we can see that again the first sub-section (**i'**)—a ninth-level heading covering "learning and contemplating the path"—is very short (351a–352b); and that it is the next sub-section (**ii'**)—a ninth-level heading covering the actual "experiential cultivation of the path"—that is the primary subject matter of the remainder of the treatise (352b–504b), including the entirety of our chapters XI and XII.

Chapter XI: Overview of the Topical Outline and Subject Matter

Having clarified the larger context within which chapters XI and XII are situated, we now can move on to consider the topical contents of these two chapters in more detail. To do so, we begin by looking at Table 6, which picks up where our previous table left off (that is, after the ninth-level sub-section [**ii'**], on the actual "experiential cultivation of the path"), focusing on the major topical headings covered in chapter XI, and showing the way in which this chapter segues into chapters XII–XIII:[60]

CHAPTER XI [The Integration of the Two Stages (cont'd)]	
[… Housekeeping …]	[348a–b]
[**b'** Purifying the commitments and vows]	[348b–351a]
[**c'** How to experientially cultivate the path]	[351a–504b]
[**i'** Learning about and contemplating the path]	[351a–352b]
[**ii'** Experiential cultivation of the path]	[352b–504b]
A'' Rejecting that either one of the two stages alone is sufficient for buddhahood	353a–368b
1'' Rejecting that the creation stage alone is sufficient	353a–355a
2'' Rejecting that the perfection stage alone is sufficient	355a–368b
B'' How to experientially cultivate the two stages in an inseparable way	368b–498b
1'' The verbal meaning of the two stages	368b–372a
2'' The number of the two stages	372a–b
3'' The proper sequence of the two stages	372b–375a
CHAPTER XII [The Creation Stage]	
4'' How to learn each of the two stages	375a–498b
a'' The creation stage	375a–442a
[…]	[…]
CHAPTER XIII [The Perfection Stage]	
b'' The perfection stage	442a–498b
[…]	[…]

Table 6: Topical Outline of Chapter XI (with connection to XII–XIII)

60 Again the titles of these sections as given here are very abbreviated. Also, I am here omitting several sub-sub sections. See Appendixes I and II for the complete titles and structure of all the sections of chapters XI–XII.

As can be seen from this table, after the few folios discussed above (348a–352b), the main substance of chapter XI is divided into two tenth-level sections (**A''** and **B''**). The first of these has two eleventh-level sub-sections (**A''1''** and **A''2''**, each with various sub-sub sections omitted in this table), and the second has four eleventh-level sub-sections (**B''1''**, **B''2''**, etc., also with various sub-sub sections omitted in this table). Finally, it can be noted that while **B''** is introduced in chapter XI, its final eleventh-level sub-section (that is, **B''4''**) marks the beginning of chapter XII.[61]

It should be noted that this second tenth-level topic (that is, **B''**, on "How to experientially cultivate the two stages in an inseparable way") in fact goes on to subsume almost the entirety of the remaining material in chapters XI–XIV (368b–498b). This is very significant, as it highlights and underscores Tsong Khapa's more general argument that neither of the two stages can be understood or practiced in isolation or independently, and that instead both of the two stages must be understood and practiced in an "inseparable," "integrated" (or coordinated) way. Thus, while the arguments behind this admonition ostensibly are the main topic of chapter XI (as the title of this chapter indicates), Tsong Khapa's topical outline structure itself strongly reinforces the message that *all* of the topics of *all* of the subsequent chapters (XII–XIV) likewise must be understood as being governed by this same admonition.

Chapter XI: Selected Key Issues, Arguments, and Themes

Prefatory Comments

Before we consider some of the key issues raised in chapter XI, we should address the brief section that appears at the outset of this chapter (348a–b). Without clarifying the intention, context, and content of this prefatory section, the reader may struggle to understand the significance of this passage, especially if s/he assumes (understandably but mistakenly) that this passage represents some sort of introduction to the whole chapter.

---

[61] Such occurrences of the topic structure continuing over chapter boundaries (rather than a particular level of topic headings concluding neatly at the end of a chapter) is quite common in scholastic Tibetan texts, adding to the overall structural complexity of such texts.

As noted above, the first part of this prefatory section in fact contains what we might consider just a bit of "housekeeping" (or perhaps "bookkeeping"). Here, in one succinct paragraph, Tsong Khapa is acknowledging that there are two previously mentioned sub-topics within his overall topical outline structure that he has not yet addressed (and that must be "closed off" now in order for the structure of his outline to proceed). The first is a sixteenth-level sub-topic that was introduced in chapter VIII almost one-hundred folios previously (253b), and the second is an eleventh-level sub-topic that was introduced in chapter V over two-hundred folios previously (136a). Tsong Khapa here simply states that although these sub-topics cover "many very important methods" (some of which he briefly lists), the reader should learn about them elsewhere, as he will not be discussing them herein, fearing prolixity.

Tsong Khapa then concludes this brief prefatory section with a second paragraph containing the following noteworthy comment:

> {348b}... In order to help you understand into which contexts you should incorporate all the meanings of Tantra when you [have to] sort them into the branches of practice for a person to attain buddhahood, in this *Stages of the Path* [*of Mantra* text] I have picked out some special[ly important points] to arrange into a source of concise meanings [for you to use].

This comment is important as it emphasizes at the outset of our chapter that while we certainly may consider the *NRC* to be a scholarly tour-de-force, Tsong Khapa himself did not intend it to be used only (or even primarily) as a scholarly resource. We are reminded here that he has written this entire treatise not merely as a source to be studied by scholars, but also as a practical text, to help the *scholar-practitioner* both with understanding as well as with practice.

Rejecting that Either of the Two Stages Alone is Sufficient

In the first major sections of chapter XI (**A"1"** and **A"2"**, 353a–368b) Tsong Khapa presents and refutes various versions of the position that either the creation stage or the perfection stage alone is sufficient for attaining buddhahood (and that the other stage is ancillary or of provisional use at best). It is interesting and important to note that in both cases Tsong Khapa cites the antagonist's position as it is presented in an Indian

Buddhist text (Āchārya Mañjushrīkīrti's *Ornament of the Essence*), and that this text itself lists several Indians who advocated each of these positions, indicating that such one-sided positions had a long (and possibly widespread) precedent.

Tsong Khapa begins the first section (**A''**) with a brief representation of the (presumably more rare, but nonetheless misguided) position that the creation stage alone is needed (**A''1''**). The gist of this position is that—since the primary purpose of achieving buddhahood is to benefit beings, and since it is a buddha's form body that directly benefits beings—it is the achievement of the form body that is the primary characteristic of buddhahood; and that thus, since it is the creation stage that directly leads to the development of the form body, creation stage practice alone is needed. Regarding the realization of emptiness (and by implicit extension the achievement of a buddha's truth body): as Tsong Khapa shows, advocates of this position tend to severely downplay the profundity (and hence the importance) of the realization of emptiness, believing that this realization amounts to "simply finding" the view that "turns back the false notions that wrongly conceptualize the import of thatness," as if such "finding" were a one-shot, "ah ha" type of insight. Other than briefly characterizing (indeed almost caricaturing) this particular position, Tsong Khapa does not bother to refute this position, presumably because he assumes that the reader already is thoroughly familiar with the refutations of similar naïvely simplistic philosophical views which he extensively presents in his many exoteric texts such as the *LRC*, the *Essence of Eloquence*, the *Ocean of Reasoning*, and so forth.

Tsong Khapa then devotes the vast majority of this section (**A''**) to representing and refuting the (arguably much more common, but equally misguided) position that the perfection stage alone is needed (**A''2''**). Indeed, much of the other major section in this chapter (**B''**)—including its three sub-sections (**B''1''–3''**, 368b–375a)—also deals extensively with this issue.[62] As Tsong Khapa shows, this mistaken position is more subtle than the previously characterized position, and seems much more plausible (and hence is more pernicious). If (as is affirmed) the three lower Tantras can only "get at" the subtle bases of purification, and if even the creation

---

[62] As indeed does much of the rest of section **B''**, which itself subsumes the majority of the remainder of the entire *NRC* (368b–498b), as noted above (p. 51).

stage of Unexcelled Yoga Tantra can at best only artificially simulate the purification of these bases, and if indeed therefore the perfection stage alone can directly utilize and transform these bases, it is natural to wonder why one should not simply bypass these other yogas and jump straight into the perfection stage practices. Based on Tsong Khapa's analyses it is evident that there were indeed many who—overly eager to practice the profound and exciting yogas of the perfection stage—were doing just this. Upon wider review it would appear that the tendency for this kind of short-sighted, premature enthusiasm for the perfection stage is a universal, perennial one. As Tsong Khapa himself notes (in section **A"2"**), precisely this type of over-enthusiasm is recorded as an objection even in the root text of the *Hevajra Tantra*. Tsong Khapa quotes a passage from that Tantra in which an interlocutor expresses great enthusiasm for the perfection stage, wondering aloud why one should practice anything other than that highest stage "of which the bliss is called great bliss." Tsong Khapa then quotes the Buddha's answer, which in part indicates that such great bliss is inexorably connected with the body: "If the body did not exist, where would there be bliss? It would not be possible to speak about bliss [without the body]." Tsong Khapa then gives his own synopsis of this exchange, clarifying its ramifications, viz. that it is precisely the creation stage yogas that are indispensably involved in the development of the body (and hence of great bliss):

> {360b}... In that [passage, the interlocutor, the great bodhisattva Vajragarbha] formulates the argument: "The beginner has no need for a *creation stage* meditation *that lacks a perfection stage meditation*, because the goal which is the orgasmic *great bliss is* [to be obtained through] the *yoga of the perfection stage*." [The Buddha] answers: "*Through the force of your faith* in the perfection stage, *you have lost sight* of the creation stage!"—and he establishes that both creation and perfection, like a flower and {361a} its scent, are the support and the supported [respectively].
>
> Moreover, [at the time of fruition] the mind's entrance into the thatness of phenomena is achieved through the perfection stage, and the body's abiding as the form body is achieved through the creation stage; [thus] intending

> that the body is the support of the mind, [the Buddha] spoke [in terms of] support and supported. Moreover, at the time of the path there is also support and supported like that.

Thus, drawing on the *Hevajra Tantra* as a source, Tsong Khapa here emphasizes that one cannot bypass the creation stage practices and jump into the perfection stage practices for the simple reason that this would entail eschewing the development of the subtle body while trying to develop only the subtle mind. Not only is this misguided, but it is not even possible, because at the subtlest levels the energy-wind bliss-body and the clear light mind are nondually integrated, with the energy-wind serving as the inseparable support for the mind. As the Buddha expresses it here in the *Hevajra Tantra*, the bliss-body is the basis of the mind; one simply cannot have (or develop) one without the other.

Tsong Khapa himself later raises this misguided position again (in **B"1"**) in terms of the artificiality of the creation stage. He presents an objector as contending that the creation stage—which creates a divine body through its fabricative methods of letters, hand-symbols, moon, sun, etc.—does not produce an actual buddha body, whereas the perfection stage—which creates a divine body through its non-fabricative methods involving the yogas of wind-energies and drops, which are the *actual import* of what is *only symbolized* by letters, etc., in the creation stage—does directly produce an actual buddha body, and that therefore one should practice only the non-fabricative perfection stage yogas. Tsong Khapa then gives an important practical answer to this misguided contention:

> {371a}...That is not so. Without having become accustomed to the fabricative methods you will be unable to perfect the non-fabricative methods, and thus, also, without having become accustomed to what arises from the fabricative methods you will be unable to actualize what arises from the non-fabricative methods. That was the intention of the previously cited boat analogy.... This [analogy] {371b} shows both that it is necessary to go to the end of the creation stage and that the creation stage alone is not sufficient.

Thus, with further elaborations surrounding all of the above answers to these objections, Tsong Khapa demonstrates not only that the creation stage yogas *can* function to prepare the subtler bases for the perfection stage yogas, but more importantly he demonstrates that these subtler bases *must* be so prepared in order for the perfection stage yogas to be able to work *the way they are intended*. Indeed, Tsong Khapa's emphasis on linking "what arises from" the creation stage practices to "what arises from" the perfection stage practices is very significant here, for it suggests the dangerous possibility *not* that practicing perfection stage yogas without the preparation of the creation stage will produce no result, but rather that it might produce something deceptively *like* a perfection stage result.[63] Tsong Khapa sounds precisely this type of cautionary note when he says (in **B"3"**):

> {372b}...The perfection stage can arise in a continuum that has been developed through the creation stage, but in one not developed by that, although a few parts of the perfection stage may arise, a perfection stage capable of traversing the path will not arise.

And near the conclusion to chapter XI he further elaborates the danger:

> {374a}...[Y]ou can see that this sequence of the path is extremely important—because if you err by not grasping this well, then no matter how much you exert yourself you will definitely not develop anything; or else you might experience something like that [perfection stage experience] which is not the actual [perfection stage experience], but you will be confused and will waste your time....
>
> In general, there seem to be two [types of] perfection stage, one which beginners are not able to meditate and one which they are able to meditate. Regarding the latter, even though they have not stabilized the creation stage,

63 This then would raise concerns similar to those raised by Asaṅga in an exoteric context. Asaṅga elaborated various types of "nirvana *simulacra*" experiences that are *not* conducive to liberation and hence are not cultivated as an integral part of the path. See *EF* for a detailed examination of this important issue.

> if they meditate [on the perfection stage] it is not the case that they cannot produce some simulated qualities; nonetheless, they will not produce [qualities] like those produced in those who did develop their continuum through the first stage. Therefore, forsaking the first stage it appears that they can produce simulated qualities of the wind-energies, psychic heat, etc.; {374b} but it is not acceptable if they jumble those all up and err with respect to the key points of the path.

Thus, taking all of the above arguments together, with ample scriptural support from the key figures of the two main Tantric exegetical traditions, Ārya and Jñānapāda, Tsong Khapa establishes—with logical reasons (causal homogeneity) and pragmatic reasons (subtle body development) pertaining to the evolution of the body aspect of any being's nondual body-mind—that the creation stage practices are the absolutely indispensable arts for the extraordinary development of the relative/bodily/perception side of buddhahood.

Chapter XII: Overview of the Topical Outline and Subject Matter

Recall from Table 6 above that all of chapter XII takes place within the tenth-level topical outline section **B''** (on "How to experientially cultivate the two stages in an inseparable way"), and that within that macro level topic, it takes place within the eleventh- and twelfth-level subheadings **4''a''** (which simply delineate that this chapter will be about the creation stage).

Having recalled this context, it now will be useful to continue to expand upon the abbreviated topical outlines discussed above, to include the details for chapter XII. Thus, within the broad topic headings just mentioned (**B''4''a''**), we can note that the entire substance of chapter XII takes place within the following two thirteenth-level topic headings: **i''** ("A general presentation of the creation stage"), occupying the first two-fifths of the chapter, and **ii''** ("An explanation of the stages of evocation"), occupying the latter three-fifths of the chapter. These broad topical headings (with some key sub-headings) are summarized in Table 7:[64]

---

[64] As in the previous tables, section titles here are abbreviated, and several sub-sub sections are omitted. See Appendixes I and II for complete information.

[B'' How to experientially cultivate the two stages in an inseparable way] […]	[368b–498b] […]
CHAPTER XII [The Creation Stage]	
[4" a" The creation stage]	[375a–442a]
i'' A general presentation of the creation stage	375a–402b
A° That for which the creation stage is an antidote	375a–391a
1° How to identify and get rid of what is to be abandoned	375a–377a
2° How to establish vivid perception and stability	377a–391a
B° The division of things to be created	391a–398b
C° How to meditate emptiness in that context	398b–402b
ii'' The stages of evocation	402b–442a
A° The yoga of the actuality of the session	403a–437b
1° The preliminaries [accumulating merit and intuition; creating the defense perimeter]	403a–410a
2° The actual yoga with its components	410a–430a
a° Creation of the measureless mansion habitat	410a–412a
b° Creation of the deity inhabitants	412a–421b
i° Actual creation [by five manifest enlightenments; by exhorting the melted deity]	412a–416b
ii° The bases of purification, and homologies with the paths	416b–420a
iii° A summary of the essential points	420a–421b
c° Completing the actual yoga [entrance of intuition hero; sealing; offering; mantras]	421b–430a
3° The follow-up to those yogas [fortifying the body; creating guests and offering votary cake]	430a–437b
B° The yoga in between sessions	437b–439b
C° Making those yogas magnificent	439b–442a

Table 7: Topical Outline of Chapter XII

Chapter XII: Selected Key Issues, Arguments, and Themes

ELIMINATING THE PRIDE AND PERCEPTION OF ORDINARINESS

In section **i''A°1°** (375a–377a) Tsong Khapa discusses the important issue of how and why the primary function of the creation stage visualizations is to eliminate the practitioner's "pride of ordinariness" and "perception of ordinariness." The former is eliminated through the cultivation of divine pride (which Tsong Khapa states is of paramount importance), and the latter is eliminated through the cultivation of the distinctive (or divine) perception of the habitat and inhabitant mandala (which is ancillary to the former). These are of course the essential goals of deity yoga in general, in any of the four classes of Tantra.[65] Here Tsong Khapa elaborates how these essential goals are accomplished in the context of the creation stage of Unexcelled Yoga Tantra in particular.

DEVELOPING STABLE VIVID PERCEPTION

In section **i''A°2°** (377a–391a) Tsong Khapa discusses how and why these creation stage visualizations are to be developed until they are vividly perceived. While vivid perception is again a goal common to deity yoga in all classes of Tantra, here Tsong Khapa explains the special creation stage arts for stabilizing such vivid perception over three phases through focusing on the various "subtle drops" (located at key points in the practitioner's body) that are the specially efficacious subtle objects of meditation unique to the creation stage of Unexcelled Yoga Tantra.

ALTERNATE CREATION STAGE SCHEMAS

In section **i''B°** (391a–398b) Tsong Khapa gives a detailed comparative analysis of alternate schemas employed (by different root Tantras, sādhanas, exegetical traditions, etc.) to divide up the key phases of the creation stage (as well as to show the relationships of these phases to the corresponding perfection stage phases), including schemas that divide it into "the four branches," "the four yogas," "the six branches," or "the three samādhis," each with its own set of sub-divisions. Each one of these schemas is complex (and sometimes obscure) in the context of its own Tantric system, and within any given system it can be difficult

[65] See above, p. 32.

enough to sort out the terminology for the sub-stages, the order of the sub-stages, the precise boundaries demarcating the various sub-stages, the overall logic or rationale for the divisions, and so forth. The difficulty of understanding any one such schema is then exponentially increased when one tries to compare multiple schemas across multiple systems. In this situation it can be very difficult to keep one's bearings, and all too easy to get lost in the myriad details of the various systems, and to "lose the forest for the trees."

Fortunately, in this very lengthy and detailed section, Tsong Khapa provides us with a comprehensive map of this "forest," situating each "tree" within its broader context, thereby offering invaluable analysis and assistance in charting a path through these various schemas for structuring the sub-phases of the creation stage (as well as the perfection stage). In this way he shows us not only how the various systems' sub-divisions of the creation stage compare and relate, but (perhaps more importantly) he reveals to us the overall common structure that underlies all of these systems. Indeed, Tsong Khapa himself seems to emphasize throughout this section that (initially at least) it is more important to understand this overall structure than it is to understand the specifics of any given schema; for it is only by clearly understanding the major components and parameters of this structure (as well as the functional intent of the order of those components) that one will be equipped to accurately assess the viability of any given schema that may present itself (e.g., in any teacher's oral Tantric precept, or in any author's written Tantric exegesis or sādhana text). Thus, after this extensive analysis, as Tsong Khapa states in his conclusion to this section:

> Those are the amazing partitions of the first stage. Therefore, {398b} if you analyze [a creation stage sādhana or explanation] taking those as a basis, then you will understand the criteria [establishing] whether or not the key points of the first stage are complete.

Now it should not be necessary (nor likely would it be useful) to discuss all the details of these various schema here in this introduction. Rather, the translation of this section should stand on its own, and the reader should find that—with some effort—by reading this translation s/he can come to understand both the details of each of these various schema as well as their relationship to the overall structure of the creation stage. However, it can be very useful in exploring this "forest" to have access to a summary of all the components of such schemas brought together into a single comparative table. Accordingly, the reader should find Table 8 on the following page helpful (indeed, the reader is encouraged to consult this table regularly while reading the translation of the *NRC* in general, and while navigating the translation of this section in particular).

* * *

Other correspondences with creation stage divisions			**Branches of service and practice (*sevā-sādhana*)**			**Other correspondences with the perfection stage**
6 sādhana branches (*ṣaḍaṅga*) [with other key steps in brackets]	5 manifest enlightenments (*abhisaṁbodhi*)	3 samādhis [creation stage only; also in Yoga Tantra]	4 Yogas (*caturyoga*) [creation stage only]	4 branches/vajras (*caturaṅga/vajracatuṣka*) [creation or perfection stage]	6 branches of yoga (*ṣaḍaṅgayoga*) [perfection stage only]	5 stages (*pañcakrama*) [perfection stage only]
[Emptiness]	1. Moon 1 (suchness)	1. ***Preliminary union***	1. **Yoga** (review place and mandala, dissolve into emptiness)	1. ***Service*** (dissolution to emptiness/ clear light)	1. ***pratyāhāra***	[creation stage to body isolation]
					2. ***dhyāna***	
					3. ***prāṇāyāma***	1. ***vajrajāpa***
[Defense perimeter]					4. ***dhāraṇā*** (incl. 8 dissolutions of death)	2. ***cittaviśuddhi*** 3. ***svādhiṣṭhāna***
1. Measureless mansion 2. Devotee hero/ empassionment†	2. Moon 2 3. Seed syllable 4. Hand-symbol		2. ***Conformative yoga*** (placing seed syllables)	2. ***Conformative practice*** (arising as seed syllables)	5. ***anusmṛti***	4. ***abhisaṁbodhi***
[Intuition hero] 3. Blessing/initiation	5. Completed deity body		3. ***Extreme yoga*** (completed deities)	3. ***Practice*** (completed deities)	6. ***samādhi***	5. ***yuganaddha***
4. Offerings 5. Praise 6. Taste nectar [Main deity yoga] [Mantra recitation] [Depart & dissolve]		2. ***Supreme mandala triumph*** 3. ***Supreme action triumph***	4. ***Great yoga*** (engaging the world as buddha)	4. ***Great practice*** (engaging the world as buddha)		

Table 8: Comparison of the Phases and Divisions of Creation and Perfection Stages

Sources: The four branches/vajras: *NRC* 391a–394a; 372a–b. The four yogas: *NRC* 394a–b; 372a–b.
The six branches (creation stage): *NRC* 395a–396b; 372a–b. The three samādhis: *NRC* 396b–398b. The five *abhisaṁbodhis*: *NRC* 412a–414a.
†Vajra empassionment has 5 sub-stages: *NRC* 395b–396a.
Cp. also: Beyer, *Cult of Tārā*, chart p. 118 and surrounding discussion; Wayman, *The Buddhist Tantras*, 47–48; *YGST*, 155–178.

Meditation on Emptiness and the "Mandala-Mind" in the Creation Stage

In section **i''C°** (398b–402b) Tsong Khapa discusses the important way in which meditation on emptiness is to be integrated into all aspects of creation stage practice. It seems that it was (and indeed still is today) quite common for there to be dangerous misunderstandings with regard to whether or not meditation on emptiness should be an integral part (or a primary part, or even any part) of creation stage meditation. A related version of this misunderstanding—which Tsong Khapa also addresses herein—contends that creation stage practices primarily (or exclusively) involve visualization, whereas by contrast perfection stage practices primarily entail meditation on emptiness.

At the outset of this section Tsong Khapa characterizes this common doubt as follows: "You may wonder: Well then, is it the case or not that in the context of the first stage one meditates just the wheel of the deities, which is the visible aspect, and then in the context of the second stage one must primarily meditate on emptiness?" (398b). He then immediately answers this, stating that "Meditation on emptiness in the context of the first stage is *extremely* necessary," offering a detailed preview of five reasons why this is so. Finally, after a lengthy analysis of multiple perspectives on this issue, at the end of this section he succinctly summarizes a key conclusion of his analyses: "Therefore, since meditation on emptiness is necessary in the contexts of *both* stages, in the context of Mantra it is not the case that all meditations on any emptiness are the perfection stage" (402a–b).

Regarding the unique way that emptiness meditation is to be integrated into Unexcelled Yoga Tantra meditations, Tsong Khapa quotes the following key passage (referenced throughout this section) from Jñānapāda's *The Samantabhadra Sādhana*:

> {399b}... There is no other suffering of existence [produced]
> From anything other than the stream of ordinary
> conceptual thought.
> The mind holding a pattern opposed to that
> Will come to have direct realization.
> Whatever [mind] has the nature of the profound and the
> magnificent
> Will not perceive [ordinary] imaginary thought.

After some further quotes and analysis Tsong Khapa comments:

> {400a}... Shrī Phalavajra, Vitapāda, and Samantabhadra ...clearly explain ['ordinary conceptual thought' to be] the self-habit, and one can know this also by the context. Therefore, the self-habit is 'ordinary conceptual thought,' the root of 'the suffering of existence,' and thus it is called 'the suffering of existence.'
>
> '*The mind opposed to that*' is explained by all the commentaries to be the mind that has the pattern of the circle of the mandala, and the way it opposes is that '*it is opposed in pattern*'—that is, the two habit patterns are necessarily really opposed. Moreover, it is the mind that has the pattern of the circle [of the mandala]—that is, the meditator himself—that '*will come to have direct realization.*'

With these passages Tsong Khapa introduces us to the important idea of an "[extraordinary] mind holding a pattern opposed to" the mind of "ordinary conceptual thought." The following essential points become clear in this and the ensuing analysis: (1) the mind of ordinary conceptual thought is not a mind involved in just any conceptual thought, but rather is a mind deluded specifically by the self-habit pattern that conceives and perceives an ordinary, non-empty world;[66] (2) the extraordinary mind is one which has both the self*lessness*-habit pattern—which extraordinary cognitive pattern directly opposes the ordinary self-habit pattern—as well as (in this Tantric context) the extraordinary perceptual pattern of a mandala; (3) thus, to qualify as such an "extraordinary mind," the mind holding this extraordinary pattern must have *both* "the nature of the profound *and* the magnificent," which entails that it must nondually integrate

[66] Thus, while in some contexts (such as the passage from 399b–400a cited above) it will sound less awkward to render the phrase *tha mal gyi rnam rtog* as "ordinary conceptual thought," we more often will render this phrase as "the conception of ordinariness." Similarly, we will render the phrase *tha mal pa'i snang zhen* as "the perception and conception of ordinariness." See the section at the beginning of chapter XII entitled "Showing how to identify and get rid of what is to be abandoned" (375a–377a) for an important, extended discussion of this idea.

both the perception of the magnificent visualized details of the form of the mandala *and* the simultaneous conception or realization of the profound emptiness of that perception.

In discussing these matters we will find it convenient to coin and use the shorthand term "the mandala-mind" to refer to the mind holding such a nondual pattern. Note that this specific creation stage elaboration of "the mandala-mind" as a nondual integration of the profound and the magnificent parallels the more general elaboration of deity yoga as nondual given above (p. 32): "a yoga in which the practitioner's (subjective) mind realizing emptiness simultaneously nondually arises or perceives itself in the (objective, perceived) form body of a buddha."

* * *

In the second main section (**ii''**) of chapter XII Tsong Khapa offers a detailed analysis and discussion of each of the creation stage practice's sub-stages of "evocation," that is, of each of the sub-sections of a sādhana practice that describe or evoke the images of the deities, etc.

The Preliminaries of Accumulating Merit and Intuition, and of Creating the Defense Perimeter

In section **ii''A°1°** (403a–410a) Tsong Khapa discusses the preliminary visualizations and rites for accumulating the stores of merit and intuition (403a–408b), as well as the preliminary processes for creating "the defense perimeter which clears away adverse conditions" (408b–410a). In these contexts the store of merit is accumulated through invoking the deity host, taking refuge, and making offerings, and the store of intuition is accumulated through meditating on emptiness after reciting the mantra *OṀ shūnyatā-jñāna*, etc., or *OṀ svabhāva shuddha*, etc. (both of which mantras Tsong Khapa explains in detail). In his discussion of creating the defense perimeter he describes two different systems, a "common" one and a "special" one.

The Actual Creation Stage Yoga with its Components [Focus on Homologies Between Bases, Path, and Fruition]

In section **ii''A°2°** (410a–430a) Tsong Khapa gives a very detailed analysis of the sub-divisions of an actual creation stage session. This constitutes the main substance of the second part of this chapter, and includes discussions of:

(a°) (410a–412a) The creation of the measureless mansion habitat.

(b°) (412a–421b) The creation of the deity inhabitants, including (i°) their actual creation through the visualization of "the five manifest enlightenments" and "the exhortation of the melted deity with sound"; (ii°) an important discussion of "the bases of purification" and their homologies with the paths; and (iii°) a summary of the essential points made in this very key section.

(c°) (421b–430a) The components completing this yoga, including (i°) the entering of the intuition hero, the sealing, the making of offerings and praises, and (ii°) tasting nectar, meditating, and repeating mantras.

A primary subject or theme that permeates these discussions (cutting across the explicitly stated topic headings) is that of the homological relationship that exists between "base, path, and result."[67] This subject is particularly prevalent throughout the two primary sub-sections (**b°** and **c°**) that constitute the great majority of this section. Accordingly, we will use this important subject as a lens through which to focus our observations throughout this part of our introduction. By focusing on and understanding this "forest level" subject, the reader will be able to make sense of and to put in place the many "tree level" details that proliferate throughout these sections.

Creation of the Measureless Mansion Habitat [ii''A°2°a°]

In the first section (**a°**), regarding the creation of the measureless mansion habitat, Tsong Khapa discusses two overall systems. One of these is a "special" system in which one first meditates a wheel with ten spokes as a protective element of the habitat, and the other is an "ordinary" system not involving this wheel. Within each of these systems he then discusses many details regarding the creation of the measureless mansion itself, which should be relatively self-explanatory upon reading.

---

[67] See above (pp. 40–46) for an extended discussion of this important subject.

This section then ends with a detailed paragraph (411b–412a) concisely summarizing all of the variations discussed.

Homologies Involved in Creating the Deity Inhabitants through the Five Manifest Enlightenments [ii''A°2°b°i°– ii°]

Throughout the second section (**b°**) Tsong Khapa gives a detailed presentation of "the five manifest enlightenments," which represents yet another schema for dividing the sub-phases of the creation stage.[68] In this very common schema the sub-phases of the creation stage are represented as five "enlightenments" or realizations which come from meditating on the following five sequential stages in the arisal of the visualized deity: suchness (represented as a moon); a second moon; a seed syllable; a hand-symbol; and the completed deity body.

As with any such creation stage schema, each of these sub-phases in the development of the magnificent aspects of the deity moves from subtler to coarser, and homologically corresponds to the subtle-to-coarse stages of development of the ordinary bases of an ordinary being (from deep sleep to dreaming to waking, or from death to between to rebirth, and so forth).

In the first two sub-sections (**i°–ii°**) Tsong Khapa gives a great many specific examples of the unfolding of the five manifest enlightenments in a creation stage sādhana, frequently emphasizing the homologies between base, path, and fruit. Some examples of this can be seen in the following representative passages:

> {417b}... When the *gandharva* enters into the unmelted [father-mother], the *nāda*, etc.—which is the syllable that is the actuality of the between-state [being]—entering between the two [lunar] mandalas is [homologized with] the context of [entering] the womb....
>
> {418a}... Here, the first moon signifies the seminal essence; the second moon [or sun] signifies the ovum,

---

[68] Compare this fivefold schema to the four other schemas discussed in the section above on "alternate creation stage schemas" (**i''B°**). See column 2 of Table 8 to see a list of the five components of this schema, and to see how these components correspond to those in the four other schemas.

> like the sun that arises from the abundance of the menses of women. Thus, in other contexts it is stated that from the consonants a sun is created, and that is also what is meant when the [second] moon is said to be red. The entry of the syllable—which signifies the between-state [being]—into the middle of those two [moons] is like the entry of the [actual] between-state [being] into the midst of the father's and mother's sexual essences [in the normal life cycle].
>
> Then, from the seed [syllable] a hand-symbol is produced, which is a five-pronged vajra, and in the *Clusters of Instructions* it is explained—gathering into sets of five—that the five prongs of one end [of the vajra] are the [embryo's] four limbs [legs and arms] and the head above the neck, and that the five prongs of the other end [of the vajra] are the five digits on the feet and hands and the five senses on the head.

And:

> {419a}... Then, regarding the exhortation of the melted [deities to arise] by song: if we homologize this with [the stage of] fruition, then having been exhorted by the four immeasurables[69] [to accomplish] the aims of beings, there is an arisal as a form body for the fortunate person; but if we homologize this with the bases of purification, then that set of four goddesses is the four elements [instead of the four immeasurables],[70] and thus the new oval embryo—which is the between-state [being] which entered—is held by earth, combined by water, developed without rotting by fire, and caused to grow by wind....

---

[69] Immeasurable love, compassion, sympathetic joy, and impartiality, here in the form of the goddesses Locanā, Māmakī, Pāṇḍaravāsinī, and Tārā.

[70] Here it is earth, water, fire, and wind that are in the form of the goddesses Locanā, Māmakī, Pāṇḍaravāsinī, and Tārā.

Summary Regarding Homologies Between Bases, Paths, and Fruits [ii"A°2°b°iii°]

In the third and final sub-section **(b°iii°)** Tsong Khapa gives a concise (420a–421b) yet extremely incisive summary of the essential points regarding the importance of properly identifying and understanding homological relationships that are the key to the rapid, powerfully potent evolutionary transformation effected by Unexcelled Yoga Tantric practice.

There are several critical passages from this sub-section that are worth excerpting at length in the context of this introduction, to bring some sharper focus and final clarity to these essential points.

Tsong Khapa begins this section with the following statement:

> {420a}... Third, regarding the creation stage we must identify the bases of purification and the means of purification; and the way of identifying [those], moreover, is the meditation which accords with how [ordinary] birth, death, and the between [occur]....

Then, after giving some concrete examples of the transformations of death, the between, and rebirth, Tsong Khapa comments on the differences in emphasis and detail in this regard offered by the Ārya and Jñānapāda traditions:[71]

> {421a}...With regard to just setting up similar properties in the process of arranging similarities with the bases of purification [that is, the ordinary birth/death experience] —ignoring the [specific] explanations that wish to identify the bases of purification and the means of purification—the acquisition of a [general] understanding such as was previously explained [using texts from Jñānapāda's tradition] is what is indispensable.... {421b} However, for the Ārya tradition the unexcelled way of [specifically] identifying the bases of purification and the means of purification which accord with birth, death, and the between [state] is the excellent explanation of the import which occurs in the treatise of Shrī Nāgabodhi [of the Ārya tradition]....

---

[71] See our discussion of some of these differences above, p. 26ff.

Tsong Khapa then concludes this sub-section with an important passage admonishing the reader to understand the bases and their homologies with the path and fruit in the context of the perfection stage, as well as the ways in which the creation stage "serves as a cause of" the perfection stage:

> {421b}... [So] in the process of exchanging the ordinary body-mind systems and achieving a deity body it becomes necessary to meditate in a way that conforms to birth, death, and the between [state]. With respect to practicing from that kind of perspective, since the paths of the perfection stage are supreme, then also in the context of the second stage [it is necessary to so meditate; so here,] relying on the power of the [perfection stage] yogas of the channels, wind-energies, and drops, etc., after you have produced in your continuum a realization of emptiness which is similar to the process of death, you arise from that, and then you must understand the [perfection stage] method of creating the deity whereby, in place of the [creation stage] moon and hand-symbol, etc., from the cause of the three intuitions together with their wind-energies you arise in the illusion and integration bodies. Otherwise, you will cut off the essential points of the path of the perfection stage which purify the bases of purification; thus, having understood the essential points of the two stages, fitting them in with the bases of purification, you should generate a firm certitude about the ways in which the first stage serves as a cause of the second. Since this is explained extremely clearly in the Ārya tradition of the Esoteric Community, you must understand it from there.

Components Completing this Yoga [ii''A°2°c°]

Within our macro section on "the actual creation stage yoga with its components (**ii''A°2°**), the final sub-section (**c°**) addresses "the components completing this yoga." Here, in the first sub-sub-section (**c°i°**) Tsong Khapa first discusses how to complete the visualization of the retinue of deities in the mandala. In this context he makes the following important statement emphasizing that for a sādhana to be efficacious—that is, for it to serve to "purify" practitioner's bases as intended—it must have been composed by an authority who understands the specific homological connections that exist between each of the deities and elements of the sādhana and each of those bases (the practitioner's sense media, etc.):

> {422b}... Although there can be various greater or lesser numbers of deities set out in a mandala, in cases where there are fewer deities, then when counting the deities which bless the sense media and the body, speech, and mind, etc. [in] the evocation of the retinue of the mandala, most authorities can match the number of bases of purification and the number of deities that are the means of purification corresponding to those [bases]. Therefore, if you do not meditate a mandala-retinue sādhana written by an authority it will be difficult to complete the essential points of the creation stage that will achieve the supreme.

After this Tsong Khapa discusses how the "intuition hero" (the intuition body-mind of the actual deity) is invited to come and enter the "devotee hero" (the practitioner visualized as the main deity; that is, the practitioner manifesting the mandala-mind, or as Tsong Khapa describes it here, "the perceptual experience of your own mind which clears away the pride of ordinariness" [422a]). He explains that "the eyes, etc., of the devotee being and the eyes, etc., of the intuition being are to be inseparably mingled down to the level of the subtlest atoms, [and] you must have a firm conviction that they have become of one taste" (422b).

He then devotes several folio sides to discussing how the practitioner confers initiation upon and "seals" the intuition hero and the practitioner's body-mind systems, sense media, elements, and so on. While many details are given here regarding which transcendent buddhas, clan lords, etc. seal which aspects of which bases (systems, media, elements, etc.), a major focus again is to emphasize homological connections, that is, to show how in each case "there is a sealing by nature to that which has the nature" (423b). Thus, for example, Vairochana Buddha seals the material body-mind system because he is the purified nature of matter (and thus is the main buddha homologically corresponding to the body base); or, to cite another type of example, "since the desire arising from perceiving taste is powerful, the tongue [deity (Lokeshvara) is sealed] by Amitābha, who is the actuality of lust" (424a); and so on.

Finally, in the last sub-sub-section (**c°ii°**) on the components completing this yoga, Tsong Khapa discusses the repetition of mantra, beginning with the following statement: "So then, having tasted nectar, you should meditate deity yoga; and when you are weary [from deity yoga concentration] you should perform repetition [of mantra]" (425a). Here Tsong Khapa indirectly references a point that he often stresses (see, e.g., 383b)—viz. that deity yoga is the principle part of a sādhana session, and that mantra repetition is of secondary importance, to be done only when one is weary from having practiced the principle part—reminding the reader of the relative priorities of a sādhana practice. Then in the remainder of this section he returns to presenting more practical information from his canonical sources, discussing many aspects of mantra repetition practice, including: the substances out of which rosaries should be made for effecting different types of actions (peaceful, prospering, dominating, and destructive); how to bless and use the rosary; how to count mantras; how to recite different types of mantras, and what to visualize in different cases; and so on.

Follow-up Practices; Practices to be Done Between Sessions; and How to Make Those Yogas Magnificent

The remaining sections of chapter XII (covering the twelve folios 430a–442a) contain many interesting and intriguing details regarding the practices to be done at the conclusion of meditation sessions as well as between such sessions. These sections are relatively clear and straightforward; thus, I will leave the discovery of the majority of these details to the reader, and in the remainder of this introduction I will provide only the briefest sketch of just a few of the main topics covered.

Follow-up Practices [ii''A°3°]

In section **ii''A°3°** (430a–437b) Tsong Khapa discusses various follow-up practices, including (**a°**) fortifying the body, creating the votary cake, and (**b°**) creating visualized guests and offering the cake to them.

At the outset of the first sub-section (**a°**) Tsong Khapa says: "When your body and mind are fatigued from having meditated..., there is the procedure of fortification" (430a). While this procedure is to be performed at the conclusion of a given meditation session, Tsong Khapa clarifies that it also may be performed at any point during a meditation session, whenever one needs to be revitalized. Following Dīpaṅkarabhadra and Shāntipa, he explains that this procedure involves visualizing that nectar streams down from a moon on one's crown, and then causing that nectar —through the force of "vitality and exertion" (here explained as being exhalation-winds and inhalation-winds)—to pervade all of the channels throughout one's body.

For the great majority of this first sub-section Tsong Khapa then turns to the topic of offering votary cakes. He begins by noting: "Votary cakes are said by many Tantras to be very important at the beginning and the end [of practice] in order to pacify demonic interference and to achieve siddhis, and thus you should use them" (431a). Having thus briefly recollected the need for offering votary cakes, he then proceeds to discuss many ritual details regarding how to create such cakes, primarily following *The Kiss Tantra* and Abhaya's *Vajra Rosary* and *Clusters of Instructions*. Then in the second sub-section (**b°**) he describes three variations (extensive, middling, and condensed) of the procedure for creating/inviting the appropriate deity host and offering the votary cake to them, before concluding with an extended presentation of varying views regarding when and how often one should perform this offering.

Practices to Be Done Between Sessions [ii''B°]

In section **ii''B°** (437b–439b) Tsong Khapa discusses what to practice between formal meditation sessions. This involves a great variety of practices that essentially carry over deity yoga (divine pride, extraordinary perceptions/conceptions, etc.) into one's daily life. This includes practices such as: perceiving one's sense faculties and sense objects as having the nature of deities; engaging in all activities with the wisdom that does not objectify the three sectors of an action; viewing all physical and verbal actions as mudrā and mantra; yogas for transforming the activities of eating, washing, sleeping, and arising; and yogas for the purification of broken commitments.

How to Make Those Yogas Magnificent [ii''C°]

Tsong Khapa concludes this chapter with section **ii''C°** (439b–442a) in which he explores some of the extraordinary ramifications of uniting the profound and the magnificent (the mind realizing emptiness arising in the form of a buddha) in creation stage practice. He begins by recapping the process and promise of this practice: when one's mind has developed the wisdom that eradicates misknowledge (the misconception of intrinsic reality), this eradicates the reified misperception of one's body-mind systems as intrinsically ordinary; and this openness in turn allows for the development of the extraordinary perception of one's body as the body of a buddha. However, he then carries this presentation of deity yoga a step further with the startling observation that this nondual conceptual/perceptual development in turn leads to the result that "that body which had the quality of being ordinary [is revealed to have] had the quality of being an incidental erroneous deception, while the buddha body [is known to] have the quality of something impossible to lose, since it abides as long as space endures" (439b–440a).

Tsong Khapa then expands upon this sense of the timelessness of the profound/magnificent buddha body by offering a further exploration of what its "magnificence" (and the unique deity yoga that develops/reveals it) entails. He cites Shāntipa who maintains that things one perceives as selfless in the Transcendence Vehicle "do not overcome dimensionality," and that they thus "have an ordinary nature because of one's [still] determining aspects of place and time," whereas "that which is not determined with respect to direction and time is great, and thus is magnificent." Tsong Khapa elaborates that it is only the Mantra Vehicle's "circle of deities, which is the counter-agent to the perception of ordinariness" that is "not measured in terms of place and time" and that is thus "magnificent" in this way (440b–441a). He concludes: "When you meditate deity yoga in terms of its being of one taste with the thatness of things and [in terms of the deity circle] having just that [nondual] nondeceptive quality, you are meditating in terms of its totality—without determining from a limited perspective the extent of the excellences, places, and times of the form bodies, etc., of all the transcendent buddhas—and thus it is magnificent" (441a).

* * *

With this brief introduction complete, I now invite the reader to enjoy our translation of chapters XI and XII of Tsong Khapa's *Great Treatise on the Stages of Mantra*, to discover the many insights Tsong Khapa and his Indian Buddhist sources offer regarding the need to integrate both the creation stage and perfection stage yogas, and regarding the amazing details, processes, and meanings of the creation stage yogas themselves.

PART TWO

Translation

CHAPTER XI

The Need to Accomplish Enlightenment Through the Integration of the Two Stages

[II.B.2.c.ii.C'3'a'iv'B''1''c''iii''B°2°b° – The rite of consecrating the deity in the initiation]

[II.B.2.c.ii.C'3'a'iv'B''2'' – The rites of the components of initiation]

{348a.4} Regarding [the sub-topic of] "The rite of consecrating the deity in the initiation,"[72] which is the second sub-topic under [the topic of] "The rite of conferring initiation on others,"[73] and [the sub-topic of] "The rites of the components of initiation,"[74] which is the second sub-topic under [the topic of] "The process of how you perform the rite"[75]: although there are many very important methods of propitiating the deity and achieving siddhi and of purifying your overall conduct of Mantra—[which include topics] such as fire sacrifice; the group host rite which repairs infractions and pleases the ḍākas [and ḍākinīs]; how to determine the components of your vows to possess and to not lack equipment such as vaja, bell, sacrifice ladle, six ornaments, ḍamaru, skull bowl, {348b} and khaṭvāṅga staff; and also the ways of determining how you have performed such activities—if I were to get into the details of that here, fearing that the text would become extremely lengthy, for the time being I will not write about them, and so you should come to know them from other [texts].

In order to help you understand into which contexts you should incorporate all the meanings of Tantra when you [have to] sort them into the branches of practice for a person to attain buddhahood, in this *Stages*

[72] This sixteenth-level sub-topic was introduced in ch. VIII at 253b.2.

[73] This fifteenth-level main topic was introduced in ch. VIII at folio 248a.1.

[74] This eleventh-level sub-topic was introduced in ch. V at 136a.6.

[75] This tenth-level main topic was introduced in ch. V at folio 135a.4.

of the Path [*of Mantra* text] I have picked out some special[ly important points] to arrange into a source of concise meanings [for you to use].

[**II.B.2.c.ii.C'3'b'** – Having become a suitable vessel, how to purify the commitments and vows]

{348b.3} Second, you may wonder: For a person who has become a suitable vessel through having received such an initiation, what should they do first with respect to purifying their commitments and vows?

Having made efforts to keep the commitments and vows in accordance with what you promised at the time of the initiation, when you meditate the personal instructions of the two stages, such as the wheel of the mandala, etc., then you will achieve siddhi. Otherwise, if you let your assumed vows disappear, then even though you strive for many aeons you will not achieve [siddhi]. The *Arisal of Saṁvara [Tantra]* says:

> Just as you were personally instructed,
> Later you should strive to practice the commitments.
> Within the continuum of having become a vessel,
> By the stages of meditating on the wheel, etc.,
> And by the superlative and authentic personal instructions,
> You will come to achieve; and otherwise not.

Moreover, *The Interpenetrating Union [Tantra]* says:[76]

> If you have not entered {349a} into a pure mandala,
> If you abandon your commitments,
> Or if you do not understand the esoteric reality,
> Then although you practice, you will not achieve anything.

And the *[Vajra] Peak [Tantra]* says:

> Even though for many hundreds of aeons
> They may make great efforts in the world,
> Four [kinds of] people, although they practice,
> Will have no achievement:

---

[76] Lhasa edition varies slightly (see my note to the Tibetan critical edition of *NRC* XI–XII, forthcoming in this AIBS *Treasury of the Buddhist Sciences* series).

> Those who have not conceived the spirit of enlightenment,
> Those who have doubt,
> Those who do not practice according to the teaching, and
> Those with no faith—[all these] will not achieve.

Furthermore, right after having become a suitable vessel through initiation, without delay, you must be guided through instruction. As [Ashvaghoṣha's] *The Fifty Verses on the Mentor* says:[77]

> Then, when by the blessing of the mantras, etc.,
> You have become a vessel of the holy Dharma,
> You should study the fourteen root downfalls
> And uphold [your vows].

The *Arisal of Saṁvara [Tantra]* says:

> If you want the supreme siddhi,[78]
> [Rather than to break your commitments,]
> It is better even[79] to let go of your life,

---

[77] This is verse 49 of the *Gurupañcāśikā*. Here "the blessing of the mantras" translates *sngags sogs byin ba yis*. However, according to Abby Petty Li's 1994 U.W. Master's thesis on this work (pp. 98–99, 126, 162–163), the first pada should read: *de nas sngags sogs sbyin ba yis* (based on *sDe-dge*, *Co-ne*, and Peking canonical sources). Apparently the *rgyud sde kun btus*, as well as Tshar chen's and Tsong Khapa's commentaries attest the byin spelling found here in this *NRC* citation. That perhaps it should indeed be *sbyin* is suggested by the fact that the immediately preceding pāda (pāda 4 of verse 48) reads *kha ton bya bar sbyin par bya* ("[A student] should offer a recitation of prayers"). Petty Li's translation of verse 49 (reading *sbyin*, as "offering," and here reaing *sngags* as "praises") is:

> Having been made a vessel for the holy *Dharma*, / Through such things as offering praises, /
> One should then read and exactly adhere / To the fourteen main Tantric vows.

On problems of authorial attribution, cf. Petty Li's discussion at pp. 1–75.

[78] "The supreme siddhi" (*dngos grub mchog*, or *mchog gi dngos grub*), and "the great siddhi" (*dngos grub chen po*)—both attested extensively herein, and throughout Tantric literarure—are epithets for buddhahood.

[79] Taking *yang bla* (and next *kyang bla*) as "it is *better* even to...." A more literal translation would be: "You should *easily* cast away your life...[before you consider breaking a commitment]"—i.e., it should be a 'no-brainer.'

> It is better even to reach the moment of death.
> You always should maintain your commitments!

And the second [chapter] of *The Illusory Net [Tantra]* says:

> Then [the mentor] should teach the commitments:
> 'Oh you child, from today onwards,
> Even though it comes down to your life or body,[80]
> Do not despise the holy Dharma,
> The spirit of enlightenment, or the teacher;[81]
> And never slander your vajra brothers and sisters,[82]
> Appease the hateful,[83] or be devoid of passion.'

{349b} Just as it states [here] that you must guard your commitments and vows even at the risk of your life, you must make effort. In particular, it states that if you are contaminated by a root downfall, then having spoiled your continuum it will be very difficult to generate any excellences. Therefore, you must make a fierce effort not to be contaminated by that [kind of root downfall]. Moreover, you must strive not to be contaminated by any other downfall; but if there is an occurrence [of a such a non-root downfall], then again you should confess in accordance with the Dharma, [re-]bind yourself, and thereby repair it.

If one who has completely attained the initiation strives to keep the commitments and is thus not contaminated by downfalls, then even if there is not much [of an opportunity] to meditate on the path, it is stated that [that person] will achieve the supreme [siddhi] within seven lifetimes, etc. [But] if you let your keeping of the commitments of the precepts diminish, then even though you protest that you were striving in other

---

[80] While all three editions of the *NRC* read "bone/clan" (*rus*), the Derge and Lhasa editions of the cited text both read "body" (*lus*) which seems to make better sense. See the note to the Tibetan edition for other variants.

[81] These would appear to be essentially the sixth, fifth, and first root Tantric downfalls, respectively.

[82] The third root Tantric downfall.

[83] *sdang la byams*—this appears to be something like the tenth root Tantric downfall: Sapan's commentary says that the 10th downfall is "Always to befriend enemies and harmful beings,...those who disrespect or harm the teaching...." (Elsewhere the tenth is cited as *gdug can gyi grogs bsten pa*—"relying on poisonous friends.")

ways, you will go to bad migrations, and thus it will be difficult to return to the happy [migrations], let alone to attain siddhi! So, Saraha's *Commentary on The [Buddha-]Skullbowl [Tantra]* quotes *The Secret Treasury Tantra* as saying:[84]

> If one has the true gift[85] of receiving initiation,
> Then one will receive initiation in life after life.
> That person, even though not meditating,
> Will achieve siddhi in seven lifetimes.
>
> Whoever has a meditation [practice]
> And abides in the commitments and vows,
> And, due to the force of evolutionary action, [still] does not achieve in this life,
> [Such a one] will achieve siddhi in another life.
>
> But if someone spoils their commitments,[86]
> It will be hard to obtain a human rebirth again,
> Let alone to achieve siddhi.

And [Padmākara's] *The Five Commitments* says:

> If you have no downfalls,
> You will achieve in sixteen lifetimes.

{350a} Furthermore, Vibhūtichandra says [in the *Luminous Rosary of the Three Vows*]:

> Even though you do not meditate, if you have no downfalls
> You will achieve in sixteen lifetimes.

---

[84] Tōh. 830. This is one of the 17 Tantras (Tōh. 828–844) within the *rnying rgyud* section of the Tōh. Derge Kangyur. I could not locate the passage cited here.

[85] *sbyin* (349b.4, MS p. 306.2)—both texts have this spelling. Again, one might want to read this as *byin* (blessing). Compare this with the discussion of the discrepancy between *sbyin* (gift) and *byin* (blessing) in verse 49 of *The Fifty Verses on the Mentor*, note 77 above.

[86] The Derge says "[But if] someone does not abide in their commitments and vows," which has the same import.

Here, whether you are a master who explains Tantras or practical instructions and confers initiations, or whether you are a student who listens to Tantras and practical instructions, or whether you are both, and whether you practice or do not practice at all, everyone who obtains an initiation should act as if it is unsuitable to transgress[87] [their vows]. With respect to achieving the supreme [that is, buddhahood], etc., in this life, [this attitude is] the sole means of progress on the path, whether you are a superior, a mediocre, or an inferior person.

[In particular,] depending upon the statement—[appearing] again and again in the Tantras and the elucidations [of the Tantras]—that the mentor is the root of all siddhis, the ancient holy ones maintained that meditating mentor yoga is of the greatest importance at the beginning of the path; and so they condensed the extensive explanation about the first root downfall into the maintaining of the commitments [as expressed] in *The Fifty Verses on the Mentor*, and [they held that] just this [avoidance of the first downfall] is the most important of the precepts.

Therefore, if you develop the utmost certainty regarding the instruction in the learning of Mantra, then those partial practices of that kind [that is, relying on the mentor]—[from among] all the things which are designated as prerequisites of the actual path—come to have the highest importance with respect to maintaining of the commitments and vows. Therefore, the intelligent should understand that the prerequisite for the two stages is inititation and the maintenance of the commitments. **{350b}** Regarding these imports, His Holiness Dragpa Gyaltsen[88] himself said:

> Though you have faith in the Vajra Vehicle, if you are not
> ripened [through initiation],
> The Buddha said that even though you meditate the
> profound,
> You will not achieve any fruit other than a bad migration.

---

87 *yang dbang thob pa kun gyis 'dar mi rung bar bya dgos pa yin*—this is neither the verb *dar ba* ('to spread,' which has no prefix in any tense) nor *'dar ba* ('to tremble, shake'—Das 680, Gold. 599). I am taking *'dar* to be the terminal form of the verb *'da' ba* (pf. *'das pa*), 'to die; *go beyond*; *disobey, break a promise, violate*' (Das 679, Gold. 599).

88 The Sakyapa Dragpa Gyaltsen, third of the five founding Sakya heirarchs. I have not yet found the source of this quote. Tsong Khapa's use of "His Holiness" (*rje bstun*) for this lama reflects his deep respect for the Sakya tradition in which he was educated.

Therefore, receive the conferral of initiation from the
supreme mentor!

One who has achieved initiation and is seeking profound
private instruction
May seek all over the vast surface of the world,
But the key import which is helpful is the practical
instructions and the commitments—
Without this it is like a decrepit house on a crumbling river
bank.

Having been well-ripened [through initiation], if you keep
your commitments,
Then even though you do not rely on the profound
personal instruction of the two stages,
The benefactor of the family of beings[89] said
"You will achieve in sixteen lifetimes."

Although I am of little learning, and lack the eye of wisdom,
Since I have seen this stated well in the immaculate
Tantras,
I pray to everyone, with folded hands:
"Receive initiation and maintain the commitments!"

This is advice from someone who knows the pith of the Tantras; and so I likewise pray!

Since making this kind of precept known is the duty of the mentor, if that [precept] is not taught, then the mentor incurs fault. But if it is taught and it is not practiced, then it is the disciple's fault. Since I already have explained this in my *Explanation of the Fifty Verses on the Mentor* and in my *Explanation of the Root [Tantric] Downfalls*,[90] you should learn about the subject of the commitments fom these other [sources]. When you learn that, then with whatever strength you have you should strive to maintain the precepts in general, and especially {351a} the root

---

[89] *'gro ba'i rtsa lag phan par mdzad pa*—presumably an epithet for the Buddha.

[90] Cf. bibliography herein ("Tibetan Texts (Other)," under Tsong Khapa) for complete citations. See Petty Li's thesis (86–91, 165, 184–91) for a discussion of these texts. See Tsongkhapa (trans. Sparham) 1999 and 2005 for studies and translations of these texts.

commitments; and within those [root commitments you should strive to maintain] the extremely important mentor-commitments, because it would be inappropriate not to maintain the vows which you undertook, with the mentors, heros, and yoginīs as witnesses.

[**II.B.2.c.ii.C'3'c'** – Grounded in the commitments, how to experientially cultivate the path]

The third has two: [i'] That you first should understand the path by learning about it and contemplating it; and [ii'] Experiential cultivation [of the path] by meditating on the import of what you have understood.

[**II.B.2.c.ii.C'3'c'i'** – That you first should understand the path by learning about it and contemplating it]

You may wonder: What should one who has received initiation and who properly maintains the commitments and vows do next?

[Shraddhākaravarman's] *Deciphering the Seven Ornaments* says:

> First, through the wisdom [born] of learning
> Generate erudition in the Tantric literature.
> Then through the wisdom [born] of thinking
> Learn the connection between word and meaning.

According to that statement, whether you are practicing yourself or whether you are teaching the path to others, first you must seek an unerring understanding through learning and thinking—because if you do not understand it yourself you cannot teach it to another; and because there is no experiential cultivation without understanding; and, since one experientially cultivates according to how much one understands, if your understanding is erroneous your practice will be erroneous, because unerring practice depends upon unerring understanding.

And so, accordingly, [Ratnākarashānti's] *The Pearl Rosary: A Commentary on the Difficult Points of the Hevajra* says:

> If you have no intelligence you cannot learn, and if you do not learn you cannot think;
> {351b} If you lack both then there is no yoga, and without yoga there is no siddhi.

And [Vīryabhadra's] *The Clear Meaning: A Commentary on the Difficult Points of [Nāgārjuna's] Five Stages* says:

> If you have both the wisdom completed through learning
> And [the wisdom completed through] thinking,
> Then real application to meditation [is possible];
> From that there will be the unexcelled siddhi.
>
> Considering in that way, the intelligent person
> Who first strives for the aim of learning
> And then continually makes effort,
> Will, as a result of that, achieve siddhi.
>
> If you have doubt about the words,
> Then how will you realize the meaning?

And [Nāgārjuna's] *The Five Stages* says:

> Whoever has veneration for and faith in the mentor
> And always strives to serve and honor [him or her] with respect,
> Is one who upholds their learning, and is the best disciple.

—thus proclaiming the upholding of learning to be a defining characteristic of [being] a disciple. And *The Interpenetrating Union [Tantra]* says:[91]

> If you do not understand the esoteric reality,
> Then although you practice, you will not achieve anything.

Moreover, if you are very intelligent and energetic, etc., you must apply yourself to the [root] Tantric literature; if not, you must apply yourself to the appropriate Mantric treatises written by scholar-adepts; or at the very least you must develop certain erudition and reflection with respect to one complete presentation of the key points of the creation and perfection [stages]. Furthermore, if you serve as a vajra master who teaches personal instructions of Mantra to others, etc., then in particular you must become skilled in {352a} the two stages and in the rites of the mandala, etc.

[91] This is the second half of the same quote cited previously (see p. 78 above).

[However, some people] view the Tantras and the great treatises that elucidate their intention as mere Dharma-props[92] that cut away outer elaborations, and they grasp at the thought that there is some indirect profound practical instruction which is hidden [in those texts] and which is not explained in them. Due to this, lacking esteem[93] for the thorough completeness of the Dharma, they prevent themselves from developing great respect for the great treatises of Mantra and from [seeing how] those [Mantric treatises] arise as practical instructions;[94] and this is a great condition for the rapid demise of those people. Therefore, you should abandon [such notions] as though they were poison! Rather, relying upon the private instructions of a superior mentor, you should strive in the art of [seeing] the great treatises arise as practical instructions. As *The Five Stages* says:

> These principles[95] are sealed
> In *The Glorious [Esoteric] Community Tantra*;
> You should know [them] from the mentor's mouth
> Following the explanatory Tantras.

This says that the ultimate practical instructions—the principles of the five stages—were placed and sealed within the root Tantra of *The [Esoteric] Community* by the Victor, and that those [principles] must be understood by relying on the mentor's speech. Thus, this says that the locus of these profound ultimate points is the root Tantras of the precious Tantric literature, and that to understand them the mentor is necessary; and that moreover it is not enough for the mentor to just say whatever occurs to him, but that {352b} he must know how to explain the root Tantras by following the explanatory Tantras.

Therefore, regarding the private instructions: Non-mistakenly explaining the meaning of the root Tantras following the explanatory

---

[92] *chos rgyab*.

[93] *zhe rtsis*—cf. Das: 1074 and 1011.

[94] It was one of Atīsha's four cardinal principles that the Buddha's teachings must be seen to arise as practical instructions (*gsung rab thams cad gdams ngag tu 'char ba*). While this is cited often in exoteric contexts, it is important to note that here in this esoteric context also Tsong Khapa insists on following Atīsha in this regard.

[95] *de nyid 'di dag*.

Tantras is what is called "the method for easily generating insight in the disciple's continuum." Thus, you should understand the 'tradition of learning from the [mentor's] mouth' also to be like that; and you should not maintain that—discarding what is written in the Tantras—it involves a gradual ear-whispered transmission [of teachings] not set forth in those [Tantras]. Thus, if it seems to you that, just because the private instruction is supreme, if you practice it for a long time, then though when you [simply] glance into the authoritative treatises on the Tantras, etc., they must surely give you certitude about many Tantric imports, but that since you carry the practical instructions, critical investigation of the import of the Tantras cannot give you any certitude at all—it is a sign either of a faulty intelligence or of a misunderstanding.

Just as you would survey the course before you race on a horse, so here, whether in Mantric or philosophical systems, you first understand through learning and critical reflection what is going to be experientially cultivated, and you then experientially cultivate the import that you have thus determined. Nevertheless, [I acknowledge that] when you have a heartfelt desire to get on with practice you may look upon studying the great treatises of Mantra as ridiculous, since it may seem that whether or not you study the Tantras a lot will make no quantifiable difference when you experientially cultivate in the future. Therefore, [I reiterate my plea here that] you who seek liberation should investigate well with careful intellectual discrimination![96]

[**II.B.2.c.ii.C'3'c'ii'** – Experiential cultivation [of the path] by meditating on the import of what you have understood]

The second has four: [A''] Rejection of the claim that one can attain buddhahood by experientially cultivating either one of the {353a} two stages alone; [B''] The way of experientially cultivating the two stages in an inseparable way; [C''] The [radical] practices that are the method for

---

[96] Although a skilled horse racer may be impatient to get on with the thrill of the race, he nevertheless will understand that the preliminary careful examination of the course is a necessary prerequisite to running a successful race. So here, while Tsong Khapa is sympathizing with those who may be impatient to get on with "practice," he is nevertheless urging them to engage in the learning and critical reflection which constitutes the necessary foundation for successful practice.

bringing out the impact[97] of those two [stages]; and [D''] The way that those [two stages] serve as the path for the three [types of] persons.

[II.B.2.c.ii.C'3'c'ii'A'' – Rejection of the claim that one can attain buddhahood by experientially cultivating either one of the two stages alone]

The first has two: [1''] Rejection of the claim that one can attain buddhahood by the creation stage without the perfection stage; and [2''] Rejection of the claim that one can attain buddhahood by the perfection stage without the creation stage.

[II.B.2.c.ii.C'3'c'ii'A''1'' – Rejection of the claim that one can attain buddhahood by the creation stage without the perfection stage]

The first has two: [a''] Expression of the claim; and [b''] Its refutation.

[II.B.2.c.ii.C'3'c'ii'A''1''a'' – Expression of the claim (that creation stage alone is needed)]

Āchārya Mañjushrīkīrti presents the antagonist['s position] in *The Ornament of the Essence*:

> The Great Ṛiṣhi Vishvamitra,[98] and the Vidyādhara Āchārya *Kumārasena,[99] and *Jinapāda,[100] and *Ratnamat,[101] and *Brahmaṇabhadramitra,[102] etc., argue: "The

97 *bogs 'byin pa'i thabs*— lit. 'a method for extracting the benefit, profit, advantage, enhancement,' hence 'a method for bringing out the impact,' or a method for bringing about the full impact, success, conclusion, result, etc. (of the two stages). Thus, it is often stated that once you have achieved a stage (e.g., a perfection stage level) you then need to do various practices (sometimes wild ones) to "extract its essence" (*bogs dbyung*), that is, to fully cement it.

98 *drang srong chen po bi shva mi tra* (Great Ṛiṣhi Vishvamitra)—*Blue Annals* I (no page reference) cites a Vishvamitra.

99 *rig sngags 'chang gi slob dpon gzhon nu'i sde* (Vidyādhara Āchārya Kumārasena?)—not in *Blue Annals*.

100 *rgyal ba'i zhabs* (Jinapāda?)—*Blue Annals* I, 12, 227 cites a Jina.

101 *rin chen ldan* (Ratnamat?)—*Blue Annals* II, 691 cites a *spyan lnga rin chen ldan*.

102 *bram ze bzang po'i bshes gnyen* (Brahmaṇabhadramitra?)—not in *Blue Annals*.

> [wisdom realizing the] natural purity of all phenomena is that which is to be practiced [only] in order to stop conceptual thought,[103] since buddhahood is achieved [rather] by merit [alone]. The path of the creation stage abandons ordinary phenomena and accomplishes the aims of sentient beings by means of the form body; and since [this] in itself is perfectly complete buddhahood, it should be achieved by [taking] the form of a deity and by infallible conduct."

Their thought is as follows:[104] {353b} The desired aim of the Universal Vehicle practitioner is *the aim of sentient beings*, and since it is *the form body* that is the [means for] directly accomplishing that [aim], then when you achieve that [form body] you have become a *buddha. Therefore, [this] should be achieved by deity* yoga *and by infallible conduct* such as the commitments and vows, since it is *by the creation stage* that *you abandon the ordinary* body and achieve the *body* [endowed] with the signs and marks. As for the statement that you need the wisdom of emptiness —that is, [the wisdom] of *the natural purity of all phenomena*—that [wisdom] *is to be practiced [only] in order to stop the conceptual thought* that wrongly apprehends the import of thatness, *since buddhahood* is the

---

[103] Tsong Khapa's citation is the same as that in the the Derge Tengyur edition (Tōh. 2490), with one important difference (underlined below). The *NRC* citation reads: *chos thams cad rang bzhin gyis rnam par dag pa ni, rnam par rtog pa dgag pa las blang ba'i bya ba nyid yin te,* In his commentary below, Tsong Khapa makes sense of this version by replacing the potentially confusing ablative *las* to give the much clearer *rnam rtog dgag pa'i phyir du blang bar bya ba*, more clearly translating the Sanskrit use of the ablative to give a reason. The Derge edition's version of the second phrase is significantly different, reading *log par rtog pa dgag pa las blang bar bya ba ma yin te*, meaning that the wisdom realizing natural purity (i.e., emptiness) "should *not* be practiced *except* to stop wrong thought." This makes better sense, but it will be noted that the negative verb coupled with an interpretation of the ablative as meaning "other than" renders this reading similar to that cited in the *NRC*. With either reading we see that these objectors wish to minimize or limit the role of emptiness awareness and to (over-)emphasize the role of merit and the development of a form body.

[104] In what follows Tsong Khapa gives almost a phrase by phrase commentary of the antagonists' thought, quoting phrases verbatim, often in a different order, and often glossing each with slightly different Tibetan words or syntax to make the meaning clearer. I have *italicized* the phrases he has directly quoted in this way.

fruition that *is achieved [rather] by* the store of *merit [alone]*. Therefore, if you [simply] find the non-erroneous view of emptiness, you do turn back the false notions that wrongly conceptualize the import of thatness, and therefore you do not err with regard to the way things really are; but if you have that [nonconceptual view] and deity yoga and [proper] conduct, then since you then have an inseparable [form of] method and wisdom, why wouldn't you become a buddha?

Although these people claim to generate a pure form of the view, they do not claim that one must become more and more accustomed to meditating on that [view]. The reason [they think this] is that they think that the establishment of emptiness in the treatises of the central way, etc., was stated [just] in order to reverse the wrong notions among those in our own [Buddhist] and others' [non-Buddhist] systems; and that therefore once one has found the unerring view, then since those wrong notions are reversed [one need not meditate on emptiness any more since] one is [then already] {354a} without the wrong notions which were to be reversed through meditation on emptiness.[105] They grasp at the words of scriptural passsages such as those we quoted previously from *The [Vajra] Pavilion [Tantra]*[106]—and [thinking that such passages] refute that the view of emptiness is the method for achieving buddhahood, it is clear that they rely on these passages as if they said that the need for the Victor to teach emptiness was only to reverse wrong notions, and that therefore if you practice by means of deity yoga involving a mandala circle then that is the [real] method for quickly becoming a buddha, and that therefore you should practice by that [method].

---

[105] Thus, due to their superficial understanding of what the realization of emptiness entails, these antagonists adopt a subitistic ("sudden enlightenment") perspective with respect to "finding" the correct the view of emptiness. Their particular subitistic perspective is rather idiosyncratic since (among other reasons)—by arguing that "buddhahood is achieved...by merit [alone]" and that "the form body...in itself is perfectly complete buddhahood"—they evidently do not consider the development of the store of intuition (or even the buddha's truth body) to be necessary.

[106] The particular passage under discussion here ("If emptiness were the method, then there could be no buddhahood...," from ch. I of the *NRC*) appears at *TT*: 117. Hopkins' footnote 35 locates this in the Peking canon at P11, vol. 1, 223.4.4–223.4.7. This key passage is also translated and discussed at length in my forthcoming book, *The Emptiness that is Form*.

These [antagonists] do not appear to be people who have not inquired into the Tantras; but they do not seem to offer a clear account regarding whether or not one should meditate the yogas of the channels, wind-energies, etc., mentioned frequently in the Tantras; so it is clear that they [must] include those [practices] under the topic of conduct.[107]

[**II.B.2.c.ii.C'3'c'ii'A''1''b''** – Refutation of that (claim that creation stage alone is needed)]

Since it is not necessary to prove to these people that they must meditate the additional path of Mantra,[108] [we primarily will need to prove to them that] they should accustom themselves more and more to emptiness meditation.[109]

Although it is indeed true that [the aspect of] a buddha which directly accomplishes the aims of sentient beings is the form body and not the truth body, and that the form body is achieved through the store of merit, still, without achieving the truth body one cannot achieve the form body, and thus one must achieve the truth body as well. Therefore, why shouldn't one depend also on the store {354b} of intuition, just as one depends on the store of merit? There is no difference in the reasons

---

[107] Recall that these antagonists maintain that one must do three things: (1) obtain non-conceptuality; (2) practice deity yoga; and (3) practice the code of conduct (*spyod pa*). Now the yogas of the channels, wind-energies, and drops (which come after the deity yoga of the creation stage and at the beginning of the perfection stage) do involve at least some level of subtle conceptuality, so Tsong Khapa here reasonably wonders how such practices might square with their beliefs (1) and (2). Since they make no clear statement about such practices, Tsong Khapa concludes that they must include such necessary practices under (3).

[108] *sngags kyi lam gzhan*—lit. "another path which is Mantra." That is, they already accept that in addition to the Transcendence Vehicle they must practice the Mantra Vehicle.

[109] Again (cf. note 105 above), throughout this section Tsong Khapa will be characterizing the anatagonist as adopting an essentially subitistic perspective (albeit an idiosyncratic one), in response to which he will be presenting the progreessive, gradualist perspective (advocated by Tsong Khapa himself, and by the vast majority of Indian and Tibetan traditions).

[for the need to depend on each one, and hence no justification for emphasizing either one over the other].[110]

Objection: There is a dependence on the store of intuition [for us] because [we] have the view which realizes the thatness of selflessness.

[Answer:] That is illogical, because if you do not want to meditate [progressively] on the view of selflessness then you will not complete the store of intuition by just ["having"] that [view]; otherwise, with regard to the creation stage, it also would be the case that once you found a [general] understanding of the habitat and inhabitant mandalas, then even without practicing it [progressively] you would complete the store of merit!

Objection: If [as we both agree] meditating the view is done for the sake of reversing wrong notions about the meaning of thatness, then [we would point out] there are no [such] wrong notions that wrongly hold the meaning of thatness in the continuum of one who has found the unerring view.[111]

[Answer:] This [position] fails to distinguish between the intellectual wrong notions and the instinctual wrong notions. Even though it is indeed true that as long as the function of the view of thatness which is developed by logic is not deteriorated one will have no theoretically posited wrong notions,[112] still there will be no reversal of the instinctual self-habit which is beginninglessly entrenched in the mind and which does not depend upon the mind being distorted by theories.[113] Were that not the case, then just as soon as one discovered the view which understands the way things are one would abandon all the things which are to be abandoned on [the path of] insight and on [the path of] meditation, and one therefore would have no need to meditate upon the creation stage

---

[110] In chapter 1 of the *NRC* Tsong Khapa argues extensively (backed with substantial canonical citations) that the form body and the truth body are mutually dependent and must be developed in coordination with each other. See *TT*.

[111] That is, once one has "found" (i.e., even had an initial glimpse of) the correct view of emptiness, all wrong notions about reality will be automatically and entirely elimintated, and hence no further meditation on the view of emptiness would be required.

[112] *grub mthas btags pa'i log rtog med.*

[113] *grub mthas blo bsgyur ba la ma ltos nas.*

either. Therefore, {355a} in order to abandon those obscurations[114] it is not sufficient to have only a [correct intellectual] understanding of selflessness; [rather] one must develop a direct realization by meditating on the import of selflessness which has been determined by the view.

When one determines the import of selflessness through the treatises of the central way, etc., one's negations—taking one's own and others' schools as antagonists—do not negate merely the wrong notions of advocates of theories. Well, then what [do they also/primarily negate]? [They negate] that which serves as the obstruction to liberation, which is precisely the instinctual self-habit; because if [liberation were] obstructed only through intellectualizations developed from theories, then those whose minds had not been distorted by theories would have no obstruction to liberation.

[So how do central way negations negate both intellectual as well as instinctual self-habit patterns?] If you are to negate the object of the instinctual self-habit you must negate the theories of substantialists, because their theories do [attempt to] prove the existence of that [self]. So the negation—by the treatises of the central way, etc.—of the claims of the substantialists of our own and others' schools is a factor in the negation of the object of the instinctual self-habit, and thus the selflessness determined through those [treatises] is the selflessness which refutes the manner of the habit of the instinctual self-habit. So although the mere finding of that view does not [by itself] reverse that [instinctual] self habit, if you familiarize yourself [with that found view through progressively meditating on it], it will reverse it.[115]

---

[114] That is, all the obscurations which are to be abandoned on the paths of insight and meditation.

[115] Tsong Khapa makes exactly this same point in his philosophical treatise, the *Essence of Eloquence* (*legs bshad snying po*). See Thurman's clear discussion of the relevant passages in his introduction to *The Speech of Gold* (1989, 136), and in the translation (297). Therein Tsong Khapa says:

> ...although such [instinctual] mental habits do not hold their objects through analysis of the meaning of conventional expressions (as do intellectual mental habits), if the objects thus held were to exist in fact, they would have to be discoverable by the analytic cognition that analyzes the manner of existence of the referents of conventional expressions.... Therefore, ...one (should) not adhere to the notion that "the texts merely negate intellectual mental habits with their objects." (1989, 136)

[II.B.2.c.ii.C'3'c'ii'A''2'' – Rejection of the claim that one can attain buddhahood by the perfection stage without the creation stage]

The second has two: [a''] Expression of the claim; and [b''] Its refutation.

[II.B.2.c.ii.C'3'c'ii'A''2''a'' – Expression of the claim (that perfection stage alone is needed)]

[Mañjushrīkīrti] presents the antagonist's position in *The Ornament of the Essence*:[116] {355b}

> Furthermore, the brahmin *Shūnyamati,[117] and the Kashmiri abbot *Prabhākara,[118] and Anantavajra,[119] and the upāsika Sitikara,[120] and the great sage *Shrī Siṁha,[121] and *Avabhāsavajra,[122] and the bhikṣhu *Mahāyānashrī,[123] and *Sudattabhadra,[124] and *Shrī Nīlāntaravāsadhara,[125] and *Jinapāda, and *Ratnamat, and *Brahmaṇa-

---

[116] This passage appears immediately after the passage cited at 353a above. Note the variants mentioned in the following notes to this pasage.

[117] *bram ze stong nyid blo* (brahmin Shūnyamati?)—not in *Blue Annals*.

[118] *kha che'i mkhan po rab snang byed* (Kashmiri abbot Prabhākara?)—not in *Blue Annals*.

[119] *a nanta badzra* (Anantavajra)—not in *Blue Annals*.

[120] *dge bsnyen si ti ka ra* (upāsika Sitikara)—not in *Blue Annals*.

[121] *mkhas pa chen po dpal gyi seng ge* (great sage Shrī Siṁha)—*Blue Annals* I, 104 cites a *glang dpal gyi seng ge*. It also cites a Siṁha at I, 22, 25, 168, 191. This may be the famous *rDzogs chen pa* by this name.

[122] *snang mdzad rdo rje* (Avabhāsavajra?)—not in *Blue Annals*.

[123] *dge slong theg chen dpal* (bhikṣhu Mahāyānashrī?)—*Blue Annals* II, 704 cites a *theg chen pa*.

[124] *legs sbyin bzang po* (Sudattabhadra?)—*Blue Annals* I, 33 cites a Sudatta.

[125] *dpal sham thabs sngon po can* (Shrī Nīlāntaravāsadhara?)—not in *Blue Annals*. Das (p. 1231) refers to a *sham thabs sngon po can*: "A *Tīrthika* Pandit who preached a perverse system of *Tantra* and used to wear a blue petticoat." (A *sham thabs* is a monk's lower robe, not really a "petticoat").

> bhadramitra,[126] and the bhikṣhuni *Nandā,[127] etc., say: "Statements regarding the creation stage and modes of conduct are stated [merely] as methods for rejecting nihilists, for establishing the fruition of relativity by relativity, and for reassuring some worldly people who are frightened by the profound meaning. But perfect buddhahood is inconceivable nondual intuition, and it is not born from a cause [such as creation stage practice] which does not correspond with that [nondual intuition]. Therefore, here, inconceivably seeing the sign of emptiness, there is a cutting off of [mental] elaborations, and by thinking along these lines a yogī will possess the highest fruition in the world [that is, buddhahood]."[128]

Since the three [final antagonists here], Jinapāda, etc. [Ratnamat and Brahmaṇabhadramitra], also appear as claimants of the former antagonists' position [above], one should investigate whether or not their appearance again here [in this latter list] is a corruption in this book.[129]

You may wonder: These people [Shūnyamati, etc.], having dispensed with the stage of creation and matters of conduct, {356a} may want to become buddhas [without those practices]; but in view of what

---

[126] On Jinapāda, Ratnamat, and Brahmaṇabhadramitra, cf. above, notes 100, 101, and 102. These three names do not appear in the Derge edition of this text. See Tsong Khapa's comment below regarding this.

[127] *dge long ma dga' mo* (bhikṣhuni Nandā?)—*Blue Annals* I, 20 cites a Nandā.

[128] This last phrase (from "therefore, here..." onwards) differs from the Derge. Tsong Khapa's version reads: *'dir stong pa nyid mtshan ma mthong ba bsam gyis mi khyab cing spros pa rnam par chad pa ni, rnal 'byor pas bsam pa'i tshul gyis 'jig rten na 'bras bu mchog dang ldan no....* The Derge reads: *'dir stong pa nyid mtshan ma <u>ma</u> mthong ba bsam gyis mi khyab cing, spros pa rnam par chad pa ni rnal 'byor pas <u>mi</u> bsam pa'i tshul gyis <u>brten</u> na 'bras bu'i mchog dang ldan no...*, which could be rendered: "here, regarding emptiness—which is the inconceivability of the <u>non</u>-seeing of signs and the cutting off of elaborations—if the yogī <u>relies</u> on the method of <u>not</u> thinking he will possess the highest fruition in the world [that is, buddhahood]." The Derge seems much better here, but either version makes the objector's apophatic position clear.

[129] Indeed, Tsong Khapa's hunch appears to be correct; as noted above (note 126), these three names do not appear in the Derge edition of this text.

reason [can they justify that this] should this be an assertion that you should meditate merely the stage of perfection?

Indeed, they have no good reason [to advocate the perfection stage alone]. However, using apparent reasons, and relying on mere words without having found the intention of the scriptures, their thought is as follows:

The object to be attained—completely perfect buddhahood—is the nondual, nonconceptual intuition; and thus also the method for achieving that logically should be the meditation of nonconceptualization; but that [nonconceptual intuition] would not be achieved through meditating on conceptual things in the creation stage, etc., because conceptual thought must be abandoned, and because from familiarization with conceptual thought you will not get any fruition other than what corresponds with just that, [namely] something that is just conceptual.

Now, if we then say that [the above antagonists' wrong thought] invalidates the statements of the Teacher that one should practice the creation stage and the matters of conduct, they then will say:[130]

The disciple to whom he [the Teacher] taught those things is the worldling who would have been afraid if he [had instead] explained the import of profound emptiness; that is, he taught [those things] as a method of reassuring certain types of [inferior] disciples. Moreover, it is necessary for [the Teacher] to teach the matters of conduct in order to refute the view of nihilism which repudiates the causality of addiction and purification, and it is necessary for [the Teacher] to teach the creation stage {356b} so that through the relativities of deity yoga, mantra repetition, fire sacrifices, substances, etc., people can achieve the relativities of the fruits of peace, etc. [prosperity, dominance, destruction], and the [mundane] siddhis such as sword, pill, etc. Therefore, the antidote to all taints is the realization of emptiness free of all [mental] elaborations, and if the yogī familiarizes himself with just that alone and increases that familiarization limitlessly, he will achieve the supreme fruit; thus, since one should meditate on just that alone, what's the use of any other meditation? As the fiftieth chapter of *The Vajraḍāka [Tantra]* states:[131]

---

[130] This is the antagonist's main argument, extending from here to the end of this section a few pages later.

[131] The passage cited here is located at Tōh. 370 (Derge rgyud, kha): 125a.1–2; Lhasa 386 (rgyud kha): 518a.5. Note that this is the fifty-chapter *Vajraḍāka Tantra* which is

(cont'd)

The fabricated activities of people
—Who apply their own minds
According to whatever grammatical or scientific
treatises[132]
Were composed by the Seers—
Give rise [only] to suffering
When they make efforts in pursuit of the Tantras.

Therefore, striving in ritual activities
Such as mandalas, etc.,
These people are separate from and outside of liberation;
They generate only addictions!

And as the fourth chapter of the second section of *The Kiss [Tantra]* says:[133]

Meditation, and commitments,
And [deity-]bodies, and [buddha-]pride,
And mantra, and mudrā—[all] create ordinary siddhis.
Why practice these?!

---

well over one-hundred folios (Derge rgyud kha: 1b–125a; Lhasa kha: 327b–518b), and not the two-folio long Tōh. 399 (P44, vol. 3; no Lhasa) entitled *Vajraḍākaguhyatantra-rāja (rdo rje mkha' 'gro gsang ba'i rgyud kyi rgyal po)*. In *TT* Hopkins mistakenly cites this latter text (Tōh. 399) in his bibliography, but he does not cite Tōh. 370. Thus, referencing the incorrect text, he does not cite any folio references for the one passage which Tsong Khapa cites from the "*Vajraḍāka Tantra*" at *TT*: 137. The passage Tsong Khapa cites there is from Tōh. 370 (Derge rgyud, kha): 2a.3–5.

[132] Taking *sgra shes bstan bcos* as *sgra'i bstan bcos* and *shes pa'i bstan bcos*.

[133] Tōh. 381; Lhasa 396 (ga). Although Tsong Khapa here refers to the *kha sbyor*, his reference to a fourth chapter (*rab byed*) of a second section (*brtag pa*) indicates that this is not the expected *rnal 'byor ma bzhi'i kha sbyor gyi rgyud* (*Catur-yoginī-saṁpuṭa-tantra*; Tōh. 376, Derge rgyud, ga; Lhasa 395, rgyud, ga). Rather it is the *yang dag par sbyor ba shes bya ba'i rgyud chen po* (*Saṁpuṭa-nāma-mahātantra*; Tōh. 381, Derge rgyud, ga; Lhasa 396, rgyu, ga). According to our Tengyur chart, both of these are A.2.b.1 = Mother Tantra, Akṣhobhya clan, Saṁvara class. Panchen Sonam Dragpa (*Overview*, pp. 51–52) identifies the first (Tōh. 376) as one of four explanatory Tantras (and also as one of three supplementary Tantras) for the *Abhidhānottara-tantra* (the root Tantra of the Saṁvara class), and he identifies the second (our text, Tōh. 381) as an "uncommon" Tantra within that same class. All of Tsong Khapa's remaining references to the *kha sbyor* herein are also to this longer Tōh. 381. Cf. my note to this passage in the critical edition of the Tibetan for further information.

Through the yoga of your chosen deity
[Comes] the ultimate [fruition] of buddhahood;
If you realize the characteristics of the characterized [goal, that is, buddhahood] {357a}
The three realms [underworld, earth, and sky] will become like sky [—that is, clear]!

In reliance upon such passages [the antagonist's position] is clear.[134] The former [passage from *The Vajraḍāka*] is cited in [Ratnarakṣhita's] *Commentary on The Arisal of Saṁvara [Tantra]* as [something used as] a means of proof by those who reject the creation stage.[135]

Ratnarakṣhita expresses the antagonist's further position as follows: Not only will you not attain buddhahood through the creation stage, but you will not even attain samādhi through it—because this [creation stage] agitates the mental continuum with many conceptual thoughts, whereas samādhi has the nature of one-pointedness of mind. Although you may indeed get a little vividness by meditating, it is like a lusty person's vivid vision of his desired female object—it abides only for an instant, not for a long time. Conceptual yoga is extremely false—even more so than the conceptualizations of worldly phenomena—like meditating on a skeleton [in Individual Vehicle meditations]. Therefore, it is erroneous and is thus of no help in the achievement of the supreme.

So there are two kinds of [antagonistic] claims here: [1] the creation stage is completely unnecessary for the achievement of the supreme; and [2] it is unnecessary for those with sharp faculties, but it is necessary for those with dull faculties.

---

[134] Tsong Khapa's interpretation of these two passsages appears below at 360a–b.

[135] The syntax is somewhat convoluted here. However, based on what Tsong Khapa says at the very end of the next section (cf. 362a end), it is clear that Ratnarakṣhita is not himself stating that the creation stage is useless; rather, like Mañjushrīkīrti above, he is stating the antagonist's position. As Tsong Khapa states below (362a), in Tōh. 1420 Ratnarakṣhita "extensively refuted those false positions."

[**II.B.2.c.ii.C'3'c'ii'A''2''b''** – The refutation of that (claim that perfection stage alone is needed)]

The second has two: [i''] The actual refutation; and [ii''] Rebuttal of objections to the refutation.

[**II.B.2.c.ii.C'3'c'ii'A''2''b''i''** – The actual refutation]

The wisdom which realizes thatness which is free from all [mental] elaborations {357b} is indeed the immediate cause[136] of the nondual intuition of a buddha. However, if you familiarize yourself with that alone, then no matter how long you may strive you will not be able to reach the supreme ultimate goal, because you will lack the factor of art. For example, although a seed is indeed the immediate cause of a sprout, if the conditions of water and fertilizer, etc., are lacking then you will not be able to grow the sprout. Therefore, it is the general system of the Universal Vehicle practitioner that the wisdom that realizes emptiness depends upon art to reach the supreme ultimate goal, and that art relies upon wisdom to reach the supreme ultimate goal. And in the Mantra Vehicle system in particular, the path has aspects of those two [art and wisdom] as the cause of the two [buddha] bodies; [so] it is necessary to meditate on [*both*] emptiness and deity yoga as I have already explained many times before.

Again, if [you claimed that] it were impossible to enter a state free of concepts through familiarization with concepts, then [you would be forced to argue that] it must be impossible to perceive vividly the object of familiarization through familiarization with concepts because a very vivid perception of that object and [a holding on to it] as a concept are mutually contradictory [which you would not want to argue]. As the Lord of Reason [Dharmakīrti] said [in the *Validating Cognition Commentary*]:

> When one is [still] chasing after a conceptual thought,
> One does not have a vivid perception of its object.[137]
> (III.283ab)

---

[136] *nyer len* (*upādāna*)—the "immediate cause" or "material cause."

[137] Here, in the context of logic (*pramāṇa*), we see the formal incompatibility of conceptual thought (*rnam rtog*) and vivid perception (*gsal snang*).

If, through a very vivid perception of an object you could not achieve a state free of concepts no matter how long it took, then you could never refute the Hindus' claim that sense cognitions are [always only] conceptual. {358a}

If [you claimed that] vivid perception could not arise through familiarization with concepts, then [1] you would be forced to make false claims such as [A] a lusty person who thought again and again about his object of lust could not possibly see its form vividly and make efforts to touch it, etc., or [B] a person with an extremely frightened mind who thought again and again about a ghost, etc., could not possibly have a very vivid vision of its form; and [2] [when dealing] with non-Buddhists who claim that liberation is impossible and who reject statements of the Blissful Lord which are said to occur in scripture—such as what the King of Reason [Dharmakīrti] said [in the *Validating Cognition Commentary*]:

> It is stated [by the Buddha] that such things as the earth-
> ugliness-totality,[138]
> Even though unreal—being manifest by the force
> Of meditation—are nonconceptual,
> And have a vivid appearance. (III.284)

—you will have cut the root of the means of proof for proving that there are noble persons, etc., even in other groups [other than Buddhists], since even though [such] non-Buddhists may not deny the example [the 'earth-totality'], which is the basis for ascertaining the concomitance of the reason which proves that yogic direct perception could possibly occur, [still] they may formulate some further denial.

Therefore, when an object of familiarization is vividly perceived it is the same whether you are familiarizing with a genuine thing or a false thing—just to familiarize is all that is intended. As the Lord of Reason [Dharmakīrti] said [in the *Validating Cognition Commentary*:[139]

---

138 *mi sdug zad pa*. Here *zad pa* = "totality" (*kṛtsna*—LC 1638. MW 304: "all, whole, entire"). This is a meditation in which one contemplates the totalities of earth, water, fire, skeleton, etc., as ugly and disgusting—i.e., one considers that everything is earth, and one sees that as ugly, etc.

139 This verse is cited again below at 381b–382a (see p. 155 below).

> Therefore, whatever you really familiarize[140] yourself with,
> Whether it is real or {358b} unreal,
> If you become completely familiarized,
> The result is its vivid, nonconceptual cognition. (III.285)

And as the eleventh [chapter] of the *Activities [of the Yoginīs Tantra]* says:

> When people impress in their mind
> Any thing whatsoever,
> That thing becomes the reality of that [mind]
> Like a jewel that adopts various colors.[141]

If it is accepted that through familiarization with a concept[ual object] there arises a vivid perception of the familiarized object, then since this is the achievement an object '*free* of concepts' (*rtog bral*), if you then refuse to use the convention '*non*conceptual' (*mi rtog pa*) with regard to that, you are just quibbling about words.

Objection: When there is vivid perception of an object, then although you are indeed free of the conceptuality which holds together word and referent,[142] you are not free from the conceptuality which perceives dualistically,[143] and therefore there is [still some] conceptuality.

[Answer:] If it were impossible to generate a mind free of concepts from a dualistically perceiving conceptuality, then since all minds short of those who had attained the exaltation of the noble ones would be dualistically perceiving conceptual [minds], it would be impossible [for anyone] to develop the nonconceptual intuition of a noble being from the [pre-noble] paths of accumulation or application. As [Maitreya's *Distinguishing*] *The Center and Extremes* says:

---

140 *goms* ("to familiarize"). The Derge has the related term *bsgoms* ("to meditate") here and *bsgom* in the third line. This would change the translation only slightly to: "Therefore, whatever you really meditate, whether it is real or unreal, if it is completely meditated, it will have a vivid, nonconceptual effect in the mind."

141 This common Indian analogy refers to the case of a clear jewel which will appear to adopt the color of any cloth onto which it is placed.

142 *sgra don 'dzin pa'i rtog bral* (or "free of the the conceptuality which grasps at the referents of words"; or "free of the the conceptuality which grasps at words and meanings").

143 *gnyis su snang ba'i rtog pa dang ma bra ba.*

> Artificial imagination
> [Comprises] mind and mental functions [in] the three
> realms.[144] (I.8ab)

And since the aftermath intuition of noble bodhisattvas also has dualistic perception, those [dualistic aftermath intuitions] also would not be a path to buddhahood.

New Objection: Well, the [well-accepted] way in which cause and fruition are said to correspond—that 'a non-corresponding fruition will not arise from a non-corresponding cause'—{359a} [means that] if the fruition is nonconceptual then also a nonconceptual cause definitely preceded it.

[Answer: If you hold so strictly to that, then also] you have to assert that one has had nonconceptual [cognition] from beginningless saṁsāra.

New Objection: A nonconceptual [cognition] which realizes suchness at the time of the path is the necessary prerequisite cause of the nonconceptual intuition of a buddha; therefore, since the mind which meditates the creation stage does not realize suchness, [your position] is refuted.

[Answer:] If you claim that there is no mind which realizes suchness in the context of the creation stage, that is extremely wrong, as I will explain. And furthermore, if [you claim that] there is no realization of suchness through the creation stage—which is a meditation in which there are aspects of color and shape on the perception side—and that for that reason [the creation stage] is therefore not a method for achieving the supreme, then [it follows that] it would be impossible for there to be

---

144 *yang dag ma yin kun rtog ni, sems dang sems 'byung khams gsum pa*. The Skt reads: *abhūtaparikalpaśca cittacaittāstridhātukāḥ* (Here "artificial imagination" or "unreal mental construction" can be used to translate *yang dag ma yin kun rtog* [*abhūtaparikalpaḥ*].) This is a famous equation, *kun rtog = sems + sems byung* (*parikalpitā = citta-caitta*). That is (in the present context), all mental states, other than the nonconceptual-intuition state of a noble, are dualistic. Vasubandhu's *Commentary* (Tōh. 4027) clarifies that "the three realms" here refers to the desire, form, and formless realms. Cf. D'Amato (trans.), *Distinguishing the Middle from the Extrmes*, AIBS, 2012, pp. 121–122.

any method for achieving buddhahood which was not a realization of emptiness,[145] and that would be an extremely absurd consequence.

[Now,] as for the assertion that the creation stage cannot achieve samādhi: if you claim that the arisal of a one-pointed virtuous mind—whether long or short in duration—is the existence of samādhi, and that therefore at least such a samādhi is not achieved [by the creation stage], then you are wrong. But if you [go even further and] say that serenity is not achieved [by the creation stage], and for that reason you reject that [the creation stage] is a path to buddhahood, then you are extremely mistaken—just like [you would be extremely mistaken to claim that] the many ways of analyzing and cultivating love, compassion, and the spirit of enlightenment [do not achieve serenity and are thus not a path to buddhahood]; there are very many [other examples] like that.

Moreover, {359b} creation stage meditation is not exclusively cultivation through analysis with discriminating thought; rather it comprises both analytic and static meditations, and I will explain below the far-reaching way in which it produces this as well as vivid perception.

The fiftieth chapter of *The Vajraḍāka*[146] states:

> In order to realize the natural yoga[147]
> You should do the fabricative meditation
> And the fabricative repetition.
>
> Once you have realized the natural yoga,
> Since—by the outer, fabricative yoga—
> You have realized the natural yoga,
> You should no [longer] do the fabricative [practices].
>
> For example, one takes up a boat
> Then goes across the water;
> When one has crossed it, one discards [the boat].
> Likewise, the fabricative [should be discarded] like that.

---

[145] *stong nyid ma rtogs pa'i 'tsang rgya ba'i thabs mi srid par 'gyur bas....* That is, *nothing* would serve as a method for achieving buddhahood *other* than the realization of emptiness.

[146] See note 131 above.

[147] *rnal ma'i sbyor ba. rnal ma* = "true, real, actual, genuine, original, pure, basic" (RY).

> Activities you do with a fabricative mind,
> Such as [meditatively constructing] mandalas, etc.,
> Clarify the outer activities;
> Therefore they are recommended for beginners.
>
> And since all the [fabricative, mundane] siddhis occur in this [fabricative creation stage],
> They are not [the concern of] the victors' knowledge of reality.

After which it continues:[148]

> [The fabricated activities of people
> —Who apply their own minds]
> According to whatever grammatical or scientific treatises
> ...

Thus, [the above quote] is a [scriptural] source for [the notion that] until you have achieved firm realization of the perfection stage which is non-fabricative, you must do the creation stage which is fabricative, and that then, [only after creation stage mastery] you can leave [the creation stage];[149] but it is stupid to claim this as a [scriptural] source for the [notion that] a beginner who [wishes to] achieve the supreme should not meditate the creation stage. Moreover, this can be understood through the boat analogy—although one leaves it once one has crossed the water, {360a} one definitely needs to rely on it until one has arrived there!

Moreover, the perfection stage involves a firm realization that is capable of [performing] emptiness and deity yogas without fabrication—without needing to use fabrication as in the creation stage.[150] But just by using the term 'perfection stage' for the mere meditation of the wind-

---

148 As cited above, p. 96 (356b).

149 *de nas 'jog pa'i khungs yin gyi*—Recall that Tsong Khapa introduced this quote by saying "...the creation stage...has both analytic and static (*'jog pa*) meditations, and I will explain below the far-reaching way in which it produces this...." However, *'jog* is then used in the immediately *following* sentence (about the boat) clearly in the sense of "to leave." This double use of *'jog* makes this section somewhat tricky.

150 The syntax is tricky here. I am taking the *stong pa dang lha'i rnal 'byor* with the *nus pa* later on (something must go with the *nus pa*, and this makes the most sense).

energy and psychic heat yogas [which are still subtly fabricative], it does not mean that you have left the creation stage; that is the meaning of the statement [above], "They are not [the concern of] the victors' knowledge of reality."[151]

Since it says [in *The Vajraḍāka* passage just above] that the creation stage is 'recommended for beginners,' it is very important for beginners; and *The Five Stages* and [Āryadeva's] *Practice Integration* explain that 'a beginner' includes everyone that has not yet completed the creation stage.

As for the passage [cited by the objector in the previous section above]:[152] 'By striving in [ritual activities] such as mandalas, etc., these people are separate from and outside of liberation and generate only addictions!'—this means that if you familiarize yourself with only the deity yoga of habitat and inhabitant [that is, the creation stage] without meditating on the perfection stage involving emptiness, etc., then you will not achieve the supreme and will therefore just become fatigued. And that is also how you should understand the meaning of the scriptural passage from *The Kiss* [also cited by the objector above][153] and other passages like that. Moreover, when [in fact] many Tantras demonstrate the virtues of the various methods of creation stage deity-meditation, then since there seems to be a vast number of sources [which state] that

---

[151] If the original *Vajraḍāka* quote was somewhat eliptical, Tsong Khapa's explanation here seems equally elliptical! There seem to be several points here: [1] the earlier phases of the perfection stage (such as those involving wind-energy and psychic heat yogas) still use constructive imagination, and *in that sense* are continuous with and do not transcend the creation stage; thus, if one uses the term "perfection stage" to refer to such constructive practices, one cannot say that such a "perfection stage" really transcends or allows one to "put aside" (*'jog*) the creation stage; [2] there are other, later perfection stage practices (such as those involving clear light, illusion body, and integration) which are non-constructive (not artificial), and these truly transcend creation stage practices; [3] the fact that (at higher levels of practice and at buddhahood) one *does* finally engage in the higher-level perfection stage practices and set aside all constructive practices (including those of the creation stage as well as the earlier phases of the perfection stage) is the meaning of *The Vajraḍāka* statement "They are not [the concern of] the victors' knowledge of reality."

[152] Here Tsong Khapa paraphrases the verse from the fiftieth chapter of *The Vajraḍāka* which he quoted in the previous section above (p. 97, Tib. 356b).

[153] Cf. above, p. 97, Tib. 356b–357a.

familiarization with the creation stage bestows the supreme—like the statement in the second section of *The Kiss*:[154]

> Thus the yogī meditates
> And thereby becomes equal to Vajrasattva

{360b}—when [an objector tries to] prove [that the creation stage is unnecessary] by relying on just the few scriptural passages [he cites], then since the former [counter-passages like the ones I cited] are much more extensive, he should [in fact] say the opposite!

Having cut off the doubt that wonders 'might it be unnecessary to meditate the creation stage?'—now to demonstrate this clearly: The second chapter of the latter section of the *[Hevajra Tantra in] Two Sections* says:[155]

> [Vajragarbha said:]
>
> > Regarding this yoga of the perfection stage,
> > Of which the bliss is called great bliss:
> > Lacking [such] perfection [stage] meditation
> > What is the use of creation [stage meditation]?[156]

---

[154] Tōh. 381; Lhasa 396 (ga): 382b. This general statement appears at the very end of the fourth chapter (*rab byed*) of the second section (*brtag pa*) of *The Kiss* (here Tōh. 381, not 376; cf. note 133 above). Since Tsong Khapa cites this brief passage in the context of proving that the creation stage bestows the supreme, perhaps this fourth chapter of the second section only discusses the creation stage, and the reader is expected to know this. This section does not explicitly mention the creation stage, but it does involve the creation of many deities in the mandala.

[155] *The Hevajra Tantra* (Tōh. 417) often is referred to by the abbreviated title *The Two Sections* (*rtags gnyis*). The following passage is from section II, chapter 2, verses 33–36; Lhasa 378 (ka): 356a–b. For a discussion of this passage, see the final chapter of my forthcoming book, *The Emptiness that is Form*. For the Sanskrit, an alternate translation, and a commentary, see Farrow and Menon, pp. 164–166. The Sanskrit is reproduced also in my *NRC* Tibetan edition.

[156] *utpattyā kiṁ prayojanaṁ* (*bskyed pa yis ni ci zhig 'tshal*). MW (p. 688) explains that "X *kiṁ prayojanaṁ*" with X in the instrumental (as here) means "what is the use or need of/necessity for X." In the 9th c. *Jewel Rosary of Yoga* (*Yogaratnamālā*) commentary Kṛiṣhṇāchārya/Samayavajra (see note 496 below) explains that Vajragarbha is raising the doubt that the creation stage may be of no real use:

> The import is: What is the purpose of actualizing the Great Bliss through long drawn-out emanations of Maṇḍala Circles when one who directs all

(cont'd)

The Divine Lord said:

> Hey! Great bodhisattva! Through the force of your
> faith [in the perfection stage]
> You have lost sight of this [important creation
> stage]![157]
>
> If the body did not exist, where would there be bliss?
> It would not be possible to speak about bliss
> [without the body].
> With the relationship of pervaded and pervader
> Living beings are pervaded by bliss.

---

his attention through the Great Bliss accomplishes? Vajragarbha is exposing the difficulty in understanding the utility of the Process of Generation. (Farrow & Menon, p. 165).

[157] *naṣṭo 'yaṁ* (*rab tu nyams*). (Note that *'di*—the Tibetan equivalent for the Sanskrit term *ayaṁ*, meaning simply "this"—is implied, but is omitted from the Tibetan translation of this phrase, presumably for metrical reasons.) Skt. *naṣṭo* (MW 532) or Tib. *nyams* (Das, 476–77) can mean "lost, damaged, wasted, deprived of, lost sight of," etc. So, *naṣṭo 'yaṁ* here means "this [creation stage] is lost, wasted, lost sight of," and so on. Note that our bracketed interpolations here—in the phrases "faith [in the perfection stage]" and "this [important creation stage]"—are following Tsong Khapa's interpretation immediately below. Farrow & Menon's translation, following Kṛiṣhṇāchārya's commentary, is very different:

> [Root text:] Bhagavān said: O Great Bodhisattva, it is said that this difficulty is removed by the strength of conviction.
>
> > [Kṛiṣhṇāchārya's commentary:] **naṣṭaḥ** (removed): The difficulty in understanding the utility of the Process of Generation is removed by the strength of conviction.

Kṛiṣhṇāchārya thus takes the implied refrerent of *ayaṁ* (in *naṣṭo 'yaṁ*) to be "this *difficulty* (*gauravam*)" (note that the word "difficulty" in Farrow & Menon's translation of the *root* text above is an interpolation—based on Kṛiṣhṇāchārya's reading—and as such should be in square brackets); and he takes the phrase *naṣṭo 'yaṁ* to mean "this [difficulty in understanding the utility of the creation stage] is removed." Thus, he has the Buddha saying simply that "your confusion about the need for the creation stage will be removed through faith." This is not a very satisfactory answer. Tsong Khapa's interpretation seems much better, especially in the context of the next verse. He interprets the implied subject (that to which the missing *'di* would refer) to be be the creation stage, paraphrasing *rab tu nyams* as *bskyed rim las nyams*, "you are deprived of the creation stage."

Just as a scent based on a flower
Would not be sensed if the flower did not exist,
So if matter, etc., did not exist
Bliss likewise would not be experienced.

In that [passage, Vajragarbha] formulates the argument: "The beginner has no need for a *creation stage* meditation *that lacks a perfection stage meditation*, because the goal which is the orgasmic *great bliss is* [to be obtained through] the *yoga of the perfection stage*." [The Buddha] answers: "*Through the force of your faith* in the perfection stage, *you have lost sight* of the creation stage!"—and he establishes that both creation and perfection, like a flower and {361a} its scent, are the support and the supported [respectively].

Moreover, [at the time of fruition] the mind's entrance into the thatness of phenomena is achieved through the perfection stage, and the body's abiding as the form body is achieved through the creation stage; [thus] intending that the body is the support of the mind, [the Buddha] spoke [in terms of] support and supported. Moreover, at the time of the path there is also support and supported like that.

Furthermore, if you do not assert that there is a beginner's context for the exceptional person who will attain buddhahood in this life, then you must assert, like the Chinese abbot [Hva shang],[158] that disciples will [attain buddhahood] instantaneously; but if you do assert that there is a beginner's context [for the exceptional person], then the assertion that that [exceptional person] does not need the first stage [that is, the creation stage] to attain buddhahood is in contradiction to all the treatises of Mantra. If you say that you take as the exceptional person the person who has long practiced Mantra in many previous lives, and that that one does not have to be instructed in the first stage, that is a remark that has lost sight of the context, since [1] this is an examination of whether or not the first stage is needed for the context of a beginner at Mantra practice who is traversing the stages of the path, and since [2] besides, for such a person as that [exceptional one], the context would be such that it would even be permissible to instruct that one having set aside a great many of the perfection stage [practices, let alone the creation stage].

---

[158] See note 164 below.

This [last remark of yours] is like saying—when examining whether or not one must progress from the path of accumulation in order to become a buddha—"Having attained the first [bodhisattva] stage, {361b} one does not have to progress from the path of accumulation."[159]

Āryadeva also composed a mind-piercing refutation of this wrong view in the *Practice Integration*:

> The Vajra-disciple asked: "Alienated individuals such as ourselves—due to having conceptual adherence to the variety of external phenomena since beginningless time—have been beings engaged in conceptual adherence to concepts caused by the natural instincts for absolutism and nihilism, etc., [concepts such as] existence and non-existence, one and many, dual and not dual, and neither existence nor non-existence. When [such beings] learn the samādhi of the perfection stage, should they learn it according to a gradual process or, alternatively, will they be illuminated in just an instant through the mentor's personal instruction?"
>
> The Vajra Master answered: "They should learn it through a gradual engagement; it is not sudden."[160]

[After this, Āryadeva] proves with many scriptural sources that it is necessary to instruct [a disciple] gradually,[161] and he states that you must [first] learn the vision of the Buddha Vehicle, and that then you must learn the creation stage.[162]

---

159 This obviously would be true, since the path of accumulation necessarily precedes the attainment of the first bodhisattva stage.

160 Here again we see how issues related to the perfection and creation stages connect to the controversy over "sudden" (*cig car*) and "gradual" (*rims kyis*) enlightenment.

161 Āryadeva immediately follows the passage cited here by Tsong Khapa with two long sūtra quotes (one from the *Journey to Lanka Sūtra [Lankāvatārasūtra]* and one from the *Hero's March Samādhi Scripture [Śūrangamasamādhisūtra]*). These sūtra passages discuss the need to learn gradually, not suddenly, as an archer first trains on a large target and progressively graduates to smaller and smaller targets, etc. (cf. Wedemeyer 2007, 143–145).

162 Immediately after the quote from the *Hero's March Samādhi Scripture* the Vajra Master goes on to say:

(cont'd)

In short, if you say that the first stage is not a path that is definitely needed for buddhahood, then [you are essentially saying] about the three lower Tantra sections that "the paths of the Transcendence Vehicle and of extraordinary Mantra have nothing whatsoever to distinguish them";[163] {362a} and since this is a repudiation of most of the treatises of the three Tantra sections and of the Unexceled Yoga Tantras, such a mantrin [as yourself] is really amazing! Two statements are not different: [1] "In the Transcendence Vehicle the exceptional disciple has a path to buddhahood in which he does not need to learn the activities of the transcendences such as generosity,"[164] and [2] "In the Mantra Vehicle, without relying on the first stage, the exceptional disciple has a path for going to buddhahood" —these are false notions, yet they seem to be extremely widespread.[165]

> Also, you who desire to learn the Hero's March Samādhi of the Vajra Vehicle should learn according to these very stages. The stages are these: first, you learn the vision [*bsam pa, āśaya*] of the Buddha vehicle. Having learned the vision of the Buddha vehicle, you learn the Samādhi of Single-mindedness on the New Vehicle. Having learned Single-mindedness on the New Vehicle, you learn the imaginative yoga [*rtog pa'i rnal 'byor*]. [He then goes on to list the subsequent perfection stage yogas which one successively learns.] (cp. Wedemeyer 2007, 145–146)

As Wedemeyer points out, citing the *sngags kyi sa lam* (trans. in *Paths and Grounds of Guhyasamaja According to Arya Nagarjuna*) by Yangchen Gawai Lodoe (a.k.a. Akya Yongdzin, 18th c.), the "Samādhi of Single-mindedness" (*dran pa gcig pa, ekasmṛti*) means gross creation stage practices, and the "imaginative yoga" (or "conceptual yoga" [*rtog pa'i rnal 'byor*]) means subtle creation stage practices. Cf. *Paths and Grounds*, 41–46. These are well-established synonyms—as Yangchen himself notes, "These terms often appear in Tantric commentaries" (41).

[163] *phar phyin gyi theg pa dang thun mong ma yin pa'i sngags kyi lam khyad par can ci yang med do*. Alternatively: "there is no special Mantric path which is 'extraordinary' with respect to (*dang*) the Transcendence Vehicle." Tsong Khapa's point is as follows: If the perfection stage were the only practice really needed to attain buddhahood, then since the three lower Tantras do not have perfection stage practice any more than the exoteric Transcendence Vehicle does, there would really be nothing finally "extraordinary" about the three lower Tantras that would distinguish them from the Transcendence Vehicle.

[164] This is a clear and direct reference to the views associated with Hva Shang Mahāyāna which were strongly rejected by Kamalashīla at the bsam yas debate (cf. especially *Bhāvanākrama III*). See my forthcoming book, *The Emptiness that is Form*, and Ruegg 1989, 93–94.

[165] *shin tu kham che ba*. The word *kham* seems to have to do with "a bit, a piece of something" (Das, 139). In this regard it also often means "a mouthful" (RY). Thus this phrase

(cont'd)

Thus, knowledgeable people who carefully compile all of the scriptures from beginning to end and then examine them will completely distance themselves [from such false views]; because finally that [type of false view] seems to be a misunderstanding of even the mere meaning of the names such as '*Supreme Bliss Sādhana*' and '*Hevajra Sādhana*,' etc., given to sādhanas by the great adepts. The great master Vāgīshvarakīrti and the paṇḍita Ratnarakṣhita in the auto-commentary on *The Seven Branches* and in the *Commentary on The Arisal of Saṁvara [Tantra]* [respectively][166] have already extensively refuted these false positions, so fearing prolixity I won't write [any more about this here].

[**II.B.2.c.ii.C'3'c'ii'A"2"b"ii"** – Rebuttal of objections to the refutation]

Objection: If [you maintain that] the creation stage is the path to buddhahood, [then we point out that] *[The Great Commentary:] Immaculate Light* says:[167]

> One who lacks the path divided into sixteen and four
> Does not attain the reality which the Buddha
> proclaimed,[168] **{362b}**

(which I am rendering here as "extremely widespread") is derived from the possible interpretation that these false notions "fill a great many mouths" (that is, that they are on many people's lips). Alternatively, this phrase might mean that such false notions "are quite a mouthful." Most generally it seems to be conveying the idea that that these false notions "seem to have broad [negative] implications."

166 The first text mentioned here (*yan lag bdun ldan*) must be the *Saptāṅga (yan lag bdun pa*; Tōh. 1888) by Ngag gi dbang phyug grags pa (Vāgīshvarakīrti). However, I could not locate an "auto-commentary" (*rang 'grel*) by this author. It is possible that Tsong Khapa here has made a bibliographical error, intending to cite Vāgīshvarakīrti's *Tattvaratnāloka-vyākhyāna* (Tōh. 1890) which *is* an autocommentary (on his *Tattvaratnāloka*, Tōh. 1889). The second text mentioned here (*sdom 'byung gi 'grel pa*) presumably is Tōh. 1420: *Śrīsaṁvarodaya-mahātantrarāja-padminī-nāma-pañjikā (dpal sdom pa 'byung ba'i rgyud kyi rgyal po chen po'i dka' 'grel padma can shes bya ba)*, by Ratnarakṣita. That these issues are raised and refuted in these Indian texts highlights the fact that these are not just Tibetan (or Gelugpa) concerns and positions, as is sometimes alleged.

167 This is a key commentary to the *Kālachakra Tantra*, written by Puṇḍarīka (an emanation of Avalokiteshvara).

168 *lam dang bral bas thob pa ma yin no*: "One who lacks the path...cannot achieve [reality by it]." The objector reads this as meaning that you do not need the creation stage at all, since you need the perfection stage to attain buddhahood. As we shall see in Tsong

(cont'd)

> [But only attains worldly siddhis] by the path of various conceptualizations
> Such as the *HŪṀ* and *PHAT* letters
> Stated on the creation stage.
> However, when free of conceptions,
> There is the reality of the perfection stage yoga,
> And there is no means of attaining reality other than that.

And:

> Through familiarizations with the meditation on the wheel
> Of the mandala which are conceptualizations of form, etc.,
> You will achieve the mundane siddhis;
> But how [could you achieve] the great siddhi[169] which you desire [that way]?

[Here, *The Great Commentary: Immaculate Light*] states that there is no path for achieving buddhahood other than the perfection stage, and that you may achieve worldly siddhis through the creation stage, but that you will not achieve the supreme siddhi [through it]; and after explaining that at the time of meditating on the lord [of the mandala] there are no deities in the east, etc., and likewise there are no faces and hand-symbols,[170] [it says:] "Therefore, the yogī should not do conceptual meditation for the sake of [achieving] the siddhi of the great seal." So, by virtue of the fact that there is no [recommendation of some] conceptual mind in which there abides a mandala-wheel, for the sake of buddhahood you should not meditate the creation stage.

Khapa's rebuttal below, Tsong Khapa says this is a misreading. He says it means: "If [*you*] are bereft of the path [of *perfection*], you cannot achieve [buddhahood by the creation stage alone]." The Sanskrit version of this takes lines cd of one verse, then one full verse, and then lines ab of a third verse; and the order is somewhat garbled, which the Tibetan canonical translation clarifies (although the case endings in Sanskrit do help to retrieve the proper order also).

169 An epithet for buddhahood. Cf. note 78 above.

170 *phyag mtshan*. A "hand-symbol" is an implement held in the hand of a Tantric deity which quintessentially symbolizes that deity. Examples include a vajra, a lotus, a skull-bowl, a chopper, a staff, and so on.

Rebuttal: If you think that such statements contradict [our position], we answer that they confirm that you do not understand the scriptures. The first verse [you cited above] clearly states that if [*you*] "lack" the perfection stage "path" of great bliss involving "the sixteen" ecstasies, {363a} then [you] cannot achieve buddhahood by the creation stage [*alone*];[171] but it does not indicate that meditating the creation stage is not necessary [at all] for the attainment of buddhahood.[172] Therefore, the statement in the second verse [of the three you cited] that "there is no means of attaining [reality] other than that" also should be understood likewise.

As for the statement [in the third verse] that you will not achieve "the great siddhi which you desire" through the creation stage, it is refuting the claim that you can attain buddhahood *just* [1] by familiarizing yourself more and more with the meditation on the habitat and on the body, color, face and hands, etc., of the deity who is the inhabitant, and [2] by [gaining] stability in the vivid direct perception of the mandala of [that] habitat and inhabitant. The meaning of the quote is that, while you can achieve ordinary siddhis through such [methods] as that, you cannot achieve the supreme [by that *alone*], and thus it does not indicate that the creation stage is [entirely] unnecessary for the attainment of buddhahood. Because, as *[The Great Commentary:] Immaculate Light* [itself] states:[173]

---

[171] The qualifier "alone" (*tzam zhig*), which is implicit here, is explicitly inserted by Tsong Khapa in his commentary on this theme below (Tib. 363b; cf. notes 178 and 179).

[172] Again, as we shall see in the section just below (Tib. 363b), Tsong Khapa stresses that it is *this* kind of *qualified* refutation "that *The Great Commentary: Immaculate Light* states again and again." The creation stage may not be a (*sufficient*) cause for attaining buddhahood, but it nonetheless *is one* of the (*necessary*) causes for such attainment—in brief: it is necessary, but not sufficient.

[173] Here—by citing the following two passages from the *The Great Commentary: Immaculate Light* (the same text the antagonist has been citing)—Tsong Khapa provides reasons (in the form of similar textual passages) for why he finds it justified to read the refutations in *The Great Commentary* as *qualified* refutations. In the first passage, in stating that you will not become a buddha by meditating on a totality-sphere, it is clear that the text is *not* saying that you should *not* meditate on totality-spheres (as a part of the path to omniscience or buddhahood); rather, it is making the more limited point that meditation on totality-spheres alone will not be a sufficient cause for attaining omniscience or buddhahood. Likewise, in the second passage, in stating that you will not become a buddha through such conceptual meditations as visualizing your body-mind systems, etc., as a mandala, it is clear that the text is *not* saying that you should *not* so meditate; rather, again, it is making the more limited point that to so meditate—*without*

(cont'd)

> Here, if you would say that "having directly realized a totality-realm[174] or a single mandala wheel you will come to realize the three realms and you will come to realize omniscience, and also for the sake of attaining the omniscient exaltation you will realize universal omniscience, path omniscience, and path-aspect omniscience," this would not be the case. For even if you have realized a totality, etc., or a single mandala wheel, {363b} it is not the case that you can call that [realization] "becoming a perfect buddha, disciple, solitary buddha, or adept."

And:

> Here, if—without[175] the yogīs' stores of merit and intuition—the body-mind systems and elements and media, etc., will be transformed into the form of the wheel of the mandala by the power of familiarization with meditation [alone], and if you claim that[176] you even will [achieve] buddhahood itself by the power of meditating on the conceptual [alone], then in such a case, some other person with an inferior store of merit who thinks "I am a king" will also, through familiarization with that [thought alone], become a king without a [sufficient] store of merit. But this is never seen to be the case!

[So, in a similar way, the line in the third verse you cite][177] is a very clear statement refuting the claim that—without accumulating other stores of merit and intuition—a direct vision of the mandala [achieved] through

---

sufficient merit and intuition, etc.—would be an insufficient cause for attaining buddhahood, just like wishing to be a king (with an insufficient store of merit) would be an insufficient cause for actually becoming a king.

174 A "totality realm" (*kṛtsnadhātu*, *zad par gyi khams*) is another term for a "totality-sphere" (*kṛtsnāyatana*, *zad par gyi skye mched*). Cf. note 138 above.

175 *ma gtogs par*—usually this is translated "except for …," but it clearly means "without" here. Das (p. 526) lists the following range of meanings: "not included, except, besides."

176 [*sangs rgyas nyid du yang*] *'gyur na* at the end of this phrase. Tsong Khapa takes *'gyur na* in this context to mean *'dod na* (cf. below).

177 To the effect that you will not achieve "the great siddhi which you desire" through the creation stage.

familiarizing oneself with just the creation stage *alone*[178] is buddhahood. Therefore, *without meditating on other paths*, through mere familiarization with the creation stage *alone*[179] one can achieve mundane siddhis, but one will not attain buddhahood: [and *that* is the kind of] refutation *The Great Commentary[: Immaculate Light]* states again and again, and you should not say that the Kālachakra tradition refutes that the creation stage is [a crucial element of] the path of buddhahood.

{364a} [In the passage I just cited,] the [literal] phrase "if [the body-mind systems, etc.] [or 'if you'] even could be transformed into buddhahood itself...."[180] means, in this case, "if you claim that you even will [achieve] buddhahood itself...";[181] but it is not a refutation [of the notion] that you will become a buddha through relying on that [conceptual meditation].[182] As *The Great Commentary[: Immaculate Light]* says:[183]

---

178 *bskyed rim tsam zhig la goms pa las*—here Tsong Khapa makes explicit the qualifier "alone" (*tsam zhig*) which was implicit above.

179 *bskyed rim goms pa tsam zhig*—again, here the qualifier "alone" (*tsam zhig*) is explicit.

180 *sangs rgyas nyid du yang 'gyur na*. Translated above (following Tsong Khapa) as "...if you claim that you even will [achieve] buddhahood itself...." The use of *'gyur* (instead of *'dod*) would literally seem to mean "if [the body-mind systems, etc.] [or 'if you'?] even could be transformed into buddhahood itself...." Although Tsong Khapa certainly is correct that a sense of claiming (*'dod*) could be inferred here, it would seem to work about as well to give a sense of becoming/transforming (*'gyur*), as follows:

> ...if the body-mind systems elements and media, etc., could be transformed into the form of the wheel of the mandala by the power of familiarization with meditation [alone], and if [the body-mind systems, etc.] even could be transformed into buddhahood itself by the power of meditating on the conceptual [alone], ...

181 *sangs rgyas su 'dod na* (lit. "if you *claim* to be a buddha").

182 It is, rather, a refutation of the notion that you could *claim* to be a buddha *just* from relying on that conceptual creation stage meditation alone.

183 Again, as above (cf. note 173), Tsong Khapa's point in choosing the following passage appears to be to demonstrate that the refutations in *The Great Commentary* are often *qualified* refutations. Here the text is *not* outright refuting the notion that "the power of familiarization with meditation" can transform the body-mind systems into the mandala; rather, as the "answer" section shows, it is refuting the (qualifed) naïve, simplistic notion that with "false pride" alone one might be able to effect such a radical transfomation. Thus, while genuine familiarization with conceptual meditation (involving pure perception, buddha pride, etc.) is an integral part of "the path of omniscience," the text here mocks the type of false pride that would purport naïvely to engage in such practice, deriding it as a "corruption of the path of omniscience."

> "The body-mind systems and elements and media, etc., will be transformed into the pattern of the wheel of the mandala by the power of familiarization with meditation"[184]—regarding this, some will wonder: "Just by that [passage],[185] has not the Transcendent Buddha stated that you [will achieve] buddhahood?"

And [it answers]:

> But regarding that corruption of the path of omniscience: Overwhelmed by false pride, one might boastfully claim "I am Vajrasattva! I have the ten powers!" [However,] this person is not a ten-powered person—he is the very opposite of a ten-powered person, limited and very deluded! Here, the buddhahood of this kind of yogī is unprecedented and extremely amazing because he is endowed with all obscurations!

In that context, it mockingly says that 'since that boastful claim to have achieved buddhahood is a great delusion that is incompatible with buddhahood, it is filled with obscurations, and accordingly that claim to buddhahood is unprecedented!'

Citing the [supposed] fact that[186] *The Great Commentary[: Immaculate Light]* [says] that you should not meditate the conceptualizations of the creation stage for the sake of the siddhi of the great seal, {364b} and citing the [supposed] fact that it [says] that at the time of meditating on the lord [of the mandala] you do not meditate on the deities in the east, etc., [these deluded] Tibetans proclaim that 'for those very 'reasons' a single mind cannot perceive in its entirety [all] the aspects of the arms of a deity, and it also cannot meditate completely the

---

184 Cf. the passage quoted just above.

185 Or perhaps "Just by that [process of meditation]...."

186 *...rgyu mtshan du...rgyu mtshan du bkod pa'i don la....* This is very odd syntax, but I believe the meaning is correctly rendered here. Part of the confusion is created by the fact that (I believe) the opening phrase *'grel chen las* does *not* introduce a quote. Note Goldstein (p. 280) (and THL [Ives Waldo]) indicates that *rgyu mtshan du byed* means "to use a false reason, to use a pretext." It seems very likely that *rgyu mtshan du bkod* would have a similar meaning.

wheel of a mandala, and therefore [conceptual meditation] is not a method for achieving the supreme.'[187] [However,] that is extremely wrong, because it is only a pseudo-refutation.[188] [And it is also extremely wrong because] if things were like that, then at the time when you meditated on any one of the branches [of perfection stage yoga] such as retraction, etc., you could not meditate on another [branch], and thus you would not [be able to] meditate completely the six branches [of yoga], and, therefore, [any such branch of yoga] could not be something to be meditated for the sake of the siddhi of the great seal. [And it is also extremely wrong] because when one sets forth a means of 'proof' like that, then the refutation [of that position] is exactly like the form of the refutation of one who does not put forth a reason when expressing a premise.[189]

Furthermore, a claim made in that manner would appear to have the same essence as the antagonist's position set forth in *The Root Commentary of the Ornament of Clear Realizations: The Personal Instruction of the Mother of the Victors*:[190]

> At the time of the former spiritual conception [of enlightenment], the positive virtues that appear in the latter spiritual conception are absent, and at the time of the latter spiritual conception the positive virtues that appear in the former spiritual conception are absent, and therefore it is incorrect that you ever will achieve enlightenment.

Therefore, {365a} the point is to show that—just like the statement in *The Great Commentary[: Immaculate Light]* itself that in the instant when you are meditating on the lord [of the mandala], then in that instant you

---

[187] This paragraph up to here is a slight rephrasing of the objector's position above (362b).

[188] TL has *ltag ched* (which is not a word), whereas the MS (326.3) and ZH (316a) have *ltag chod*. Das (542) says *ltag chod* = *ltag gcod* = "...changeable, fickle, inconstant" (*ltag* is the nape of the neck). THL (Ives Waldo) says that *ltag chod* = "inconstant, fickle, changeable, merely apparent refutation/contradiction, wrong answer."

[189] In other words, one can easily refute such a person simply by pointing out that they are just insisting on a premise without giving any (real, valid) reason.

[190] Source unidentified. See my note to the Tibetan critical edition for discussion.

are not meditating on the eastern deity, etc.—at the time when you meditate thinking "This is the right face," you do not meditate thinking "This is the left face"; but it is *not* to show that the mind that perceives the right face cannot perceive the left face, etc. Because—while [indeeed] two concepts cannot be simultaneously produced [in the mind], as the Lord of Reason [Dharmakīrti] says [in the *Validating Cognition Commentary*]:

> One does not see two concepts simultaneously. (III.178b)

—still, two different aspects contained within one concept[191] can be perceived by direct perception, like a mind that has a conception of a striped thing. Otherwise, when you perceived an eye it would preclude your perceiving a nose, and when you perceived the middle of an eye it would necessarily preclude your perceiving the two corners of the eye, and therefore you would not be able to perceive anything about [any] concept. Such a [false] claim is refuted in many ways by the auto-commentary of *The Seven Branches*[192] [when, for example, it refutes the erroneous assertion that] [1] since when you see a person's front you do not see their back or insides, etc., therefore you cannot see a [whole] woman, etc.; and similarly that [2] [you do not see] the pillars stuck inside the walls of a house, therefore [you cannot see] the totality of a house, etc.; and the *Commentary on The Arisal of Saṁvara [Tantra]*[193] also refutes [such erroneous assertions].

Objection: Although we [both] allow that indeed when one is meditating on the right face one does not meditate on {365b} the left face, how does that serve as a reason that proves that the creation stage is not that which is to be meditated for the sake of the supreme siddhi?

Rebuttal: Granted, [but your quibble here is beside the point]; the point is: those scriptural references[194] refute the claim that [the creation

[191] *rtog pa gcig la gzung rnam mi 'dra ba gnyis.*

[192] Cf. above, note 166.

[193] Again, cf. note 166.

[194] Especially the scriptural references from the *The Great Commentary: Immaculate Light* which were misconstrued by the objector at the outset of this section (p. 112)—those that state "how [could you achieve] the great siddhi which you desire [through the creation stage]?' etc.

stage *alone*] realizes the suchness of things, but they do not negate that [creation stage] meditation is a [necessary] partial method[195] for [achieving] the siddhi of the great seal.

Again, the need for refuting that [the creation stage *alone* could produce the realization of suchness] is as explained before: [recall that] the person who asserted the antagonist's position—which was refuted in the commentary—claimed that by familiarizing oneself with the meditation of the deity wheel one gets a vivid perception, and that when one realizes that, then the [five] body-mind systems become the five [buddha-] clans and the elements become the mothers, and then one becomes a buddha [who realizes suchness]. In that [antagonist's] system they do not claim that there is a need for any auxilliary path which meditates the suchness of things; but since they also do not claim that one can attain buddhahood *without* realizing the suchness of things, they are forced to claim also that just the meditation on the deity wheel [entails] the meditation on the meaning of suchness; and therefore *that* is what is being refuted.

That being so, the import of the [present objector's] thesis is: "With respect to the aim of [achieving] the siddhi of the great seal, conceptual meditation involving individual discriminations regarding the wheel of the mandala is not the meditation of the thatness of ultimate reality [and hence such conceptual meditation will not achieve the desired aim]."

The reason [they give for this] is: "Because it is not a totality."[196] The import [of that reason] is: "Because when you meditate on your [kind of] meditational object, you must meditate on it only sequentially, and you cannot meditate on it all once"—that is what it means.

The proof of that {366a} they set forth as follows: 'When you meditate on the lord [of the mandala,] then you do not meditate on the deities of the east, etc.; and when you meditate on the right face [of the lord] then you do not meditate on the left face, etc.' And the proof of the concomitance [between the thesis and reason they say] is established by [the fact that when] the meditational object is the meditation of the thatness of selflessness, it is only allowable that it be meditated all at one time.

195 *thabs tsam.*

196 *thams cad med pa.*

Furthermore, as for the assertion that such a claim [that the creation stage is unnecessary] is the system of the Kālachakra—this contradicts *The Great Commentary[: Immaculate Light]*'s establishment of the sequence of the chapters;[197] it contradicts its identifications of the immediate purpose and the ultimate purpose from among the [five] topics of textual analysis;[198] and it contradicts [its] explanation of the fruit of the seven childlike initiations, viz. that when you directly manifest the mandala wheel, you become a lord of the seventh stage in this very body, or at least if you are free of the ten non-virtues when you die, then you become such [a seventh stage lord] in another life due to the store of merit.[199] There are [many such] sources, but I will not discuss them here, fearing prolixity.

Objection: Vajragarbha's [Hevajra] Commentary explains that because the nondual intuition is not produced from a conceptual cause—which [cause] would be non-corresponding in kind with the nonconceptual—the conceptual yoga of the creation stage is not suitable as a cause of buddhahood. Therefore, how could it be correct to refute that? Because it is stated [in that *Commentary*]:

> We always see that effects
> Are produced from causes like them;
> Thus from a Koṭava seed
> A Salu fruit is not produced.

---

[197] Which includes a chapter on the creation stage.

[198] Here *dgos pa* and *nying dgos*, respectively. These are two of the five "topics of textual analysis" (*dgos 'grel*), points necessary to determine when analyzing a text: The text itself (*abhidhāna, rjod byed*), its topic (*abhidheya, brjod bya*), the immediate purpose (*prayojana, dgos pa*), the ultimate purpose (*prayojanaprayojana, dgos pa'i dgos pa = nying dgos*), and the relevance or connection between them (*sambandha, 'brel ba*). Cf. Broido, Michael M. "A Note on *dgos-'brel*." *Journal of the Tibet Society* 3 (1983): 5–18.

[199] Cf. my note to the Tibetan edition for the citation. The point here is that the first seven initiations in the *Kālachakra* system *are* necessary, and that they are related to the creation stage practice of creating a divine body (or as stated here, "directly manifesting the mandala wheel"), which is related to merit. During initiation (and subsequent sādhana practice), once you have received the seven initiations you say a mantra "now I am the seventh stage lord," indicating that you have achieved the seventh bodhisattva stage, called the "far-reaching" or "far-advanced" (*dūraṅgama, ring du song ba*). And it is only *after* (and on the basis of) this that you then are matured to practice the perfection stage.

From a conceptual seed {366b}
A conceptual fruit will be produced;
From a nonconceptual [seed]
A nonconceptual fruit will be born.

Rebuttal: That [passage causes us] no problem. Its intended meaning is as follows: Just as a Koṭava seed is not suitable as a seed for a Salu fruit, so the creation stage which is meditating merely on the form of habitat and inhabitant deity is not the material cause[200] of the nonconceptual intuition. But this does not refute that the creation stage is needed as a supporting condition[201] for the nonconceptual intuition. For example, water, fertilizer, and earth are not the material cause of the barley sprout, but they are certainly necessary for its production.[202] Even that very [*Vajragarbha's Hevajra*] *Commentary* says:

First, in order to cultivate a field,
One plants the Koṭava [seeds];
Then later, on the cultivated field,
One plants the seeds of the Salu—it is like that.

So this uses the example that in a field which has been well cultivated by having first planted the Koṭava one later plants the Salu fruit. Then:

In the pure field of the human birth
One plants the seed of the non-objectifying compassion;
Thereby, because of that,
There arises the wish-fulfilling tree of emptiness.

---

200 Cf. note 136 above.

201 *lhan cig byed rkyen* (*sahakāri-kāraṇa* or *-pratyaya*)—an "accompanying condition" or "supporting condition."

202 In this case the barley seed would be the material cause of the barley sprout, and the water, fertilizer, and earth would be its necessary supporting conditions. In the example below the Salu seed is the material cause of the Salu tree and its fruit, and the Koṭava seeds (in addition to water, etc.) provide the necessary supporting conditions. For more on "material causes" (*nyer len*) and "supporting conditions" (*lhan cig byed rkyen*), including definitions, examples, and discussion, see Daniel Perdue, "Substantial Causes and Cooperative Conditions" in ch. 12 of *Debate in Tibetan Buddhism* (Ithaca: Snow Lion, 1992), 544ff.

This explains that when you have purified the field [of your human existence] through the creation stage you then can meditate the perfection stage which is the non-objectifying compassion, the great bliss, and that thereby you easily can produce the fruit. So this [*Vajragarbha's Hevajra Commentary*] is actually a source proving the *need* for the prior development of the creation stage.

Thus, it does not say that any conceptual thought is useless, nor that nonconceptualization {367a} is just not thinking; rather, since the cause of the nondual intuition of the buddha must be preceded by the path of knowing the thatness of selflessness without conceptualizing the signs of the two kinds of selves [objective and subjective], the point [that it is emphasizing] is that it is necessary to have a cause that corresponds in kind [with its effect]. Thus, moreover, you must understand this without contradicting what that [*Vajragarbha's Hevajra] Commentary* states:

> From among the profound and magnificent Dharmas,
> To those who are bereft of good fortune
> I have taught what is pleasant:
> Mudrā, mandala, mantra, etc.
>
> 'By means [only] of mudrā, mandala, mantra, etc.
> You will become a teacher
> [Like] Buddha Vajrasattva, etc.!'
> —Future masters who teach that are a class[203] of demons.

The meaning of the first verse is as follows: To those who are Mantra disciples who do not have the good fortune[204] for [receiving] the perfection stage, [a master] should teach the creation stage [that is, "mudrā, mandala, mantra, etc."]; and to all those [same] disciples to whom he does teach the creation stage, he should not teach the perfection stage since they are born without the good fortune for it in that life. The second [verse means]: A master who teaches that [corrupt perspective] cited previously from *[The Great Commentary:] Immaculate Light*,[205]—viz.,

---

[203] Reading *rigs*, in agreement with Derge (contra the reading *ris* in the *NRC* editions).

[204] *skal ba*—here and below this almost has the sense of "destiny."

[205] Cf. the two *Immaculate Light* passages cited above (363a–b), where it discusses: "Here you may think that if you can directly perceive...the wheel of a mandala, then you

(cont'd)

that once you have familiarized yourself just with the yoga of the circle of deities, then when that becomes vivid, that is buddhahood—is a teacher who is in the category of demons.

Moreover, *Vajragarbha's [Hevajra] Commentary* quotes the root Tantra of *Hevajra*:[206]

> Seeing the three types of beings {367b}
> Trapped in the net of conceptual thought
> I teach this or that method
> According to whom it liberates.
>
> To those bound by instincts for conceptual thought,
> I first teach conceptual procedures;
> When they know the nature of conceptual thought,
> [I teach them] they should enter nonconceptual thought.
>
> In order to engage the immature ones,
> [I] the world savior teach them how to create
> The mandala wheel mansion
> And the deities,
> The attracting of the intuition [heroes] and the conferral of initiation,
> And likewise the wheels, channels, seminal essences, and wind-energies;
> And [I] do not [teach] the definitive meaning
> Investigated elsewhere.[207]
>
> Who looks for the way of the mandala, the deities,
> The attracting of the intuition [heroes],
> The conferral of initiation, the seeds, and wind-energies,
> Does not understand Hevajra.

---

will...become omniscient, etc.," and "Here, if...the yogī...will be transformed into the form of the wheel of the mandala by the power of familiarization with meditation [alone], and if you claim that you even will [achieve] buddhahood itself by the power of meditating on the conceptual [alone]...."

206 The following cited verses appear in Vajragarbha's text (Tōh. 1180) at 58a.3–6. However, I have not been able to locate these verses in the root text of the *Hevajra Tantra* (Tōh. 417; Lhasa 378, kha), or in any other text.

207 *ma yin nges don gzhan du dpyad*. The Tibetan is somewhat obtuse here.

This clearly demarcates first the creation stage and then the perfection stage meditations.

[Some persons may argue] it is not like that; and depending on just a few scriptures that state that the creation stage is interpretable in meaning and is a [mentally] elaborated phenomenon, [such persons] may abandon meditation on that [creation stage]. [Furthermore,] like the passage [above]—which stated "[I teach] seminal essences, and wind-energies [and I do not teach the definitive meaning.... Who looks for these] does not understand Hevajra"—one can see more than a few Tantras and treatises which state that the [perfection stage] yogas of the channels, wind-energies, and drops are also interpretable in meaning and are [mentally] elaborated phenomena; and one also can see many assertions that [even such perfection stage yogas] are not necessary for the most advanced persons; and thus [such persons may come to conclude erroneously that] even those [perfection stage yogas] are not definitely necessary to meditate to attain buddhahood through the Mantra path. And thus, in the final analysis, {368a} [such persons] will have come to the conclusion that the only path there is that one must meditate will be just some sort of narrowly focused completely nonconceptual mind; and thereby they will have abandoned all the scriptures.

Therefore, the wise should far distance themselves from and abandon the following two positions, having understood them as essenceless messages: [1] that in the [exoteric] Transcendence Vehicle, since the deeds component is interpretable in meaning and [mentally] elaborated, all one needs to rely on is mere emptiness; and [2] that in the [esoteric] Mantra Vehicle, since the meditation of the creation stage, [mantra] repetition, etc., are conceptual, elaborated, and interpretable in meaning, then if one knows the definitive meaning [such practices] are unnecessary. Rather, [the wise] should train sequentially in the path of the integration of [exoteric] art and wisdom and the integration of [esoteric] creation and perfection, and they should enter into the path of the great champions, which entails two approaches: understanding the import of the central way which is free of fabrications, and keeping the commitments. As [Mañjushrīkīrti's] *The Ornament of the Essence* says:

> If you engage [practice] having seen just one mere part, you definitely have not found the path to truly perfect buddhahood. Therefore, you should live free of partial

> views regarding that: you should have a realization free of [mental] elaborations regarding the way of the view, you should engage sequentially in the samādhis of the creation stage and the perfection stage,[208] and you should keep your commitments. Those who understand the way of practice which proceeds sequentially will definitely generate the supreme vehicle; directly realizing thatness by the path of Vajradhara, {368b} they will acquire the desired qualitites. Therefore, you should apply the stages of the path, together with the two approaches—this is what you should undertake.

Having given those two previous antagonist's positions,[209] I now will present our own system.

[II.B.2.c.ii.C'3'c'ii'B'' – The way of experientially cultivating the two stages in an inseparable way]

The second has four: [1''] The verbal meaning of the two stages; [2''] The determination of the number of the two stages; [3''] The determination of the proper sequence of the two stages; and [4''] The way of learning each of the two stages.

[II.B.2.c.ii.C'3'c'ii'B''1'' – The verbal meaning of the two stages]

A certain past mentor said that according to the Ārya Father and Sons' tradition, the ordinary [processes of] taking birth and of dying are creation and perfection, and that these are sequential, involving sequential establishment and sequential dissolution [respectively]. Thus, the bases of what is to be purified [viz. one's ordinary body-mind continuum] are the *actual* creation [one's birth/life] and perfection [one's death],[210] and the

---

[208] The Derge says only that "one should engage sequentially in the concentrations of perfection stage," omitting the clause "the creation stage and the...." This makes less sense given the overall thrust of this *Ornament of the Essence* text (Tōh. 2490); this omission may well be another corruption in this text.

[209] Viz. (1) that one can attain buddhahood by the creation stage without the perfection stage (explored at Tib. 353a–355a); and (2) that one can attain buddhahood by the perfection stage without the creation stage (explored at Tib. 355a–368b).

[210] *bskyed rdzogs dngos.*

two paths—which are the means of purifying what is purified through meditating according to that process—are [what are called] the *metaphoric* creation and perfection.[211] [This is so, said this past mentor,] because as [Āryadeva's] *Practice Integration* explains:

> Birth should be called superficial truth
> And the name for death is ultimate truth.
> The discovery of those two stages through the kindness of the mentor
> Is [what leads to] buddhahood in the future.

[However,] that is not the position of the Ārya Father and Sons—because the meaning of "creation" in the term "creation stage" is not accepted as a birth-creation by the proper cause of the ordinary body, and because the passage from the *Practice Integration* does not indicate that [actual physical] birth is the creation stage. [Rather,] just like when [Chandrakīrti's] *Illumination of the Lamp* **{369a}** states:[212]

> Individually indicating the arts of achieving the stages of designation and perfection,[213] ...

the creation stage is often referred to as the *stage of designation*,[214] and therefore it is designation by the mind or creation by the mind, not physical creation by the elements, etc.

[Moreover], before that passage in the *Practice Integration* it states that you should project the following mental intention: 'if after completing the creation stage I do not happen to succeed in the practice of a perfection stage achievement, then at the time of death I should realize ultimate truth, and then having died, at the time of birth I should arise in the superficial-truth illusion body.'[215] Thus, [1] that verse [in the

---

[211] *bskyed rdzogs btags pa ba.*

[212] The *Pradīpoddyotana* (Tōh. 1785) by Chandrakīrti is one of the most important commentaries on the *Guhyasamāja Tantra* (Tōh. 442).

[213] *brtags pa dang rdzogs pa'i rim pa.*

[214] *brtags pa'i rim pa.*

[215] Note here that (1) death correlates with ultimate-truth (clear light), (2) birth correlates with superficial-truth illusion body, and that (3) *both* of these are references to sub-stages

(cont'd)

Practice Integration] indicates the import of achieving buddhahood through transforming [death and birth] in that way, and it does not indicate the [actual] birth and death of some other sentient being [in one's future continuum]; and [2] "those two stages" [in the third line of the verse] refers to two [*perfection*] stages [viz. the clear light of death and the illusion body],[216] as I have strived to explain previously,[217] and it does not indicate that [ordinary] birth and death are the two stages. Otherwise, the praise that 'the discovery of the two stages through the kindness of the mentor is [what leads to] buddhahood in the future' would be meaningless, because all sentient beings have already discovered two stages like that [that is, ordinary birth and death]! So when you cite that passage as an authority, since a yogī merges death and the clear light, and since he makes birth into the illusion body, both ["death" and "birth" in this context] must be accepted as [references to] the *perfection* stage.[218]

---

of the perfection stage (i.e., they are levels or practices within the perfection stage). The relevance and importance of this will become evident in the remainder of this paragraph.

[216] Cf. the previous note (above), and the last sentence of this paragraph.

[217] I have not been able to find a discussion of this passage elsewhere in the *NRC*. Presumably his "previous explanation" of this occurs in one of his other previous works.

[218] So in the preceding paragraph we see that the past mentor whose views Tsong Khapa is critiquing has made *two* different mistakes: (1) He mistakenly thinks that actual birth and death are what he wants to call the "actual creation and perfection " (and that the Tantric practices constitute what he calls the "metaphoric creation and perfection"); and (2) He mistakenly thinks that the phrase "those two stages" (in the verse from the *Practice Integration* which he cites) refers to the creation and perfection stages.

Regarding the first mistake, this has two mistakes within it: (1a) While it is true (as we shall see later) that the processes of actual birth and death (and the between) constitute what are called "the bases of purification," it is not correct to refer to these bases themselves as constituting some kind of ("actual") creation and/or perfection (stages). Moreover, (1b) it is not correct to correlate the creation stage with birth and the perfection stage with death. Rather, practices involved in *both* stages need to correlate with all three of the stages of birth, death, and the between. (Much of the next chapter, ch. XII, discusses this; for a summary, see the section entitled "A Summary of the Essential Points," p. 236ff.; Tib. 420a–421b.)

Regarding the second mistake, while it is of course often the case that the phrase "the two stages" refers to the creation and perfection stages, Tsong Khapa demonstrates (by showing the *context* of the *Practice Integration* verse, through citing a prior passage from that text) that in this case the phrase must refer to two perfection stages (i.e., two levels or practices within the perfection stage).

Another [past mentor] has argued:[219] According to the system of the *Bodhisattva Commentaries*,[220] perfection (*rdzogs pa*) is the supreme siddhi, without [needing to] extract the impact,[221] {369b} and the process (*rim pa*) of achieving that is the perfection stage (*rdzogs rim*); and since they create enthusiasm for the supreme, ordinary siddhis are called "creation" (*bskyed pa*), and the process (*rim pa*) of achieving them is taken to be the creation stage (*bskyed rim*). Thus, [the two stages are] designated from the point of view of their effects [supreme and ordinary siddhis].

[Response:] Although indeed those texts do say many times that the perfection stage is the means for achieving the supreme, and that the creation stage is the means for achieving the ordinary siddhis, one never sees the *terms* 'creation' and 'perfection' explained like that. Therefore, following Virūpa and Ḍombipa, it is better to say that [these terms] are principally names associated with paths [and not their effects]; and thus, the etymological analysis of [the terms] 'the creation stage' and 'the perfection stage at the time of the path' is that they are posited with respect to paths only. As Shāntipa says [in *The Pearl Rosary*]:

> 'Stage' (*rim pa*), 'aspect' (*rnam pa*), 'portion' (*cha*), and 'part' (*phyogs*) are all synonyms. Stage of what? Of yoga.[222]

Regarding the ascertainment of the bases upon which the terms for the two stages are established, and the ascertainment of their etymological analyses: the latter is the more difficult, because to ascertain this one has to distinguish the uncommon distinctive characteristics of creation

---

[219] In characterizing the following position Tsong Khapa uses honorific verbs (*bzhed pa*, *gsung*, etc.), indicating that has high regard for the person who proposed this (perhaps Bu-ston?).

[220] *byang chub sems dpa'i 'grel pa rnams*. According to Stearns (*The Buddha from Dölpo*, p. 316 n27), the *sems 'grel skor gsum* (or *Bodhisattva Trilogy*) refers to Tōh. 1347, 1180, and 1402.

[221] Cf. note 97 above.

[222] Note that all of these terms pertain to paths (e.g., a "section of the path") and not to the effects or end results of those paths (one would not speak of a "section/part" of the result). Cf. also below, p. 132 (Tib. 372a), where Tsong Khapa mentions this passage again, and then further clarifies that *rim pa* here does not refer to "a temporal process" (*dus kyi rim pa*) either.

and perfection; and thus, the meaning being extremely profound, the really great ones do not explain clearly or in great detail the actual analyses of these etymologies.

The Vajraḍāka Tantra gives the two stages the alternate names "fabricative yoga" and "natural yoga,"[223] and [Kṛiṣhṇāchārya's] *Drop of Spring* states:

> Having abandoned the fabricated mandala,
> All fabricated things—such as
> Actions involving fabricated fire offerings, {370a}
> Actions involving fabricative meditation,
> And fabricative repetitions
> —Are abandoned through the mode of the natural yoga.[224]
> You should fully engage the outer fabricated,
> In order to realize the natural.

Thus it declares, together with an example of a boat. Therefore, "creation stage," "designative stage," and "fabricative yoga" are names for the first stage;[225] and "perfection stage," "non-designative stage," and "natural yoga" are names for the second stage.[226] [The stage with] the three [names] "creation," etc., being created by the mind, involves designation and fabrication; and in parallel with that, [the stage with the three names] "perfection," [etc.,] is perfected or achieved in that it is not designated by the mind.

Well then, what is the meaning of these being achieved or not achieved through the power of mental fabrication?

Both of the stages, each relying on its various methodologies within its own context, are indeed similar in causing you to become perfected as a divine body; however, they are dissimilar in the way that they do this. Thus, in the creation stage you perfect yourself as a divine body through the methods of [visualizing] vowel and consonant letters, with moon and sun coming from those, then seed letters and hand-symbols, etc., [ultimately

---

[223] *bcos ma dang rnal ma'i rnal 'byor*. Cf. above, p. 103 (Tib. 359b).

[224] *rang bzhin rnal 'byor*.

[225] Respectively: *bskyed pa'i rim pa*; *brtags pa'i rim pa*; and *bcos ma'i rnal 'byor*.

[226] Respectively: *rdzogs pa'i rim pa*; *ma brtags pa'i rim pa*; and *rnal ma'i rnal 'byor*.

arising as a divine body]; being mental creation, this is just designation. In the perfection stage, through the force of making fit for action the [actual] referents of what were [merely] symbolized [in the creation stage] by vowel and consonant letters, moon and sun, etc.—[e.g.,] the white and red spirits of enlightenment {370b} and the wind-energies—and through the power of actualizing the three intuitions of luminance, radiance, and imminence, you arise from mere wind-mind as an [actual] illusory divine body; and thus this is perfection as a divine body without designation or fabrication by the mind.

Therefore, the creation stage method for perfecting the body involves mental fabrication, and the divine body that arises from that method is also fabricated. The perfection stage method for perfecting the divine body involves the yogas of channels, wind-energies, and drops, etc., and does not involve mental fabrication; and through that methodology emptiness is actualized, and after that the body of a deity arises, and that is not designated by the mind. Thinking of that, [Āryadeva] said in the *Practice Integration*:

> Beginning from the creation stage up through the conclusion of body isolation, there is merely an imaginative orientation that is characterized by the three vajras [of body, speech, and mind], etc.; therefore, even in body isolation one does not [yet] have the [actual] form of the deity, ...

So he states that until one has attained the illusion body there is no divine body other than that which is just mentally imagined in the context of the three isolations and the creation stage; and thus the divine body of the three isolations is merely included in the category of the perfection stage, but it is not the actual intuition body.[227]

Objection: If that is the case, then one should create the divine body only through the methods of the perfection stage such as the yogas of wind-energies and drops which are the import of what is symbolized by letters, etc. {371a} What is the point of the fabrication which creates a divine body through the methods of letters, hand-symbols, moon, sun, etc.?

---

[227] So within the five stages of the perfection stage, it is only *after* the end of the three isolations (stages 1–3) and after the self-consecration, which then launches one into the actual illusion body (stage 4), that one really has a real divine body for the first time. Cf. Wedemeyer 2007, p. 243.

[Answer:] That is not so. Without having become accustomed to the fabricative methods you will be unable to perfect the non-fabricative methods; and thus, also, without having become accustomed to what arises from the fabricative methods you will be unable to actualize what arises from the non-fabricative methods. That was the intention of the previously cited boat analogy:[228] for example, if in some place on the far side of a river there are provisions of food and drink which you want to enjoy, but which you are unable to enjoy because of being obstructed by the river, then you can get to the far shore by relying on a boat. Likewise, if you want to enjoy the enjoyments of the perfection stage, but because of being obstructed by the river of the perception and conception of ordinariness[229] you do not have the power to enjoy them, then by relying on the boat of the creation stage you can get to the shore where the perception and conception of ordinariness are eliminated. [Furthermore,] while the boat is the method for getting to the far shore, you [still] need some other method for obtaining the enjoyments of the food and drink [once you have arrived there]. So, likewise, although the creation stage is that which causes the maturing of the continuum for the production of the perfection stage, you [still] need something else—such as the yogas of wind-energies and drops, etc.—as a method for [obtaining] the enjoyments of the emptiness and the deity body of the perfection stage. This [analogy] {371b} shows both that it is necessary to go to the end of the creation stage and that the creation stage alone is not sufficient.

Therefore, regarding deity-creation yoga—although [all classes of Tantra] are similar insofar as they include the creation of a deity body from methods such as letters and hand-symbols and moon, etc., still, from the perspective of those methods, the ability to set up the distinctive relative circumstances that ripen one's continuum for the development of the yogas of psychic heat and the drop—which are the signified meanings of all of those things [letters, hand-symbols, moons, etc.]—[that ability] does not exist in the [Tantras which are] not Unexcelled. Such a thing [which so ripens] is spoken of as the creation stage. Thus, it is the case that the lower Tantras do not have the creation stage; and if [one wanted

---

[228] See the quote from the *The Vajraḍāka* above (p. 103, Tib. 359b).

[229] *tha mal pa'i snang zhen*. See introduction, p. 64 (esp. note 66) above.

to maintain that] there was a creation stage teaching in their root Tantras, that vajra word[230] should have both interpretable and definitive [levels of] explanation, and thus one would have to accept that [those lower Tantras] had *both* creation *and* perfection [stages][231]—this can be understood by looking at *The Illumination of the Lamp*'s way of explaining the *Intuition Vajra Compendium [Tantra]*.[232]

Regarding the meaning of the terms for the two stages, [Ratnākarashānti] states in the *Hevajra* commentary, *The Pearl Rosary*:

> Creation of a deity through the process of mantras, symbols, etc., is the yogī's creation: whatever is involved with that is the stage of creation. Perfection is orgasmic creation: the yogī should meditate considering his own nature as a practitioner, etc., to be the thatness, etc., of orgasmic [bliss], [itself] the nature of thatness; that is the stage of perfection.

The former of these [statements] is as I explained before; while the latter, {372a} being in the area of the perfection stage, [shows that] it also requires the body of a deity.[233]

According to the explanation in that [*Pearl Rosary*] commentary, [the term] 'stage' (*rim pa*) should be [understood as referring to] an 'aspect,' a 'portion,' or a 'part,'[234] and not to a temporal phase.[235]

---

230 I.e., that purported creation stage teaching.

231 In Unexcelled Yoga parlance "interpretable meaning" correlates to creation stage practice (among other things), and "definitive meaning" correlates to perfection stage. Tsong Khapa is arguing here that if one wants to maintain that the lower Tantras have one of these, then one must also maintain that they have the other—and this would be an unacceptable consequence for just about any Tantric exegete.

232 This is one of the five explanatory Tantras of the *Esoteric Community Tantra*.

233 Tsong Khapa is quoting *The Pearl Rosary* to support his earlier point that the perfection stage as a whole must also include meditation on a (subtle) deity body, since the experience of bliss requires a body.

234 *rnam pa*, *cha*, and *phyogs*, respectively. Cf. above, p. 128 (Tib. 369b).

235 *dus kyi rim pa*. We are only left to wonder if Tsong Khapa intends that this interpretation should be applied generally in all contexts.

[Finally], although Subhagavajra explains it as follows [in *The Stages of the Path of the Universal Vehicle*]:[236]

> Regarding 'creation': when one creates the moon, etc., that is 'creation.' The other [word] is 'stage.' Regarding 'perfection': [it is] the intuition of the great void—there is 'perfection' in the method of that [intuition]. Or, by perfecting that [intuition], one perfects all excellences; and thus it is perfection. The other [word] is 'stage.'

—the previous explanation [from *The Pearl Rosary*] is preferable.

[**II.B.2.c.ii.C'3'c'ii'B''2''** – The determination of the number of the two stages]

Second, *The Further Tantra* of *The [Esoteric] Community* states:[237]

> The Dharma taught by the buddhas
> Is based upon the two stages:
> The stage of creation, and
> The stage of perfection.

You may wonder: What is the reason for stating that the path is determined to have two stages?

Since each of the two stages has both meditation on a circle of deities on the perception side as well as [meditation on] on emptiness, the determination of the number is not in terms of deities and emptiness. Therefore, the reason for determining that there are two stages is as stated in *The Further Tantra* of *The [Esoteric] Community*:

> Through division into shared and supreme
> It is held that service is of two types.
> The shared one is in terms of the four vajras,
> And the supreme one is in terms of the six branches.

---

[236] This is Subhagavajra's only canonical text. According to the Tengyur chart, this is in the Tengyur's general section E, "Other Tengyur Texts Pertaining to All Four Tantras," subsection 4, "Distinctions Among the Three Yānas and the Four Tantras."

[237] Tōh. 443: *Uttaratantra (rgyud phyi ma)*. The eighteenth chapter of the *Esoteric Community Tantra* (Tōh. 442), but considered a separate explanatory Tantra. See Wedemeyer 2007, pp. 40–41, for an interesting discussion of this verse.

What is to be obtained includes both temporary and ultimate siddhis, and thus their means of achievement also is determined to be the two stages.[238]

Here, {372b} [the the four vajras schema is] 'shared' [between the two stages] in two ways. It is shared with respect to cause: in the first stage you must create in your continuum both of the siddhis, the supreme siddhi and the [ordinary] eight siddhis etc. It is shared with respect to effect: siddhis such as the eight siddhis, etc., come to be an effect of both stages.[239] The meaning of [the above passage from] that Tantra is expressed by [Chandrakīrti's commentary] *The Illumination of the Lamp*:[240]

> Thus, having shown that through the process of the four [branches of] yoga you should propitiate Vajrasattva, now it states that through the process of the six branches you should perfect [yourself as] Great Vajradhara.

So it is the determination of these two—the propitiation and the perfection of Vajrasattva—that determines there to be two stages. The meaning of the first is stated again in *The Illumination of the Lamp*:

> Thus, having constantly practiced in four sessions, you completely mature the root of virtue, and having thereby

---

[238] However, as we shall see next, there is *not* a one-to-one correspondence between creation/perfection stages and shared/supreme service, or between creation/perfection stages and temporary/ultimate siddhis.

[239] So in both stages it is necessary to create both types of siddhi—thus there is not a one-to-one correspondence as one might have thought based on the previous paragraph.

[240] Although *The Illumination of the Lamp* does not comment on *The Further Tantra* (the eighteenth chapter) of *The Esoteric Community* in general, it does cite and comment upon the verse cited above (see *YGST*, 38, 44, 155–56). Note that the phrase "the four yogas" (*sbyor ba bzhi*, *caturyoga*) used in the following *Illumination* passage normally would to refer to the rubric that is specific to the creation stage only, and not to that which is shared between the two stages. This normal usage here would be problematic, since *The Further Tantra* verse on which this is commenting, above, is discussing the "shared service." However, in the last sentence of this section below Tsong Khapa clarifies this particular usage of the phrase "the four yogas" as follows: "The 'four yogas' are the four branches of service and practice" (*sbyor ba bzhi ni, bsnyen bsgrub yan lag bzhi'o*). By clarifying that in this instance the phrase "the four yogas" refers to "the four branches" (*yan lag bzhi*, *caturaṅga*), he resolves this apparent problem, since "the four branches" is an alternate term for "the four vajras" (*rdo rje bzhi*, *vajracatuṣka*), which was the term used in *The Further Tantra* quote above. See Table 8 in the introduction for further clarification of these categories.

> clearly realized the vajra-like samādhi, in this very life
> you will achieve the siddhi of the great seal.

Thus, having set up the many distinctive relative circumstances as previously explained, you mature your continuum. The *'four yogas'* [in this case] are the [shared] four branches of service and practice.

[**II.B.2.c.ii.C'3'c'ii'B''3''** – The determination of the proper sequence of the two stages]

The perfection stage can arise in a continuum that has been developed through the creation stage; but in one not developed by that, although a few parts of the perfection stage may arise, a perfection stage capable of traversing the path will not arise. Thus there are many statements that first you meditate the creation stage and then you meditate the perfection stage. There is the example of the boat given in *The Vajraḍāka [Tantra],*[241] {373a} and likewise the similar explanations given in [Jñānapāda's] *Drop of Liberation* and [Kṛiṣhṇāchārya's] *Drop of Spring.* Moreover, the second chapter of the later section of the *[Hevajra Tantra in] Two Sections* states:[242]

> With the yoga of the creation stage
> The disciplined one should meditate [a mentally]
> elaborated [world].
> Making [this] elaborated [world] dreamlike,
> He should make elaboration itself non-elaborative.

And *The Five Stages* states:

> To those abiding well in the creation stage
> Who are ambitious for the perfection stage
> The perfect buddhas have taught
> This method that is like the rungs of a ladder.

---

[241] See above, p. 103 (Tib. 359b).

[242] This is book II, chapter 2, verse 28, on p. 162 of Farrow and Menon. They give it as follows: *utpattikramayogena prapañcaṁ bhāvayed vratī/ prapañcaṁ svapnavat kṛtvā prapañcair niḥprapañcayet//* "The holder of the Vow must conceive the differentiated world by means of the method of the Process of Generation. Making the differentiated dream-like, utilising the differentiated, transform it into the undifferentiated."

And the *Practice Integration* states:

> So that those beings who are beginners
> Could engage in ultimate reality
> The perfect buddhas have set forth
> This method, like the rungs of a ladder.

And Ḍombi Heruka states:

> Sumati! First meditate the creation stage, [utilize] the hand gestures, and
> Do not separate yourself from being definitely mindful of all [the types of] mantras: purifying, atttacting, creating, and armoring![243]
> Later, Sumati, overjoyed in the stream of moments, be single-minded on thatness;
> Meditating the perfection stage, abandon existence and always contemplate the orgasmic [intuition]!

Therefore, to conduct yourself through the second stage without having conducted yourself through the first stage is contradictory to all the authoritative texts. Thus, if you have a heartfelt desire to practice the path of great yoga, you must in the beginning {373b} cultivate the conduct of the first stage.

Well then, you may wonder: Is it that until one has firmed up the first stage one does not meditate the second stage, or is it that in the beginning of the [meditation] session one meditates the first stage and in the latter part of the session one meditates the second stage?

The Ārya Father and Son maintain the former position. The *Practice Integration* states:

> When you have learned the spirit of the [general exoteric] Buddha Vehicle, then you learn the single-minded samādhi [of the creation stage] in the new [esoteric] vehicle. When you have learned the single-minded samādhi in the new vehicle, then you learn the conceptual yoga

243 These seem to be four types of mantras, though I have not yet located such a list in any reference work.

> [of the creation stage]. When you have learned the conceptual yoga, then you become fully established in the samādhi of a beginner [on the subtle creation stage]. When you have become established in the samādhi of a beginner, then you engage in the division into the one hundred clans [of the body isolation]. When you have known body isolation through the division into the one hundred clans, then you abide in the body-vajra samādhi. Having remained in body isolation, you enter into speech isolation through the door of the vowels and consonants. When you have come to know vitality and its control[244] through the process of vajra repetition, then you fully remain in the speech-vajra samādhi....

This explanation cuts to the essential point: When you have learned the first stage, then [you learn] the second stage, and moreover when you have learned various earlier parts of the second stage then you learn the various later parts.

Furthermore, as Ghaṇṭāpa and [his disciple] Lavapa[245] state in their *Supreme Bliss Sādhana*[s]:[246] {374a}

> By meditating uninterruptedly with devotion in that way [on the creation stage], your mind becomes firm, and then you can meditate the perfection stage samādhi.

That also was the position of Dīpaṅkarabhadra;[247] you can understand this from the context [in his work] about the fourfold division into beginners, etc.

---

244 *prāṇa* (*srog*) and *āyāma* (*rtsol ba*).

245 Lva-ba-pa/Kambala (*lva ba'i na bza' can*). Dowman's *Masters of Mahamudra* (pp. 179–185) clarifies that Lva-ba-pa and Kambala are two names for the same mahāsiddha. (Actually, *lwa ba* is the Tibetan for the Sanskrit *Kambala*, "blanket.") According to Tibetan tradition, Kambala was a disciple of Ghaṇṭāpa (Dowman: 183).

246 Ghaṇṭāpa states this in his *Five Deity Supreme Bliss Sādhana*, and Lva-ba-pa states it in his *Supreme Bliss Sādhana*.

247 On Dīpaṅkarabhadra (*mar me mdzad bzang po*), cf. Wayman's *The Buddhist Tantras*, pp. 111–113.

[Among Tibetans,] the great Tibetan mantrika, Master Gö [Khugpa Lhaytsay], and his followers also advocated that position. But those who practice the Tantras following Master Nyugu Lungpa and Master Marpa hold the position that in the beginning of the [meditation] session you meditate the creation stage and in the latter part of the session you meditate the perfection stage.

Here, you can see that this sequence of the path is extremely important—because if you err by not grasping this well, then no matter how much you exert yourself you will definitely not develop anything; or else you might experience something like that [perfection stage experience] which is not the actual [perfection stage experience], but you will be confused and will waste your time. However, if you do not err with respect to this sequence, then whatever you meditate will get to the essential point, and thereby you will quickly develop a straight-forward path; and through the force of that you will very quicky develop the higher [stages of meditation].

In general, there seem to be two [types of] perfection stage, one which beginners are not able to meditate and one which they are able to meditate. Regarding the latter, even though they have not stabilized the creation stage, if they meditate [on the perfection stage] it is not the case that they cannot produce some simulated qualities;[248] nonetheless, they will not produce [qualities] like those produced in those who did develop their continuum through the first stage. Therefore, forsaking the first stage it appears that they can produce simulated qualities of the wind-energies, psychic heat, etc.; **{374b}** but it is not acceptable if they jumble those all up and err with respect to the key points of the path.

Nevertheless, until you have firmed up the first stage, if within the confines of meditating primarily on that [first stage] you practice wind-energy [yogas], psychic heat, etc., on the side, in accordance with what is circumstantially necessary, then it is certainly less objectionable.

Regarding mere meditation on emptiness: this being shared with the [exoteric] Transcendence Vehicle, the three lower Tantra classes also have [emptiness] meditations, which they tie in with deity yoga; however, given that those [lower Tantras] do not have the perfection stage, the claim that mere meditation on emptiness is perfection stage meditation

---

[248] *rjes mthun pa'i yon tan*—simulated or virtual qualities.

is extremely ill-considered. Therefore, even in the context of the first stage, meditation on emptiness is also very necessary.

> Having little experience in the boat which is effort in investigation,
> And not relying on a spiritual friend who is a skilled captain,
> [Fools] do not see the ocean of the treatises of Secret Mantra
> [And thus develop] wishful systems for travel by partial paths.
>
> Having well refuted [such partial paths], I say you must travel this path which delights experts,
> Which, producing in order the two stages,
> Is not an incomplete path to the stage of a Victor!
> [Thus in this chapter] I have illuminated the excellent tradition of the Champions.

[This completes] the eleventh chapter of *The Critical Elucidation of the Key Instructions in All the Secret Stages of the Path of the Great Vajradhara*,[249] showing {375a} the need to accomplish enlightenment through the integration of the two stages.

---

249 Tsong Khapa slightly abbreviates the full title here at the end of this chapter (and all chapters).

CHAPTER XII

The Creation Stage

[II.B.2.c.ii.C'3'c'ii'B''4'' – The way of learning each of the two stages]

Fourth: There are two parts to the way of learning each of the two stages: [a''] The way of learning the creation stage; and [b''] The way of learning the perfection stage.

[II.B.2.c.ii.C'3'c'ii'B''4''a'' – The way of learning the creation stage]

The first of these has two parts: [i''] A general presentation of the creation stage; and [ii''] An explanation of the stages of evocation.[250]

[II.B.2.c.ii.C'3'c'ii'B''4''a''i'' – A general presentation of the creation stage]

The first of these has three parts: [A°] That for which the creation stage is created as an antidote; [B°] The divisions of the creation stage to be created; and [C°] How to meditate emptiness in that context.

[II.B.2.c.ii.C'3'c'ii'B''4''a''i''A° – That for which the creation stage is created as an antidote]

The first of these has two parts: [1°] Showing how to identify and get rid of what is to be abandoned; and [2°] Showing how to establish vivid perception and stability.

---

250 *mngon (par) rtogs (pa)* (Skt. *abhisamaya*). Translated herein as "evoke/evocation." While this term generally can be translated more literally by the phrase "clear realization," in Tantric ritual contexts such as this it often specifically refers to the sections of a sādhana practice which describe (or evoke) the image of the deity(ies), etc., to be visualized/evoked. In these contexts one also could translate *gsal btab* (herein translated as "visualize") as "evoke" as it implies "visualize" under the idea of "verbally summon in contemplation."

[**II.B.2.c.ii.C'3'c'ii'B''4''a''i''A°1°** – Showing how to identify and get rid of what is to be abandoned]

The special things to be abandoned on the creation stage are the perception of the ordinariness of the habitat and inhabitants, and the pride involving the conception of the habitat and inhabitants as ordinary. In the fourteenth chapter of *The [Vajra] Pavilion [Tantra]* it says:

> True meditation is renowned
> For the destruction of ordinary features...

and in [Āryadeva's] *Practice Integration* it is stated:

> Further, in this regard, those body-mind systems, sense fields, and media that are established from beginningless time on the basis of the pride of ordinariness are thus demonstrated in reality to be made from the subtle atoms of all transcendent buddhas.

[These passages] state that in the Tantras it is shown that you should meditate on the body-mind systems, etc., as buddhas, as an antidote to establishing yourself from beginningless time in the body-mind systems due to the pride of ordinariness. {375b} While this [passage] is concerned with the context of [the sub-stage of] body isolation, the two special things to be abandoned by both that [sub-stage] and the [whole] creation stage are similar. The meditation involving the creation of a distinctive perception of habitat and inhabitants—done in order to get rid of this kind of perception and conception [of ordinariness]—does not exist in the Transcendence Vehicle; it is a distinctive characteristic of the Mantra Vehicle. The creation stage involving meditation on the habitat celestial mansion and inhabitant deities was taught as the antidote to both the perception and the conception of ordinariness. Thus, through familiarization with the perception which gives rise to the habitat celestial mansion and the inhabitant deities, you will get rid of the perception of ordinariness, and through familiarization with the habit pattern which ascertains the thoughts "I am Akṣhobhya," "I am Vairochana," etc., [you will get rid of] the pride of ordinariness. Having eliminated the pride of ordinariness, [your sense of identity] is transformed into divine pride. For example, when intuition is well grounded, and you have eliminated whatever was your previous self-centered habit pattern, the thought "I am a deity" begins to develop. Accordingly, after developing the fabricated thoughts "I am Akṣhobhya" and "I am Vairochana," etc., [your sense of identity] will be transformed into divine pride.

Here we see four possibilities. For some, though unfabricated divine pride arises, there is no clear perception of habitat and inhabitants. For others, though there is clear perception of habitat and inhabitants, there is no divine pride that is not fabricated. For others there are both, and [for others] there is neither. In [Nāgārjuna's] *Integration of the Scripture [with the Sādhana]* it is stated:

> Thus, beginners {376a} take the commitments and vows when entering [the mandala], and receive initiation, and being free from the pride of ordinariness, they meditate deity yoga in four sessions.

Since the expression "get rid of the pride of ordinariness" is stated frequently in other scriptures as well, [we can deduce that] meditation on [developing] the pride of the habitat and inhabitants' mandalas as an antidote to the pride of ordinariness is paramount, whereas meditation on [developing] the distinctive perception of the habitat and inhabitants in order to overcome the perception of ordinariness is ancillary to that.

The 'perception of ordinariness' to be eliminated is not the perception by sense consciousnesses of vessel and contents;[251] rather, it is the perception in the mental consciousness of vessel and contents as ordinary. Regarding the way that the creation stage terminates both that [perception of ordinariness] as well as the pride of ordinariness: in this context it is not useful to raise [the example of] the kind of elimination of seeds [which occurs] when one eliminates [seeds] on the path of liberation from this world. Moreover, this is not the kind of evident elimination of seeds [which occurs] when one eliminates [seeds] on worldly paths, wherein there is [just] a deteriorization of seeds.

So then how are [the perception and pride of ordinariness] terminated?

If there are no other incidental contrary conditions, then when you maintain [the perception of] the habitat and inhabitant mandala as well as

[251] *snod bcud*—lit. "vessel and contents"; i.e., the environment and its inhabitants (another phrase for *rten dang brten pa*, translated herein as "habitat and inhabitants").

the pride of that [perception], and when you have the ability to transform pride as previously explained and you visualize both mandalas, then you produce an extremely vivid perception just like that which is visualized. Thus, with that way of overcoming the perception {376b} of ordinariness in the mind,[252] you overcome both the perception and conception of ordinariness.

Furthermore, it is not enough to be able to overcome [the perception and conception of ordinariness] to a small, partial extent; it must be very firm. When vajra masters—who have been made fit for action using this kind of method in their prior retreats—place the obstructors of the earth rites[253] under their command, etc., they produce the unfabricated pride of Vajradhara, etc., when they themselves create the pride of such and such a [deity], with declarations such as "I am glorious Vajradhara." For those who do not do it like that, there is mere verbal pride; so it is said that the prior retreat is crucial. However, since the distinctive pride and perception that are not merely verbal must at first be produced through familiarization with the meditation on the fabricated pride and perception which are merely verbal, in the beginning you should strive for that.

When through great familiarity you become absorbed in deity yoga, no further perceptions arise in the eye consciousness, etc. Then the mental consciousness, through intensely engaging that [internal perception of a divine] object, erodes the potentiality of the antecedent condition for the production of the eye consciousness, etc., and thereby those [sense consciousnesses] temporarily are not produced. This [non-arising] is a [temporary] non-arising of further perceptions of color, etc., but those perceptions are not [permanently] terminated by the creation stage. As Dharmakīrti said [in the *Validating Cognition Commentary*:

> Consciousness attaching to [one among] other object[s],
> Becomes powerless to apprehend yet another object.
> (II.112cd)

---

[252] *yid ngo'i*—"in the mind," or "as an object/sphere of the mind" (*sems kyi nang ngam blo yul*, acc. TTC).

[253] *sa chog*—earth occupying rites performed prior to making a mandala. These include votary cake offerings to local deities, etc., who might otherwise act as obstructors (*bgegs*) to the meditator.

Therefore, {377a} when through [developing] the distinctive perception you obtain the power to terminate the perception of ordinariness on the level of the mental consciousness, you thereby will achieve what is necessary. Then even though in actuality you will not [yet] have become a deity [through that perceptual practice], if you develop the unfabricated pride of being a deity [on the basis of that divine perception], you thereby will achieve what is necessary.

[II.B.2.c.ii.C'3'c'ii'B''4''a''i''A°2° – Showing how to establish vivid perception and stability]

In the second there are three: [a°] Meditating on whatever is clearly realized; [b°] How to bring about vivid perception; and [c°] How to achieve stability.

[II.B.2.c.ii.C'3'c'ii'B''4''a''i''A°2°a° – Meditating on whatever is clearly realized]

Well, you may wonder: Is it the case that learning on the creation stage is like learning on the perfection stage—that is, does one meditate on each visualized object, switching to the subsequent one [only] when the former one is firm; or does one meditate a single sādhana in its entirety, from beginning to end, in a single session?

Regarding [a comprehensive answer to] this, given that an analysis of the phases pertaining to the creation of paths in the continuum of a single person who is meditating on the path reveals that there are four [phases for such a person], we must understand the statements that analyze just how much meditation and what kind of meditation [is to be done by a person] in those [different phases]. So, as Dīpaṅkara[bhadra] states [in *The Mandala Rite of the Glorious Esoteric Community, The Four Hundred and Fifty (Verses)*]:[254]

> The *beginner* arises at dawn
> And recites well, as before [on previous days].

[254] Tōh. 1865 (Derge rGyud, DI): 74b.2–4. In the passage below I have italicized the descriptive names of each of the four phases.

> The one for whom *intuition has slightly settled*,
> Who has adopted the disciplines of mantric ethics,
> [And] blessed the eyes, the body, etc.,
> Recites at twilight with full attention.
>
> The one who has attained the *slight mastery of intuition*,
> Who practices radiation and retraction,
> Perfected and in all respects,
> Should rely on yoga day and night.
>
> The one who has attained *true mastery of intuition* should
> meditate,
> Should accomplish the aims of beings
> With bodies having the nature of reflected images[255]
> Having {377b} three supreme wheels in the elemental atoms.[256]

In this passage, the parts about beginners, those who have had a slight settlement of intuition, and those who have attained the slight mastery of intuition pertain to the context of the creation stage. The attainment of the true mastery of intuition pertains to the context of having reached the heights of the perfection stage.

[Phase 1: Beginner]

Here, during the phase of the first [beginner's] context, it is necessary to completely meditate all the procedures of the creation stage as they occur in your own sādhana. This is because, as Shāntipa says [in his *Commentary to Dīpaṅkarabhadra's The Four Hundred and Fifty Verses*]:

> The phrase [in the above passage] "the beginner... recites well" means that the beginner should correctly recite all of the procedures without exception...

and as Shrīdhara states—after having divided [sādhana practice] into four [yogas][257]—that in the first [beginner's] context it is necessary to meditate

[255] At this most advanced level it is as if the practitioner's body-mind systems have become a mirror in which are reflected the deity's body-mind systems.

[256] Reading *khams kyi rdul nang khams gsum mchog* with Derge. This indicates that all substance becomes the body, speech, and mind mandalas of all buddhas.

[257] On the division of a sādhana into four yogas, cf. above, 372a–b, and below, 394a–b.

all four yogas; and as [Abhayākaragupta states] in the twelfth cluster [of his *Clusters of Instructions*]:

> The beginner should do it all, just like that, not incompletely.

All of these statements are in agreement.

Now, you may wonder: Until what point are [people still] called "beginners"?

In *The Jewel Lamp Commentary* on the seventeenth chapter of the *Black Enemy* [*of Death Tantra*, Shāntipa] says:

> Furthermore, the beginning yogī meditates during all four yogas and in all three session breaks until he seems to perceive directly just the coarse appearance of the limbs of the deity.

And in his *Commentary on [Dīpaṅkarabhadra's] The Four Hundred and Fifty [Verses]* he says that "beginner" includes everyone who has the ability to instantaneously directly manifest the coarse body mandala, and who from this has their first meditation in which there is entrancement in the slight settlement of intuition, {378a} up to but not including those who are able to instantaneously clearly give rise to all of the coarse mandala.

In [Nāgārjuna's] *The Five Stages* and [Āryadeva's] *Practice Integration* everyone is called a "beginner" until they have completed the creation stage; [but the context of those statements relate to] being a beginner with respect to the perfection stage, whereas the statements here [by Shāntipa] are analyzing "beginner" in the context of the first stage alone, so these are not in contradiction.

[Phase 2: Slightly Settled Intuition]

Regarding the slight settlement of intuition, [Shāntipa's] *Commentary on [Dīpaṅkarabhadra's] The Four Hundred and Fifty [Verses]* says:

> Whoever [1] has the ability to instantaneously manifest the coarse body mandala, but cannot manifest the subtle [deities], Kṣhitigarbha, etc., and Kāyavajra, etc., and who [2] possesses Mantric ethics and discipline—through attaining the power of [all] that, he is called "one with slight mastery of intuition."

In the root text [by Dīpaṅkara, this last phrase, "slight mastery of intuition,"] has the same meaning as "slight settlement of intuition." Here [in Shāntipa's commentrary], 'coarse' means the deities set up in the mandala, and 'subtle' means the deities set up on the eyes, etc., of those [mandala deities].

Regarding the way that you instantaneously manifest the coarse [deities]: [at first,] when you are a beginner, when you visualize those [deities] they arise gradually as you visualize them; but when that is no longer the case [i.e., when you are more adept,] it is not as if they cannot arise clearly, {378b} and so when you visualize those deities everything from the major limbs and minor parts on up can arise clearly all at once. Moreover, it is insufficient that this should happen only sometimes or in certain contexts; it must be firm. As the twelfth cluster [of Abhayākaragupta's] *Clusters of Instructions* says:

> Those whose minds are firm in beginning yoga, who have attained the signs as explained, they have slight mastery of intuition, and meditate emanating the mandala instantaneously.

Regarding meditation on the evocation:[258] it is not the case that there is more and less meditation involved in regard to subtle and coarse deities [respectively]. Nevertheless, it is easier for the coarse to arise, and it is more difficult for the subtle to arise. For example, there are degrees of difficulty between the visualization of the eye of the principal Mañjuvajra and the visualization of the complete Kṣhitigarbha inside of that [eye]. In this context [of meditation on the evocation], although there is no explicit mention of the measureless mansion, it is necessary also to be able to manifest that instantaneously.

Objection: If it were the case that as long as one cannot manifest the subtle [deity] Kṣhitigarbha then one [still] is to be regarded as having [only] slightly settled intuition, this would contradict the explanation in [Ratnākarashānti's *The Jewel Lamp:] A Commentary on the Black Enemy [of Death Tantra]* which states that [this stage extends] up to [and including] the seeing of the body of the subtle [deities]:

---

[258] *mngon (par) rtogs (pa)*. Cf. note 250 above.

> One is said to have slightly settled intuition from the time when one sees the coarse limbs [of the deity] until one directly manifests the subtle [deities] Kāyavajra, etc.

[Answer:] This is not contradictory. Because even though the bodies of the subtle [deities] may clearly arise gradually as one visualizes them, as long as one has not achieved a measure of stability in their clearly [arising] instantaneously, one [still] is to be regarded as having [achieved only] slightly {379a} settled intuition.

Well, you may ask, are there or are there not any differences between the way this one [with slightly settled intuition] and the beginner meditates the evocation?

There are. In the *Commentary on [Dīpaṅkarabhadra's] The Four Hundred and Fifty [Verses]*, [Shāntipa discusses the way that one with slightly settled intuition meditates on the evocation as follows]:

> Therefore, in all sessions and breaks you should instantaneously manifest the mandala and bless the eye, etc., and the body, etc. Having done the preliminaries of propitiating, offering, praising, and tasting nectar, you should recite conscientiously.

Again, in this context, because you must meditate dividing into various sessions, he says "in all sessions and breaks." Regarding the way that you perform the creation during each session, he says "instantaneously"—thus, the habitat and inhabitant mandalas are to be manifested like that; and then you perform the blessing of your sense media, etc. Now, although the actualities of the sādhana [here] are indeed similar to [those for] beginners, there is a difference. [If you are at the phase of slightly settled intuition, then] when you create [a coarse deity] like Akṣhobhya you do not have to visualize by sequentially reciting his three faces, hands, feet, eyes, nose, etc., and his major limbs and minor limbs; [rather,] these are immediately recalled at one time. Therefore, there are great differences in the extent of the procedures involved in verbally reciting [the coarse visualizations] and in the meditational methods that are associated with that. Nevertheless, when you meditate on the subtle deity bodies [at this phase], {379b} you [still] do have to meditate visualizing slowly and in sequence. [Finally, in the cited passage,] "propitiating" means generating the supreme mandala triumph[259] through the male and female uniting sexually. Also, although not stated here, the entry of the intuition being is necessary.

Now, you may wonder whether this [Mañjuvajra Esoteric Community system as explained above by Dīpaṅkarabhadra and Shāntipa][260] is similar to what is stated in [Ratnākarashānti's *The Jewel Lamp:*] *A Commentary on the Black Enemy [of Death Tantra]*:

> Beginning with maintaining the four sessions and breaks up to the extreme application, he should think instantaneously and meditate with reverence on the great yoga.

[*Answer:* Although] there is a difference in [the statement] in the *Mañjuvajra [Esoteric Community]* regarding 'when you already have created the fruitional Vajradhara and you have blessed his eye, etc., ...' and [the statement] in *The Black Enemy [of Death] Tantra* regarding 'After having already generated the supreme mandala triumph you then bless the eye, etc., of the deities...,' there is a similarity in the emphasis on the subtle deities.

[Phase 3: Slight Mastery of Intuition]

Regarding the attainment of slight mastery of intuition, in [Shāntipa's] *Commentary on [Dīpaṅkarabhadra's] The Four Hundred and Fifty [Verses]* it is stated:

> One who is able to manifest the mandala instantaneously through the yoga of completely radiating and retracting it in all aspects is said to have attained "mastery of intuition." This is turn comes about from actually having attained the settling of intuition, and not without having

---

259 Supreme mandala triumph is one of "the three samādhis," which comprise a schema for dividing up the phases of the creation stage. See below (p. 184ff.; Tib. 396b–398b).

260 *Dīpaṅkarabhadra*'s *Four Hundred and Fifty Verses*, as well as Shāntipa's *Commentary* on that text—cited directly above—are both commentaries on the *Mañjuvajra Esoteric Community* Tantra system. Cf. note 284 (to Tib. 391a) below, which explains that there are two *Esoteric Community* variants, *Guhyasamāja-Akṣobhyavajra* and *Guhyasamāja-Mañjuvajra*.

> attained it; and for that very reason, that mastery [still] is called "slight."

This refers to everything beginning from somewhat being able to instantaneously manifest even the subtle bodies up until one reaches the attainment of true mastery of intuition; concerning this, {380a} there are occasions that occur on both stages.[261] [The sentence] "This is turn [comes about from]..." shows that each of the latter [stages] must come from each of the former, [that is, from the stage of] beginner, etc. Therefore, this refutes some Indians who claim that these [former] stages are not necessary for one functioning with sharp faculties.

[Regarding the relationship between multiple stages and multiple levels of ability:] In the third chapter of the *Arisal of Saṁvara [Tantra]* it is stated:

> Meditation on the creation stage mandala
> Should be contemplated by the dull and mediocre.
> For the sharp, in the space of an instant
> There is the mandala of mere mind alone;
> So he should meditate the perfection stage
> With the instantaneous kind of yoga.

Now the *Commentary* on that [by Ratnarakṣhita] says that it is with respect to an individual continuum that first there is [a phase of] 'having dull faculties' wherein one must visualize gradually, then there is [a phase of] 'having mediocre faculties' wherein one perceives more completely through repetitions, and then there is [a phase of] 'having sharp faculties' wherein one has the ability to meditate the mandala of the perfection stage. So, just like an individual person's phases as child, middle aged, and elderly, this is stated in such an arrangement in accordance with an individual yogī's stages of greater or lesser familiarity. Thus it says [in Ratnarakṣhita's *Commentary*]:

> Moreover, these classifications regarding dullness, etc., come about with respect to the stages of one individual's

---

[261] While the phrase "both stages" generally refers to the creation and perfection stages, it seems that in this case this most likely refers to the "stages" (or phases) of the slight settling of intuition and the mastery of intuition.

> level of familiarity, just as one would classify the phases of that same individual into childhood, etc. So the different classes of persons are [references to the phases of one person,] like childhood etc., which are distinct from [references to] different persons. {380b}

There are many other reasonings of that type. If those are not understood, the beginner—having fixated on the [mistaken] thought that one with sharp faculties does not need the creation stage—will abandon the first stage. Therefore, you should not mix up [1] the stages of faculties posited with respect to [whether different persons are] attaining supreme or ordinary siddhis, and [2] the stages of faculties posited with respect to the phases of realization generated in each individual person.[262]

[Phase 4: True Mastery of Intuition]

While the second phase [of faculties, that of mediocre faculty] pertains to when the subtle deities' limbs and members, etc., can be perceived instantaneously, but are not firm, the third [phase, when one has sharp faculties,] pertains to when they are firm. As it says in the twelfth cluster of [Abhayākaragupta's] *Clusters of Instructions*:

> One who has a firm mind with regard to all of the mandalas with which he is familiar is one who has mastery of intuition. He furthers the aims of beings by radiating and retracting; having manifested the spirit of enlightenment from his understanding of reality he should eliminate the subtlest taints.

This states that firmness is necessary [to qualify for this fourth phase]. In [Ratnākarashānti's *The Jewel Lamp:] A Commentary on the Black Enemy [of Death Tantra]* it says:

> When the [subtle deities] Kāyavajra, etc., are seen as autonomous just like a fruit in the palm of your hand,

[262] That is, you should not mix up (1) the stages of ability which characterize different persons' attainments of different levels, and (2) the stages of ability which characterize one individual person's successive levels of attainment; otherwise, you will think that any sharp, intelligent person can jump immediately into the perfection stage.

> you have attained mastery of intuition, and thus you practice without distinguishing between session and break. Then you should meditate the perfection stage, which will be explained.

The statement [here] that '[Kāyavajra, etc.] must be seen as autonomous' is similar in meaning both to [the statement in the previous passage that] 'having manifested the spirit of enlightenment, he eliminates the subtle taints' and to [the statement here that] 'then you should meditate {381a} the perfection stage.' The statement [here] that when you have arrived at this [stage] it is not necessary to separate sessions and session-breaks means that each day, having newly established the evocation at the outset, it will suffice to have one session of creation without a lot of meditation.

Now, having arrived here, with regard to the need to meditate the creation stage, [Shāntipa's] *Commentary on [Dīpaṅkarabhadra's] The Four Hundred and Fifty [Verses]* states:

> In order to reach the ultimate, which is the goal, that yogī should practice that very yoga day and night.

He says that [that yogī who has arrived here at this high phase of true mastery of intuition still] should meditate that very [creation stage] yoga[263] which is able to manifest instantaneously all the subtle and gross deity bodies. The mere arrival here is not the conclusion of the creation stage; the creation stage still must be consummated, and then one must practice the perfection stage.

Regarding one who has attained true mastery of intuition: [Shāntipa's] *Commentary on [Dīpaṅkarabhadra's] The Four Hundred and Fifty [Verses]* [next] explains that this is one who has reached the limit of his own purpose and is able to accomplish the purposes of beings by means of mere contemplation. The twelfth cluster of [Abhayākaragupta's] *Clusters of Instructions* explains that this is one who—having realized the siddhi of the great seal—is able to accomplish the purposes of others

---

263 The fact that the phrase "that very yoga" here refers to creation stage yoga which can "instantaneously manifest all the subtle and gross deity bodies" is evident from the various passages preceding this in Shāntipa's *Commentary*, cited more-or-less in sequence above from 378a–381a.

boundlessly. Also, [Ratnākarashānti's *The Jewel Lamp:] A Commentary on the Black Enemy [of Death Tantra]* states:

> Then, one who—when he arises from being in the ascertainment of emptiness—is able to transform perceptions in any way he wants, is called "one who has achieved true mastery of intuition." He is established as "a person who has achieved independence, {381b} freed in activity through certainty [of emptiness]."

In explanations such as those, it is very clear how creation and perfection [stages] are to be produced in order. Moreover, other authoritative treatises also have very many teachings regarding how one first meditates the creation stage, after which one then produces the perfection stage. Therefore, you should do the practice of the two stages like that.

[**II.B.2.c.ii.C'3'c'ii'B''4''a''i''A°2°b°** – How to bring about vivid perception]

Second, regarding the way of producing creation stage realization in your continuum, it is said that some Tibetan lamas like to first achieve firm serenity with respect to vivid perception of one deity, and then meditate on the evocation in its entirety, and that some, after having [first] meditated the complete evocation and done the whole recitation in four sessions, [then] gradually achieve vivid perception visualizing one part of one deity. In the sādhanas [themselves], except for their explaining that one meditates on the complete evocation, neither of these two preferences appear.

Regarding this first stage, you must separately understand two things: one, the method of producing vivid perception, and two, the method of achieving very firm stability.[264] In that regard, in general the vivid perception of the form of an object is achieved just by mentally imprinting that object again and again; thus it comes about in accordance with what is merely familiarized. As the Lord of Reason [Dharmakīrti] said [in the *Validating Cognition Commentary*]:

---

[264] Vivid perception is the exclusive topic of this entire section. Tsong Khapa addresses the topic of stability beginning in the next section (p. 160, Tib. 385a).

When overwhelmed by suffering from desire or fear,
Or deceived by a dream of a thief, etc., {382a}
You will see what is unreal
As if standing right before you. (III.282)

—a lustful person, by mentally imprinting the object of his lust again and again, directly sees his desired object as if it were right in front of him. Thus, in order to produce vivid perception it is not necessary first to achieve stability; and also it is not the case that it will not be produced if you do not familiarize yourself with each part.

Furthermore, in order to produce vivid perception it is not necessary to familiarize yourself with a real [physical] object;[265] because once you have familiarized yourself with any object, whether false or not, it is natural that a vivid perception of it will be produced. Again, as the Lord of Reason [Dharmakīrti] said:[266]

Therefore, whatever you really familiarize yourself with,
Whether it is real or unreal,
If you become completely familiarized,
The result is its vivid, nonconceptual cognition. (III.285)

And as was stated in the [*Activities of the Yoginīs*] *Tantra* cited above,[267] one's mind adopts the form of whatever thing it becomes attached to, as illustrated by the example of a crystal jewel.

In that regard, when a beginner meditates the [preliminary] practices from accumulating the stores up until [the stage of] retracting, he should develop a forceful habit pattern with a definite attitude, meditating by visualizing each thing in fine detail, not just having things arise [haphazardly]; because both a vividness of form and a habit of pride are necessary. At first, having limited [his meditation session] to a reasonable length, {382b} from the beginning to the end he does not allow himself to come under the influence of either mental dullness or scattered

---

265 So, for example, in the context of sādhana practice it is not necessary to have a physical image (a statue, picture, etc.) of the deity in front of you in order to meditate on it.

266 This is the same verse that was cited at 358a–b (p. 101 above). See note there for Derge variants.

267 Again, cf. 358b.

distraction, and he expends great effort at uninterruptedly engaging his mind with whatever object of meditation. Thereby, allowing his practice to get longer and longer, eventually he practices from the beginning to the end of each [longer] session without any obstacle of dullness or scattered distraction being able to interrupt him. Moreover, during that [beginners'] phase, since he has not meditated for a long time, as long as his mind is not yet very powerful and for the most part he does not see [things] vividly, conviction is paramount, and thus he must meditate with intense conviction. As is stated in [Shāntipa's] *Commentary on [Dīpaṅkarabhadra's] The Four Hundred and Fifty [Verses]*:

> [In] these three yogas[268] intense conviction is paramount, and [vivid] vision is not paramount, because the time [spent in visualizing] is slight or small. Therefore, they are referred to as "endowed with intense conviction."

Analyzing both [vivid] perception and [divine] pride with discriminating wisdom, they are cultivated, and thereby they must be produced gradually; so you should not count on their [just] suddenly occurring depending on your [meditative] experience. For, being fit for the creation stage necessarily entails that what one visualizes arises and what one does not visualize does not arise, and that what does arise does not surpass the measure of just what one is visualizing; so mixed experiential feelings do not bear scrutiny when it comes down to such measures. Therefore, when visualizing, having previously created the resolve "I am going to meditate this way," if you are capable of giving rise [to a visualization] without any diminution or excess from the measure [you have set up], {383a} then you are fit to meditate. However, if [at first] you cannot get to what is essential even after having established a [specific] measure from the beginning, then once your mind has come to have a greater familiarity, it will be so [achieved]. Apply the same reasoning with regard to [cultivating divine] pride.

As for the need to do things that way [in general], also in the meditations on impermanence and compassion, etc., through cultivation

268 The passage prior to this mentions "these yogas involving arising having been produced from the drop, the subtle [object], and the three secrets" (*thig le dang phra mo dang gsang ba gsum las skyes shing byung ba'i rnal 'byor 'di rnams*).

involving focusing on each respective object, an experience [of each object] is produced gradually; or at the time when you want to, you can produce [either insight] if you meditate visualizing each object. However, [just] mixing in your experiential feeling and suddenly producing an intense thought of those [objects, impermanence or compassion,] is tantamount to not having any [real] place to produce them when you want.

In general, the creation stage is necessary not just because through the visualization of oneself as a deity there is a transformation into a distinctive pride and perception. For if it were only that, then even all of the lower classes of Tantra would have the complete essentials of the creation stage, and since [visualization of just] one deity would be sufficient, meditation on the [whole] circle of the mandala would become pointless. Therefore, [the unique necessity of the creation stage is due to the fact that through it alone,] by meditating the complete set of the habitat and inhabitant mandalas that purify [respectively] the ordinary vessel and contents that are the bases of purification—[which complete set is] the import of the Tantra, as elucidated by the great scholar-adepts—one correlates the many distinctive relativities of the bases of purification and the means of purification, and [thereby] one thoroughly develops the roots of virtue which [later] produce the superlative realizations of the perfection stage. Thus, since it is meditation on a [complete creation stage] mandala circle in four sessions [per day] that has the power to develop your continuum, {383b} you must complete [the kind of] vivid perception which comes from practicing a complete [creation stage] sādhana again and again.

Now, as for the way of bringing about this vivid perception, according to the textual systems of the great ones, if you practice by placing an equal emphasis on each part of everything [to be visualized], then everything to be vividly perceived will be produced together, and that will be very powerful. However, practicing the entire sādhana in this way, if at times you do not get a vivid perception of each individual part, then if the procedures which ripen your continuum are complete, this will be very powerful; and when you get that, you [at least] will produce a vivid perception of everything in a coarse way. In many Indian treatises there occur statements such as: "After having grasped the types of procedures for creating the deity, then you should meditate [on that]; and when you get tired while meditating, you should recite [mantras]." Although such pithy sources may not clearly explain both what it is to practice with individually discriminating analysis and what it is to place the mind one-pointedly on the deity body, in these contexts it nevertheless still is necessary to achieve vivid perception of the deity, and thus visualizing again and again with the analytic meditation of individual discrimination is of principal importance.

In that regard, in both contexts—when you are first practicing the creation procedures, and when you have completed the sections of the creation procedures prior to reciting [mantras]—after you have visualized the form of whatever habitat and inhabitant, you also must create the individual pride thinking "this and that are the actual [mandalas and deities]." {384a} Thus you practice both [vivid perception and pride]. So these contexts are said to be supreme for taking the pride of the fruitional-stage land, retinue, Teacher, etc., as the path, and for recollecting the Buddha. Thus, this is not [just passively] recollecting merely the forms of the bodies, colors, faces, hands, etc., of Vairochana and Akṣhobhya, etc., and then generating the pride merely of that [impersonal, disassociated recollection]. Rather, you must have the conviction of [personally being] the actual Buddha who has terminated all defilements and has mastered all excellences. By familiarizing yourself in this way, distinctive perception and pride both must come about naturally, just as when you familiarize yourself with a treatise and recite it [effortlessly]. As [Ratnākara-shānti's] *The Pearl Rosary* states:[269]

> Siddhi is achieved when the mind has become firm, that is, when each day you naturally perceive yourself in the form of a deity and have that [deity] pride.

Therefore, through meditating both [vivid perception and divine pride], once you have achieved the ability to prevent the perception and conception of ordinariness—from the beginning to the end of each great [sādhana] session—through the force of transforming into the distinctive perception and pride, then at that time you must firmly establish your mind [in that transformed state], which here entails getting rid of the incidental contrary

[269] The Derge (rgyud, ga, 273b.1–2) reads slightly differently: "Siddhi is achieved when the mind has become firm, that is, when the perception of yourself in the form of a deity and the establishment of [that deity] pride continually naturally occur." Cf. the Tibetan critical edition.

conditions of body and mind. For that, it is not necessary that you have uninterrupted consistency of the thought "I am that deity"; rather, it will be sufficient that you activate the initial production of unfabricated pride, which will be able to prevent the pride of ordinariness. {384b} This is similar to when, for example, someone channels a non-human spirit: without the thought "I am that non-human spirit," his mind [simply] is deviated into another mind, and as long as the function of that [deviation] does not decline, the notion "I am that previous human" will not be produced.

Regarding how long you must meditate before producing a direct vivid perception of the deities, the *Thousand [Verse] Commentary on the Compendium of Reality [Tantra]*[270] [by Ānandagarbha] states:

> Thus, you should meditate every day until you directly see the great mandala of the Vajradhatu. Or if you have already achieved the three samādhis, you should meditate for six months or a year.

Also, other teachings regarding the duration of meditation [required for direct vivid perception] do not explain that it is longer than a year. Thus, if you understand well the way of cultivating, keep the commitments and vows, and strive uninterruptedly with great effort, you will complete the vivid perception of the deities of the mandala without requiring a very long time. As Āryashūra stated in the *Compendium of Transcendences*—using the [cautionary] example of fire not starting due to rubbing fire sticks together forcefully but not for a long time, taking many rests in between—you must practice continuously:

> With uninterrupted yoga
> You should strive to achieve contemplation
> If you rub [fire sticks], yet rest again and again,
> Fire will not ignite! {385a}
> Likewise, in the process of yoga, too,
> Do not give up until you achieve excellence!

---

270 The root text here, known as the *Compendium of Reality "Sūtra,"* is in fact a Tantra (Tōh. 479). The commentary on this Tantra by Ānandagarbha is Tōh. 2510.

[II.B.2.c.ii.C'3'c'ii'B''4''a''i''A°2°c° – How to achieve stability]

In the third part there are two sections: [i°] The way of meditating on the subtle drop in the first two phases; and [ii°] The way of meditating on the subtle drop in the third phase.

[II.B.2.c.ii.C'3'c'ii'B''4''a''i''A°2°c°i° – The way of meditating on the subtle drop in the first two phases]

One may think [the following mistaken set of thoughts]:

[Objections:]

In the context of the first stage, when one achieves vivid perception—which becomes familiar through repeatedly mentally imprinting the subtle and gross habitat and inhabitant mandalas—just that is sufficient; one need not achieve serenity [during the creation stage]. For, in the context of the second stage, there are many methods cited for achieving a firm samādhi that stabilizes the mind through the yogas of channels, wind-energies, and psychic heat, etc.

Furthermore, if [you assert that] one achieves serenity here [in the first stage], and that one has to do this with the [creation stage] yogas of the subtle drop, etc., then [this is untenable,] because: the authoritative treatises such as [Nāgārjuna's] *Abbreviated [Practice]* and [Jñānapāda's] *The Samantabhadra Sādhana* explain that one must do these [yogas] after the supreme mandala triumph and before [mantra] repetition [in the daily sādhana], and thus they state that they are combined with repeated imprinting of analytic meditations;[271] therefore, serenity will not be achieved by these [creation stage yogas in this way]. Because, as previously explained in [Kamalashīla's] *Stages of Meditation*, in [Buddhaguhya's]

[271] Supreme mandala triumph involves performing the analytic meditation of constructing the mandala in the most minute detail and then having it absorb the ordinary world with its imperfections. The objector here is noting that since the creation stage subtle drop yogas come after the supreme mandala triumph, they therefore take place in the context of having created (and continuing to maintain) the analytic meditation involved in the supreme mandala triumph. As we will see in the next sentence, he now will object that serenity could not be developed within this analytic context.

Commentary on The Contemplation Addendum [Tanta],[272] etc., even one who has gained a fully qualified serenity will have his stability diminish if he does too much analytic meditation; and if this is what is stated for one who is [actually] in serenity meditation, what need to mention the case of one who has not yet gained serenity? {385b} And because, as Āryashūra stated [in the *Compendium of Transcendences*], when one practices contemplation, it is unsuitable if one shifts [one's attention] unstably among many objects, from one object to another object:

> One should stabilize mental thought
> By way of stablizing upon a single object.
> Shifting to many objects,
> The mind will be disturbed by addictions.

[Answer:]

Here, we should explain. If you meditate mentally imprinting the form again and again, you indeed can create vivid perception by just that, but firm stability will not be gained that way; it will be like the vivid perception of one habituated to lust or terror. Therefore, it is not sufficient to merely transform [your identity] into the distinctive perception and pride; rather, it is necessary [within the creation stage] to abide with solidified stability, since [1] without that, you will not discover the antidote which enables one to stop the perception and conception of ordinariness; and since [2] meditation on the creation stage is for stopping that; and since [3] in order to achieve fitness of mind through vivid perception of both the subtle and gross complete habitat and inhabitant mandalas, you definitely must achieve serenity. Therefore, there is no doubt that you must achieve serenity while on the first stage, and moreover that this must be done by the yoga of the subtle drop.

[Now,] meditation on the complete habitat and inhabitant mandala within the subtle hand-symbol or subtle drop is not a meditation which occurs either for beginners or for those of slightly settled intuition; {386a} rather, it is a meditation for those [starting] from the third phase. The third phase commences when one has the ability to instantaneously manifest

---

[272] This commentary by Buddhaguhya (Tōh. 2670) is cited numerous times throughout the Action and Performance Tantra chapters of the *NRC* (see *YT*). The *Contemplation Addendum Tantra* itself (Tōh. 808) is one of four General Action Tantras (Kriyā Tantras).

the deities established in the eye, etc.; the ability to radiate and retract the subtle mandala is stated to be the achievement of [the third phase,] the slight mastery of intuition.[273] As has been stated [above by Dīpaṅkara-bhadra]:[274]

> The one who has attained the slight mastery of intuition,
> Who practices radiation and retraction,
> Perfected and in all respects, ...

Regarding drop yoga: Jñānapāda, father and sons, explained that this is meditation on the samādhi hero who is located on the hand-symbol at the heart of your intuition hero. Even beginners meditate that in that context. Regarding the purpose of that [meditation], the master Shrī Phala-vajra said [in his *Commentary on (Jñānapāda*'s*) The Samantabhadra Sādhana*]:

> If the yogī who truly strives in such meditation becomes mentally distracted or depressed, at that time he should meditate on the drop yoga, etc. Therefore, [Jñānapāda] says, "Having thus imagined, [you should meditate on the symbol at the immaculate moon in your heart...]," etc.

He states that when striving in the meditation of the supreme mandala triumph, etc., you should meditate drop yoga in order to prevent the influence of mental dullness or distraction. Thus, beginners who meditate drop yoga do not achieve serenity in that context; {386b} rather, they prevent that instability of not being able to focus continuously on the [visualized] objects due to mental dullness or distraction during creation stage meditation. Thus, [they do so] in order to achieve mental firmness that is able to focus continuously. So in those contexts, even though they have not found samādhi which rests for a long time on a single object [of visualization], it is very important to block mental dullness and distraction with respect to meditating the evocation.

Furthermore, in this [context] holding the mind on the subtle drop blocks the wind-energy from moving outside, and thus functions as a

---

[273] The third phase is discussed again briefly below (see Tib. 388a, and note 278); and then is the primary topic of the next major section.

[274] See above, p. 146 (Tib. 377a).

cause of staying within. As Tathāgatavajra states [in his *Auto-commentary to the Commentary to Lūipa's Evocation*]:

> That contemplation which involves the application of subtle *āli* and *kāli*[275] in the navel, or the application of drops, etc., in the heart, etc., reverses the emergence of the vital [wind-energy]; because of that impact, it is called "vitality control."

Therefore, if you hold the mind forcefully at the upper and lower openings, or at the navel or the heart center, etc., in [the form of] a letter, subtle drop, etc., then these vital places of meditation and objects of visualization gradually create the conditions for the wind-energy to stay within. Thereby, even though it is mixed with many visualizations of analytic meditation, because the wind-energy is gradually controlled, meditation is able quickly to block the above [mentioned obstacles of] distraction, etc., and therefore it is different from the ways of attaining samādhi explained in other treatises.

You may wonder: Well, [precisely] how does one practice meditation on the subtle drop in the phases of beginner and of slightly {387a} settled intuition?

[Answer:] The drop yoga meditation is stated in [Dīpaṅkarabhadra's *The Maṇḍala Rite of the Glorious Esoteric Community*,] *The Four Hundred and Fifty [Verses]*:[276]

> Saviors emanated by light rays from your heart
> Dispel [all beings'] own wrong notions,
> Making [these] beings into the nature of buddhas
> Who enter into the seed [syllable] of your heart.

---

[275] Vowel and consonant syllables.

[276] When reading the following verses and Tsong Khapa's commentary which follows, it will help to consult the following hierarchical diagram of the elements discussed (ordered from outermost at the top to innermost at the bottom):

Your heart
  Intuition hero's heart
    Hand-symbol
      Moon
        Seed syllable

> Meditating your own mind as luminous
> In the form of a moon heart-drop
> Abiding within the hub of the heart-center symbol,
> Strongly meditate the intuition hero.
>
> You should awaken the vajras of mind, speech, and body
> With wreathes of light.
> [Then] imagining that that [light] [re]enters your heart center,
> Your own intuition nectar streams down.
>
> Then the masses of light [filling] the whole interior of your body
> Emerge from your pores,
> Radiating in all directions
> And totally fulfilling the needs of beings.

The process of that is as follows. With great radiance you imagine that savior buddhas are emanated by the light rays of the seed [syllable] which rests on the moon contained within the hub of the hand-symbol at the heart center of the intuition hero in your own heart center; that they dispel the wrong notions—the two obscurations—of [all] sentient beings, make these beings into buddhas, and invite them [back to you]; and that they unite them with the seed syllable [at your heart], make the seed indivisible from the drop, and [the drop indivisible] from your own mind. Then, with those light rays you gradually illumine the interior and the exterior of the hand-symbol, and the intuition hero, {387b} and his location, and the body, speech, and mind vajras, and their locations, interior and exterior. Then, just as that was gradually illumined, likewise later it is done again in reverse, collecting into the drop of [its] origin, and you imagine a streaming of intuition nectar. After that, you illuminate your entire body, and then with the light rays which emit from all your pores you illuminate [all] beings.

Shrī Phalavajra explains that if you become mentally dull, you meditate like that on radiating light, clearing away the dullness, until it has been cleared away; and that if you become distracted, you visualize just the drop, focusing one-pointedly and meditating until you pacify your distraction. Regarding the statement by that master that when getting rid of dullness you can wake up the intuition hero by the process of radiating and retracting up to the count of ten inhalations and exhalations—that should be done according to the explanation in [Abhayākaragupta's] *Clusters of Instructions* that at the time of your exhalations light radiates out and at the time of your inhalations it retracts.

Thagana[277] describes a yoga involving a drop which is a thorough transformation of the mantra, and a variant in which the drop is meditated as the mantra itself.

Also, in [Nāgārjuna's] *Abbreviated [Practice]* it says:

> When you have created the entire mandala,
> And have come to reside in the center of the chakra,
> Then you should begin the yoga of the subtle.

This describes completing the supreme mandala triumph and meditating the yoga of the subtle at the nose-tip of [yourself as] the lord; {388a} and *The Illumination of the Lamp* explains that this means that at the *upper* nose-tip you meditate a subtle *hand-symbol*, that at the *secret place* nose-tip [you meditate] a subtle *drop*, and that within the latter you meditate on the habitat and inhabitant mandalas. Further, it is in the first two phases that you meditate just the subtle hand-symbol and drop, and it is [starting] from the third phase that you also should meditate the two mandalas within the subtle.[278]

Now, commenting on the statement in [Āryadeva's] *Practice Integration* that it is *after* you are settled with single[-pointed] mindfulness that you train in the conceptual yoga, *The Illumination of the Lamp* says:

> When you train in the conceptual yoga within the white-mustard seed[-sized drop] itself, both animate and inanimate things should be imagined as Vajrasattva.

Thus, [taking these two statements together,] the meditation on the deity —the animate essence—and the measureless mansion—the inanimate

---

[277] On the author Thagana, see *The Blue Annals*, pp. 160, 372, 847. He may be the same as Smṛitijñānakīrti?

[278] The next entire paragraph briefly continues this discussion on the meditation of drop yoga within the context of the third phase (involving the meditation of the inhabitant and habitat mandalas within the subtle drop). The remainder of this section then returns to the stated topic at hand, viz. "The way of meditating on the subtle drop in the first two phases." The meditation on the subtle drop in the third phase then will be the exclusive focus of the next section below (Tib. 389b–391a).

vessel—within the subtle hand-symbol and the subtle drop must be done after you are settled with single[-pointed] mindfulness. The meanings of 'settled with single[-pointed] mindfulness' in the Ārya system and of 'arrived at the third phase' in the Jñānapāda system are similar.

According to the Ārya system, in the first two phases, when you meditate the subtle at the upper door you imagine the [subtle] hand-symbol of the lord—a blue five-pointed vajra, just as big as a white-mustard seed—at the [upper] nose-tip; and having held that one-pointedly, when you meditate the subtle at the lower door the enlightenment spirit of the father-mother in sexual union melts and you meditate on the subtle drop—{388b} [about the size of] a mere mustard-grain—at the [secret place] nose-tip. Furthermore, one who has a great propensity for dullness should meditate at the upper nose-tip, and one who has a great propensity for distraction should meditate at the lower nose-tip.

As a method for stabilizing the mind, we have finished explaining two of the ways drop yoga is meditated. Another [third] way involves meditation at the heart center, as follows. You imagine that light rays of the samādhi hero [at your heart] radiate from your *avadhūtī* [central channel]. Then the enlightenment spirit abiding in the great bliss wheel at the crown melts and, descending via that [central channel] path, dissolves into the drop of whatever samādhi hero—such as the *HŪṀ*, etc.—in your heart, and you hold your mind [on that].

A [fourth] way involves meditating the drop yoga at the navel, as follows. You visualize the four [seed syllables] *AṀ, HŪṀ, OṀ, HAṀ,* respectively at the four holes of the central neural knots of the four chakras—navel, heart, throat, and crown. Then the wind-energies abiding in the wheel of the secret place agitate the fire, and the light rays of the *A* letter blaze with the nature of psychic heat, melting the three upper syllables, which fall into the *AṀ* syllable at the navel. They become indivisible from that, and you orient yourself towards the drop, which has the nature of orgasmic joy, and you hold your mind [on that]. Shākyarakṣhita also explained that you meditate the form of a drop. Lavapa states that the four chakras and the colors and orientations of the syllables are as follows, from the bottom up: variegated facing up, blue facing down, red facing up, and white facing down. {389a} He explains that you should meditate the channel-chakras and their letters very clearly; this he took as a component of the creation stage. Thus, the occurrence of the phrase [in Tantric commentaries] "aspiring to thoroughly develop meditation" is [best understood] according to Shākyarakṣhita's explanation [that this means] to thoroughly perfect meditation.

Thus, when you have held your mind on the previously visualized object, you stably meditate that from the drop there are fine streams of light rays all blazing with tongues of flame. The nectar melted by that light oozes out, fills the drop, and cools the streams of light. Then, you meditate with the mind one-pointedly on the drop until you see the signs of having achieved firmness.[279] When you have seen the signs of firmness, you imagine that the radiance of those streams of light rays clarifies the variety of things [throughout the universe], and you look at the entire [universe] as if it were a myrobalan nut in the palm of your hand. Then, samādhi quickly will be completed.

Abhaya explained the two drop yogas of the heart center and the drop yoga of the navel, and combined [these] with the Mother Tantras as the drop yoga of the Jñānapāda tradition. The third one[280] depends on *The Kiss [Tantra]*, *The Vajraḍāka [Tantra]*, etc. That also is the system in which in the syllables in the four channel-chakras are not set forth extensively, rather the four main [syllables] are set forth.

[II.B.2.c.ii.C'3'c'ii'B"4"a"i"A°2°c°ii° – The way of meditating on the subtle drop in the third phase]

Second—{389b} having thus made the mind firm by the yoga of the subtle drop in the first two phases, [the third phase entails] the way of meditating the complete mandala within the subtle after cultivating well—again and again—a vivid perception of the mandala deities and of the deities established in their eyes, etc. In [Dīpaṅkarabhadra's] *The Four Hundred and Fifty [Verses]* it says:

> Again, meditate the subtle [mandala] in your own symbol
> Abiding at the nose-tip of the science[-consort],
> The introspectively known muni-chakra....[281]

[279] These signs are mentioned in the next section below (Tib. 390b, p. 169).

[280] This refers to the discussion just above beginning "Another [third] way involves meditation at the heart center, as follows."

[281] The phrase I am rendering as "muni-chakra" (*thub pa'i 'khor lo*), in addition to appearing here in Tōh. 1865, appears also in several other texts, including Tōh. 1855–6, 1868,

(cont'd)

This states that here you should meditate the complete mandala in the center of the lord's hand-symbol—only [the size of] a barley grain—at the nose-tip of the mother. Shrī Phalavajra explains that you can choose the [meeting-point of the] two nose-tips of the secret places of the father and mother. And Vitapāda[282] states that if your mind becomes dull while meditating the mandala in the center of the symbol in the dome of the vajra-jewel, then there is a private instruction that you should meditate it on the upper nose-tip; and that if you are meditating it in the hand-symbol in the lotus of the science[-consort] and your mind becomes dull, then the central prong of your five pronged vajra becomes a goad hook and draws it up, and you meditate it at the nose-tip of the mother. Thus it is not certain [that the subtle mandala should be meditated] in any one location.

Here, Vitapāda explains that the light rays of the heart seed [syllable] attract the buddhas, who melt into enlightenment spirit, stream into the secret place, and become the hand-symbol, in the center of which you meditate [the mandala]. And [Abhayākaragupta's] *Clusters of Instructions* describes as 'subtle yoga' both [1] that [meditation], as well as [2] the previously explained {390a} meditation of the complete mandala in the

---

1871. The following passage from Thagana's *Commentary on the Samantabhadra Sādhana* (Tōh. 1868, 224b.2–3) seems most relevant and helpful:

> *yang na rang gi zhes bya ba la sogs pa la lha'i mtshan ma phra mo* ***rang gi rig ma****'i sna'i rtse mor zla ba'i dkyil 'khor la gnas pa 'od zer dang bcas pa'i* ***thub pa'i 'khor lo****'i nang du chud par bsgom par bya ste, de yang snying rje rgyur gyur pas na rang gi shes rab dam pa yang dag par gzung ba nyin mtsan du rtag tu bsgom par bya'o, ,*

And this from one of Shridhara's texts (Tōh. 1924; Derge rGyud, MI, 22b.3–4; not cited in *NRC*):

> *bsgrubs pa nyid ni bla na med pa'i 'gro ba'i don ma lus pa'i, sgrub pa brtags pa'i ngo bo dang bral bas yang* ***rang gi rig pa*** *dang, tha mi dad pa* ***thub pa'i 'khor lo****'i bdag nyid, yid bzhin nor bu lta bu'i 'od 'phro ba bstan pa'i rang bzhin slob ma la sbyin no zhes bya ba 'di yang sbyin pa'o,,*

Note also that the phrase *thub pa'i 'khor lo* appears in a quote below at 438a, quoting there from *The Samantabhadra Sādhana* (Tōh. 1855–6).

282 Tsong Khapa cites the views of Vitapāda frequently throughout the *NRC*, usually (as here) without referencing any specific text. Vitapāda has nine texts in the Tengyur: Tōh. 1866, 1870, 1872–78. Here it seems evident that Tsong Khapa would be referring to Tōh. 1873, which is Vitapāda's commentary on Dīpaṅkarabhadra's *Four Hundred and Fifty*.

center of the drop of the navel that has streamed into the secret place; and it explains that the location [for this meditation] is at the nose-tip of the vajra or the lotus, whichever is appropriate.

In the explanatory citations in *The Illumination of the Lamp*, the meditation within the subtle drop and the meditation in the lotus of the mother are clear; and it is obvious that the two secret places are similar.

Shrī Phalavajra explains that having completed the meditation that meditates the drop yoga [in the first two phases], [in the third phase] you meditate the subtle, which is the meditation on the deity [mandala] inside of the hand-symbol. Also, Vitapāda explains that the meaning of "again" [in Dīpaṅkara's quote above] is that—having meditated on drop yoga [in the first two phases]—you yet again meditate on the subtle for the purpose of making the mind firm; thus, he combines the arrival at the third phase with the drop yoga, and [he says that] it is after the achieving of mental firmness that there is meditation on the subtle [mandala].

Therefore, even in the Ārya tradition, [beginning] from that context, you learn stabilizing the mind on the subtle symbol at the upper door, and having stabilized that you learn the radiation and retraction of the symbol. Having learned that, you learn the the radiation and retraction of the deity, which is the symbol created as the deity; and after having finished learning that, you meditate the subtle, which is the complete meditation of the deity [mandala] at the nose-tip of the secret place. Alternatively, you stabilize the mind on the upper subtle hand-symbol, and you meditate the subtle, which is meditating the complete meditation of the deity [mandala] at the lower. Then when that is stable, you radiate the hand-symbol from the upper door, {390b} and you radiate and retract the deity [mandala] from the lower door.

As for the way of creating the subtle mandala, [Abhayākaragupta's] *Clusters of Instructions* explains that it is created in an instant; this is instantaneous creation. Until that is stable, you do not radiate. Having achieved the signs of stability, you practice radiating and retracting. All the rest is similar.

Regarding the signs [of having achieved stability], Shāntipa, Vitapāda, Shrī Phalavajra, Thagana, etc., explain that you see the five signs [of death]: a mirage, smoke, etc. In *The Illumination of the Lamp* stability is described as the meditated vajra, etc., remaining without changing.

Further, the thought of the *Compendium of Reality Tantra* is that after the complete meditation of coarse deity yoga, you meditate on the subtle; and regarding the time-frame for that [subtle deity yoga], the *Light on Reality*[283] explains that to firm up the subtle you use two months, and that for radiating and retracting you use one month. This [explanation] is made with respect to attaining serenity through visualizing the subtle.

Therefore, in the two contexts of a beginner and of one with slightly settled intuition you do subtle drop meditation for the sake of getting rid of dullness and distraction, while you principally meditate the evocation in four sessions. Having concentrated on the subtle drop, when you attain the stability which makes the mind firm, from this third phase onward you should analyze the contexts of your practices—the need to meditate the subtle drop, the boundary [of that meditation], and how to meditate [it]—because these seem to be the superlative practical instructions of the first stage.

Shākyamitra explained that when the subtle is firm at the upper door, {391a} you attain fluency of body and mind; and since that is described as the occasion of achieving serenity in many great treatises, such as [Asaṅga's] *Volumes on the Stages*, etc., it is the attainment of serenity. Then, according to other treatises, the repeated practice of radiating and retracting by means of discriminating wisdom is similar to the practice of transcendent insight, which is oriented towards whatever exists. Therefore, one who practices [both] like that achieves the supreme samādhi that integrates serenity and insight. When such a yoga is firm, the creation stage is said to be culminated—that is the system of both of the *Esoteric Communities*.[284]

In the context of the Unexcelled Yoga's subtle drop practice, when you have held your mind well, the left and right wind-energies no longer go outside, and they abide within. Depending upon that, the elements stream down from the crown, the great bliss is created, and also the mind is free from dullness and distraction. In this state you develop the samādhi

---

[283] *Tattvāloka* (Tōh. 1293), by Bodhisattva. This text seems to be of uncertain origin. See the "comments" section of the bibliographic entry for this title.

[284] The two *Esoteric Communities* are *Guhyasamāja-Akṣobhyavajra* and *Guhyasamāja-Mañjuvajra*. The latter, which now appears to be in relative disuse, went from Marpa and perhaps some early Sakyas like Drogmi through Khyung-po Lhas-pa to Bu-ston and down to Tsong Khapa.

that can abide with solidified stability on its object, and you are able to pass long periods of time thus, etc. There are procedures for creating such experiences, but fearing prolixity, I do not write them [here]; you should learn them from your mentor.

[**II.B.2.c.ii.C'3'c'ii'B''4''a''i''B°** – The division of things to be created in the creation stage]

In the second there are two: Showing [1°] the segmentation into the four branches and the four yogas; and [2°] the segmentation into the six branches and the three samādhis.

[**II.B.2.c.ii.C'3'c'ii'B''4''a''i''B°1°** – The segmentation into the four branches and the four yogas]

Regarding the division of the general segments comprising the creation stage, *The Esoteric Community* {391b} states these to be the four branches of service and practice. *The Further Tantra* of *The [Esoteric] Community* states:

> In all Yoga Tantras,
> [Four rites] are always praised by the yogī:
> First is the rite of service;
> Second is conformative practice;
> Third is practice;
> Fourth is great practice.

[1. The Branch of Service (sevā, bsnyen pa)]

In this regard, in the root Tantra of *The Esoteric Community*, the service branch is described:

> You should meditate the supreme enlightenment,
> The application of the samādhi of service.

The meaning of '*service*'—which is called 'service' on both stages—accords with what is stated in [Chandrakīrti's] *The Illumination of the Lamp*:

> The things to be learned by those who serve and who seek liberation are called 'service.'

Vitapāda explains that this has the meaning of 'approaching' (*nye ba*).

As for shared service—the analysis of which is fourfold—when one gives an etymological explanation of the [Sanskrit] term *sevā* [service], it has a meaning pertaining to what is to be served and to what is to be apprehended. *The Illumination of the Lamp* explains that, although in the *Instruction on Initiation*[285] it is suchness [that is to be apprehended], in [its] extensive explanation service is explained as apprehension with respect to the spirit of enlightenment, so this means "to be apprehended by this [spirit of enlightenment]" and not that "this [spirit of enlightenment] is what is to be apprehended." Therefore, it is the spirit of enlightenment apprehending emptiness that is '*service*'; and doing just that one-pointedly and applying it to the mind is '*samādhi*.'

The '*supreme enlightenment*' is enlightenment [that arises] from the suchness coming from the analysis {392a} of the meaning of the *shūnyatā* mantra;[286] and 'to meditate' on that is called 'service.' The service that apprehends thatness must be taken as explained by Karuṇashrīpāda [in his *Illumination of the Lamp Commentary*][287] who [refers] to the meditation on emptiness that comes after [visualizing] the defense perimeter; thus, it is not definite that it is only the meditation on emptiness that imaginatively withdraws into clear light.

'*Application*' [occurs] from creating the earth element to imaginatively withdrawing everything into the body; [this] is the '*samādhi of service*' and the '*application*' of those.

Since the intention of *The Illumination of the Lamp* is to take the samādhi of service as above, and to include the things in between as its branches, you should examine whether [these] are considered to be the branches of service. Accordingly, the intention of *The Illumination of the Lamp* is precisely the explanation given by the commentary of *The Further Tantra* [of *The Esoteric Community*] and by Karuṇashrīpāda, viz. that one should place the branch of service from the ground of intuition up to withdrawing [all of the deities] into the visualized body. In harmony with this, when we connect this with other treatises, [it seems that] the branch

---

[285] *Sekoddeśa* (Tōh. 361); in the Kālachakra section of the Kangyur.

[286] *OṀ shūnyatā-jñāna-vajra-svabhāva ātmako 'ham!*

[287] This is Karuṇashrīpāda's sole text in the Tengyur.

of service begins from meditating on emptiness and goes until creating the measureless mansion with its seats.[288]

[2. The Branch of Conformative Practice (upasādhana, nye bar sgrub pa)]

The branch of conformative practice is described in the root Tantra of *The Esoteric Community*:

> In conformative practice, the supreme practice,
> You explore the vajra media.

In *The Illumination of the Lamp*, [Chandrakīrti] explains, {392b} and Nāropa agrees, that conformative practice is [presented as] creating the form of the great seal from meditating on the sun, etc., and perfecting the [deity] body.

Regarding the meaning of the expression "*conformative practice*" [in the verse cited above], Karuṇashrīpāda explains [the first part of this expression] as follows [in his *Illumination of the Lamp Commentary*]:

> "Conformative" (*upa-*, *nye bar*) means "near" (*nikaṭa, gam du*), as it conforms to the thoroughly purified great seal, and [conforms to] the great seal, in terms of just the thorough purification of the primal Savior.[289]

The object to which one is conforming is the so-called 'thoroughly purified deity body which is the great seal intuition body.' Conforming to that is the body of the primal Savior. That very [body] becomes the beatific body, which is achieved from wind-mind in the context of the perfection stage. When it is thoroughly pure, it is the intuition body of the perfection stage; whereas when it is not pure, it is the mantra body. Thus, their difference is only that of their degree of purity.

Well, you may wonder, then are not the rest of those [procedures in the sādhana] included in conformative practice?

---

[288] In Tibetan the term "seats" (*gdan*) appears here, which makes this terminus of the service branch slightly short of that indicated in the previous text. The terminus would be the same if the term here were "inhabitant [deities]" (the nearly homophonous Tibetan term *brten*).

[289] *Dang po'i mgon po'i sku*, a major *Esoteric Community* deity. Alternatively, this could be rendered as "the first Savior," if taken to be a reference to the stage in the sādhana when the deity first appears in this way.

Bhavyakīrti[290] etc. explain that they are something else; but Karuṇa-shrīpāda explains that conformative practice includes everything up to extreme yoga, and this is very much in agreement with the summary of *The Illumination of the Lamp*.

You then may wonder, well, if that is so, then in what way are the rest [of those procedures] described by the term 'conformative practice?'

The creation of the primal Savior is conformative practice, and the remaining [practices] are either its factors, or else—as they have commonality with the principal element of conformative practice—they are included in conformative practice.

Regarding '*practice*' (*sgrub pa*)—you should accept that [the meaning of] this accords with the the explantion that Karuṇashrīpāda {393a} gives when he discusses the remainder of the expression ["*conformative practice*" in *The Esoteric Community* verse above], viz. that this is to practice—that is, to establish (*bkod*)—the body of the great seal.

'*Vajra*' is [a reference to] the thirty-two [deities] from Vairochana up to Shumbharājā. Karuṇashrīpāda explains that the '*media*' of that [vajra] is [a reference to everything] from the matter body-mind system up to the soles of the feet, which indicate the [thirty-two] places where letters are established.[291]

'*Discern*' (*rnam par dpyad*) means to establish the body mandala while knowing the cause and effect of such establishment. Although it is stated that this is similar to establishing it in the body of the primal Savior, [here] you must establish it in the body which is going to become the emanation body.

If we connect all this with other treatises, [conformative practice] runs from creating the lord by means of the five manifest enlightenments[292] up to [transformatively] blessing the [sense] media.

---

[290] Bhavyakīrti has three texts listed in the Tōh. catalogue: 1405 in the *Supreme Bliss* section of the Tengyur, and 1793 and 1838 in the *Esoteric Community* section.

[291] The thirty-two places in the body where letters are established are the five body-mind systems, the five elements, the six sense fields, the six sense realms, the five limbs, and the five activities. Purifying these purifies all of the elements of ordinary life.

[292] On the five manifest enlightenments, cf. note 299 below, and especially the section on this topic beginning on p. 217 (412a ff.).

[3. The Branch of Practice (sādhana, sgrub pa)]

The root Tantra [of *The Esoteric Community*] describes the branch of practice:

> Practice is said to be invocation,
> Meditating on the lord of mantra.

'*Mantra*' means *OṀ*, etc. The '*lord*' of that means the triply-nested spiritual heroes; for the sake of meditating on those and for blessing body, speech, and mind, you invoke the three vajras and make the commitment of practicing with yourself as experientially identical with the three vajras —this is '*practice*' (*sgrub pa*). Therefore, this is '*practice*' because one practices the three doors as the three vajras, one by one and indivisibly, and as the triply-nested spiritual heroes.

[4. The Branch of Great Practice (mahāsādhana, sgrub pa chen po)]

The root Tantra [of *The Esoteric Community*] describes the branch of great practice:

> When performing great practice
> You have the form of the vajra holders [who arise from]
> their own mantras.
> Imagining the lord on your head ornament,
> You will achieve the intuition {393b} vajra.

'*Intuition vajra*' means the mantra practitioner endowed with the yoga of his own deity who has entered the trance preceded by the union of vajra and lotus. '*Vajra holders*' refers to those deities who have arisen from '*their own mantras*,' such as Vajradhṛk, etc.[293] When you imagine '*the form*' of those [deities]—after having meditated the great seal and having been sealed with your clan lord—you achieve siddhi. *The Illumination of*

[293] Vajradhṛk is the essence mantra of Akṣhobhya in the *Esoteric Community*. This refers to the supreme mandala triumph. Prior to this one already has achieved the samādhi of uniting with the consort ("the trance preceded by the union of vajra and lotus"), in which union all internal seeds have melted and have come to the tip of the vajra. In that seed in the tip of the vajra in the yoni of the consort the mandala is fully created. From this mandala Akṣhobhya deities (called *vajri* deities) emerge with the expression "Vajradhṛk!" and travel up through his heart and throughout the universe, transforming all hate into the ultimate perfection of wisdom, before then returning to the mandala.

the Lamp says that '*great practice*' is supreme mandala triumph and supreme action triumph, which accomplish the great aim of others; thus, since supreme action triumph is mentioned there, it too should be understood as great practice.

[Comparative Observations]

The implication of such a statement is that we should consider the first three branches as 'preliminary union'[294] and as the branches for accomplishing one's own aims. Having thus interpreted it, the Ārya system includes the [two preliminary] practices of accumulating the stores and [creating] the defense perimeter as branches of the actual sādhana. Therefore, other than those [two], the four [branches] of service and practice must comprise all the yogas of habitat and inhabitant [mandalas], and thus one should not apply the four branches to the inhabitant [mandala] as a whole and just to each deity.[295]

The Jñānapāda system maintains that there are individual sets of four branches of service and practice used for the lord, for the consort, and for the deities of the supreme mandala triumph, and that those are the lesser, middling, and great four branches, respectively. Also, in the context of [creating the deities of] the supreme action triumph {394a} the three—lesser, middling, and great [four branches]—are used. They maintain that service means creating the devotee hero; conformative practice means blessing the sense-media; practice means blessing body, speech, and mind; and great practice means being initiated and sealed by the clan lords. Further, Vitapāda explains that service is coming close to not staying in the world or in peace; conformative practice is approaching practice; practice is practicing the three doors as the three bodies; great practice is receiving initiation as a Dharma King of the three realms is, because among all practices it is distinctively noble.

---

[294] *dang po sbyor ba*. "Preliminary union" is the first of "the three samādhis" (the remaining two being supreme mandala triumph and supreme action triumph), an alternate schema for dividing up the phases of the creation stage. See below (p. 184ff.; Tib. 396b–398b).

[295] In Tsong Khapa's time there was a common misconception that a sādhana should be divided into (1) the entire inhabitant mandala; and then into the deities of the three buddha bodies: (2) the truth body, (3) the beatific body, and finally (4) the emanation body. Tsong Khapa states the above to remedy this misconception.

According to their position, the creation stage of each respective[296] deity has four branches of service and practice. However, a complete set of four branches of service and practice must have all three—the lesser, middling, and great [four branches]—and therefore that is what is necessary for the stage of creation of a mandala circle.

[The Four Yogas]

Those are the divisions of the general partitions which comprise the creation stage according to the explanations of the Yoga Tantra; but the *Black Enemy [of Death] Tantra*, in accordance with the Father Tantra position, gives the following four general partitions which comprise the creation stage:

> First there is meditation that is yoga,
> Second there is conformative yoga,
> Third there is extreme yoga,
> And fourth there is great yoga.

The same *Tantra* gives a more extensive {394b} explanation of those, as follows:

> The completion of Vajrasattva
> Is said to be yoga.
> Its corresponding cause, the deity body,
> Is known as conformative yoga.
> The full completion of the entire retinue
> Is said to be extreme yoga.
> The blessing of the body, speech, and mind,
> And of the deity's eyes, etc.,
> The entrance of the intuition [hero] into the circle,[297]
> And the making of great offerings and praises,
> Are called great yoga.

---

[296] *re re ba*. Not in Tibetan dictionaries, but LC says this = *itaretara*, *ekaika*.

[297] Tōh. 467 (Derge rgyud, ja): 150a.5–6. The Derge includes another line here: "And the tasting of nectar" (*bdud rtsi myang ba dag dang ni*). All three editions of the *NRC* are missing this line. See my note to the Tibetan edition of this passage for more details.

Likewise, the nineteenth [and final] chapter of the *Red [Enemy of Death] Tantra* says the exact same thing.

Now in general, according to what is stated in *The Further [Tantra of the Esoteric] Community*, 'yoga' means the indivisible union of art and wisdom, but here [it means] the samādhi of the causal Vajradhara,[298] which has the nature of the intuition of the reality realm, which takes place within the [first of the] five manifest enlightenments.[299] Regarding 'conformative yoga'—Shāntipa explains that 'conformative' (*anu-*, *rjes su-*) means 'similar' (*'dra ba*), thus it is similar to the previous yoga, that is, it is the yoga of the fruitional Vajradhara. Moreover, from among those [four], when deity yoga becomes very extensive it is 'extreme yoga' —that is, when there is the completion of the retinue which entails the father and mother entering into union, radiating the retinue of deities born in the lotus, and then installing [each deity of] the retinue in its respective location. Then, Shrīdhara explains that 'great yoga' means everything from the blessing of the [deity's] body, speech, and mind, etc., the entrance of the intuition [hero], {395a} the sealing through receiving of initiation, the offering, praising, and tasting of nectar, and the recitation, up until the intuition retinue is invited to depart and the devotee [hero] gathers [the visualization back into himself]. The yogas between sessions are not included [among the four yogas], and the [preliminary] practices of accumulating the stores, [creating] the defense perimeter, and creating the habitat are not included among the four yogas.

Kumārachandra summarizes 'yoga' as running from the inviting of the deity host[300] up until the causal Vajradhara. [Nāgārjuna's] *Abbreviated [Practice]* has the preliminary union as part of the four yogas—that

[298] The causal Vajradhara is sometimes explained as being one's beatific body, whereas the fruitional Vajradhara is one's emanation body. This connects in a sādhana to bringing bardo and birth, respectively, into the path. Alternately, the causal can be the present practitioner, and the fruitional the actual state of Vajradhara one will become.

[299] Here, the five "manifest enlightenments" (*abhisaṁbodhi*, *mngon byang lnga*) are the five wisdoms/buddhas in the form of emptiness, moon, seed syllable, emblem, and then deity body. See the section on this topic beginning on p. 217 (412a ff.).

[300] *tshogs zhing* lit. = "field of assemblage [of deities]," that is, a field or a host of holy beings in whom one can take refuge, on the basis of which one can thereby create merit. In this Tantric context this refers to various other deities in and around the mandala.

is the system of the *Vajra Rosary Tantra*,[301] and this [preliminary union] is done in terms of meditating the circle of the mandala as a whole, without applying it [over again] to each respective deity.

[**II.B.2.c.ii.C'3'c'ii'B''4''a''i''B°2°** – The segmentation into the six branches and the three samādhis]

[The Six Branches][302]

Regarding the system of dividing up the general segments which comprise the creation stage according to the Mother Tantra system, the seventh chapter of *The [Vajra] Pavilion* says:[303]

> [1] Having completed the Buddha's residence
> And [2] having meditated the five events
> —The true actuality of Samantabhadra—
> Perform the sādhana of your own special deity.
>
> Thereupon, you should establish the mandala, [3][304]
> [4] Offer, [5] praise [6], and [enjoy] nectar, etc.
> When you have meditated with this sequence,
> It is said to be the six-branched yoga.[305]

---

301 Cf. below, 396b–397a.

302 Note that these six branches of the creation stage should not be confused with the six branches of yoga (*ṣaḍaṅgayoga*) of the perfection stage.

303 See my note to the Tibetan edition for Derge and Lhasa variants in the cited passage.

304 As we will see below, everything from meditating the five aspects through establishing all of the deities of the mandala constitutes the second branch. The third branch, then, should be the conferral of initiation (as we also will see below). This branch seems to be conspicuously absent here in these root verses from *The Vajra Pavilion Tantra* as cited by Tsong Khapa (and in the Derge and Lhasa variants mentioned in the previous footnote). Of course, the "etc." at the end of the next line could implicitly include this third branch.

305 Cp. the translation by Stephan Beyer, *The Cult of Tārā* (115). Also, cp. Beyer's chart (p. 118) with Wayman's chart (*Buddhist Tantras*, p. 47)—both are based on this section of the *NRC*. Cf. also Table 8 in the introduction herein.

Thus [the creation stage] is collected into six branches. The meaning of that [collection] is given by the great adept Durjayachandra, [in his *Six-Branch Sādhana*]:[306]

> Meditate the six branches: [2] Empassion by Vajra[sattva],
> [1] Meditate the details of the Buddha's {395b}
> measureless [mansion],
> [3] Confer initiation, [6] enjoy the nectar,
> [4] Make offerings, and [5] give praise.
> The yogī who meditates these six branches
> Will quickly achieve siddhi.
>
> [1] The palace is Buddha Vairochana,
> [3] Initiation is transcendent Buddha Akṣhobhya,
> [6] Enjoyment of nectar is Amitābha,
> [5] Praise is glorious Ratnasambhava,
> [4] Offering is Amogha[siddhi]'s genuine offering,
> [2] Empassionment is Vajrasattva.

Thus he formulates [the creation stage] into six branches from the perspective of the six [buddha-] clans.

[The First Branch]

Regarding that, *The [Vajra] Pavilion* says:[307]

---

[306] Tōh. 419 (rGyud NGA): 44b.1–2. Lhasa 379 (rGyud KA): 400b.4–6. The Derge and Lhasa editions both vary somewhat (in identical ways) from Tsong Khapa's citation here (cf. my Tibetan edition). Beyer (115) translates this passage, citing it as appearing in the following two of Durjayachandra's texts: the *Six-Branch Sādhana* (Tōh. 1239), and the "*Superb Embrace," a Sādhana of the Mandala Rite* (Tōh. 1240); cf. Beyer (485, note 175) for the references to the Peking editions which he consulted. (According to the Tengyur chart, both are commentaries on the *yab skor* of *Hevajra*, to which *The Vajra Pavilion* belongs; Tsong Khapa also mentions both of these texts together by name below, at 411a). While I found the passage cited here in the Derge edition of the *Six-Branch Sādhana*, I did not find it in the Derge edition of the "*Superb Embrace*" (it is of course possible that the Peking edition consulted by Beyer varies from the Derge). Note that Beyer seems to have mistranslated this passage in several places, as when he says: "...contemplating the *separation* of the divine mansion of Buddhahood," and "*What is* this six-limbed yoga?"

[307] For some reason Beyer (115–116) attributes the following quote to Indrabodhi.

[1] Meditate the reality-source,[308]
And therein imagine the Buddha's abode.[309]

And:

The Great Victor Vairochana
Is created from the reality realm syllable;
That should establish the Buddha's abode.[310]

So, according to these passages, meditation on the measureless mansion, the abode of the Buddha arisen from Vairochana, is the first branch. The reason for that is: since matter is the support of body and mind,[311] and since Vairochana is the reality of the matter body-mind system of the transcendent buddhas, that [Vairochana] should create the habitat [mandala], the measureless mansion.[312]

[The Second Branch]

The second branch is shown by [those verses] in *The [Vajra] Pavilion* up through the following:[313]

---

308 *Dharmodaya* (*chos kyi 'byung gnas*). Here visualized as a cosmically huge tetrahedron of white light. See note 393, below.

309 Beyer (116) mistranslates *sangs rgyas gnas* as: "visualize the Buddha *placed* therein...."

310 Again Beyer (116) mistranslates *sangs rgyas gnas* as: "he arrays the Buddhas *in place*." This is odd, since he then correctly translates this phrase in Tsong Khapa's commentary (below) as "the *place of* Buddhahood...."

311 *gzugs lus sems kyi rten yin*. We are interpreting this as *gzugs ni lus sems kyi rten yin*.

312 In the following pages there will be a "reason" for each of the six associations between a creation stage branch and a transcendent buddha. These "reasons" are summarized in the right hand column of the chart on p. 47 of Wayman's *The Buddhist Tantras*.

313 The following verses together with Tsong Khapa's commentary are translated in Beyer (116). Note Beyer's chart (p. 118) seems to reverse what is numbered here as iv and v in this *Vajra Pavilion* quote. However, as he explains (107–108), he is trying to follow the standard sequence of "the four limbs of approach and evocation" found in *Guhyasamāja*.

> [2] You should meditate the five events:
> [i] First imagine [yourself as] the divine male;[314]
> [ii] Then radiate the circle of ḍākinīs;
> [iii] The *gandharva*[315] then enters, and falls;
> [iv] The goddesses of the quarters recollect the melted
> [deity] and exhort [it];
> [v] Having been exhorted, the leader of the circle
> Places [Vajra-]delusion, etc., {396a} in the eyes, etc.
> And the three vajras in the three places.
> So the Vajra[sattva] empassionment [just described]
> Is the intuition [hero] entering manifestation....

Among the six branches, there is no one who does not accept that these [events] comprise the branch of empassionment: from the five manifest enlightenments you create [yourself as] the father-mother causal Vajradhara; after that, having blessed the two secret places, you generate the pride of empassionment, after which you emit the goddesses of the circle and set them in [their] places; [then] the [intuition hero as] melted [*gandharva* between-state deity], having been exhorted by song, arises, and the intuition being having entered you [as father-mother causal Vajradhara], you effect the blessing of [your] eyes, etc. Accordingly, everything from the initial meditation of the five manifest enlightenments which creates the inhabitant deities, up through bringing the intuition being into the fully created circle of the devotee hero and [performing] the blessing—[all that] is the mandala which is produced from yourself, having made yourself into Vajrasattva and developed his pride of empassionment, and thus it is the second branch.[316]

The reason why you develop empassionment from the perspective of [being] Vajrasattva is [as follows]: the development of empassionment is [done] so that, in this context, the deities of the circle [can be] emanated from the enlightenment spirit of the father-mother; thus [you as]

---

[314] *skyes bu* (*puruṣa*); here the devotee hero (*samayasattva*).

[315] The *gandharva* is the bardo being, here homologized with the intuition hero (*jñānasattva*). For an extensive discussion of the *gandharva* and the topic of the melting of the *gandharva* and/or the father-mother, see below, p. 231ff. (Tib. 417b ff.).

[316] In simple summary: the first branch is the creation of the habitat mandala, and the second branch is the creation of the inhabitant mandala.

the lord must become empassioned, and that very [lord] is asserted to be Vajrasattva.[317]

[Branches Three Through Six]

Four branches are shown by each of the following phrases in *The [Vajra] Pavilion*:

> [3] The eight science[-goddesses] confer initiation; {396b}
> [6] You should enjoy nectar;
> [4] The eight goddesses make offerings;
> [5] You should praise the leader of the circle.[318]

Initiation is done from the perspective of Akṣhobhya, because the initiation in this [context/phrase] is the water initiation, and that is the essence of Akṣhobhya.[319]

Enjoyment of nectar is done from the perspective of Amitābha, because Amitābha is Speech Vajra, and the enjoyment of nectar satisfies Speech Vajra.

Offering is done from the perspective of Amoghasiddhi, because, since Amoghasiddhi is the [lord of the] action clan, he is the authority with respect to actions involving offering to buddhas and accomplishing the aims of sentient beings.

Praise is given from the perspective of Ratnasambhava, because praise is the expression of excellence, and when one makes [a division of excellence] into the five—[those of] body, speech, mind, miraculous actions, and excellences—Ratnasambhava is the [praise of the] excellences.

Since Vajrasattva is the inseparability of those five [excellences], the six clans are involved in all of the yogas of habitat and inhabitant [mandalas]; further, the remaining repetitions, etc., being marked by those [clans], also involve them.

---

[317] Cp. the last two paragraphs with Beyer (116).

[318] Beyer (117) attributes this passage to "Indrabodhi" for some reason. Also, he mistakenly translates the final line as "and one should praise the conjured retinue."

[319] The reason (*phyir*) goes back to the *ni*, not just back to the *yin la*. The "that" (*de*) refers back to *dbang bskur ba mi bskyod pa*, not to the immediately preceding *chu dbang*. The structure is "A is the case, because of B and [because of] C," not "A is B, because of C." The initial phrase is elliptic—it would have been clearer if Tsong Khapa had said: *dbang bskur ba mi bsyod pa'i sgo nas byed pa yin pa ni OR...byed pa yin te*. The next three paragraphs follow a similar pattern.

[The Three Samādhis][320]

The *Vajra Rosary [Tantra]*, an explanatory Tantra common to both the Yogī and Yoginī Tantras,[321] divides up the general segments that comprise the creation stage into the three samādhis: preliminary union, supreme mandala triumph, and supreme action triumph. So it states:

> Yoga, {397a} conformative yoga,
> Extreme yoga, and great yoga[322]
> Are included in the preliminary union.
> Thus, likewise, there is the supreme mandala triumph
> [And] the supreme action triumph, the supreme yoga.

By adding the two yogas of the two supreme triumphs to the four yogas [mentioned in the first two pādas] one gets six yogas, but they can also be called the three samādhis or yogas since the first four can be included in the preliminary union. A partitioning of the sādhana by these three samādhis occurs often in the Mother Tantras as well. Moreover, those [three samādhis], being used as conventions from the Yoga Tantras, Mother Tantras, and Common Tantras, it is not the case that those [partitionings] are mutually incompatible with 'the four [branches of] service-practice' and 'the six branches,' etc.

Concerning the three samādhis: the 'preliminary union' used in the Unexcelled [Yoga Tantras] is the samādhi of the father-mother lord who is the emanator of the deities of the mandala; since it occurs at the beginning of the remaining two [samādhis] it is 'preliminary,' and since it nondually unites art and wisdom it is a 'union.' Although here [only] the 'lord' is mentioned, this [preliminary union] comprises everything from creating the habitat to creating the father-mother. [Next,] once those two [father and mother] have completed the deities of the mandala who are emanated from [their] spirits of enlightenment, then setting [those deities]

---

[320] For more on the three samādhis, cf. Beyer, pp. 117–18; Cozort, p. 51; *YGST*, 160ff.

[321] Tsong Khapa's description here of the *Vajra Rosary Tantra* (Tōh. 445) as being "an explanatory Tantra common to both the Yogī and Yoginī Tantras" is rather surprising since this Tantra is classified as an explanatory Tantra of the *Esoteric Community Tantra* (Tōh. 442), which is a Father (or "Yogī") Tantra.

[322] On this set of "four yogas," see above (p. 177ff., Tib. 394a–395a).

in their [respective] places is the full completion of the retinue that is to be placed in the mandala, {397b} and hence it is the supreme mandala triumph. [Finally,] after that the deities' accomplishing deeds such as purifying fields, etc., is the supreme action triumph.

[Comparative Observations]

Regarding [all] that, according to the Ārya tradition: up through the preliminary union there are extensive procedures for the creation of [all] three bodies; therefore that is said to be the consummation of one's own aim, and they include in that [preliminary union] the first three of the four branches of service-practice. The two supreme triumphs are the deeds of one who has attained buddhahood,[323] and they are, moreoever, precisely the [fourth branch of service-practice,] great practice. Therefore, from the point of view of taking as the path the realm, body, and deeds of the fruitional time, they make the partitions from the perspective of the three samādhis and the four branches of service-practice. Moreover, regarding the key points which are set up in relation to the purification of the bases to be purified as well as to the achievement of the perfection stage, I have already explained these extensively in my *Commentary to [Nāgabodhi's] Graded Presentation [of the Esoteric Community Practice]*.[324]

Many such as Shāntipa, etc., connect the three samādhis respectively with the nature body, beatific body, and emanation body, because according to them one practices the three samādhis in order to take the three bodies as a path. Thus, [1] the preliminary union is the achieving of one's own aim first, the means of emanating the hosts of deities, and so it is regarded as the nature body or the truth body; and [2] the form bodies —which emerge by the power of that [truth body] and which are the means of achieving others' aims—are the first things which emerge [from that truth body], and thus the supreme mandala triumph [is regarded as]

---

323 *sangs rgyas nas kyi mdzad pa* (same at MS: 286b, 5). The awkward phrase *sangs rgyas nas* is probably short for *sangs rgyas <u>zhal snga</u> nas*, an honorific (Buddha "presence").

324 Tsong Khapa's *rnam gzhag rim pa'i rnam bshad*. The *Graded Presentation* itself (Tōh. 1809: *vyavasthāli/vyavasthāna; rnam gzhag rim pa*) is an Indian Esoteric Community creation stage commentary. There are several variants in the name of this Indian text and its author. See the "comments" section of the bibliographic entry for this title.

the beatific body; and [3] while staying in one's own place {398a} the hosts of deities which one [simultaneously] radiates from each [syllable/beatific deity form] perform the aims of sentient beings throughout the ten directions, and thus the supreme action triumph is posited as the emanation body.

The yogas of the first stage are partitioned into six branches in order that one may understand that they do not exceed being interpreted from the perspective of the six clans.

All of the yogas of the actual creation stage are contatined in the four yogas: the first two yogas involve the minor practice of [visualizing] the lord father-mother; and by adding to that the complete practice of [visualizing] the circle of deities we get the third yoga, the middling yoga; and in the final [yoga] one visualizes [one's creation] as being of one taste with the intuition hero, and one performs the blessings, etc., of the eyes, etc., and thus that is posited as the great yoga. [You should know this] in order to understand that the first stage has [yogas with] minor, middling, and great powers to dispel your resistances.[325]

Jñānapāda's tradition, moreover, presents the minor, middling, and great [yogas] in terms of their dispelling the gross, middling, and small resistances by adding each later [yoga] to each previous one; so you should consider whether or not this is similar to Vitapāda's explanation. Further, Jñānapāda's tradition makes an analysis of the creation stage from the perspective of taking it as a path having seven branches—its point is extremely great, but I have already explained it previously.[326]

Those are the amazing partitions of the first stage. Therefore, {398b} if you analyze [a creation stage sādhana or explanation] taking those as a basis, then you will understand the criteria [establishing] whether or not the key points of the first stage are complete.

---

325 *mi mthun phyogs* (*vipakṣa*) are a person's resistant tendencies or counter-tendencies.

326 We have not yet determined which other Tantric commentary by Tsong Khapa contains this discussion. To do so would be interesting and valuable in establishing the chronology of his writings.

[II.B.2.c.ii.C'3'c'ii'B''4''a''i''C° – How to meditate emptiness in that context]

You may wonder: Well then, is it the case or not that in the context of the first stage one meditates just the wheel of the deities, which is the visible aspect, and then in the context of the second stage one must primarily meditate on emptiness?

This should be explained. Meditation on emptiness in the context of the first stage is *extremely* necessary. This is because [1] the first stage is the means for developing the continuum of methods which fully produce the realization of the perfection stage, and if one does not meditate on emptiness [in that context] then such a development cannot possibly be accomplished. Because in the Mantra Vehicle [2] many Tantras state that before one creates the wheel of the deities, which is the visible aspect, one recites the mantra "*OṀ Svabhāva...*" and meditates on the meaning of the mantra, which is the ultimate truth of selflessness, and so they state that it is necessary to practice [emptiness meditation] from the outset; and because [3] in the context of the first stage it is necessary to take all three bodies as the path, and therefore it is necessary to meditate emptiness when taking the truth body as the path; and because [4] it is necessary to purify all three bases of purification—birth, death, and the between—and therefore it is necessary to meditate emptiness when purifying death; and because [5] limitless Tantras and commentaries say not only once that it is necessary to perform all of the yogas of habitat and inhabitant, etc., from within an illusory state. Moreover, {399a} *The Five Stages* says:[327]

> Employment of mantras and mudrās,
> Constructs such as mandalas, etc.,
> And all activities involving fire offerings and votary cakes,
> Always should be performed as like an illusion.
>
> Pacifying, and prospering,
> Likewise dominating, and destruction,
> And attracting, etc.—all [such actions]
> Should be performed as just like rainbows.[328]

[327] This is in the middle of chapter III on self-consecration (*svādhiṣṭhāna*, *bdag la byin gyis brlab pa'i rim pa*). The Derge varies greatly in places; cf. my note to the Tibetan.

[328] *dbang po'i gzhu* = Indra's bow = a rainbow = "like an illusion."

Enjoying sensual play, etc.,
Partaking of song and music, etc.,
And engaging in the arts,
Should be performed as like the moon [reflected in] water.

Forms, sounds, and likewise smells,
Tastes, and tangibles—
Fully engage these with the eyes, etc.,
[Having] discerned [them] as illusory.

What more is there to say?
For the yogī on the Vajra Vehicle
Whatever he may perceive
Should be considered in reality to be only an illusion.

Especially on this [Vajra] path, Jñānashrī says in his *Dispelling the Two Extremes [of the Vajra Vehicle]* that if you do not continuously recall the view once you have found it, your heart-commitment will deteriorate; and in [Mañjushrīkīrti's] The *Fourteen Root Downfalls* it says:

With respect to things free of names etc.,
To conceptualize them [as substantial] is the eleventh [root downfall].[329]

Thus, it is not merely appropriate if you do [continuously recall the view of emptiness], but it will create a fault if you do not.

In the context of the first stage, regarding the way to indivisibly unite both the perception that has the pattern of the circle of the mandala and the wisdom that realizes the meaning of selflessness, and {399b} the way to thereby stop the self-habit which is the root of the suffering of existence—Jñānapāda's tradition is clear; as [Jñānapāda's] *The Samantabhadra Sādhana* states:

There is no other suffering of existence [produced]
From anything other than the stream of ordinary conceptual thought.[330]

---

[329] Cf. Dudjom Rinpoche's *Perfect Conduct*, p. 121 regarding this.

[330] *tha mal rnam rtog*; or "conceptions of ordinariness." See introduction, p. 64 (esp. note 66) above.

> The mind holding a pattern opposed to that
> Will come to have direct realization.
> Whatever [mind] has the nature of the profound and the magnificent
> Will not perceive [ordinary] imaginary thought.

In order to cut any doubt regarding this—Thagana's *Commentary* on that [passage mentions that] someone might think: 'If all of this striving to make a detailed explanation of the way to meditate deity yoga is [supposed to be] for the sake of liberating one from saṁsāra, [well then] meditating this path of the first stage of yours is not going to liberate you from saṁsāra,' [implicitly] because it involves no meditation on selflessness! And in answer to that objection [Thagana] explains that those passages show that the first stage *is* the way to oppose the root of saṁsāra.

Moreover, Vitapāda states [in his *Commentary on [*Jñānapāda*'s] The Four-Branched Samantabhadrī Sādhana*]:

> Since the abbreviated treatment [in *The Samantabhadrī Sādhana*] teaches that, it declares that that very inconceivable nature of the circle of the mandala[331] previously stated is the remedy for the suffering of existence.

—which is also like other commentaries within Jñānapāda's tradition.

Here, regarding the explanation by certain Tibetans and Indians that the phrase "ordinary conceptual thought" {400a} means just unreflective concepts[332] [involving ordinary] perceptions wherein there is no perception

---

[331] The inconceivable aspect of the mandala is of course its emptiness. It is thus the profound emptiness aspect of the visualized mandala that is being said to function as an antidote to the self-habit pattern and hence to the sufferings of saṁsāra. Recall also in the quote above from *The Samantabhadra Sādhana* that we are talking about a "[mind]... which has the nature of the profound *and* the magnificent." So, the magnificent aspect is the vibrant, intricate details of the visualized mandala, whereas the profound aspect is one's own simultaneous cognizance of the *emptiness* of that vibrant vision. *Both* of these aspects must be present for such creation stage practice to cut the self-habit which is the root of suffering. *This must be kept in mind throughout the following discussions.*

[332] *snang ba rang dga' ba'i rtog pa*. The term *rang dga' ba* literally means something like "whatever pleases one," or "self-indulgent." This phrase *rang dga' ba'i rtog pa* then means "whatever thoughts happen to arise, without being examined," hence "ordinary, unreflective thoughts."

of the form of the deity—that definitely is not what Jñānapāda asserts. As Thagana's *Commentary* on this [*Samantabhadra Sādhana* by Jñānapāda] states:

> 'Ordinary conceptual thought' is conceptual thoughts of 'I' and 'mine.'

And furthermore, as Shāntipa states in his *Commentary on [Dīpaṅkarabhadra's] The Four Hundred and Fifty [Verses]*:

> Here, where "ordinary conceptual thought" is described as being an inner mental formulation having the pattern of 'I' and 'mine,' and subject and object, then with the expression "the suffering which is the very nature of existence" the entire phrase is "it [ordinary conceptual thought] is the chief cause of the suffering which is the very nature of existence."

Also, Shrī Phalavajra, Vitapāda, and Samantabhadra [in their respective *Commentaries* on Jñānapāda's *Samantabhadra/-ī Sādhanas*][333] clearly explain ['ordinary conceptual thought' to be] the self-habit, and one can know this also by the context. Therefore, the self-habit is 'ordinary conceptual thought,' the root of 'the suffering of existence,' and thus it is called '*the suffering of existence*.'

'*The mind opposed to that*' is explained by all the commentaries to be the mind that has the pattern of the circle of the mandala,[334] and the way it opposes is that '*it is opposed in pattern*'[335]—that is, the two habit patterns[336] are necessarily really opposed. Moreover, it is the mind that

[333] All three of these authors wrote such commentaries; thus, we may surmise here that by grouping these authors together Tsong Khapa may be referring to these texts. If so, these texts are: Tōh. 1867 (Shrī Phalavajra's only text in the Tengyur); Tōh. 1872 (by Vitapāda); and Tōh. 1869 (by Samantabhadra).

[334] *dkyil 'khor gyi 'khor lo'i rnam pa can kyi sems*. This phrase occurs several times in the discussion below. I have contracted this phrase to "the mandala-mind" when interpolating it in brackets. See Introduction, p. 63ff.

[335] *rnam pa 'gal ba*.

[336] *'dzin stangs gnyis*. That is, the self-habit pattern which conceives/perceives a non-empty, ordinary world, and the selflessness-habit pattern which conceives/perceives the empty, extraordinary world of a mandala.

has the pattern of the circle [of the mandala]—that is, the meditator himself—that '*will come to have direct realization*.'

The reason why '[it is] *opposed* {400b} *to that*' is shown by the quote "[*Whatever (mind) has the nature of the*...] *profound*..." etc.[337] in [the fifth phrase cited from] *The Samantabhadra Sādhana*—which means that at the time when that 'mind' that has the pattern of the circle [of the mandala] is created, it '*will not perceive ordinary 'conceptual thought*.'

[Here one might object:] When that [mandala-mind] is created, since one does not experience the self-habit, that [mandala-mind] cannot stop that [self-habit]; but the meditation on the medium[338] of infinite space will reverse it.[339]

In answer [to that objection] Shāntipa states [in his *Commentary to Dīpaṅkarabhadra's The Four Hundred and Fifty Verses*]:

> [The mandala-mind does stop the self-habit,] because the mind that has the pattern of the mandala does engage in clearing up all untrue conceptions.[340] And it is not that it [the self-habit] is just naturally not perceived [by the mandala-mind].

And:

> [A mind abiding in any of] the [four] media of infinite space, etc., does not engage with selflessness, because

---

[337] In Tibetan the syntax is such that the pāda begins with the word "profound," whereas in English it is necessary to begin with "In whatever mind...."

[338] *skye mched* (*āyātana*). There are three "realms" (*dhātu, khams*), the third of which is "the formless realm" (*arūpadhātuḥ, gzugs med pa'i khams*). However, within the latter the four subdivisions or "levels" (*bhūmi, sa*) are not further *dhātu*s but rather "media" (*āyātana, skye mched*): hence the *āyātana* of infinite space (*ākāśānantyāyatanaṁ, nam mkha mtha' yas skye mched*), of infinite consciousness, etc. Thus, the common translation "the *realm* of infinite space," etc., obfuscates this distinction. Tib. *skye mched* literally is that in which something is "produced and extends"—hence a "medium." Thus, we should speak of three "realms" (*dhātu*), the third of which is the formless realm, which in turn has four "levels" (*bhūmi*), the first of which is the "*medium*" (*āyātana*) of infinite space. (Cf. *Mahāvyutpatti*, trans. Csoma de Körös, pp. 141–143.)

[339] This is a paraphrase of various objections raised (then next answered) in Shāntipa's text.

[340] For the upcoming discussion, recall what was emphasized in note 331 (and discussed in the Introduction, p. 63ff). What Shāntipa calls "the circle of the mandala" or "the mandala-mind" always includes the aspect of an awareness of emptiness; so mere visualization of a mandala (without such awareness) will not do.

> that [mind] does not reverse the self-view; and it also does not involve a reversal of the suffering which is caused by that [self-view]. Furthermore, here, old age, death, etc., [which occur] in the continuum from lifetime to lifetime, are the truth of suffering. That which is the cause of that, the view of self, etc., is the truth of the origin [of suffering]. That which is the antidote to that, the circle of the mandala, is the truth of the path. Because it totally annihilates the origin of suffering, the total transformation of the locality[341] that [itself] has the characteristic of [being] a continuity of mind is the truth of cessation—and this here is ultimate reality.

So [Shāntipa] beautifully distinguishes the processes of [1] [the mind abiding in] infinite space, {401a} which—since it has no mental orientation toward selflessness—will not damage the self-habit when it is meditated, and which thus also will not liberate one from existence when it is meditated; and [2] the mind that has the pattern of the circle [of the mandala], which—since it does [necessarily] engage with selflessness, which refutes the object that is habitually grasped as a self—is able to reverse the self-habit.

Moreover, [saying that] the self-habit's being overcome by the wisdom that realizes selflessness is from the perspective of '[holding] an opposed pattern' is [to say that] it is from the perspective of whether or not the mind is distorted; and establishing that gets back to whether or not it has supportive validating cognition.[342] This is like what the Lord of Reason says [in the *Validating Cognition Commentary*]:

> Whatever things have validating cognitions
> Will refute other things [that do not]. (IV.99cd)

---

[341] *gnas yongs su gyur pa* (*āśraya-parāvṛtti*)—which I am translating here as "the total transformation of the locatedness/locality/place/site [that is the mind]"—is what often is translated as "a transformation of the basis." This is the Yogācāra view of an "inner revolution" (*parāvṛtti*), resulting in the elimination (or purification) of the *ālayavijñāna* (the *āśraya*), leaving only the pure mirror-like intuition.

[342] That is, the self-habit mind is distorted and is not supported by validating cognition, whereas its opposite, the mind cognizing selflessness, is *not* distorted and *is* supported by validating cognition.

[Concerning this key] place of doubt that arises [even] for realized experts, you wise people have to understand that [1] [this] debate against [their assumption that it is not the case that] without the view of selflessness that undermines the self-habit, the root of bondage, one loses the essence of the path that liberates from saṁsāra, and [2] our [above] ways of answering [their counter-arguments] are necessary in the context of both stages.

Seeing one time—from a perspective like that [above]—the means of refuting that which is to be refuted, then as you familiarize yourself with [that as] the antidote, and intensify your familiarization with that, you gradually will block the resistances, and thereby in the end you will uproot them. As [Jñānapāda's] *The Samantabhadra Sādhana* states:

> That [selflessness-habit] which occurs even once {401b}
> Against those [tendencies] counter to it, as it progresses
> and expands
> [Stimulates] intensifications of insight and learning
> And utterly blocks your counter[-tendencies].[343]

The meaning of this is what is stated in *The [Validating Cognition] Commentary* [by Dharmakīrti]:

> All reliances, [some to be] decreased and [some to be]
> increased,
> Have their [respective] resistances.
> Familiarizing yourself with those [reliances],
> You become habituated [to them],[344] and thereby,
> Gradually, your contaminants will be eliminated. (I.220)

---

[343] On the "counter[-tendencies]" (*mi mthun [phyogs]*) or "resistances," see note 325 above. The syntax of this entire verse again is very obtuse. What is supplied in brackets could of course be determined only with reference to Tsong Khapa's set-up commentary.

[344] As the commentary in the next footnote shows, *bdag 'gyur ba* is an abbreviation for *bdag <u>nyid du</u> 'gyur ba*, which is an appropriate translation of the Sanskrit *sātmībhāva*. MW (p. 1200) defines *sātmībhāva* as "the becoming a custom or habit, conduciveness, suitableness" (and *sātmīkṛta* as "one who has made anything part of his nature, i.e., become accustomed to (acc.)").

Here, using [the next passage] from *The [Validating Cognition] Commentary* [beginning] "Non-harming and...,"[345] Shāntipa proves the non-reversal of [radical] transformation. And using [the passage from the *Validating Cognition Commentary* containing the phrase:] "If there is a self, then there is a notion of other...,"[346] Shrī Phalavajra proves that the self-habit is the root of saṁsāra. And in the context of determining the view of [Jñānapāda's] *The Samantabhadra Sādhana*, Thagana and Shrī Phalavajra determine the view by citing many passages from *The [Validating Cognition] Commentary*. And also many other Mantric paṇḍits make many proofs using the *[Validating Cognition] Commentary* as a source. Therefore, [while some people may erroneously] view the treatises of the two Lords of Reason[347] to be of no use in the context of the inner sciences in general and in the context of Mantra in particular, since [those people have only] meager intellect and experience in traversing the path of reasoning, [their] proclamations about that [erroneous view] to others are not up to the system[348] of taintless reasoning that is developed through the path that is engaged by the intellect whose depth is so hard to fathom, and therefore [their proclamations] {402a} are rash nonsense which is impossible even to mention in the presence of the learned who are able to analyze the meaning of scriptures with subtle reasoning.[349]

---

345 This is *Pramāṇavārttika* I.221 (in the *svārthānumāna* chapter). The full verse in Tibetan is: *'tshe ba med dang yang dag don, ,ngo bo nyid la phyin log gis, ,'bad du zin kyang mi bzlog ste, ,blo ni de phyogs 'dzin phyir ro, ,* (Derge 103a.2). The Sanskrit is: *sarveṣāṁ savipakṣatvān nirhrāsātiśayaśritām / sātmībhāvāt tadabhyāsād hīyerannāsravāḥ kvacit //* Shākyamati also wrote a useful commentary on this text (*Pramāṇavārttikaṭīkā, tshad ma rnam 'grel gyi 'grel bshad*).

346 *Pramāṇavārttika* II.221c: *ātmanisati parasaṁjñā* (*bdag yod na ni gzhan du shes*). See the note to the Tibetan edition for the full verse and citations.

347 *rigs pa'i dbang phyug rnam gnyis*. Here it is made clear that for Tsong Khapa the epithet "Lord of Reason" can refer either to Dignāga or to Dharmakīrti.

348 Reading *rnam gzhag ma lcogs*. TL and ZH have *ma lcigs*; MS has preferred *ma lcogs*. Even better woiuld be *mi lcogs*. For *lcigs pa*, THL (Ives Waldo) gives "to realize, understand"; and for *ma lcigs pa*, THL (Dan Martin) gives "*ma theg pa*... [not able to hold up]." For *lcogs*, RY gives "to be able to cope, handle; to be able, capable of/ to handle, cope with." Das (401) cites it as a verb ("to be able"), and as an adj. ("able").

349 The syntax of this long sentence is rather difficult. I am taking the previous *smra ba ni* as the subject. Thus, the X and Y of the *yin* work out as follows: "their proclamations

(cont'd)

Regarding that yoga in which the mind that has the pattern of the circle [of a mandala] engages with the thatness of selflessness: according to Shrī Phalavajra's explanation, [such a nondual mind] is generally operative in all three samādhis, and this also is Jñānapāda's thought. Thus, although it is indeed the case that in the context of the first stage one principally meditates the circle of deities that is the perception side, nonetheless one does train oneself in everything arising as an illusion by developing intense certitude about the import of the intrinsic identitylessness of all things. So, [1] [first there is] the meditation on [building up] the circle of deities; then having visualized the objective deity, after that [one engages in] [2] the yoga of the nonduality of the profound and the vivid in which the subjective mind that is certain about the import of the intrinsic identitylessness of [that deity] form—[which mind has] a habit-pattern involving certain knowledge—while engaging in emptiness, arises as the objective form of the habitat and the deities who are the inhabitants. So you should perform the practice, by alternating [2] [this yoga of the nonduality of the profound and the vivid] with [1] evocation meditation.[350]

Having seen the power of this import, the root Tantra of the *Hevajra* says:[351]

> With the yoga of the creation stage,
> The ascetic should meditate an elaborated [world].
> Making [this] elaborated [world] dreamlike,
> With this very elaboration he should make it un-elaborative.

And the explanatory Tantra on that, *The [Vajra] Pavilion*, says:

(*smra ba ni* = X), because [these people] are of small intelligence (*blo nyams chung ngus* = subord. clause), are (*yin*) not up to a presentation (*ma lcogs pa* = Y) of taintless reasoning." Then I am taking the *smra ba ni* as also carrying down to be the subject of the final implied *yin* in the final verb *bab col lo*.

350 This long run-on sentence is rather difficult. The final phrase hangs together as a complete thought: *...[2] zab gsal gnyis med kyi rnal 'byor yang [1] mngon rtogs sgom res kyis bya'o*. (In my rendition the phrase "the yoga of the nonduality of the profound and the vivid" [*zab gsal gnyis med kyi rnal 'byor*] had to appear in the beginning, so I had to repeat it in brackets at the end.)

351 This same verse was quoted above at 373a (cf. also note 242 at that location).

> For example, the moon [reflected] in water,
> Oh friends, is neither true nor false.
> Likewise here, the wheel of the mandala
> Has a nature which is transparent and vivid.

Therefore, {402b} since meditation on emptiness is necessary in the contexts of *both* stages, in the context of Mantra it is not the case that all meditations on any emptiness are the perfection stage. On the other hand [on the perception/body side], since in the context of the creation stage there is an extreme development of the yoga of a deity body—which [body] is like the moon [reflected] in water, or a rainbow in the sky, like an illusion which though perceived is yet identityless—one must distinguish that [highly developed creation stage illusory deity body] from the illusion body of the self-consecration [stage of] the perfection stage.[352] As the *Practice Integration* states:

> Even meditators who engage in the ways of the Sūtra [Vehicle] or who abide in the creation stage and who express the examples, "all things are like an illusion and like a dream and like reflection," although they aspire [to that divine illusion body] they will not know through example the divine body, which has the nature of mind, and which will be perfected only through intuition from the private instruction of the self-consecration.

Thus, Jñānapāda explains the yoga of the nonduality of the profound and the vivid in which one develops certitude about emptiness and [has one's certain subjective mind] arise as the objective aspect, the deity;[353] and [many other] Indian adepts explain [like this] using precisely

---

[352] The self-consecration (*svādhiṣṭhāna*) stage is the third of the five stages of the perfection stage. The Tibetan phrases Tsong Khapa is cautioning us to distinguish here are: (1) *lha'i sku...sgyu ma dang 'dra ba'i rnal 'byor*, and (2) *sgyu ma'i lus*. Overall, the correlated points Tsong Khapa is making in this paragraph may be summarized as follows: (1) creation stage, like perfection stage, *also* has emptiness meditation; likewise (2) perfection stage, like creation stage, *also* has a deity body (which body, however, must be distinguished from that of the creation stage; on both stages there are illusory bodies, but these are "illusory" in different senses).

[353] *...gzung rnam lhar shar ba'i zab gsal gnyis med kyi rnal 'byor*. This is almost exactly the same phrase discussed above in note 350.

this [explanation by Jñānapāda] as a source—as the Great Adept Shrīdhara says in *The Sādhana of the Black Enemy [of Death]*:

> The truth is not other than this;
> The supreme ones such as Jñānapāda, etc.
> Clearly explain these very things.

—and there are also many others who follow this [great master Jñānapāda].

[II.B.2.c.ii.C'3'c'ii'B''4''a''ii'' — An explanation of the stages of evocation]

The second has three: [A°] The yoga of the actuality of the session; [B°] {403a} The yoga in between sessions; and [C°] The way of making those yogas magnificent.

[II.B.2.c.ii.C'3'c'ii'B''4''a''ii''A° — The Yoga of the Actuality of the Session]

The first has three: [1°] The preliminaries to the actual yoga; [2°] The actual yoga with its components; and [3°] The follow-up [to those yogas].

[II.B.2.c.ii.C'3'c'ii'B''4''a''ii''A°1° — The Preliminaries to the Actual Yoga]

The first has two: [a°] The accumulation of the stores [of merit and intuition], which establish the favorable conditions [for the practice of yoga]; and [b°] The defense perimeter which clears away adverse conditions.

[II.B.2.c.ii.C'3'c'ii'B''4''a''ii''A°1°a° — The Accumulation of the Stores (of Merit and Intuition), which Establish the Favorable Conditions (for the Practice of Yoga)]

[Initial Conditions and Preliminaries; Accumulating the Store of Merit]

[Jñānapāda's] *The Samantabhadra Sādhana* states:

> This [human] liberty and opportunity[354] is very unstable,
> And it is difficult for worldly people to meet the holy.
> Therefore, you should achieve that supreme attitude
> Which is dedicated to wisdom and method.

---

[354] *dal 'byor* = *kṣaṇa-sampat* = eight liberties and ten opportunities of the perfectly endowed precious human life.

According to this, it is extremely difficult to find [a human life endowed with] liberty and opportunity, and further [such a life] is enormously tenuous, and having met with a holy savior it is extremely difficult to find accomplishment on a pure path—finding certitude about this pattern, you must make [such] accomplishment the essential [purpose of life]. Moreover, since [such] accomplishment is [found via] the supreme Vajra Vehicle, and since we have seen that it is necessary to practice that beginning from the first stage, then regarding the place where you should practice that [first stage], that same [text] states:

> On the side of a mountain
> Adorned by supremely beautiful trees,
> With very pure water and perfect trees,
> You should practice the lord called Mañjughoṣha.

So, in an isolated, pleasant place you should perform Mañjuvajra, etc.; in your dwelling {403b} you should anoint [yourself] with sandalwood, etc., strew flowers, and equip [yourself] with implements such as vajra, bell, etc.

There, at the beginning of the session, if it serves as a complement to your samādhi, you should perform an ablution; but if it makes no difference [to your samādhi] to omit it, then that also is appropriate. Since Saroruha[355] and Kṛiṣhṇachārya[356] stated that preliminarily one should offer a votary cake, at the start [of the actual session] you should meditate Vajrasattva and repeat the one-hundred syllable [mantra], as the mentors of the past preferred, in order to make up for lapses in your commitments and [possible] failure [to offer] the votary cake.

The key points regarding the body are as follows: *The Commentary on The [Vajra] Pavilion [Tantra]*[357] states that you should sit in the vajra position on a comfortable seat in a meditation hut, with your hands in the

---

[355] Saroruha = *Saras* + *ruha*, "lake born" (Tib. *mtsho skyes*). While *mtsho skyes* is usually the Tibetan translation for the Sanskrit name Saroruha, it also can be the translation for Sāgara and (especially when *mtsho skyes rdo rje*) for Padmavajra.

[356] Kṛiṣhṇāchārya is also known as Kanhapa.

[357] *The Commentary on The [Vajra] Pavilion [Tantra]* (cited here by Tsong Khapa only as the *gur 'grel*) is likely Tōh. 1194, by Indrabhūti.

equanimity [position]; and the brahmin Bhṛiṅgāra[358] explains that letting your eyes fall on the tip of the nose, with your teeth slightly separated, you should keep your body immovable. Regarding the direction you should face, Vitapāda explains that in [practicing] *The Esoteric Community* one faces east, but that in [practicing] *Supreme Bliss* one faces south, etc.; so you should [orient yourelf] in accordance with your scripture.

Then, there are many places in which there is no clear explanation about placing a seed [syllable] in your heart and creating yourself as a deity; however, there are also very many places in which there is the placing of the seed [syllable] of a temporary principal deity. So, [as an example of the former, Abhayākaragupta's] *Clusters of Instructions* says that having created yourself as a temporary principal deity, and having purified that in emptiness, you then perform the instantaneous creation together with the mother; whereas [as an example of the latter] Lavapa explains that you make the light rays of the seed [syllable] in your heart pervade [yourself throughout]—from within your body out to the tips of your body hairs—and that thereby {404a} you will produce the pride of yourself having become a desire[-realm] deity. Thus, either way [with or without a seed syllable] is appropriate.

Shrī Phalavajra explains that [as an intermediate step, before arising as a deity,] a hand-symbol marked with a seed [syllable] arises from the seed [syllable] at the heart, but many others explain a seed [syllable] without a hand-symbol, so again it can be done either way. [Moreover,] for Shrī Phalavajra there is a deity host[359] which emanates from the tips of the light rays of the seed [syllable]; for Lavapa, etc., the deity host is clarified by the light rays; and for Abhaya, etc., the deity host is invited by the light rays. [So again,] since there are many [different] explanations, there is no one definite approach.

With regard to inviting [the deities], the twelfth cluster [of Abhayākaragupta's *Clusters of Instructions*] explains that, in the way that one splits off a second [flame] from a single lamp, you summon [the deities] from Akanishṭha into the space nearby in front of yourself; and that

---

[358] Bhṛiṅgāra has two entries in the Tengyur: Tōh. 1482, 2137.

[359] *tshogs zhing*. See note 300 above.

having summoned [them] you then retract the light rays [back] into the seed [syllable].

Regarding the deity host, many such as Lavapa and [Abhaya's] *Clusters of Instructions*, etc., explain that it takes the pattern of whichever mandala circle is the object of your meditation, but Jñānapāda, etc., take it to be in terms of general buddhas and bodhisattvas, so [again] there is no one definite [approach]. *The Vajra Pavilion* states:

> Make offerings to the mentor who holds the vajra,
> Perform the seven-fold purification,
> Conceive the spirit of enlightenment—

This states that you accumulate the stores [of merit and intuition] in relation to the deity host, and here it also explains that the mentor is the deity host; {404b} and many [texts] such as *The Commentary on The [Vajra] Pavilion [Tantra]*[360] explain that the mentor and the lord of the mandala are to be taken as not different; and Lavapa explains that you should meditate [the mentor] as Vajrasattva adorned with all ornaments sitting upon a jewelled throne with a lotus [cushion] in front of the lord of the charnel grounds to the east of the mandala.[361]

Regarding the seven[-fold] purification, *The Commentary [on The Vajra Pavilion Tantra]* explains that this consists of: confession of sins, rejoicing [in your own and others' virtues], dedication, going for refuge, requesting [teaching], invitation [to the deities to stay], and relying on the path.[362] If you make offerings before those [seven], many texts explain

---

360 See note 357 above.

361 In Unexcelled Yoga Tantra in general there are eight charnel ground lords, and Indra normally presides over the eastern charnel ground. However, since Lavapa was a Chakrasaṁvara yogī, this may be a reference to the main protector of that mandala, namely the Skeleton Couple (Kiṅkara).

362 This "sevenfold purification" (*bdun po rnam par dag pa*) appears to be an alternate name for the "sevenfold rite" (*saptāṅga-pūjā*), also known as the "unexcelled rite" (*anuttara-pūjā*). The list of seven given here is somewhat atypical. A more standard list within the Indo-Tibetan traditions is: salutation, offering, confession, rejoicing, requesting teaching, inviting to stay, and dedication. For a discussion of the history and the variations of this sevenfold rite, see Crosby & Skilton (trans.), *The Bodhicaryāvatāra*, Oxford: Oxford University Press, 1995, pp. 8–13.

that it is the goddesses that emanate from the seed [syllable] at your heart that make the inner and outer offerings, etc.

Regarding going for refuge: there are many descriptions of going for refuge which are common to the two Universal Vehicles [exoteric and esoteric], but the sādhanas by Lavapa and Saroruha describe going for refuge by taking the lord of the mandala to be the Buddha Jewel, the mantras and mūdras described by him to be the Dharma Jewel, and the deities of the retinue to be the Saṅgha Jewel. The twelfth chapter of *The Vajraḍāka* and the fourth chapter of the third section of *The Kiss* state that in these contexts [of going for refuge] you should uphold the vows of the five clans, and thus you should uphold [your vows] singling out both common and extraordinary vows; and Buddhaguhya explains you must do this as the method of strengthening the vows you have taken. {405a}

Then, Lavapa explains that according to a statement in the *[Hevajra Tantra in] Two Sections*, you also should meditate on the four immeasurables,[363] and that after that, thinking that you have been blessed by those [four], you should recite the hundred syllable [mantra]. Then, Shrīdhara, etc., explain, you should invite the deity host to depart, and Lavapa explains that you should imagine that they disappear; but the majority of others are unclear about what you should do [regarding the deity host].

[Abhayākaragupta's] *Clusters of Instructions* explains:

> You should recite while realizing the meaning of those [preliminaries].[364]

Thus, [while reciting the preliminaries described above,] without coming at all under the influence of dullness or distraction, you must master being continuously engaged without being interrupted by other concepts except for the thoughts of the specific context, and, with the meanings of those [thoughts] taking the form of arising clearly in your mind, you should not just generally wander through the words. In order for things to go like that, first you must gain certainty about the count and the sequence of

[363] Immeasurable love, compassion, sympathetic joy, and impartiality.

[364] Abhaya's admonition at this point in his *Clusters* comes after he has described a long list of preliminaries similar to those discussed here in the *NRC*.

what is to be meditated, and you must practice having projected a intense resolve, thinking, "I should not let it go any other way!" However, if you were to practice [just] by concluding whatever [parts you wanted], it would not be suitable; so you should understand that in all cases you should divide [the recitation] into short segments, and then practice accordingly the resultant pieces.

[Accumulating the Store of Intuition]

Shāntipa's *Realization of the Black Enemy [of Death]*[365] and [Abhaya's] *Clusters of Instructions*, etc., explain that those [preliminaries discussed above] are the accumulation of the store of merit, and that meditation on emptiness is the accumulation of [the store of] intuition. Thus the store of intuition {405b} is meditation on the import of the mantra "*[OṀ] shūnyatā...*," etc., or "*[OṀ] svabhāva...*," etc. Here, the mantrin, having perceived that sentient beings are tightly bound by the net of views, thinks "Oh! Although these beings have the nature of nirvana, through such a darkness of delusion they themselves do not realize it—I should make them realize their own nature!" and he [thereby] meditates on the ultimate spirit of enlightenment. *The Samantabhadra [Sādhana]* states:

> Perceiving with compassion that this entire world
> Is bound in the net of [unrealistic] views,
> In this way the mantrin should meditate
> The authentic, unequalled spirit of enlightenment.

[The meaning of OṀ shūnyatā-jñāna-vajra-svabhāva ātmako 'haṁ]

Regarding that [mantra], *Shūnyatā* is emptiness: since things lack a nature and a cause and an effect,[366] they are empty of those [qualities].

---

365 *dgra nag gi mngon rtogs*. It is not clear what text Tsong Khapa is citing here. There is no text in the Derge Tengyur by Ratnākarashānti (rin chen 'byung gnas zhi ba) that has both the words *dgra nag* and *mngon rtogs* in the title. The most likely candidate by him is *The Blossoming Kumudā Flower: A Sādhana of the Black Enemy of Death Tantra* (Tōh. 1935), which could be abbreviatated as *dgra nag gi sgrub thabs* (indeed, Tsong Khapa appears to be using this abbreviation for this text below, at 427a).

366 These three correspond respectively to the three doors of liberation: emptiness, signlessness, and wishlessness. *rang bzhin dang bral ba = stong pa nyid* (*śūnyatā*), *rgyu dang*

(cont'd)

Jñāna is the mind that is of one taste with that emptiness, which is emptiness and signless[ness] and wishless[ness].

Vajra is adamantine, which is just that inseparability of both the object, emptiness, and the subject, intuition; [it is adamantine] because it is not destroyed by resistances, it overcomes resistances, and it has no beginning or end. Just as the reality realm has no beginning or end, so one can also metaphorically say the same thing about the mind that perceives it; because, since it perceives suchness, it is the same as it in kind.

Svabhāva is intrinsic reality—that is, purity {406a} with respect to intrinsic reality[367]—because it abides as the intrinsic reality free of incidental stains.

Ātmaka is nature, and *Ahaṁ* is "I." [So the last part of the mantra means:] "That which is the nature which is pure with respect to intrinsic reality, I am precisely that!"

Therefore, although the phrase "intuition of emptiness" [*shūnyatā-jñāna*] expresses a general subjectivity that is one's own realization of emptiness, it also expresses a strong orientation toward the ultimacy of the intrinsic identity of reality.[368] Furthermore, the term "adamantine" [*vajra*] is oriented toward ultimate purity, and the term "intrinsic reality" [*svabhāva*], even when [speaking] ultimately, [means] purity [emptiness] of intrinsic reality, which [pure intrinsic reality] lacks anything extra;[369]

---

bral ba = *mtshan nyid med pa* (*animitta*), and *'bras bu dang bral ba* = *smon pa med pa* (*aprahanitā*). These three come up in the next sentence.

367 *rang bzhin gyis rnam par dag pa nyid* = "purity with respect to intrinsic reality" = "emptiness with respect to intrinsic reality" = "emptiness of intrinsic reality" = "lack of intrinsic reality." Tsong Khapa here presents the classic Centrist formulation that the intrinsic reality of things is their lack of intrinsic reality.

368 *chos nyid kyi rang gi mtshan nyid kyi mthar thug par lhag par mos pa yin.*

369 *mthar thug pa'i dus na yang rang bzhin rnam dag la lhag po med pa.* (Note that the term *rang bzhin rnam dag* in this phrase translates the Sanskrit *svabhāva-śuddaḥ* which is present in the other mantra: *OṀ* *<u>svabhāva-śuddhaḥ</u>* *sarva-dharmāḥ* *<u>svabhāva-śuddho</u>* *'haṁ*). All versions of the text attest *lhag <u>po</u>* (not just *lhag pa*); so rather than translating this as a verbal (adj., adv., etc.), I am translating this here as a substantive, "an [implied] extra thing." In the final phrase I am reading the syntax as in *X la Y med*, "X does not have Y." So X (*rang bzhin rnam dag*) is doing double duty—predicate of the first phrase, and subject of the second—as if it read: *rang bzhin gyi dgra ni rang bzhin rnam dag yin, rang bzhin rnam dag la lhag po med.*)

(cont'd)

and the terms "nature" [*ātmakaḥ*] and "I" [*ahaṁ*], in their very purity, are established as purity with respect to intrinsic reality. That is the presentation of Shāntipa's ideas.

The syllable *OṀ* is comprised of the three letters *A*, *U*, and *Ṁ*, which are one's body, speech, and mind, and the actuality of the single taste of emptiness and compassion of those three is defined as its nature.

Moreover, *The Samantabhadra [Sādhana]* sets forth the three [doors of] liberation:

> Since [things] lack an essence, they are empty;
> Likewise, since they lack a cause, they are signless;[370]
> Since they are free from conceptualizations, [one] is surely
> liberated
> From any wish for anything at all.

—at the end of which there is an expression of the previous mantra [*OṀ shūnyatā-jñāna*...]; so this verse shows the meaning of that mantra.

Regarding the way in which this meditation on the meaning of the mantra "*Shūnya*...," etc., {406b} involves meditation on the meaning of the three doors of liberation, Vitapāda presents the three—'emptiness,' 'signless[ness],' and 'wishless[ness]'—as being distinct on the verbal level, but he states that on the ultimate level just 'empty of essence' alone

---

This is a very important passage, for it *could* be construed to show a very non *gzhan stong* view being propounded by Ratnākarashānti: because "purity" is almost always synonymous with "emptiness" (a lacking) in these contexts, and so here he is saying that *even when speaking ultimately* the term "intrinsic reality" really means "*lack* of intrinsic reality," and it does *not* imply that there is anything that exceeds such a purely negational lack (that is, on this reading, he would be propounding emptiness as an absolute negation, not a choice negation). On the other hand, it seems that one *could* find a *gzhan stong* reading here; for one can render *svabhāva-śuddhaḥ* (*rang bzhin rnam dag*) as "natural purity" (instead of "purity *of* intrinsic nature"), and one certainly could read *lhag po* as *gzhan* and *med pa* as *stong pa*, such that *lhag po med pa* = *gzhan stong* (lack of anything extra = empty of anything extrinsic), and then the whole phrase could be rendered "natural purity is extrinsically empty [that is, empty of other]." However, in the next definition we *do* have the phrase *rang bzhin gyis rnam par dag pa nyid*, "purity with respect to intrinsic reality."

[370] The Derge Tibetan has *rang bzhin rgyu*... instead of *de bzhin rgyu*..., which changes the meaning of this line to "Because they lack an intrinisc cause, they are signless."

incorporates the other two. [This statement] agrees with the statement of the savior Nāgārjuna in the *Accumulations for Enlightenment*:[371]

> Since [things] lack intrinsic reality, they are empty;
> Being empty, how could they have signs?
> Since all signs have been eliminated,
> Why would the wise wish [for anything]?

Therefore, although three [doors] are set forth, the [door of the] liberation of emptiness alone includes the other two.[372]

Furthermore, using the reasoning of the lack of unity or plurality, Vitapāda and Shrī Phalavajra set forth the import that is determined to be the identitylessness of things; thus the penetrative view regarding the identitylessness of things—the object brought to mind in this context—is *shūnyatā* [emptiness], whereas the subjectivity is *jñāna* [intuition].

Once you have reversed the function of subject-object differentiation governed by misknowledge regarding just that [*shūnyatā-jñāna*], when you have entered into [their] inseparability, like water poured into water, that is *vajra*.

Although that understanding must newly generate the realization of the indivisible, unelaborated nature of things, [still] the pure nature—wherein one cannot in reality individually distinguish object and subject—exists indistinguishably [as much] in the fruitional [newly achieved] as in the causal [previously unachieved] stage,[373] {407a} and thus it is *svabhāva* [the "*intrinsic* nature"].

---

[371] This text is the **Bodhisaṁbhāra[ka]*, ascribed to Nāgārjuna, and extant only in Chinese as the *pú tí zī liáng lùn* (Taisho 1660; the verse cited here is v. 64, appearing at iv 532a.19–.20). Chr. Lindtner notes that "the fact that the scope of the text was known to Bu-ston...renders it likely that a Tibetan version may have existed, and perhaps still does" (*Master of Wisdom*, p. 305; special thanks to Paul Hackett for the above citations). This apparently well-known verse is cited also in several other indigenous Tibetan texts; and the same verse is quoted in Candrakīrti's *Bodhisattva-yogācāra-catuḥśataka-ṭīkā* (Tōh. 3864; Derge vol. 103, YA), at folio 191a.3–4.

[372] And hence the meditation on emptiness involved in the use of the mantra *OṀ shūnyatā*... also automatically entails meditation on signlessness and wishlessness.

[373] That is, fom the ultimate perspective, there is no distinction between the time when one *has* achieved it (= fruitional stage) and the time when one is *striving* to achieve it (= causal stage). So although the realization (the subjectivity) of the nature of things (the object realized) appears to be generated anew, paradoxically, since the "object" to be realized (the

(cont'd)

That [intrinsically empty nature] abiding naturally in yourself,[374] and also yourself not existing as some thing separate from that [empty nature]—such is the meaning of *ātmaka* ["nature"] and *ahaṁ* ["I"].[375]

That [above analysis] is an explanation in which the three liberations [are presented] as the meaning of the mantra. Alternatively, it can be explained in terms of the mantras of the three vajras. *OṀ* is the body-vajra. "The intrinsic nature which is the vajra of the intuition of emptiness" [*shūnyatā-jñāna-vajra-svabhāva*] indicates the mind-vajra; that is obvious. The reason why "I am" [*ahaṁ*] is posited as the speech-vajra is that since the self is without substance it is mere linguistic designation.

Alternately, the meaning of the mantra can be explained in terms of the five clans. *OṀ* is the mirror-like intuition. 'Emptiness' [*shūnyatā*] is the equalizing intuition. 'Intuition' [*jñāna*] is the individuating intuition. '*Vajra*' is the [all-]accomplishing intuition. 'Nature' [*svabhāva*] is the extremely pure intuition.[376] The final two [words, *ātmako 'ham*,] definitively show the natural self (*bdag nyid*) to be the actuality of the great Vajradhara who is the nature (*bdag nyid*) of the five intuitions.

Those [latter] two explanations are no more than understandings arrived at by applying separate differentials[377] to the [explanation of the] intuition that amounts to emptiness in the former explanation of the meaning of the mantra. Moreover, that all three explanations are statements made by the Lord himself in the Tantras is explained and made clear [by Abhaya] in *The Clusters of Instructions*.

---

pure nature) is not something which can be expressed in terms of object/subject duality, one cannot really distinguish between a before (ignorant subject) and an after (awakened subject). This is a very interesting point: in this context (realization of the nature of things) cancelling subject/object dichotomy necessarily cancels temporal cause/effect dichotomy. In a sense one has "always" realized the pure nature—it cannot be "attained"—which is precisely why it is called "nature."

374 *bdag nyid la* (here: "in one's self"). It also may be that *bdag nyid* is here being used in the sense of "nature" (Tib. *dag nyid* also translates Skt. *ātmakaḥ*) such that Tsong Khapa is somehow glossing equivalent terms (e.g., "That [*svabhāva*] naturally abides as the self-nature [*ātmakaḥ*]").

375 This again would seem to completely reject a *gzhan stong* view.

376 Here the "extremely pure intuition" (*viśuddhi-jñāna*) is short for the more common "extremely pure Reality-realm intuition" (*dharmadhātu-viśuddhi-jñāna*).

377 Tib. *ldog pa [= apoha] so sor phye ba*.

[The meaning of OṀ svabhāva-shuddha-sarvadharmāḥ svabhāva-shuddho 'haṁ]

The Kiss [Tantra] and *The Four Seats [Tantra]* say in this context:

> First, reflecting upon emptiness
> Will wash away the stains of embodied beings. {407b}

...and so on. Since [these Tantras] state that it is determined that the eighteen elements lack intrinsic reality, and since many Indian treatises also have taught the view of selflessness in this context, then when considering the import of the mantra *[OṀ] Svabhāva...*, etc., the claim that 'the import of this [mantra] is not the view realizing identitylessness but is rather the meditation of gross dualistic perception vanishing like a rainbow' does *not* reflect the intent of any of the Tantras or authentic treatises. As Shāntipa states [in his *Commentary on [Dīpaṅkarabhadra's] The Four Hundred and Fifty Verses*]:

> Furthermore, other blessing mantras should be understood according to this verbal meaning of "*vajra-svabhāva-ātmako 'haṁ*."

So although the words may differ, the meaning of mantras that indicate emptiness such as *svabhāva-shuddha*, etc., should be recalled from what was previously explained. Many such as Shāntipa and Vitapāda explain that this mantra has the functions of stabilizing and blessing, so after you have first clearly recollected the meaning of the mantra, you should bless with that mantra.

* * *

When by means of the individuating wisdom you have determined that all the things of saṁsāra and nirvana are not established ultimately, then even though [this analytic determination in itself] does not reverse the dualistic perception with respect to the objects which appear to that mind, still, since the [very] import of [such determined] certain knowledge [does entail] the reversal of dualistic perception, you do not need [to develop some] further additional apprehension of the thorough pacification of dualistic perception. Accordingly, you should develop certainty, thinking 'All things are free of the two extremes, they have the characteristic of lacking intrinsic reality, {408a} they are the reality realm free of all [mental] elaborations'; so, as [Shāntideva] states in *Engaging in the Bodhisattvas'*

Way of Life, all things have a non-objectifiable nature and are radically immersed in emptiness:[378]

> When neither something nor nothing
> Remains before the mind,
> Then, since there is no other alternative,
> There is radical peace, free of objectification. (IX.34)

Well, you may wonder, [if the above mentioned analytically determined certitude is sufficient,] then what is the purpose of meditation on emptiness here [in the creation stage]?

[Answer:] [Ratnākarashānti's] *The Blossoming Kumudā Flower: A Sādhana of the Black Enemy [of Death Tantra]* states that the Lord is created both by the store of merit, first, and then later by the store of intuition; and Kamalarakṣhita[379] describes that as the supreme [way] of guarding against obstructions. Now while those do indeed comprise a partial [explanation of the] purpose [of meditation on emptiness], as for the principal purpose: as will be explained later, while the [creative] meditations are for the upholding of the pride of the form body, the upholding of the that pride is required to empower the direct realization of the truth body; so that is the point of it. This is corroborated by the Adept Ḍoṁbipa's explanation [in his *Nairātmya Sādhana*] that once one has entered into emptiness, one re-emerges [only] due to the recollection of one's previous prayerful vow:[380]

> The yogin should recollect the prayerful vow,
> Made prior to the meditation on natural emptiness.

---

[378] This is verse IX.34 in the Tibetan editon (verse IX.35 in the Sanskrit). For an extended discussion of this verse, with reference to Indian and Tibetan commentaries, see Williams 1998, pp. 21–28.

[379] Tsong Khapa does not indicate here which of Kamalarakṣhita's texts he is referencing, nor does he do so any of the other times he mentions him. Kamalarakṣhita wrote the following five texts: Tōh. 1932, 1934, 1947, 1952, all *Yamāri* texts, and Peking 4802 (Dharma Index supplemental No. 4713), a *Vajrabhairava Sādhana*.

[380] In other words, the relative spirit of enlightenment of love and compassion for beings creates a power or momentum that pushes a realizer of emptiness toward buddhahood, and does not just leave him stuck in an isolated experience of emptiness (like an Individual Vehicle saint). This reinforces Tsong Khapa's main point that the relative meditations on the form body deepen the realization of the truth body.

—and this likewise is corroborated by statements in Saroruha's *[Hevajra] Sādhana* and in Ghaṇṭāpa's *Hevajra Sādhana [Sole Hero]*, etc. {408b}

Furthermore, you withdraw all perceptions into the clear light so that you may arise as a deity; and there also is a need for all the subsequent visionary meditations to arise like illusion, etc., through the force of the intense certainty generated in your previous view. The lack of perceptions when you have entered into emptiness is nonconceptual intuition; and—as explained in [Ratnākarashānti's] *Hevajra Sādhana, "An Elimination of Errors"*—the arisal from there into the perception of the defense perimeter meditation has the nature of a pure mundane intuition;[381] though [here] the defense perimeter is just an example, so [in fact] all the perceptions of the habitats and the inhabitants—the things to be imagined as taking form, which arise here and there—also are the objects of nondualistic intuition; this is very important. Therefore, since there are many [reasons why it is] necessary to meditate emptiness here [in the creation stage], you should meditate it until you find a fierce certitude [about it], which will [not happen] in a very short time![382]

---

381 In Ratnākarashānti's sādhana, his description of the perception of the defense perimeter arising as "a pure mundane intuition" (*dag pa 'jig rten pa'i ye shes*) occurs directly after the emptiness mantra *OṀ śūnyatā-jñāna-vajra*.... Here, his qualification "*pure* mundane" would seem to be equivalent to the qualification "extraordinary" (*thun mong ma yin pa*)—and hence "nondual' (*gnyis med*)—used in other Tantric treatises (cf. the discussion above, surrounding p. 190, note 336, regarding the idea that the the mandala-mind is extraordinary both because it has an unconventional, enlightened form, and because it simultaneously and nondually is perceived/conceived as being empty). Thus, the perceptions evoked in a sādhana likewise can be described as "pure mundane": "mundane" or "worldly" in the sense that they still are perceived forms, but "pure" in the sense that these forms simultaneously and nondually are perceived as lacking intrinsic reality, that is, as being empty. Thus, at the end of this sentence, as an equivalent gloss of Ratnākarashānti's phrase "perception [that]...has the nature of *a pure mundane intuition*," Tsong Khapa substitutes the phrase "perceptions [that]...are objects of *nondualistic intuition*" (*snang ba...gnyis su med pa'i ye shes kyi gzung ba*).

382 *yun ha cang thung ba min pa'i nges pa drag po rnyed kyi bar du bsgom par bya'o*. It seems that this should read *ma rnyed kyi bar du bsgom par bya'o* (a standard idiom, hence our emendation; though none of our editions do read that way).

[**II.B.2.c.ii.C'3'c'ii'B''4''a''ii''A°1°b°** – The defense perimeter which clears away adverse conditions]

In the aftermath of such meditation on emptiness and before the meditation on the defense perimeter you either can meditate or not meditate on the syllables which symbolize the between state. The first [option] can be done in three ways; as the twelfth cluster [of Abhayākaragupta's *Clusters of Instructions*] states:

> There is a case in which a seed [syllable] is sandwiched between two red *HOḤ* syllables, or a case in which there are three letters, or [a case in which] there is just the *nāda*—each of these three ways {409a} is done for the sake of creating the body, speech, and mind.

Thus, this presents a syllable *HŪṀ* between two *HOḤ* syllables; the three [syllables] *OṀ ĀḤ HŪṀ*; and just the *nāda*. Moreover, those who do not meditate like that, [in one of those three ways,] explain that they use as appropriate the [same] syllables that they later use to create the lord, whereas those who follow Lūipa explain that they place just the *nāda* until they have created the base support of the defense perimeter.

Regarding the ordinary defense perimeter: from *RAṀ* there arises a sun; and from a *HŪṀ*, which is on that, there arises a crossed vajra, the center of which is marked with a *HŪṀ*, from which light rays radiate. [Those light rays] are like the [supernova] fire at the time of [cosmic] destruction, and they are explained to be like a blazing [forcefield-]wall of vajras, and also like a dome, etc.[383] Abhaya and Samantabhadra assert that those very light rays which are radiated turn into vajras [like bullets] and make up the wall, etc.; and all of those [vajra bullets], moreover, are explained by *The Further [Tantra of the Esoteric Community]* to be crossed

[383] From the circular vajra ground the vajra forcefield rises up with cylindrical walls (the "wall" [*prākāra, rva ba*] part), and it is capped with a hemispherical roof (the "dome" or "pavilion" [*pañjara, gur*] part). Monier Williams (p. 703) says that a *prākāra* is "esp. a surrounding wall elevated on a mound of earth...." The militaristic connotation of this definition helps to justify the militaristic translation of *srung 'khor* as "defense perimeter." Regarding the supernova flames: many commentaries explain that these flames are not unrelated to the vajra forcefield; they are in fact radiated out from the forcefield. These flames burn up any elementals that might have been able to penetrate the vajra forcefield.

vajras. The *[Hevajra Tantra in] Two Sections* agrees with this when it states:[384]

> On that sun is a *HŪṀ*, [from which] emerge crossed vajras, and
> Those very [crossed] vajras bind themselves into a wall and
> A dome—thus you should contemplate.

Abhaya asserts that it is a seamless whole and [that the ends of the vajra-crosses are each] five pointed. Abhaya asserts that you meditate that above there is Akaṇiṣhṭha and that below it rests upon a golden ground; {409b} but Lavapa states that with respect to its size it is as big as the practitioner wants, and that the shape of the wall is square.[385] You make the dome on top, and on top of the wall which is under that [dome] a [flat] canopy ceiling, and outside above and around the sides a [forcefield] network of [vajra] arrows. It is clear that Prajñārakṣhita's explanation[386] that one makes a network of arrows that have the form of five-pronged vajras is [an explanation which is describing] the shape of the arrow-heads.[387] Outside of all that, you should imagine that there is a wall of [supernova] flames.

Regarding the special defense perimeter, which is a defense perimeter wherein you place [yourself as] a [Vajra-]hūṁkara[388] in the hub of a ten-spoked golden wheel, and the ten Fierce Ones on the ten spokes: Abhaya asserts that that is common to the majority [of sādhanas]. This is a meditation in which the lord of the defense perimeter is inside the hub of the [wheel's] spokes—since the twelfth cluster [of Abhayākaragupta's *Clusters of Instructions*] mentions:

---

384 *Hevajratantra* I.3.3. Cp. Farrow and Menon, p. 39.

385 *Chakrasaṁvara* has a square wall.

386 Prajñārakṣhita has forty-five texts in the Tengyur. Tsong Khapa here is referring more likely to discussions scattered throughout this entire corpus than to one particular text. Later on (429b), Tsong Khapa does explicitly reference Prajñārakṣhita's commentary (Tōh. 1465) on Lūipa's *Chakrasaṁvara Sadhana*, so it is possible here that he is referencing that text as well.

387 Arrows with five-pronged vajra tips. Typically these would be "vajra bullets," just the *tips* of the arrows, i.e., the arrow-heads alone (with no shafts), shooting around at light speed.

388 *HŪṀ mdzad*—this is a reference to the deity Vajrahūṁkara (or Shumbharājā, *gnod mdzes rgyal po*, a.k.a. Yakṣharāja, *gnod sbyin rgyal po*), who is the source of the ten fierce deities mentioned next.

> ...the great being who abides in the space which is at the center of the hub of the ten spokes...

And:

> ...below the great being who is inside the hub of the wheel...

[And] since [it also] states that the four elements are created therein, it shows that the hub has an empty space inside. Then, taking the upper and lower points which are inside the hub to be the upper and lower spokes,[389] and having set the upper and lower Fierce Ones on those two,[390] you should arrange the other eight in the directions and quarters without [them] touching the spokes. Abhaya asserts that the golden wheel spins clockwise with a fierce motion, not stopping even slightly, and that it radiates the light of a blazing fire. However, Ḍombipa says that the lord of the defense perimeter is [Vajra]hūṁkara, {410a} and does not discuss any spinning of the wheel; but when [he says] Uṣhṇīṣhachakravartirājā is the lord [when using the wheel] to reverse [curses],[391] [he says] the wheel spins counterclockwise. [And Ḍombipa's] *The Tenfold Thatness* states that when meditating at the time of sleep you recite the mantras such as "*Namaḥ samanta...*," etc., seven times.

If the harm of obstructor demons is small, then the common [defense perimeter] will do; but if it is great, then you should meditate [the special one with] the ten Fierce Ones together with their retinues, summon the obstructor demons, and transfix them with the ritual stake, etc. If

---

389 The upper and lower "spokes" are actually like an axis, one going upwards and the other downwards from the center. Then there are the eight spokes connecting the rim and hub within the two-dimensional plane of the wheel. The whole object looks like a gyroscope. The ten "spokes" represent the "ten directions," which indicate "everywhere" in Indian and Tibetan convention. Unlike a gyroscope, which spins steadily on a central axis such that the wheel part spins only in a two-dimensional plane, this whole protection wheel spins wildly in all directions (the laws of physical motion not applying in emptiness). The idea is that any negative entity that somehow gets past the outer flames and vajra wall and then gets in to the interior, from any angle, will be chopped up by the wildly spinning spoke-blades.

390 Uṣhṇīṣhachakravartirājā (*gtsug tor 'khor los sgyur ba'i rgyal po*) is above and Shumbharājā (*gnod mdzes rgyal po*) is below.

391 *phyir zlog*.

the obstructor demons have great magical powers, then you should very intensely [practice] emptiness and the defense perimeter; but if that which is to be defended against gets inside of the defense perimeter, then you must employ the policy of putting the created mandala inside the hub of the spokes, as I have explained before.[392]

[**II.B.2.c.ii.C'3'c'ii'B''4''a''ii''A°2°** – The actual yoga with its components]

The second has three: **[a°]** Creation of the measureless mansion habitat; **[b°]** Creation of the deity inhabitants; **[c°]** The components which complete it.

[**II.B.2.c.ii.C'3'c'ii'B''4''a''ii''A°2°a°** – Creation of the measureless mansion habitat]

[So] there is a [special] system in which you do meditate a wheel with ten spokes, etc., and [an ordinary] one in which you do not do so.

Of those two, the party that does meditate it [creates the habitat] as follows. The Ārya tradition asserts that after the [creation of the special ten-spoked] defense perimeter you purify [everything] in emptiness; then you create the four mandalas of wind, fire, water, and earth; and then, having merged those into one, you create the vajra ground, upon which is a *BHRŪṀ*, from which you create the measureless mansion. Nāgārjuna's *Abbreviated [Practice]* states:

> You should meditate that standing in the middle of the
> realm of space
> Are two *HŪṀ* [syllables, between which is] the seed
> [syllable] *YAṀ*, from which arises
> A wind mandala. **{410b}**

The "realm of space" in that passage means the reality-source,[393] and "middle" means the lotus; and in accordance with the explanation in

---

[392] I have not yet been able to locate where Tsong Khapa previously explained this.

[393] *Dharmodaya* (*chos 'byung*). Here and in the following discussions this "reality-source" is visualized as a cosmically huge tetrahedron of white light (point down, flat on top) inside of which (about half way down) everything else will be visualized. Tsong Khapa provides a scriptural reference and description for this below (p. 216; 411b).

[Abhaya's *Vajra*] *Rosary* that a vajra-cross is created from the merging of the four elements into one, a vajra-cross is created from the four elements in the center of the reality-source and lotus, but the measureless mansion is not created from that.

Although the treatises of others of the Father and Sons [Ārya tradition] are not clear on this, [the Ārya] Nāgabodhi states [in his *Twenty Verse Esoteric Community Mandala Rite*]:

> The arched porticos have vajra points;
> Outside of that in the surrounding sphere
> Are garlands of vajras shining with beautiful light.

This clearly refers to the vajra forcefield, and thus you should meditate the reality-source, etc., in the middle of what was created: the pavilion, the [flat] ceiling, the vajra ground, and also the radiations of light.

[Regarding the Jñānapāda tradition:] In the twelfth cluster [of Abhayākaragupta's *Clusters of Instructions*] there is one [method that involves] creating the habitat without dissolving the ten spokes with their Fierce Ones, and creating the four elements together with Mount Meru inside of the hub [of that still-present defense perimeter];[394] and [another method that involves visualizing] yourself as the lord of the defense perimeter transforming into Vajradhara, and then—from a total transformation of that—creating the reality-source inside of which you create a lotus upon which is vajra-cross upon which you then create the measureless mansion.[395]

The party that does not meditate the special [ten-spoked] defense perimeter [creates the habitat] as follows. In the *Supreme Bliss [Sādhana]*

---

394 According to this first option, the four elements fuse together into a multi-colored vajra-cross, then that vajra-cross creates a Mount Meru, then upon that Mount Meru there is a lotus, then another vajra-cross, then a mansion—and *all* of that is inside the hub. Note that this particular variant is similar to what was discussed at the very end of the previous section, which dealt with how to handle particularly persistent obstructor demons (*bgegs*) by creating the whole mandala in a miniature form within the hub of the still-present defense perimeter.

395 According to this second option, *everything* (the entire defense perimeter—including the wheel and its hub—as well as oneself as Vajradhara) dissolves and then transforms into the reality-source tetrahedron, which then gives rise to the other things. So in this variant the lotus, vajra-cross, and measureless mansion are not within any hub.

by Lūipa, after the [common] defense perimeter, having arisen from the meditation on emptiness, then from the wind, fire, water, earth, Mount Meru, and vajra-cross upon which is a lotus, and upon which are the five manifest enlightenments, you simultaneously create all of the habitat and inhabitants. {411a} According to Abhaya, the intent of that [procedure of Lūipa's] is that you raise up [the mandala of the habitat and inhabitants] having created the vajra[-cross] on top of the lotus, without the reality-source. [However,] The Great Lord [Atīsha] explains that you do meditate the reality-source. According to Lūipa and his followers, you create the habitat and inhabitants at once, whereas according to [some who work with] the two *Esoteric Communities*,[396] and to Lavapa, Saroruha, and Ḍombipa, etc., you create [them] sequentially. Ḍombipa and Saroruha explain that in the *Nairatmya* [*Sādhana*] and *Hevajra Sādhana* the reality-source is inside of the common defense perimeter, and that within that you create in sequence the four elements, earth, water, fire, and wind; and that by combining as one [all of that] with your own consciousness, you then create the measureless mansion. However, it is not that [Ḍombipa and Saroruha] are not asserting that there is a lotus and a vajra-cross; because Ḍombipa's direct disciple Durjayachandra explains it that way in his *Six Branch [Sādhana]*, and in his *Superb Embrace*[397] he explains that you meditate that inside of the reality-source there is a *HRĪḤ* from which [arises] a lotus, and an *AḤ*[398] from which [arises] a vajra-cross, upon which [then arise] the four elements, and that upon that there is a *BHRŪṀ* from which [arises] the wheel. [Finally, note that] here, and also in [Ratnākarashānti's *Hevajra Sādhana,*] *An Elimination of Errors*, it is explained that you meditate that the measureless mansion is [created] from the merger of the four elements; thus there is no certitude that the creation of the measureless mansion from the melting of the elements is [a procedure found] only in the Yoga Tantra—[it is found also in Unexcelled Yoga Tantra,] however, it is something that occurs only in some places, and not always.

---

396 Cf. note 284 to 391a.

397 Tōh. 1239 and 1240, respectively. Cf. also note 306 above.

398 All three texts have short *AḤ* (not the expected long *ĀḤ*).

When there is no creation of the defense perimeter inside of which is the reality-source and the lotus and the vajra-cross and upon which is **{411b}** the measureless mansion, then there is no meditation on the sequential stacking of elements—these are the *Esoteric Community* traditions of Jñānapāda and Shrīdhara.

Regarding the way in which the reality-source is created: according to many such as Jñānapāda, etc., it is created from the melting of Samantabhadra, which is another name for "Vajradhara"; according to Lavapa, etc., it is created from [the seed syllable] *E*; according to [Ratnākarashānti's *Hevajra Sādhana,*] *An Elimination of Errors*, etc., that which [just] has the nature of Vajradhara is made to arise instantaneously in the form of the reality-source; so any of those ways is allowable.

Moreover, many [treatises] such as the *Clusters [of Instructions]*, etc., explain that the reality-source has a white color, a tetrahedral shape[399] which is narrow at the bottom and vast at the top, and is empty inside; so you should meditate the measureless mansion inside of something which has the form of an upright tetrahedron.

Also, many—such as [those of] the Ārya tradition of the *Esoteric Community*, and Lavapa, etc.—create the measureless mansion from *B[H]RUṀ,*[400] but Jñānapāda, etc., explain that from *B[H]RUṀ* there [arises] a wheel, and that from that [wheel] Vairochana arises, and that [the measureless mansion] is created from a transformation [of Vairochana]—those two clearly are brief and extensive [explanations of essentially the same process].[401]

The creation [of the measureless mansion] from the combination of the elements, and also the creation of both the inhabitants and the habitat from the five manifest enlightenments, are as already explained.

In this way, regarding the creation of the measureless mansion, you either can create it or not create it by progressively stacking the elements;

---

399 *zur gsum* literally means "triangular," but here this is a polyhedron with three sides and a base (hence a tetrahedron), with the base at the top and the point down.

400 In most contexts this always is spelled *BHRŪṀ*, but here all three *NRC* editions spell it *BRUṀ* consistently throughout this passage.

401 Clearly these are respectively brief and extensive, although Tsong Khapa reverses the terms, saying *rgyas bsdus su mngon no*. When Tsong Khapa wrote his own *Esoteric Community* sādhana he used Jñānapāda's more extensive process.

and regarding its creation, you either can create it or not create it inside the hub of the ten spokes; and the party that does not create it {412a} can either melt or not melt the elements; and regarding the melting you either can meditate the elements as [melting] in an emergent order or as [melting] in a reverse order;[402] and having melted the elements there is both the creation of the vajra-cross and the creation of the measureless mansion; and then you either can create or not create Mount Meru. Moreover, regarding the creation of the measureless mansion [itself, normally] it is created suddenly; but [to make it] vivid you should place [each individual part/deity] sequentially, that is, you should project[403] the general mental image of each individual [part/deity] with its [deity] seat.

[**II.B.2.c.ii.C'3'c'ii'B''4''a''ii''A°2°b°** – Creation of the deity inhabitants]

The second has three: [i°] The actual way of creating the deities; [ii°] The bases of purification, and homologies with the paths; and [iii°] A summary of the essential points.

[**II.B.2.c.ii.C'3'c'ii'B''4''a''ii''A°2°b°i°** – The actual way of creating the deities]

The first has two: [A°°] The way of creating [the deities] by the five manifest enlightenments; and [B°°] The way of creating [the deities], the melted [deity] having been exhorted with song.

[**II.B.2.c.ii.C'3'c'ii'B''4''a''ii''A°2°b°i°A°°** – The way of creating (the deities) by the five manifest enlightenments][404]

The Ārya Father and Sons assert that the five manifest enlightenments are the following five enlightenments: the enlightenment [that comes] from suchness, from the moon, from a seed [syllable], from a hand-symbol, and from the completed body—you should understand this

---

[402] The emergent order (*lugs 'byung*) of the elements is earth, water, fire, wind; the reverse order (*lugs ldog*) is wind, fire, water, earth.

[403] *lhongs pa* (pf. of *lhong ba*)—most dictionaries provided no relevant definition (RY had "...to transform, to dissolve"). However, THL (Richard Barron) indicates that *lhongs* can be an alternate spelling for *slong ba* (which can mean "to generate, make rise," etc.).

[404] For a good discussion of the five manifest enlightenments in the context of the creation stage, cf. *YGST* (229), and Lessing and Wayman's *Introduction* (1978, ch. 1).

from other [texts I have written]. Apart from them, the majority of others assert that [the five manifest enlightenments] are enlightements [that arise] from the five intuitions, as is stated in the third section of *The Kiss*:

> [1] The moon possesses the mirror-like intuition,
> [2] A like [moon] is equality intuition itself,[405]
> [3] The seed [syllable] and the hand-symbol of each individual deity
> Should be asserted to be individuating [intuition].
>
> [4] Everything becoming one is the all-accomplishing [intuition],[406]
> [5] And the complete reflected image is the pure [reality intuition].[407]
> The procedure declared by the experts
> You should meditate in a five-fold form.

Now, {412b} there is no certainty that a *sun* is created from the consonants—because in the context of the procedure of the creation of Vajrasattva that same [text] states that you should meditate two moons:[408]

> In the center of the moon's disk
> Enlightenment has a second moon.

---

405 *de bzhin mnyam nyid ye shes nyid*. It might seem that this line should read "suchness is equality intuition itself" (taking *de bzhin* to be short for *de bzhin nyid*). However, as Tsong Khapa stated in the sentence introducing this quote, it is the first manifest enlightenment (alluded to in the first line of this verse) that it associated with suchness (and the mirror-like intuition, represented by a "moon"). This second line, which mentions the equality intuition, alludes to the second manifest enlightenment, which is associated with a (second) moon (as will be made clear below). This agrees with what Wayman's research shows (*YGST*, 229), and with what Kaydrup states (Lessing and Wayman, 1978, 28–35). Thus, here we are reading the *de bzhin* as referring to "a like [moon]."

406 *bya nan tan = bya ba nan tan du grub pa'i ye shes* (*kṛtyānuṣṭhāna-jñāna*), lit. "earnest activity intuition."

407 *dag pa = chos kyi dbyings rnam par dag pa* (*dharmadhātu-viśuddhiḥ*).

408 As will become clear shortly, in some systems one meditates that there are two lunar disks, and in others one meditates that there is one lunar disk and one solar disk. The option of a sun being created from the consonants is discussed several paragraphs below.

[Regarding vowels and consonants:] In that same context in *The Kiss* it does not set forth more than [a single set of] sixteen vowels and thirty-four consonants. With regard to the doubling [of those letters], while Jñānapāda does not give a clear explanation,[409] Dīpaṅkarabhadra does state [in *The Mandala Rite of the Glorious Esoteric Community*]:

> The vowels are endowed with the [32 major] signs,
> [The consonants] *Ka*, etc., have the light of the [80 minor] marks,[410]

and thus [it would seem that] one should be doubling, but it is extremely unclear; and therefore Shāntipa, in his commentary on that [i.e., in his *Commentary on (Dīpaṅkarabhadra's) The Four Hundred and Fifty Verses*], [first] sets out the system of those who do not assert there is a doubling, and then gives his own system in which one does make them double. Shrīdhara also explains that one doubles.[411] Regarding the Mother Tantras, while Lavapa's and Lūipa's *[Supreme Bliss] Sādhanas*,[412] etc., explain that one doubles, Shāntipa's *Hevajra Father-Mother Sādhana ["An Elimination of Errors"]* explains that one creates from the vowels and consonants which are not doubled; whereas Ḍombipa's *Nairātmya*

---

[409] Jñānapāda does not have any commentaries in the Tengyur range pertaining to *The Kiss* (Tōh. 381; according to the Tengyur chart commentaries on this should be in the Tōh. range 1401–1606). Thus, Tsong Khapa here must be referring to Jñānapāda's works in general, or perhaps to his primary work on the creation stage (acc. *YGST*, 94), *The Samantabhadra Sādhana* (Tōh. 1855).

[410] There are fourteen long and short Sanskrit vowels. By adding anusvāra and visarga to these one can get 16 "vowels," and by doublibng that one gets 32. Likewise, with some creative additions to the 34 or 35 consonants one can get 40 "consonants," and by doubling that one gets 80.

[411] I have not yet determined which of Shrīdhara's texts discusses this. He has two commentaries (Tōh. 1540 and 1586) in the Tengyur range pertaining to *The Kiss* (Tōh. 1401–1606), neither of which appear to discuss the topic of doubling. However, there are over thirty other texts in the Tengyur attributed to Shrīdhara, one (or more) of which must discuss this.

[412] Lavapa's *Sādhanas* are Tōh. 1401 (*Cakrasaṁvara, 'khor lo sdom pa*) and 1443 (*Cakrasaṁbara, 'khor lo bde mchog*). Lūipa's *Sādhana* is Tōh. 1454 (*Vajrasattva*).

Sādhana and Durjayachandra's *Hevajra Sādhana*[413] both double and do not double—so it is unclear.

If you do meditate with doubling [the vowels and consonants], then according to Lūipa's explanation you place each of them clockwise and counter-clockwise; but Shrī Phalavajra asserts that you place white vowels on the inside and red consonants on the outside; and Vitapāda {413a} asserts that you place the vowels below and the consonants above—so those are the systems in which you previously array the vowels and consonants and *then* create [the moon]. For Shrīdhara you place the consonants upon a moon which was [already previously] created from the vowels—so any of these ways is suitable.

The Jñānapāda tradition and Shrīdhara and Lūipa declare that you create a *moon* from the consonants; but you make a *sun* according to most of the *Hevajra Father-Mother* sādhanas and according to Lavapa's *Thirteen Deity Supreme Bliss Sādhana*.[414]

Regarding the second moon: Shrīdhara and Abhaya explain that you meditate that it is red; the latter, stating that you meditate that it has the form of a full moon, explains that when *The Kiss* refers to the moon as "having the nature of a voluminous triangle"[415] that it is a case of [an effect] being designated with the name of the cause,[416] since a lily-white moon which is symbolized by *A*[417] is being created within the triangular reality-source.

---

[413] This again must be a reference either to Durjayachandra's *Six Branch [Sādhana]* (Tōh. 1239), or to his *Superb Embrace* (Tōh. 1240), as these are the only two relevant texts which he wrote in the *Hevajra* range (1180–1345). Cf. notes 306 and 397 above.

[414] Lavapa wrote several *Supreme Bliss (Chakrasaṁvara)* sādhanas and sādhana commentaries: Tōh. 1401, 1443, 1444. None of the titles specify thirteen deities.

[415] Tōh. 381; Lhasa 396 (ga): 390a: *bcom ldan zla ba'i dkyil 'khor gyi, ,yon tan khyad par ji ltar lags, ,bcom ldan 'das kyis bka' stsal pa, ,gru gsum rgya cher rang bzhin can, ,* Here in the phrase *gru gsum rgya che* it could be that *rgya che* (lit. "greatly vast") is how Tibetans specify that the triangle is three-dimensional (that is, a tetrahedron)—literally perhaps "spacious" or "volumetric."

[416] *rgyu'i ming gis 'bras bu la btags pa* = an effect designated with the name of the cause. This is a standard phrase; here in an abbreviated form omitting *'bras bu la*.

[417] All three editions have *mtshon* ("symbolized"), not *mtshan* (which might be expected and would mean "a moon *marked* with an *A*"), so I have translated accordingly.

Regarding the reason why the vowels are doubled: in [Abhaya's] *Clusters of Instructions* it is explained that the sixteen vowels represent the sixteen parts of the seminal essence of the places within the body, and that by dividing those into art and wisdom one gets thirty-two, and that it is for that reason that the vowel syllables also are doubled. [Abhaya] cites [the *Supreme Bliss Tantra* (?)]:[418]

> The Lord said:
>
> The syllable *A* is at the root of the big toe,
> The syllable *Ā* is in the calves,
> The syllable *I* {413b} is in the pair of thighs,
> The syllable *Ī* is at the secret place.
>
> The syllable *U* is at the root of the navel,
> The syllable *Ū* is in the upper stomach.
> The syllable *Ṛ* is in the center of the breast,
> The syllable *Ṝ* is likewise in the hands/arms.
>
> The syllable *Ḷ* is in the place of the throat,
> The syllable *Ḹ* abides on the lips,
> The syllable *E* is on the sides of the cheeks,
> The syllable *AI* is in the eyes.
>
> The syllable *O* is at the root of the ears,
> The syllable *AU* abides thoroughly in the head.
> *Ṁ* and *Ḥ* remain on the crown,
> According to experts you should contemplate like that.
>
> On the white side they are placed like this,
> On the black [side] [they are placed] like that in reverse.[419]
> For women this is the vajra-mind,
> And also for men, at all times.

---

[418] At the end of this quote we simply get *zhes drangs te*. It is unclear what text Abhaya is citing here. It could be the *Laghu-Chakrasaṁvara*, since after the quote it says that the *Saṁvarodaya (sdom 'byung)* agrees with it, and since the *sdom 'byung* is a commentary on *Chakrasaṁvara*. However, I have not yet found this passage in any text.

[419] In other words, you array the letters from head down to toe instead.

—and what is stated in the *Arisal of Saṁvara [Tantra]*, etc., also agrees with that. [Ratnarakṣhita's] *Commentary on The Arisal of Saṁvara [Tantra]* states:

> Regarding "the left," which is '*the white side*': relying on the left side of the body one has [the letters] ascend from the big toe to the crown; and regarding '*the black side*': relying on the right side of the body one has [the letters] descend from the crown to the big toe...

—and therefore these are the sixteen parts of the spirit of enlightenment.

To help us understand the division into art and wisdom [Abhaya's *Clusters of Instructions*] cites the *[Hevajra Tantra in] Two Sections*:[420]

> The form of the seminal essences is the lord,
> And its bliss is explained to be the beloved [consort].

—so since the sixteen things represented by the vowels have the two [aspects of] art and wisdom, that is the meaning of "also dividing the sixteen vowels into two." {414a} The statement in [Abhaya's] *Clusters of Instructions* that there is a dividing into thirty-two due to there being sixteen parts which are the reverse of the negatives of the seminal essences and the blisses[421] must also be [understood as] a dividing from the perspective of there being such and such places in the body as previously explained.

---

[420] *Hevajra Tantra*, Part I, ch. 8, verse 48 (Farrow & Menon, p. 105):

> *śukrākāro bhaved bhagavān tatsukhaṁ kāminī smṛtam /*
> *[khu ba'i rnam pa bcom ldan 'gyur, de yi bde ba 'dod mar bshad, ,]*
> Bhagavān is of the nature of Semen; that Bliss is the Beloved.

In the *Jewel Rosary of Yoga* commentary Samayavajra/Kṛiṣhṇāchārya (see note 496 below) says that this verse (only the first half of which is quoted here) explains "how Wisdom and Means arise with a form." He explains that *bhagavān* "Refers to the Means which is the totality of the two Bodies, the Bodies of Enjoyment and Creation." Regarding *tatsukhaṁ* ("that Bliss") he says "That Bliss which was said to be the space-like Knowledge, is the Beloved, meaning Wisdom." He also adds that "Here, 'semen' is the Means facet."

[421] *khu ba <u>min pa</u> dang bde ba <u>min pa las ldog pa</u>'i cha bcu drug yod pas*—this use of an opposite of a negative (*min pa las ldog pa)* is a bit strange here; presumably Abhaya used it here, so Tsong Khapa is just repeating it. In this passage we have a reference to what amounts to a *gzhi ldog* ("ground differential") as opposed to a *rang ldog* ("auto-differential"). The Tibetans took Dharmakīrti's apoha (*ldog pa*) theory and elaborated it into these two. The *rang ldog* is a thing as a conceptual thing, almost like a *sāmanya* (general image) in the mind, whereas the *gzhi ldog* is the object "outside" to which the thing refers. So, for

(cont'd)

Then, to the thirty-four consonants from *Ka* through *Kṣha* one adds [repeats of] the six *Ḍa*, *Dha*, *Ya*, *Ra*, *La*, and *Va*, and thereby one gets forty, and then one doubles that [to eighty]; [but] there are many dissimilar ways to add letters to the thirty-four consonants [to reach a base set of forty]. Moreover, the reason why one makes the consonants into eighty is:[422]

> The consonants are classified into the five elements—if one divides each of those into four one gets twenty—as within [each of] those four, from the element of earth through wind, wherever there is one there are the four [others].

So, according to this passage, it is because each of the four [elements] is fourfold, and the [fifth] element, joy, [or] space, [also] has four joys. And since each of those twenty elements has its *rajas*-energy,[423] there are forty. And by dividing those into both art and wisdom, which are bliss and emptiness,[424] one gets eighty—that is what [Abhaya's] *Clusters of Instructions* states. What this means is: the symbolic meaning of the *kāli* [consonants] is the *rajas*-energies, but this is a system in which one individually counts the five elements of that and the parts which are the *rajas*-energies, and therefore the symbolizing syllables are also divided like that.

---

example, the *rang ldog* is just the concept of "cup" that does not really reach the cup; it is the opposite of the opposite of a cup in the mind. The *gzhi ldog* is sort of the cup, whatever is out there, but as subject only to a double negative reference. Again, this passage uses *min pa las ldog pa* in a way similar to how Tibetans used *gzhi ldog*. The first chapter of Tsong Khapa's *legs bshad snying po* discusses this topic in a Vijñānavāda context (cf. Thurman, *Central Philosophy of Tibet*).

422 The following passage may be a well-known citation (*lung*) as Tsong Khapa does not mention the source. It is not from Abhaya's *Clusters of Instructions*, and I have been unable to find it elsewhere in the Kangyur.

423 *rdul* translates Sanskrit *rajas*. Although this often means "mote of dust" or "atom," it can also mean the red element or the female bodhicitta (or "female essence"). In this context it does not make sense to speak of two atoms. So perhaps it is assumed that each element has a male energy aspect (*sattva*) and that since each element also has a female energy aspect (*rajas*) the number doubles (from twenty to forty).

424 *stong pa dang bde ba'i thabs shes*. Tsong Khapa here reverses the usual correspondece between these two sets of two. I have reversed this in English in order to restore the conventional correspondence.

Moreover, [Abhaya's] *Clusters of Instructions* states:

> Also, regarding these seed syllables, such as the syllable *A*, etc.: with respect to whether the signified and the signifier are the same or different, they {414b} are analyzed as being not different, and thus that is also how they should be presented; for example: "the syllable *A*, [which is] the realm of space," etc.

So according to this you should understand that the signified and the signifier are not different also in terms of their intent.

Regarding the way in which the syllables are classified into the five elements: *Ka, Ṅa, Ña, Ṇa, Na, Ma, Ha, and Kṣha* are the space consonants. *Gha, Jha, Ḍha, Dha, Dha, Bha, Ya, Ya,* and *Sha* are the wind [consonants]. *Ga, Ja, Ḍa, Ḍa, Da, Ba, Ra, Ra,* and *Ṣha* are the fire [consonants]. *Kha, Cha, Ṭha, Tha, Pha, Va,* and *Va* are the water [consonants]. *Ca, Ṭa, Ta, Pa, La, La,* and *Sa* are the earth consonant syllables.[425]

Then, Shrīdhara and Vitapāda explain that the two moons which were produced by the vowels and consonants become one; but many such as [Abhaya in] the *Clusters of Instructions*, etc., do not explain that.

[Hand-symbols:] Then, you meditate that between the two moons—or the sun and the moon—there is a seed [syllable appropriate] to the context from which comes a hand-symbol marked with the seed [syllable]. Regarding the production of the hand-symbols, the *Hevajra Father-Mother Sādhanas* by Durjayachandra and by Shāntipa state that you produce both the hand-symbol of the father and that of the mother, but

[425] Coding this with patterns, we get the following chart:

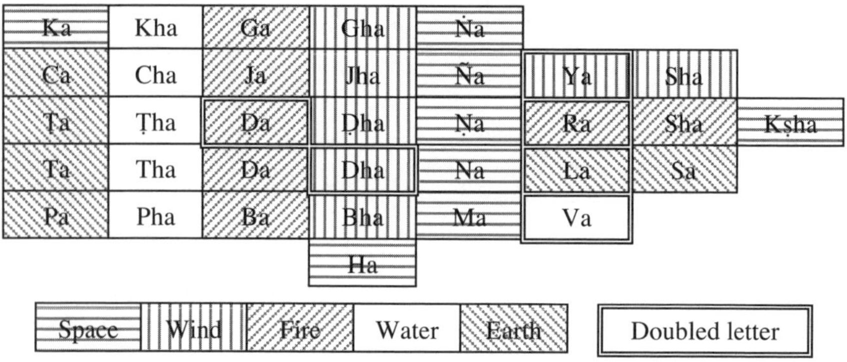
Ka
Kha
Ga
Gha
Ṅa
Ca
Cha
Ja
Jha
Ña
Ya
Sha
Ṭa
Ṭha
Ḍa
Ḍha
Ṇa
Ra
Sha
Kṣha
Ta
Tha
Da
Dha
Na
La
Sa
Pa
Pha
Ba
Bha
Ma
Va
Ha
Space
Wind
Fire
Water
Earth
Doubled letter

The Samantabhadra Sādhana, etc., does not explain there being more than the one hand-symbol [of the father]. Then, you should envision that light rays radiate from the seed [syllable] on the hand-symbol, accomplishing the aims of all sentient beings, and then gather back again, merging into one; but there are also many who explain that you just merge the light rays into one without making them [first] radiate out and then gather back. {415a}

[Body:] From that you envision [that there emerges] the completely perfect embodiment of the father-mother.

Regarding how those are assigned to the five intuitions—the *Clusters of Instructions* explains that the evolving fruition and the corresponding fruition of the vowels and consonants are respectively: [1] the mirror-like [intuition] and the thirty-two signs; [2] the equalizing [intuition] and the eighty marks; [3] the hand-symbols marked with the seed [syllable] and the individuating [intuition]; [4] radiating and gathering [the light rays] and then merging them into one and the all-accomplishing [intuition]; and [5] the completion of the [deity] embodiment and the ultimate reality intuition. And even when one asserts that the second [disk] is a sun [the foregoing explanation] is similar; this tradition explains it often [that way]. Shrīdhara explains that: [1] the two moons are the mirror [-like intuition]; [2] the unification of those two is the equalizing [intuition]; [3] the seed [syllable] is the individuating [intuition]; [4] the hand-symbols are the all-accomplishing [intuition]; and [5] the completion of the [deity] embodiment is as before [that is, the ultimate reality intuition]. And Vitapāda also explains that the unifying of the two moons is the equalizing [intuition].

If there is no song exhorting the melted [deity], then the first four manifest enlightenments are the causal Vajradhara and the fifth is the fruitional Vajradhara; and if there is [such an exhortation] then all five cause the completion of the causal Vajradhara, and the completion of the seed [syllables] from the syllables that represent the between state is not done in the context of the causal Vajradhara—that is the system of the *Clusters of Instructions*.[426]

[426] This last phrase (from "if there is…") is somewhat obscure.

[**II.B.2.c.ii.C'3'c'ii'B''4''a''ii''A°2°b°i°B°°** – The way of creating (the deities), the melted (deity) having been exhorted with song]

Second, once you have melted such a causal Vajradhara and then exhorted with song, then when you do create the fruitional Vajradhara, in general many other [texts] state that you do it in this [very] context of exhorting the melted [deity] with song; but [Nāgārjuna's] *Abbreviated [Practice]* states [that you create the fruitional Vajradhara] in the context of the supreme action triumph {415b}, and that although there is a melted [deity] it is not a melted [deity which emerges after] having passed through a between-state syllable, but that rather the method of melting is just a [direct] entry into clear light.

Moreover, regarding the melted [deity] in this context of the preliminary union, according to what *The [Vajra] Pavilion* states:[427]

> [iii] The *gandharva* then enters, and falls;
> [iv] The goddesses of the quarters recollect the melted [deity] and exhort [it];...

According to the interpretation that the melted state [comes about] through [the *gandharva*] having entered you as the syllable which symbolizes the between state, then the Jñānapāda tradition and Shrīdhara, Durjayachandra, etc., explain that you place the three seed [syllables *OṀ ĀḤ HŪṀ*] between two *HOḤ* syllables; and as was previously explained[428] there is also [the further] entrance into the [*anusvāra*] seed drop and the *nāda*, etc. Lūipa intends the interpretation that you enter just the *nāda* in the context of the previous [five] manifest enlightenments.

Regarding the way of entering, Shrī Phalavajra asserts that from the beginning [the *gandharva*] enters through the mother's lotus; but Vitapāda asserts that it enters the father's mouth, travels through the vajra path, and then enters the mother's lotus; and still others explain that it enters through the crown-aperture—thus there is no one certain door [of entry].

Once it has entered, the conditions are thereby set, and it melts due to the lust of the father and mother, and it then is caused to abide in the

[427] This and more also was cited above on p. 182 (*NRC* 395b–396a).

[428] Cf. above, p. 210 (Tib. 408b–409a).

form of a drop. Then it is exhorted by the songs of the goddesses Locanā,[429] etc., and there are many developments—from the drop into a seed syllable, and from a hand-symbol into a deity[430]—this is the way of creation [by] the three procedures.[431] Also in this context there is a creation from the five manifest enlightenments, as [Abhaya's] *Clusters of Instructions* explains:[432]

> The two repetitions of the fivefold {416a} manifest enlightenments are for the sake of realizing that "there is only great bliss in the cause as well as in the fruition."

In the context of creating the retinue, Durjayachandra explains that the causal Vajradhara father-mother unite and then emit the eight goddesses [of the Hevajra mandala], following what is stated in *The [Vajra] Pavilion* [from the *Hevajra* corpus]:[433]

> You should meditate the five events:
> [i] First imagine [yourself as] the divine male;
> [ii] Then radiate the circle of ḍākinīs; ...

Since in [Ratnākarashānti's *Hevajra Sādhana,*] *An Elimination of Errors*,[434] etc., in the context of the fruitional Vajradhara there is emission from the womb, then it is uncertain even in *Hevajra* that there is just one way; and in the Jñānapāda system, etc., there are very many ways in which the fruitional Vajradhara father-mother creates the circle from the womb.

Moreover, regarding the body-colors of the causal and fruitional Vajradharas, Durjayachandra explains that in *Hevajra* the former is white

---

429 All three texts have just *spyan* instead of the more complete *spyan ma*.

430 *thig le las sa bon dang phyag mtshan las lhar rdzogs pa mang ste*—I am here reading this with this distribution. It could perhaps preferably distribute as follows: "there are many developments (*rdzogs pa*)—from the drop into a seed syllable and hand-symbol, and then into a deity."

431 The three procedures are: (1) seed syllable, (2) hand-symbol, and (3) deity.

432 That is, great bliss exists at both the causal time and at the fruitional time, so there can also be five manifest enlightenments in the causal time and five in the fruitional time.

433 This and more also was cited above on p. 182 (*NRC* 395b–396a).

434 Cf. note 381 above.

and the latter is blue; but in [Ratnākarashānti's *Hevajra Sādhana,*] *An Elimination of Errors*, it is explained that they both have the same color; and in the *Mañjuvajra [Esoteric Community]*[435] it is explained that the colors and the hand-symbols [of each] are different, [though] the number of faces and hands are the same; etc. So, since there is a variety [of traditions regarding this], you should not be one-sided [about such subjects].

The Clusters of Instructions explains [three possibilities regarding being melted:] [1] At a time when you are not an appropriate disciple for the occasion [of this practice], you remain with only a great bliss body [that is, you stay melted]; [2] at a time when you are [an appropriate disciple], you appear in the form body and accomplish the aims [of beings], **{416b}** and for that purpose you are exhorted to arise by song; and [3] you stay unmelted, so that, for the sake of others, you stand firm without withdrawing even for an instant the appearance of your body.

[**II.B.2.c.ii.C'3'c'ii'B''4''a''ii''A°2°b°ii°** – The bases of purification, and homologies with the paths]

Second, the *Kālachakra Root [Tantra] and Commentary*[436] and [Nāgabodhi's] *Graded Presentation [of the Esoteric Community Practice]*[437] have an explicit presentation of the creation of the deity which corresponds with the bases of purification,[438] but other [texts] are not

---

[435] Cf. note 284 (to Tib. 391a) above which explains that there are two *Esoteric Community* variants, *Guhyasamāja-Akṣobhyavajra* and *Guhyasamāja-Mañjuvajra*. Tsong Khapa's reference here to *'jam rdor* (*Mañjuvajra*) is probably a reference to the general *Guhyasamāja-Mañjuvajra* tradition rather than to a specific text. However, the *Blue Annals* I, p. 373, does use the abbreviated title *'jam rdor* to refer to the following specific text: Tōh. 1880: *Śrī-guhyasamāja-mañjuśrī-sādhana* (*dpal gsang ba 'dus pa'i 'jam dpal gyi sgrub thabs*), by Samantabhadra.

[436] *Dus 'khor rtza 'grel*. This likely is a reference to the shorter "root" *Kālachakra Tantra* (*laghu-kālacakra*) which is combined with *The Great Commentary: Immaculate Light* (*Vimalaprabhā*), and not the actual root Tantra (the *mūla-kālacakra*, or *dus 'khor rtza*).

[437] Cf. note 324.

[438] The bases of purification (*sbyang gzhi*) in Unexcelled Yoga Tantra consist of the states of death, intermediate state, and life—these are what are to be purified (into the three buddha bodies). In addition, on a cosmic level all of the elements of the universe are also purified into the mandala, and thus those elements also may be considered the bases of purification. So here Tsong Khapa is saying that these two texts make it clear that the normal processes of creation (either the processes of rebirth for the individual, or

(cont'd)

quite that explicit. [Moreover,] the previously cited *[Vajra] Pavilion* states only a little about the process by which [you as] a between-state[-like being] enter the womb of the mother of [yourself being born as] the causal Vajradhara. Because of this, and because the symbolisms of the other bases of purification are extensively detailed in the *Clusters of Instructions*, we should explain it according to what is stated there.

So, a person who has previously collected the evolutionary action that is the cause for taking rebirth in the womb dies and attains the between state; then the between-state being enters the womb of the mother and, having remained there, finally gets born outside; then having taken a wife he performs the deeds of producing sons and daughters, etc. [So] having taken [all of those ordinary life-cycle] processes as the objects of correspondence, it is in correspondence with those that you meditate the creation stage.

And so, visualizing the [refuge] field of assembly and then accumulating the many stores [of merit and intuition] is like accumulating the evolutionary action that is the cause of birth in existence, and that then is to be homologized with the path of accumulation. As the *Clusters of Instructions* states:

> Thus, like the circumstance of a past existence [of a bodhisattva], [this is] the place of accumulation [of the stores] for bodhisattvas—because it has properties similar to actual accumulation. {417a} Here, accumulating the merit of generosity, etc., is [akin to accumulating] virtue and non-virtue previously.

The paths of both the aspiring and activated [spirits of enlightenment], etc., in this context are common with the Transcendence Vehicle, and this has the same meaning as [Āryadeva's] statement in the *Practice Integration* that one first educates oneself in the Buddha Vehicle; and therefore this means that [even in the Vajra Vehicle] you must meditate the paths that are in common [with the Transcendence Vehicle].

Although Lūipa states that it is after the defense perimeter that one accumulates the stores in relation to the deity host, many [other] scholar-

---

the elemental cosmogonic "big-bang" for the universe) are re-interpreted/ re-appropriated/ homologized in the creation stage process.

adepts explain that one should do it before that—so here we are explaining the majority system; and again, although [Nāgārjuna's] *Abbreviated [Practice]* and Lūipa state that it is after the defense perimeter that one does the meditation on emptiness, here we are explaining the majority system that one meditates it before.

Next, there is meditation on emptiness. This is like dying, because when the body-mind systems—which are the bases of the self- and property-habits—are determined to be identityless, the perceptions of them become stilled, and thus this is like casting off one's old body-mind systems [when one dies].

Then the paths involving everything from there on up to [but not including] when the between-state syllable enters are homologized with the path of application; as the *Clusters of Instructions* states:

> [This is] the stage of imaginational practice,[439] which is like the context connected with the confrontation with death because it entails {417b} the actuality of applying the discernment of thatness. Following that there is the occasion of the uninterrupted path of the stage of great joy,[440] which is the actuality of the final instant when one has just ceased the final instant of being close to the end, which is the context of applying [things] as if it was the context of the between state after the cessation of the previous existence.[441]

---

[439] *mos pas spyod pa'i sa*. This is a technical term. The *Mahāvyutpatti* (ACIP R0061) has an entry (896—Sec. 32 [missing in Koros' edition]) for *mos pas spyod pa'i sa'i ming* (*adhimukti caryā bhūmi nāmāni*), with the following five entries (or four if 896 = 897?) under it: 897 (1) *mos pa spyod pa'i sa (adhimukit* [sic] *caryābhūmiḥ)*; 898 (2) *snang ba mched pa (āloka labdhaḥ)*; 899 (3) *snang ba mchad pa (āloka vṛddhiḥ)*; 900 (4) *de kho na'i don gyi phyogs gcig la rjes su zhugs pa (tattvārthāika deśānupraveśaḥ)*; 901 (5) *bar chad med pa'i ting nge 'dzin (anantarya samādhiḥ)*. Also, RY has the following entry for *mos pas spyod pa'i sa bzhi*: "the four stages of devoted conduct, [1] *snang ba thob pa*, [2] *snang ba mched pa*, [3] *de kho na'i phyogs gcig la rjes su zhugs pa*, [4] *bar chad med pa'i ting nge 'dzin*."

[440] *rab tu dga' ba'i sa* = *Pramudita*, the beginning of the path of vision, right after the path of application.

[441] This paragraph seems awkward because of the succession of "final instants," but the translation follows the original Tibetan precisely. The main point is the analogy between (1) transitioning from death to entering the between-state process, and (2) transitioning

(cont'd)

The uninterrupted path of the first [bodhisattva] stage arises at the conclusion of the path of application—which is called the great supreme [mundane] realization[442]—because after that the ten [bodhisattva] stages are homologized with the [creation stage] context of being in the womb [in the sādhana], and further because [Maitreya's] *The Ornament of [Universal Vehicle] Sūtras* states with respect to the supreme [mundane] realization:[443]

> At that time you quickly obtain
> The uninterrupted samādhi.[444] (XIV.26cd)

Everything from when the between-state syllable enters up to [but not including] the completion of the deity body is homologized with the ten [bodhisattva] stages on the paths of vision and meditation; as the *Clusters of Instructions* states:

> Following that, just like being in the context of the womb which comes after the cessation of the [previous between-state] form which was just like the between-state being, you should know [this to be] the context of the ten stages which comes after the cessation of the [previous] uninterrupted path of the bodhisattvas, because these [later] stages possess obstructions.

Regarding this, there are two [possibilities, involving the *gandharva* entering the Vajradhara melted or unmelted].[445]

---

from the application path—the last moment of being an unreflexively egocentric being in supreme mundane experience—to just before becoming a noble being (an *ārya*) on the vision path by melting into a nonconceptual experience of emptiness.

442 *['jigs rten pa'i] chos mchog* (Skt. *dharmottara*; *[laukika] agradharma*). This is the fourth stage of the path of application, after heat (*drod*), peak (*rtse mo*), and tolerance (*bzod pa*). It represents the highest realization or state of being within the mundane world, before one then transcends the world for the first time as a noble (*ārya*).

443 This is XIV.26cd, which is translated as follows in the AIBS publication: "26. Then… she soon experiences unobstructed meditative concentration." (*The Universal Vehicle Discourse Literature*, AIBS, 2004, p. 180)

444 This is the final (fourth or fifth) "stage of practice involving the imagination" (*mos pas spyod pa'i sa, adhimukti caryā bhūmi*). Cf. note 439 above.

445 The next few paragraphs discuss the latter option (involving no melting). The former option (involving melting) is discussed below (418a–b).

When the *gandharva* enters into the unmelted [father-mother], the *nāda*, etc.—which is the syllable that is the actuality of the between-state [being]—entering between the two [lunar] mandalas is [homologized with] the context of [entering] the womb, and [this stage continues] up through the [production of the] seed [syllable] and hand-symbol and the radiating and retracting [of light]. {418a} For those who do not declare that the between-state syllable enters from the side, the seed syllable that is between the two [lunar] mandalas is just there from the beginning, and this is the between [state].

Here, the first moon signifies the seminal essence; the second moon [or sun] signifies the ovum, like the sun that arises from the abundance of the menses of women. Thus, in other contexts it is stated that from the consonants a sun is created, and that is also what is meant when the [second] moon is said to be red. The entry of the syllable—which signifies the between-state [being]—into the middle of those two [moons] is like the entry of the [actual] between-state [being] into the midst of the father's and mother's sexual essences [in the normal life cycle].

Then, from the seed [syllable] a hand-symbol is produced, which is a five-pronged vajra, and in the *Clusters of Instructions* it is explained—gathering into sets of five—that the five prongs of one end [of the vajra] are the [embryo's] four limbs [legs and arms] and the head above the neck, and that the five prongs of the other end [of the vajra] are the five digits on the feet and hands and the five senses on the head. [However], regarding the hand-symbols like the skull-bowl in *Hevajra* and the staff in the *Red Enemy [of Death Tantra]* [which are not five-pronged vajras], one wonders whether it is suitable to have taken them as signifiers of just taking a body in the womb.

When there is a melting [of the the father-mother deity with the *gandharva*], then the completion of the causal Vajradhara from the five manifest enlightenments is like the father and mother, and then from the entry of the between-state [being] up until [its] body is completed is homologized with the state of the womb. In that [context], the *nāda* is explained as having the nature of the concentrate of the three syllables [*OṀ ĀḤ HŪṀ*], {418b} and the three syllables are extensive as if they were the signifiers for the between-state [being]. Regarding [the variant system of the seed syllable] being inserted between two red *HOḤ* syllables,[446] the *Clusters of Instructions* sets forth two systems of interpretation: one asserts that it is for the sake of signifying the obstruction [caused] by the intensity of lust in the between [state], and one asserts that it is for the sake of signifying the lust which is the bliss which has the nature of the art and wisdom which emerge from the father and mother; but some Indian treatises explain that it is for the sake of [signifying] being bound by the profound and the magnificent.

Regarding the way in which the syllable of the between-state [being] enters, the *Clusters of Instructions* states:

> Because of just that, thinking about this, the Blessed Lord revealed in the Tantras: "In some divine cases the *gandharva* sentient being enters through the golden door, and in some cases through the mouth, and in some cases other ways."

"The golden door" is the crown [aperture]; the explanation in *[Nāgabodhi's] Graded Presentation [of the Esoteric Community Practice]* that the between-state being enters through Vairochana's door means the same thing. "Other ways" is explained in the Abhidharma as entry through the vagina—so there are three doors of entry [i.e., crown aperture, mouth, and vagina]. Moreover, regarding the causes for entering those ways, the *Clusters of Instructions* states that: [1] through desiring to suck the honey of the lips [one enters] through the mouth; and that [2] through desiring to grasp by the hair, etc., one enters through Vairochana's door; and that [3] if there is a strong desire for birth and one is attached to the father and to the female then one enters into those doors to mother; but that some say [that even the first] two systems involve desiring only the mother, and {419a} the final one involves entering through the vagina. The *Vajra Rosary Tantra* and the *Drop of Mahāmudrā [Tantra]* declare that one enters from the mouth of the father, and they comment that that is also the intention of the *Arisal of Saṁvara [Tantra]*.

Since there is a variety of ways in which the between-state [being] enters, treatises also state many procedures for creation. When [in the ordinary birth process] the between-state [being] enters the womb, then

---

446 Cf. above, in the passages surrounding 409a and 415b.

just as both the father and mother faint with bliss, so here also [in Tantra], in correspondence with that, when the syllable of the betweeen state [being] enters the womb of the [deity] mother, both the [deity] father and mother are caused to melt.

Then, regarding the exhortation of the melted [deities to arise] by song: if we homologize this with [the stage of] fruition, then having been exhorted by the four immeasurables[447] [to accomplish] the aims of beings, there is an arisal as a form body for the fortunate person; but if we homologize this with the bases of purification, then that set of four goddesses is the four elements [instead of the four immeasurables],[448] and thus the new oval embryo—which is the between-state [being] which entered—is held by earth, combined by water, developed without rotting by fire, and caused to grow by wind; that is what is stated in the *Relativity Sūtra*. Kamalarakṣhita[449] explains that the exhortation by song and the goddesses who do the exhorting are included within the drop.[450] Even though the four goddesses of the mandala have not yet been produced [in the sādhana], at the time of melting, [this arisal of the deity through song] frequently is made to happen by great exhortations by those four, and thus there is no contradiction.

Then, regarding the completion of the embodiment of the lord father-mother: there is the birth outside from the womb, and then there is the father's and mother's creation of the male and female deities of the supreme {419b} mandala triumph [sequence], and this is similar to the context of producing sons and daughters; as the *Clusters of Instructions* states:

---

[447] Immeasurable love, compassion, sympathetic joy, and impartiality, here in the form of the goddesses Locanā, Māmakī, Pāṇḍaravāsinī, and Tārā.

[448] Here it is earth, water, fire, and wind that are in the form of the goddesses Locanā, Māmakī, Pāṇḍaravāsinī, and Tārā.

[449] Cf. note 379 above.

[450] The drop here symbolizes the subtle body-mind—which is the subtle wind-energies and the mind of the three luminances—that has emerged from the extremely subtle clear light mind-energy-body. At that subtle point, the between-state being experiences itself like a still candle flame, and the four goddesses—personifying love, compassion, sympathetic joy, and impartiality as the elements of earth, water, fire, and wind—invite the subtle body-mind to use them to manifest a coarse embodiement with corresponding senses.

> Having completely apprehended the fruition, in order to individually enjoy all objects of experience there is birth, because there is individual enjoyment of the objects of experience of all the senses. Thereupon, the similarity with the context of causing the production of a son, etc., is the context of radiating an emanation body deity.

—and that is homologized with the stage of non-learning.

Such a kind of fruitional Vajradhara is like a son; and the cause and effect that were explained as Vajradhara [related to] the previously explained first two manifest enlightenments are similar to this being like father, mother, and child; and the explanation that the two middle manifest enlightenments [2 & 3] are the causal Vajradhara [represents] a causal system which is a little different from that, but that is easy to understand.

Accordingly, in order to demonstrate the connection, the *Clusters of Instructions* quotes *The Kiss*:

> [One homologizes] the ten months with the ten stages—
> The sentient being is the lord of the tenth stage [when born outside].

The intention of that is: from entering the womb until you are born outside is homologized with the ten [bodhisattva] stages, and thus one must assign [the stages] in between those [that is, stages 1–10] to the paths of vision and meditation, and [one must assign] being born to the path of non-learning. Then whatever there is up until you have entered the womb is assigned to the path of application. Moreover, accumulating the stores [of merit and intuition] with respect to the deity host is the path of accumulation, and thus [everything] from meditation on emptiness [onward] must be assigned to the path of application—{420a} that is the thought intended.

Also, when Shrī Phalavajra wrote the [*Commentary on Jñānapāda's*] *Samantabhadra Sādhana* as the remedy for birth, death, and the between, his explanation of the way of meditating which conforms with those three also fits with this [present explanation].

[**II.B.2.c.ii.C'3'c'ii'B''4''a''ii''A°2°b°iii°** – A summary of the essential points.]

[Creation Stage]

Third, regarding the creation stage we must identify the bases of purification and the means of purification; and the way of identifying [those], moreover, is the meditation which accords with how [ordinary] birth, death, and the between [occur], and thus here also we must express the way of taking birth.

[*Birth*] So regarding that, the one who takes birth is [yourself,] the mantrin who meditates the path. Regarding what kind of body you have when you take birth, you take birth as the body of a causal lord father-mother Vajradhara. The place where birth is taken is [the environment] from the vajra wall up to the measureless mansion with a seat; manifestly there, upon the center of the seat of the measureless mansion. Regarding what kind of evolutionary action you have accumulated when you take birth, [you take birth] with the stores [accumulated] through prostrating, offering, and producing the spirit [of enlightenment] oriented toward a special field [viz. the refuge field], and [accumulated through] through keeping your vows.

[*Death*] With regard to assuming such a special deity body, since it would not be possible for you to assume it without abandoning the ordinary body-mind systems, it is taken once you have thoroughly pacified the perception and conception of ordinariness by means of emptiness.

[*Between*] Once you have abandoned your previous ordinary body-mind systems [through death/emptiness], then since you will not be born as a deity body without [first passing through] the between-state path—which [must occur] prior to achieving the later special body of a deity—after meditating on emptiness {420b} you need the [between-state] yogas of abiding as a *nāda*, etc., as long as you are not completed as a fruitional Vajradhara.

Here, Shrī Phalavajra presents an objection [in his *Commentary on* (Jñānapāda's) *Samantabhadra Sādhana*]:[451] "Immediately after having meditated emptiness, why should one then abide as the five syllables such as the syllable *HOḤ*, etc., instead of [just immediately] accomplishing

[451] Tsong Khapa is here paraphrasing Shrī Phalavajra's text. The full Tibetan text can be found in my note to this passage in the Tibetan edition.

the aims of beings by taking the body of a deity?" And in answer to this he states that since this sādhana was made to be a remedy to the three states of existence,[452] there must be a meditation which corresponds to the between state—this is excellent.

Then, when [you as] the causal Vajradhara [who emerged] from the five manifest enlightenments—[here] in the form of a between-state being—see the complete father-mother pair enter into union, there is an entry into the mother's womb [by you as the causal Vajradhara between-state being]. Shrī Phalavajra is clear on this [in his *Commentary on (Jñānapāda's) Samantabhadra Sādhana*]:

> Then the glorious Vajrasattva enters into the experience[453] of great bliss, and seeing that all sentient beings without exception are thoroughly enmeshed with evil, he creates the desire genuinely to develop excellent migrations and lands, and he produces the following determination: "With respect to this meditation of the seal of the reality-source, any sentient being with affective and cognitive obscurations who merely enters that will achieve buddhahood, and therefore for the sake of achieving All-Goodness, I must enter into this very place!" Thus having made a very firm intention like that, in the form of the five letters of the between state {421a} he enters like a candle flame into the secret lotus of the wisdom [consort].

This passage shows how you should enter, having seen what sort of necessity, and you should understand accordingly.

---

452 That is, birth (life), death, and the between state.

453 *nyams su bstar ba* means something like "experience." I could not find it in any dictionary. Das (561) gives a meaning for *bstar ba* as "to appreciate; to be aware of." He then says "*bstar chog pa* = *nyams su len chog pa* to be able to comprehend, appreciate." Goldstein (494) says *star* (pf. *bstar*) = "to string," and that *lag len star ba* = "to put into practice, to apply." The most frequent Skt. equivalent in LC (819) for *bstar* is *sajja-*. In MW it appears that this can be either from *sat* + *ja*, or from the root *sañj*. Also, *nyams su* is often the upasarga *anu-*. So we might have the Skt. *anusajja-* (for which I can locate no meaning).

[*Birth (again)*] Then, the arisal of the melted [deity] once exhorted by song is the occasion of the achievement of fully completed birth, which was already explained. If you understand well the reasons for this exhortation by song of the melted [deity], then you will come to understand the incorrectness of those who claim that at the level of buddhahood the aim of the disciples arises from just the truth body without the form body, and [you will understand] how a form body is indispensable to actually accomplishing the aims of sentient beings, and thus [you will understand] the things that a Universal Vehicle practitioner should take as principal in regard to the different aspects of the art of the cause of that [buddhahood].

Having taken such a birth, what do you do? What occurs after that [in the text] teaches that you completely create the deities of the supreme mandala triumph, and [in the supreme action triumph] you accomplish the aims of beings by purifying the individual evolutionary actions of those [deities] who were produced. If you produce the lord father-mother from just the five manifest enlightenments but you do not perform the melting, still you should understand the way of proceeding by using that as an example, and then it will be easy to understand.

With regard to just setting up similar properties in the process of arranging similarities with the bases of purification [that is, the ordinary birth/death experience]—ignoring the [specific] explanations that wish to identify the bases of purification and the means of purification—the acquisition of a [general] understanding such as was previously explained is what is indispensable to [understand] the literature of *Mañjuvajra [Esoteric Community]*, *Supreme Bliss*, *Hevajra*, and *The Enemy of Death*. {421b} However, for the Ārya tradition the unexcelled way of [specifically] identifying the bases of purification and the means of purification which accord with birth, death, and the between [state] is the excellent explanation of the import which occurs in the treatise of Shrī Nāgabodhi —but since I have already explained that extensively in my *Commentary to [Nāgabodhi's Graded] Presentation [of the Esoteric Community Practice]*,[454] I will not elaborate [further here].[455]

[454] Cf. note 324.

[455] This paragraph squares with some of what Wayman observes regarding the differences between the Ārya and Jñānapāda traditions. See introduction above, p. 27.

[Perfection Stage]

[So] in the process of exchanging the ordinary body-mind systems and achieving a deity body it becomes necessary to meditate in a way that conforms to birth, death, and the between [state]. With respect to practicing from that kind of perspective, since the paths of the perfection stage are supreme, then also in the context of the second stage [it is necessary to so meditate; so here,] relying on the power of the [perfection stage] yogas of the channels, wind-energies, and drops, etc., after you have produced in your continuum a realization of emptiness which is similar to the process of death, you arise from that, and then you must understand the [perfection stage] method of creating the deity whereby, in place of the [creation stage] moon and hand-symbol, etc., from the cause of the three intuitions together with their wind-energies you arise in the illusion and integration bodies. Otherwise, you will cut off the essential points of the path of the perfection stage which purify the bases of purification; thus, having understood the essential points of the two stages, fitting them in with the bases of purification, you should generate a firm certitude about the ways in which the first stage serves as a cause of the second. Since this is explained extremely clearly in the Ārya tradition of the Esoteric Community, you must understand it from there.

[**II.B.2.c.ii.C'3'c'ii'B''4''a''ii''A°2°c°'** – The components which complete it (the actual yoga)]

The third has two: **[i°]** The entering of the intuition being and the sealing, then the making of offerings and praises; **[ii°]** Tasting nectar, {422a} meditating, and repeating [mantras].

[**II.B.2.c.ii.C'3'c'ii'B''4''a''ii''A°2°c°i°** – The entering of the intuition being and the sealing, then the making of offerings and praises]

[The Devotee Hero]

When you have grasped the essential point of the procedures for creating the principal deity like that, it is easy to understand the ways you create the retinue—[so] you [then] should complete the devotee [hero]. Regarding that, the body of a deity beautified with face and hands, which is the perceptual experience of your own mind which clears away the pride of ordinariness, is the devotee hero. [Abhaya's] *Clusters of Instructions* states:

> Some say it is also the seed [syllable], and some say it is only the seed [syllable].

Thus there are two systems, one in which the deity's body together with its seed [syllable] is called the devotee hero, and one in which the seed [syllable] alone is called the devotee hero.

Now regarding the etymology of the term "devotee hero" (*dam tshig sems dpa'*), the original [Sanskrit] term is *samayasattva*—which means *sameti* [*sam eti*] or 'come together/ approach' (*yang dag par 'gro ba*)[456] and *milati* or 'collect/gather/unite' (*'du ba*).[457] Thus, [Abhaya's] *Clusters of Instructions* states:

> For the sake of [realizing] the actuality of the nondual intuition that was taken as the nature of that, there is the devotion/commitment (*dam tshig*) [by the *dam tshig sems dpa'* or devotee hero] "May the intuition hero approach and unite [with me]."[458]

---

456 Here Tsong Khapa shows that the *aya* in *samaya* comes from the verb √*i* ("to go") by giving the third person singular form *eti*. So he analyzes it as *sam* + *eti* = Tib. *yang dag par 'gro ba* (LC also gives *yang dag 'gro* = *samaya*). Now MW (1164, col. 1) gives the following range of meanings for *sam* + *eti* (from √*i*): "to go or come together, ... encounter, ...to come together in sexual union, ...to come to, arrive at, approach, visit, seek, enter upon, begin, ...to consent, agree with, ..." Immediately thereafter he gives the following range of meanings for *samaya*: "coming together, meeting, ...coming to a mutual understanding, agreement, compact, covenant, treaty, contract, ..." It is presumably this latter range of meanings ("agreement, covenant," etc.) that led the Tibetans to translate *samaya* as *dam tshig* and not *yang dag par 'gro ba*.

457 Here he adds that *sam* + √*i* has the same meaning as the verbal root √*mil* (third person singular *milati*). MW (817, col. 3) gives the following definition for √*mil*: "to meet, ...encounter, join, fall in with, ...come together, assemble, concur...," which indeed is equivalent to the Tibetan verb *'du ba*.

458 *ye shes sems dpa' yang dag par 'gro 'du'o*. The devotee hero makes the devotion/commitment that he/she will truly gather in and unite with the intuition hero. Abhaya seems here to be playing on the double meaning of *samaya*, "to come together": the devotee hero and intuition hero "come to a mutual agreement" (that is, make a commitment/pledge) that they will "come together" (that is, unite). No one word in Tibetan (or English) seems to capture both of these meanings, so the Tibetans chose *dam*

(cont'd)

That is the meaning of the first of the two terms "devotee" and "hero." As for the meaning of the term "hero," that same [text] states:

> Moreover, it is a "hero"—because of its accomplishment of the aims of sentient beings, and because it is the referent conventionally designated as a purified sentient being.

Question: Well now, how can a syllable which is a seed take on the meaning of the term 'sentient being?'

[Answer:] That same [text] states: 422b}

> Moreover, a seed—like a zygote—is a sentient being.

So here [Abhaya] gives the example that although [a zygote] does not have a form with face and hands, we still give it the conventional designation 'sentient being.'

Although there can be various greater or lesser numbers of deities set out in a mandala, in cases where there are fewer deities, then when counting the deities which bless the sense media and the body, speech, and mind, etc. [in] the evocation of the retinue of the mandala, most authorities can match the number of bases of purification and the number of deities that are the means of purification corresponding to those [bases]. Therefore, if you do not meditate a mandala-retinue sādhana written by an authority it will be difficult to complete the essential points of the creation stage that will achieve the supreme.

[The Entering of the Intuition Hero]

In that regard, when the intuition hero enters, like the statement in the *Compendium of Reality [Tantra]* that the eyes, etc., of the devotee being and the eyes, etc., of the intuition being are to be inseparably mingled down to the level of the subtlest atoms, you must have a firm conviction that they have become of one taste. Thus, [statements that you should have] an intense conviction in your oneness with all the transcendent buddhas mean that you should believe in your equality [with

---

tshig (lit. "solemn word," in the sense of a commitment, pledge, promise); hence *samayasattva* (*dam tshig sems dpa'*) often is translated in English as "pledge hero." "Devotee" has the advantage that it somewhat captures the double meaning: this hero is devoted to uniting with intuition.

them], and [statements that you should have] occasionally a conviction in your oneness with [all] beings mean that [due to everything's] suchness, which is natural purity, you should realize your similarity [with them]; and therefore you should develop the conviction that the intuition hero that will arise in your own mental continuum and your very self are of one nature, {423a} and you should develop the conviction [that you have the same nature as other beings] through [realizing] the equality [of your own intuition hero] with the intuition hero of others' continuums—that is what [Abhaya's] *Clusters of Instructions* states.[459]

[Sealing]

Regarding the conferral of initiation upon the intuition hero that has entered: most treatises speak about the conferral of a water initiation; they say that it is conferred by a stream of water that has the nature of the spirit of enlightenment and that usually comes from a vase but that sometimes comes from within a skull-bowl; so the water of intuition washes all taints along with their underlying instincts. Therefore, you are sealed by the seminal essence of initiation abiding in the crown, and then that [fluid] transforms [on top of your head into the form of one of the five clan buddhas] according to [which] division of the clans [you are practicing]. However, Saroruha's *[Hevajra] Sādhana* and Atīsha's *Analysis of Lūipa's Evocation* explain that you are sealed once you have been conferred [all] *four* initiations. Here, if you know the statements regarding the way of sealing in [Abhaya's] *Clusters of Instructions* you will get an understanding of sealing in general, so thus I will explain those [now].

Holding [the intuition heroes] upon your crown out of respect is sealing; moreover, by that [process] they are not caused any suffering but are only caused satisfaction.

Sealing with the lord of the clan means that, since a son follows the father, you understand that [like a son] you are produced from that [clan lord father]. Regarding that, when the six buddhas mutually seal

---

[459] This whole passage is difficult in Tibetan. Note the parallel construction at the end:

***rang** gi sems rgyun la 'byung 'gyur **gyi** ye shes sems dpa' dang bdag nyid gcig **tu** mos par byed la*
***gzhan** rgyud **kyi** ye shes sems dpa' dang mnyam pa nyid **kyis** mos par byed do.*

Thus, I rendered this as I did.

each other, then the four such as Vairochana, etc., are sealed by Akṣhobhya, because Akṣhobhya is the mind; and the four [other body-mind systems]—matter, sensations, conceptions, and {423b} volitions—are no more than the body of the mere mind. That means that you should understand the four [other buddhas/body-mind systems] to be mind. Abhaya does not posit the [(four latter) body-mind systems as] external, so his system is to posit the three [middle body-mind systems of] sensations, etc. [conceptions and volitions], as existing in the context of mind (*sems*);[460] there is a sealing by nature to that which has the nature.[461] Mind/spirit (*sems*), moreover, is the spirit of enlightenment (*byang chub kyi sems*), which arises from emptiness;[462] thus Akṣhobhya's sealing of Vajradhara is the seal of fruition upon the cause, and Vajradhara's sealing of Akṣhobhya is the sealing of the cause upon the fruition. The statement that Vajradhara is the crown of the five clans is made because he subsumes the five intuitions within his nature. Regarding the sealing of the rest of the six clans, Mohavajra [Vajra Delusion], etc.—those with names such as Kṣhitigarbha [Earth Essence], etc.—are each aspects of the samādhis of the five transcendent buddhas, and therefore they are sealed by the five transcendent buddhas.

Objection: It would be [more] logical that the five [deities] such as Kṣhitigarbha [Earth Essence], and the five such as Rūpavajrā [Matter Vajra], and the four such as Locanā [Buddha Eye], etc., should all be sealed by Vairochana since they are all aspects of the body-mind system of matter.

[Answer:] There is no fault here. When assigning the five body-mind systems to the five transcendent buddhas, each one of the five again

---

460 Wayman discusses this at *YGST*, 207. He notes that long ago Buddhaghosa's *Visuddhimagga* explained that in the context of the twelve links of relativity the *nāma* in *nāma-rūpa* stands for the three middle body-mind systems. Wayman goes on to note that in other contexts it is quite common for *nāma* also to include the fifth body-mind system of consciousness (*vijñāna*).

461 So, in other words, Akṣhobhya seals these other body-mind systems because he is the main buddha corresponding to the nature of mind.

462 Again, as Wayman points out (*YGST*, 208), while discussing the body-mind systems the *Esoteric Community Tantra* (XVIII, 47) states: *svabhāvaṁ bodhicittaṁ tu sarvatra bhavasambhavam //* (My translation: "[The body-mind systems'] intrinsic nature is the spirit of enlightenment, the source of existence everywhere.")

has a set of five buddhas [assigned to it], and therefore it is not contradictory that one body-mind system like the matter body-mind system should have a transcendent buddha of another body-mind system as its clan lord. **{424a}**

Regarding the system of sealing the deities of the twelve sense media: the eye deity [Kṣhitigarbha] is sealed by Vairochana, because he is very clear. The ear [deity (Vajrapāṇi) is sealed] by Akṣhobhya, because he is equal to space. Because in the between state—and, in other contexts—pleasure is produced in sensation through perceiving smell, the nose [deity (Ākāshagarbha) is sealed] by Ratnasambhava. Since the desire arising from perceiving taste is powerful, the tongue [deity (Lokeshvara) is sealed] by Amitābha, who is the actuality of lust. [The deity of] the bodily sense faculty [that is, the touch deity (Sarvanivaraṇaviṣhkambhin), is sealed] by Amoghasiddhi, because wind-energy, which is the actuality of Amoghasiddhi, courses throughout the body. Because the mentality follows after all of the sense faculties, the mind [deity (Mañjushrī) is sealed] by Akṣhobhya.[463]

Following after the sense faculties, the sealing of the [deities of the sense objects such as] matter, etc., is stated [one way] in *The Samantabhadra Sādhana* and it is stated in another way in [Nāgārjuna's] *Abbreviated [Practice]*.[464] The deity of matter, Rūpavajrā [(Matter Vajra) is sealed] by Vairochana, because matter is the basis of delusion. Shabdavajrā [(Sound Vajra) is sealed] by Ratnasambhava, because sounds of praise, etc., generate pride. Gandhavajrā [(Scent Vajra) is sealed] by Amitābha, because perceiving scents such as saffron, etc., generates desire. Rasavajrā [(Taste Vajra) is sealed] by Amoghasiddhi, because tastes satisfy all limbs and course in all those.[465] Sparshavajrā [(Texture Vajra) is sealed] by Akṣhobhya, because touch pervades all the senses.

---

463 This mapping of deity pairs and senses accords with *YGST* (240–41), but differs from his chart at *YGST*, 247.

464 It would seem that Tsong Khapa next describes (only) Nāgārjuna's system (based on the *Esoteric Community*), since the correspondences listed next match the chart at *YGST*, 132.

465 The meaning of this is unclear. Tsong Khapa is speaking as if tastes corresponded to a certain type of wind-energy (which would "course" throughout all the limbs, etc.), and indeed Amoghasiddhi is usually associated with wind-energy (as in the above paragraph). Perhaps taste and touch (*ro* and *reg bya*) were reveresed in this text?

{424b} Dharmadhātuvajrā [(Mental-object Vajra) is sealed] like that also [that is, by Akṣhobhya].

From among the four elements, the deity of the earth element [(Locanā) is sealed] by Vairochana, because, since it is hard and resistant, it is the basis of great delusion. Water [(Mamakī) is sealed] by Akṣhobhya, because, being like space, even if one cuts it or pierces it, it fills in again like before. Since it is luminous, fire [(Pāṇḍaravāsinī) is sealed] by Amitābha; and because it moves all around, wind [(Tārā) is sealed] by Amoghasiddhi.[466]

The eye, etc., [is sealed] by Mohavajrā [Delusion Vajra], because it is the actuality of the consort of delusion.

Regarding the system for sealing the fierce deities: starting from the east [and going around clockwise] to the north-east there are pairs of fierce deities [E and SE, S and SW, etc.],[467] and there are two that are above and below. These [ten deities in five pairs] are respectively [sealed by] Vairochana, Ratnasambhava, Amitābha, Amoghasiddhi, and Akṣhobhya, because they are each respectively the enjoyment of and the exhaustion of delusion, pride, lust, envy, and hatred. In the *Mañjuvajra Esoteric Community* there are eight fierce deities [all sealed] by Akṣhobhya, because [all eight] have the actuality of being distinctively produced from the mind and are the actuality of ferocity [and Akṣhobhya connects

---

466 Compare these four reasons to the four different ones given in the *Jewel Rosary of Yoga* commentary to *Hevajra* (Farrow & Menon, 174–175).

467 ...*khro bo gnyis gnyis*—this might seem to imply that there are two (that is, a *yab-yum* pair) in each of the eight directions, totalling sixteen. However, I take this to mean that he is counting in groups of two. So, for example, E and SE are the first group of two—there is *one* deity in each of these directions, and (as we shall see next) each of these is sealed by Vairochana; etc. This then totals eight deities, each pair sealed by a different buddha. Then finally there is one deity above and one below, each sealed by the fifth buddha Akṣhobhya. This way there is the normal total number of Ten Fierce Deities (borrowing also from Wayman's table at *YGST*, 132):

Yamāntaka and Acala	E, SE	Vairochana	delusion
Prajñāntaka and Ṭakkirāja	S, SW	Ratnasambhava	pride
Padmāntaka and Nīladaṇḍa	W, NW	Amitābha	lust
Vighnāntaka and Mahābala	N, NE	Amoghasiddhi	envy
Uṣhṇīṣhachakravartin and Sumbharāja	up, down	Akṣhobhya	hatred

with the mind and with hatred]. However, Yamāntaka and Padmāntaka are as above [that is, connected with Vairochana and Amitābha].

In some treatises the five clan lordsare included within the spirit of enlightenment, and that has the import of showing their non-difference from its actuality. In place of statements about the five clan [lords] and the four mothers [found] in such [treatises] as the two *Esoteric Communities*: in the *Supreme Bliss* there are the five [made up of] the lord and the [four] ḍākinīs, {425a} and the four [made up of] the goddesses *ltung byed ma*,[468] etc.; and in *Hevajra* there is the lord and the four such as Gaurī, etc., and the four such as Pukkasī, etc.; and in the *Red Enemy [of Death Tantra]* there are the five such as Dveṣha-yamāntaka, etc., and the four such as Charchikā,[469] etc.; and in place of Kṣhitigarbha, etc., there is Mohavajra, etc. Thus, [in each of these alternate systems] the sealings and also the symbolisms likewise should be understood, as appropriate.

[Offerings and Praises]

Then, the inner and outer, etc., offerings and praises should be done according to how they occur in your own particular treatise; and as is often stated, you should do these with the attitude that the object of the offerings and praises and the agent [of the offerings and praises] and the offerings and praises [themselves] are like illusions, appearing in a manner which lacks intrinsic reality.

[**II.B.2.c.ii.C'3'c'ii'B''4''a''ii''A°2°c°ii°** – Tasting nectar, meditating, and repeating (mantras)]

So then, having tasted nectar, you should meditate deity yoga; and when you are weary [from deity yoga concentration] you should perform repetition [of mantra].

Regarding that, the substance of the rosary [beads to be used for mantra repetition] should be as stated in the thirtieth [chapter] of *The Kiss*:

---

468 We have not found the Sanskrit name for this goddess. Perhaps Āpattikā?

469 All Tib. editions spelled this differently. MW (390) mentions that *Carcikā* is f. for *Carcaka*, which is a deity name = Durgā, Brahma. It means repetition of a thought (deliberation) or of a word (recitation).

Crystal,[470] mother of pearl, and pearl,
White substances, etc., and other things,
Are the attributes of a rosary
That are specific for [471] peaceful activities.

Gold, silver, copper, and
Lotus seeds are specific for
[Activities of] prospering—such a rosary
Should be counted on by a wise person.

Using all scent[ed substance]s which have
The scents, etc., of saffron, etc.,
Having made them into little beads[472]
Is very well-known to be good for dominating [activities].
{425b}

Rudrākṣha [berries],[473] *Phenila* [berries?],[474]
And likewise the bone of a [human] being
Should be used for fierce activities.

It is explained that [in the first verse] 'white substances' means bone, the word 'etc.' means an especially white stone, and that 'other things' means a white jewel.[475] In *The Four Seats* there appears the following:

---

470 All *NRC* editions here read *sa* (Tibetan for "earth"). However, the Lhasa canonical edition of the passasge from *The Kiss* cited here (Lhasa 396; GA: 462a–b) reads *shel* (Tibetan for "crystal"), which seems to make more sense.

471 *khyad par du* (*viśeṣataḥ*, *viśiṣṭa*, etc.) is present in each verse, though in different, seemingly random places (in the original Skt. the word position would have been less relevant).

472 *ri lu* (all three Tib. edititions). The Tib.–Tib. dictionary (*Dag yig gsar bsgrigs* [Current Tibetan Dictionary] p. 744) has the following clarifying entry: *ri lu—"ril bu" yi 'bri tshul gzhan* [*ri lu* is another way of writing "*ril bu*"].

473 Tib. here reads *ru rak sha*. Das (1186) says that this is a Skt. word: "a kind of berry, prob. the smaller species of *rudrākṣa*, of which the rosaries used by *Tantrik* lamas are often made."

474 Tib. *lung thang*. Das (1216) says that *lung thang* = *lbu ba 'dzin* (which he does not define). *lbu ba* (935) means "bubble, foam, froth, scum" (Skt. *phena*). LC (1909) says *lung thang* = *ariṣṭa* or *phenila*. MW (719) says *phenila* = "foamy, frothy...," but also "a kind of tree, Vāsav.; Zizyphus Jujuba, Bhpr.; Sapindus Detergens, L.;...Hingcha Repens, L.;...."

> Saffron, or else
> All scent[ed substance]s in particular,
> When made into little beads and cooked[476]
> Are well-known to be used for dominating [activities].

The Vajraḍāka also explains [that you can use] coral and red sandalwood. [In the fourth verse from *The Kiss* above,] 'being' means a human being. [Finally,] that same text [*The Kiss*] states an auspicious material[477] common to all [types of action]:

> For all actions—peaceful, prospering, dominating, and
> destructive—
> Use bodhi [seeds].[478]

Moreover, regarding the number of rosary beads, that same text [*The Kiss*] states:

> To practice mantras, fifty [beads are generally used];
> Half of that for dominating [activities].
> One hundred for peaceful,
> And for prospering, eight more;

---

[475] The second *pāda* reads: *khams ni dkar po la sogs gzhan*. I am breaking Tsong Khapa's commentary as follows:

> *khams dkar po ni, rus pa dang sogs kyi sgras rdo'i khyad par dkar po dang gzhan ni, nor bu dkar por bshad do.*

Alternatively, one could read this commentary by breaking after the *sgras*, which would yield the following translation: "It is explained that [in the first verse] 'white substances' (*khams dkar po*) is a term for bone, etc., and thus for an especially white stone, and that 'other things' is a white jewel." I think my rendition above makes more sense.

[476] *ri lur byas shing tshos byas pa*—all the meanings for *tshos* in Das (1036) and Goldstein (930) have to do with either dyeing/painting/coloring, cooking, or imbuing/permeating. Das says specifically that *tshos byed pa* = "to paint, colour."

[477] *shis pa*. While this could be a typo for *shes pa* (which would render "this is common to all of them, it should be understood, ...") all three editions of the *NRC* have *shis pa*.

[478] Each *NRC* edition has a different spelling for this—TL: *bo de tse*; MS: *bo de tsi*; ZH: *ba da tse*; ACIP: *bo de tsam*. Das (877) has an entry for *bo dhi rtsi*—which would seem to be the same word spelled in a *fifth* (probably more accurate) way—which he defines as follows: "Rosary used to count the recitation of the names of *Bodhisattvas*, probably made of a kind of *peepul* [*Ficus religiosa*] wood." This is what today are commonly called "bodhi seeds."

For destructive, sixty—
[Those are the numbers] one uses for particular activities.

Regarding [the phrase] 'to practice mantras' [in the first line]—since [the remaining lines] accord with [the four] 'particular activities,' [the opening phrase] relates to practicing mantras of all activities.

Regarding the rosary cord, *The Vajraḍāka* explains that this should be made of golden thread or of cotton-wool thread woven by a young woman with an impeccable body;[479] you should wind up nine [such threads].

Then, with the pride of yourself being Vajradhara, you should instantaneously meditate that the fingers of your right hand are the actuality of a five-pronged vajra, {426a} upon which is a letter *AḤ* from which is produced a sun that is blessed with an *AḤ*; and you should instantaneously imagine that the fingers of your left hand are in the form of the petals of a lotus, upon which is an *AḤ* from which is produced a moon that is blessed with that [letter *AḤ*]; and having [thus] meditated, [you should imagine that] the central cord of the rosary which is held between those [hands] has the nature of Vajrasattva, and that the [other] eight threads on the cardinal and intermediate sides [of the central thread] have the natures of Padmapāṇi, Maitreya, Gaganagañja,[480] Samantabhadra, Vajrapāṇi, Mañjushrī, Sarvanivaraṇavishkambhin, and Kṣhitigarbha, and that the rosary beads have the nature of the five clans such as Vairochana, etc.; and having instantaneously imagined that the thread-holder [triple-bead][481] is a stūpa comprised of a collection of qualities such as strength, fearlessness, etc., cause Vajrasattva, etc.—[the other deities] just as they are in themselves—to enter [into the stūpa], summoning them by the light rays of the seed [syllable] at your heart; then bless [the rosary] with the mantra:

---

479 *gzhon nu ma yan lag ma nyams pas*. Tib. *yang lag* (Skt. *aṅga*) here likely means "body" (not just "limbs" or "attributes"). This probably is an idiom/euphemism for a virgin, or at least a woman who has not yet given birth.

480 *nam mkha' mdzod* = *Gaganagañja*, acc. LC (1051). Also, the *Mahāvyutpatti* (C. Körös VI [20], no. 58, p. 9) has the bodhisattva *Gaganagañja* = *nam mkha'i mdzod*. This must be an alternate name for *Ākāshagarbha* (Tib. *nam mkha'i snying po*).

481 *mdo 'dzin*, the rosary's top triple bead which holds the threads together.

> *Akkharukāraṇuru asohi amanat avisāruganị A, Asaṁkhu alika kusijja itangtavisaru, OṀ pade pade mahājñānaṁ sarvabuddha mahābhāve HŪṀ HŪṀ HŪṀ HO HO HO ĀḤ KHAṀ Svāhā!*[482]

Moreover, you should confer initiation [upon the rosary deities] with the water of the vase, and then you should make offerings [to them]. {426b} From "*OṀ pade*" onwards occurs in the eighth section of *The Kiss*. Those [mantra syllables] are explained in [Abhaya's *Vajra*] *Rosary* and *Clusters of Instructions*—and [they involve] the consecration that is in the systems of *The Kiss* and *The Four Seats*. If you do a brief consecration [of the rosary]:

> Regarding the rosary: meditate Speech-Vajra and make it one with the intuition hero; imagine that from a thorough transformation of that matter, the form of the rosary [arises]; then having sprinkled it with the water of the vase and made offerings, repeat the essence [mantra] of Speech-Vajra one-hundred and eight times.

—so [Abhaya's *Vajra*] *Rosary* states.[483]

Regarding the way of counting, [the forty-fifth chapter of] *The Vajraḍāka* states:

> For peaceful [activities] you should place [the rosary] on your forefinger;
> For prospering [activities] you should put it on the middle finger.

---

[482] There are many odd spellings in the first part of this mantra. Insofar as any of the sounds in this first part may constitute actual words, the "word" breaks are uncertain. Some possibilities include:

> *Akkha*—does not seem to exist. *Akkā* (MW 2) = mother, woman; Akhkhala (4) = an exclamation of joy.
>
> *karūkara* (255) = (n.) the joint of the neck and the back-bone.
>
> *kharu* (337) = (mfn.) white; foolish, idiotic; harsh, cruel; ... [many other meanings].

[483] Much of the preceding discussion also is paraphrased from this same section of Abhaya's *Vajra Rosary*. See my note to the Tibetan edition.

> It is said the ring finger is for dominating [activities];
> The little finger should be used for destructive [activities].
>
> Using the thumb as an iron hook,
> Imagine that all the deities are summoned.
> If you repeat mantra with intense absorption,
> You will achieve—have no doubt about this!

This is also in *The Kiss*.[484] *The Kiss* states:

> From that very thing you will achieve;
> If you do not [do it] completely clearly, it will be long
> [before you achieve].

In the commentary it states that if you meditate that the meditation of your hands as a vajra and lotus is the indivisibility of emptiness and compassion, and if you count with the right hand and you have the reality of the understanding that the deity's body lacks intrinsic reality, then you will achieve, and otherwise you will not achieve.

Regarding [what was stated in *The Vajraḍāka* about] going through the rosary with the visualization that your thumb is an iron hook and that you summon the deities with that, {427a} *The Kiss* and *The Four Seats* also state that; and regarding [*The Vajraḍāka*'s statement that you should repeat mantra with] 'intense absorption'—that is, [with] the mind not wandering elsewhere—that is explained with great insistence in many treatises, and thus it is very important that the mind not wander.

Regarding how quickly, etc., you should repeat, Shrī Phalavajra states [in the *Commentary on (*Jñānapāda*'s) Samantabhadra Sādhana*]:

> "Clear" means distinct,[485] with measure, not disjointed—neither too long nor too slow, also not disturbed by inhaling and exhaling; and not "clear" due to loudness which agitates the senses due to the strain—

484 I could not find these verses in *The Kiss Tantra* (either in Tōh. 376, Lhasa 395, or in Tōh. 381, Lhasa 396). However, very similar verses do appear in the *Arisal of Saṁvara Tantra*, Tōh. 373, Lhasa 389 (GA): 25b.

485 *gug skyed*.

Since the explanations by Shāntipa and Kamalarakṣhita[486] also accord with this statement, you should do it like that. "Measuredly" [refers to] the long or short measure of the syllables.

Regarding reciting vocally [out loud] or not vocally: the *Hevajra Sādhana, "An Elimination of Errors,"* [by Ratnākarashānti], and the *Supreme Bliss Sādhana*[s] by Ghaṇṭāpa and by Lavapa[487] state that you should do both the vajra repetition and the fierce repetition; but in their *Sādhana[s] of the Black Enemy [of Death Tantra]* Shāntipa and Kamalarakṣhita state that you should do only the fierce repetition and not the mental repetition—this is clearly a distinctive characteristic of *The Enemy of Death*.

Regarding the two [types of] repetitions, Shrī Phalavajra quotes two passages—[the *Commentary on (*Jñānapāda*'s) Samantabhadra Sādhana* states]:[488]

> With the vajra word you should repeat—
> The vajra word abandons sound...

and *The [Esoteric] Community* states:

> Intuiting the commitments of the fierce [deities], {427b}
> Your vajra[-tongue] resounds in the mandala[-body],
> And you hear the letters and words of the mantra—
> That is proclaimed the 'fierce repetition.'

The Illumination of the Lamp explains that 'fierce' means the mantra of *The Enemy of Death*, etc.; and 'intuiting the commitments' means knowing the rites of banishing, etc.; and 'mandala' means your own body; and 'vajra' means the tongue, the resounding of which is the recitation heard by yourself or another.

Regarding the visualization of what is repeated: Ghaṇṭāpa and Lavapa state [in their respective *Supreme Bliss Sādhanas*][489] that the

---

[486] Cf. note 379 above.

[487] Ghaṇṭāpa's *Five Deity Supreme Bliss Sādhana*, and Lva-ba-pa's *Supreme Bliss Sādhana*. Cf. note 246 above.

[488] I have not found the source from which Shrī Phalavajra here is citing.

[489] Again, Ghaṇṭāpa's *Five Deity Supreme Bliss Sādhana*, and Lva-ba-pa's *Supreme Bliss Sādhana*. Cf. note 246 above.

mantra to be repeated comes out of the seed [syllable] at your heart, [travels down and out] from the tip of the vajra at the secret place and into the mother's vagina, then [it travels up and] out of the goddess' mouth and enters into your own mouth, and then it [travels back down and] enters the seed [syllable at your heart again, whereupon] you meditate that it circles around again like before; and imagining that all of the mouths and all of the yoginīs are repeating mantra [in that way], you repeat. However, Saroruha explains [in his *Hevajra Sādhana*] that it first [begins] from the goddess' mouth, then enters your own mouth, and then circles around.

[Abhaya's] *Clusters of Instructions* states that mantra repetition is fourfold. [1] Vehicle repetition: with the pride of the equality of all things, the mantra rosary enters your own mouth, comes out of the vajra and goes into the lotus, whereupon it ascends the central channel and emerges from the mother's mouth and enters into your own mouth; and [thus] meditating that it circles around, you repeat the mantra rosary with relaxed and peaceful syllables. [2] Fierce repetition: the mantra [rosary] first {428a} enters the mother's mouth and cycles as above; it is comprised of dense, harsh syllables. [3] Ferocious repetition: this is when you fiercely enunciate the essence [mantra], etc. [4] Commitment repetition: this is when you enunciate the essence and near-essence mantras [around] the seed [syllable] in your heart center, and you radiate the host of deities of the mandala to accomplish the aims of beings; then by means of the wind-energy which functions in such a way as to simultaneously draw up both the mantra and the rosary string, [the mantra] enters the seed [syllable] at the heart; and when you have completed the recitations of the mantras of the various deities, they each radiate out and gather back in. According to that, the first two [have to do with] the gentleness and harshness of mantra rosaries; and the third [has to do with] all three—the mantra rosary, the essence [mantra], and the near-essence [mantra]—and the fourth is the repetition of the essence [mantra] or the near-essence [mantra only]. Moreover, the fourth one is mentioned in *The Samantabhadra Sādhana*, which explains that the radiated deities fill the expanse of space.

Regarding this, Dīpaṅkarabhadra says [in *The Maṇḍala Rite of the Glorious Esoteric Community (The Four Hundred and Fifty [Verses])*]:

> The intuition body radiates while repeating:
> With recitation and vitality [(*prāṇa*, *srog*) during exhalation] it should radiate [deities]; and
> With mantra control [(*āyāma*, *rtsol*) during inhalation] it should gather back [the deities].

This states that when you exhale [while reciting a mantra] you radiate [deities], and when you inhale [between mantras] you gather back the deities.[490] However Shāntipa [in his *Commentary on [Dīpaṅkarabhadra's] The Four Hundred and Fifty [Verses]*] states his own interpretation [of Dīpaṅkarabhadra's quote]:[491]

> Depending on the mantra's length you recite it one, two, or many times with a long exhalation, which is '*vitality*'; and then when you gather back [your vitatlity with inhalation], the recitation and radiation [keeps happening] at the same time. If you repeat like that your mind will be undistracted.

{428b}—and then sets forth [the more literal] interpretation [of Dīpaṅkarabhadra's quote]:

> Others [say that] when you repeat each mantra it is the time of radiation, and that [only] after that comes the time of gathering back.

---

490 Note that Dīpaṅkarabhadra's presentation here connects with the first half of the following interesting observation made by Wayman:

> The four [of the five] winds, leaving out *vyāna*,...are *prāṇāyāma* [Tib. *srog rtsol*]. This word does not ordinarily signify in the Buddhist Tantra, 'restraint of breath' but rather *prāṇa*, in-breathing, and *āyāma*, out-breathing; or *prāṇa*, the passage of winds through the orifices, and *āyāma*, the out-going mental component that 'rides on the wind'. (*YGST*, 71)

However, Dīpaṅkarabhadra and Tsong Khapa here reverse these equations, saying that *prāṇa* (*srog*) = out-breathing, and *āyāma* (*rtsol*) = in-breathing (so it would seem that Wayman mistakenly reversed these). Note also that below (cf. Tib. 430b, and note 508) Tsong Khapa explicitly equates *srog rtsol* with *'byung 'jug gyi rlung* (exhalation- and inhalation-winds).

491 The next two passages from Shāntipa are condensed quotes with numerous elisions. Cf. notes to the Tibetan edition.

If you recite according to the statements of Ghaṇṭāpa and Lavapa —that you visualize that the lord recites with as many mouths as he has,[492] and that all the retinue deities recite—it is said that you can multiply your count [accordingly].[493] As [Ratnākarashānti's *Hevajra Sādhana,*] *An Elimination of Errors*, states:

> You should visualize that from all of the [lord's] mouths and from all of the goddess' mouths mantras are being recited. Regarding this, due to the repetitions of all the [eight] goddesses you should multiply eightfold[494] the repetitions made by yourself as a deity.

Thus, there are three visualizations regarding [mantra] repetitions: [1] [those involving mantras visualized as coming] from the mouths of the father-mother; [2] repetitions which are visualized with respect to the retinue; and [3] visualization that deities are radiated from the mantra and are gathered back.[495] And according to the *Hevajra Sādhana [An Elimination of Errors]* explanation by Shāntipa and by [Kṛiṣhṇa-]Samayavajra [in the *Hevajra Commentary, "The Jewel Rosary of Yoga"*][496] there are two [more] repetition[-visualizations]: [4] [one in which] you repeat the mantras as if they are written by the mind, and are arrayed by the mentality, standing up and going around the seed [syllable] in the heart, blazing like a row of lamps; and [5] [one in which] you visualize that all of the mouths and all of the deities are reciting—so there are five

---

[492] *gtso bo lta bu la zhal du yod kyis 'don pa*

[493] *de dag gi grangs kyi 'gyur yod par gsungs te*—that is, every mouth of every deity in the mandala is reciting, and as each one counts for one recitation, there are as many recitations going on simultaneously as there are mouths in the mandala reciting!

[494] The Derge reads "a hundred-fold" (*brgya* instead of *brgyad*).

[495] This is expressed elliptically and, unless edited, makes little sense. Perhaps some textual corruptions have crept in. Much of this section (including the preceding paragraphs and the ones coming up) seem hastily and elliptically written.

[496] Regarding the author of the *Hevajra Commentary, "The Jewel Rosary of Yoga"* (*Yogaratnamālā*), there seems to be some confusion (or conflation, or equivalency) between the names Samayavajra and Kṛiṣhṇa. See my discussion of this in the "comments" section of the bibliographic entry for this title (p. 297). For a complete translation of the *Yogaratnamālā*, see Farrow and Menon (1992).

[repetition-visualizations in total]. Jālandharipa explains [in his *Hevajra Sādhana, "A Vajra Lamp"*] that the former one of those is 'the sphere repetition' and the latter is 'the commitment repetition.'[497] In these contexts, you also visualize the wind-energies and do the vajra repetition of the three letters [that is, you align the wind-energies with the three letters], {429a} but as this has been explained by many such as [Abhaya in] the *Clusters of Instructions* and by Prajñārakṣhita,[498] etc., I will not write about it [here].

You should enter into your count the repetitions [that you do] in the actual [formal] session with a single-pointed mind free of the faults of repetition; but once you have given up the actual [formal] session you do not enter into your count whatever repetitions you do in between sessions, although there is nothing wrong with repeating [then]. As Akṣhobhyavajra states in *The Sādhana of the Black Enemy [of Death]*:

> Even when you get up [from the session] you should visualize the esoteric mantra body and repeat [mantras, even though] it does not help your count.

Regarding the colors of the mantra: Saroruha's explanation classifies according to the colors of the [different types of] action—peaceful, increasing, powerful, and fierce [mantras] are white, yellow, red, and black. [However,] just as in the context of the prior retreat you do not need to change the color of the deities, so likewise you should vary [or not vary] the color of the mantras in accordance with [whether or not you vary] the deities. Or alternatively, you should do it like Tibetan lamas say: in order to bring the deities under control make [the mantras] red.

Subhagavajra explains [in *The Stages of the Path of the Universal Vehicle*]:[499]

---

[497] *gong bu'i bzlas pa* and *dam tshig gi bzlas pa*. Presumably "former" and "latter" refer to the last two [of the five] discussed, those described by Shāntipa and Samayavajra. Note that the latter (the commitment repetition) is the same name as Abhaya's second of four given a few paragraphs above (at 428a).

[498] Cf. note 386 above.

[499] Cf. note 236 above.

> The technique [to be used] at the time of the repetition should be understood on the basis of the context: [repeat mantra] like whirling a fire-brand or like throwing a roped harpoon or like a bunch of feathers[500] or like winding up twine[501] or like binding with chains.

Tibetan lamas connect the first with peaceful [activities], the second with fierce, the third with increasing, and the last two with powerful, and they {429b} thereby explain the [various] types of letters and light-rays of the mantras; however, I have not seen anyone else[502] clearly explain this. [In fact] Saroruha says that [just the one method involving the mantra] circling from mouth to mouth, which is a circling like a fire-brand, is to be classified according to the colors of [all] four actions; and as Prajñendraruchi says in *The Blazing Jewels [Sādhana]*:

> Then the wise one repeats the mantra—
> It should circle around from the mouths of the father and mother
> Like the wheel of a fire-brand.
> The color should be classified according to the classification of action.

Therefore, that [one method of fire-brand circling] has the set of four actions.

Thus, from the entry of the intuition hero up until the repetition constitutes the branch that completes the deities that you have created; but recollecting the symbolism [should be done] for the most part according to what Durjayachandra said—he said that when you are unable to concentrate, then you should recollect the symbolism—thus you should do it when you have become weary from deity yoga. And then there are many

---

500 Das (337) says *sgro* means feather, but *sgro ga* and *sgro gu* mean 'rope, cord, strap,' etc., and *sgro ga* can also mean "the little bubbles in sparkling beverages." Could this be "a bunch of sparkling bubbles" ?

501 All three texts read *the gu bsgril*. No dictionary has *the gu*. However, Das (563) has an entry under *tha gu* (= Skt. *dāma*) which says that a "vulgar" spelling for this is *thi gu*. This word means "a wreath, a short cord or rope; twine for making garlands; a chain or fetter."

502 That is, canonical Tantric commentaries by Indian siddhas.

explanations [of what to do] in the context of the main part of the session, like the explanations by Shāntipa, Durjayachandra, and Ḍombipa. Saroruha and Jayasena[503] explain that it is after the votary cake that you recollect the symbolism, and according to that you would do [the recollection of the symbolism] in between sessions.

As we can see with the elucidations of the intention of Lūipa's *[Supreme Bliss] Sādhana* by Prajñārakṣhita and others, and with the explanation in Saroruha's *[Hevajra] Sādhana*, there are very many who assert that the serial withdrawal into clear light has the [same] import as the 'dissolving [yoga]' which is stated in [Nāgārjuna's] *The Five Stages*, **{430a}** and thus if you do that, you should practice while remembering the view [of emptiness].

[And there are many other miscellaneous related topics—for example:] There is an explanation that even the subtle drop is to be meditated within each context; [and one topic is the system of] meditating in [such] contexts, and especially the system for stopping dullness and distraction, which [thereby] achieves firm mental stability for visualizing. And [there is the topic of] the system for cultivating mindfulness and alertness; and [the topic of] the gauge of when one has achieved serenity, etc. These [topics] are common to both Mantra and Transcendence [Vehicles], and since you must definitely understand them from what I have already extensively explained in the stages of the path that is common to the vehicles, you should look there.[504]

Regarding the context of meditating the deity and emptiness, Tathāgatavajra explains [in his *Auto-commentary to the Commentary to Lūipa's Evocation*]:

> Moreover, regarding this, from the morning session to the midnight session you should abide meditating only the deity. Then, you should meditate emptiness...

—this is in terms of [when one is] meditating emptiness separately.

---

[503] Jayasena has five books (Tōh. 1518, 1519, 1521, 1522, and 1589) in the Saṁvara section of the canon (Tengyur chart: A2b1), and one (Tōh. 3775) in the "Miscellaneous" section of the canon (Tengyur chart: E7).

[504] That is, in Tsong Khapa's text, *Great Treatise on the Stages of the Path* (*lam rim chen mo; LRC*).

[**II.B.2.c.ii.C'3'c'ii'B''4''a''ii''A°3°** – The follow-up (to those yogas of the actuality of the session)]

The third has two: [a°] The procedure for fortifying the body and creating the votary cake; and [b°] The procedure for creating the guests and offering [the votary cake to them].

[**II.B.2.c.ii.C'3'c'ii'B''4''a''ii''A°3°a°** – The procedure for fortifying the body and creating the votary cake]

When your body and mind are fatigued from having meditated in that way, there is the procedure of fortification.[505] You should refresh your weariness according to the method stated by Dīpaṅkarabhadra in the [*Mandala Rite of the Glorious Esoteric*] *Community Tantra* [*(The Four Hundred and Fifty [Verses])*]:

> On your crown a moon with a moist *OṀ*
> Drips the water of the holy mind
> Causing the satisfaction of body, speech, and mind
> —[Thus] should [it] fall according to the rite.

That method involves imagining that in a finger-width-span of space above your crown[506] {430b} there is a moon mandala marked with an *OṀ* from which nectar falls, moistening each and every atom of your body down to your feet. Moreover, Shrī Phalavajra explains [in the *Commentary on (*Jñānapāda'*s) Samantabhadra Sādhana*] that you imagine that the nectar is attracted by the light rays of your exhalation- and inhalation-wind, and that it then falls on the crown and drips. Shāntipa explains [in his *Commentary on [Dīpaṅkarabhadra's] The Four Hundred and Fifty [Verses]*]:

---

[505] *rtas par byed pa'i cho ga*. In the heading we have *brtas*, and here we have *rtas*. Das (557) cites *brta ba* (pf. *brtas*), which he defines as "to grow wide, expand; be copious, abundant...inflate...." Gold (487) cites *rtas* (pf. *brtas*), which he defines as "to protect, to defend, to look after." Combining the meanings of "to expand" and "to look after" in the context of the body being tired (*dub*), we have derived the translation "to fortify" for *brtas*/*rtas pa*.

[506] *spyi bor mtho gang tsam gyi bar snang la*—Das (602) says that *mtho*, *mtho gang*, and *mtho re tsam* have to do with "a span, from the tip of the thumb to the tip of the middle finger when extended."

> The light rays of the *OṀ* draw it [energy] in from the ten directions, and by vitality and exertion[507] you make it enter within and run throughout the whole mass of channels such that it pervades the whole body.

That is the way it descends inside by 'vitality and exertion,' that is, by exhalation- and inhalation-winds.[508] He explains that when your weariness is refreshed by that, you then should do additional repetition and meditation; so, since it is to be done whenever you are weary, it is not definite that it is [to be done] only at the end of the rite.

Then, as *The Samantabhadra Sādhana Root-Commentary*[509] explains, when you want to end the session you again make offerings and praises to the mandala, taste nectar, and then request the mandala to depart; but this is a request to depart which entails that the mandala deities gather back into the lord, not that they go elsewhere.

When you practice this way, you should make a votary cake at the end of [each of] the four sessions—as *The Latter [Tantra of] Clear Expression* states:

> With the process of this procedure
> You should give [one] in the four session-breaks.

—and other [texts] are also similar [regarding this]. When you do not practice [this way], you should give the votary cake at the end of the final session. Moreover, Saroruha explains that it [the votary cake offering] is to be done after you have gathered the mandala inhabitants back into yourself; {431a} but the *Clusters of Instructions* explains that it is once you have made the votary cake that you gather the mandala inhabitants into oneself—so you can either do it at the very end of the final session or in betweeen sessions, whatever makes you happy.

Although there is a variety of votary-cake rites, the intentions of *The Kiss*, *The Four Seats*, and *The Vajraḍāka* are for the most part similar—so [now] I will explain the intention of *The Kiss* according to what is stated in the *Clusters of Instructions*.

---

507 *srog dang rtsol ba* (*prāṇa* and *āyāma*).

508 *srog rtsol te, 'byung 'jug gi rlung*. Again we see this equation (see above, note 490).

509 Presumably the *Commentary on [Jñānapāda's] The Samantabhadra Sādhana* (Tōh. 1867), by Shrī Phalavajra.

Votary cakes are said by many Tantras to be very important at the beginning and the end [of practice] in order to pacify demonic interference and to achieve siddhis, and thus you should use them. At that time [when you do use them], the ninth section of *The Kiss* states:

> [Do it] on the fourteenth day of the waning moon,
> Especially on the eighth day, and
> On the tenth day of the waxing [moon].[510]

—these are special times, but otherwise it is stated that you should offer [votary cakes] each and every day.

Regarding the deity yoga of the giver—the *Guhyasamāja-Akṣhobhya-vajra* states that you have choices with respect to the creation of yourself as Vajrasattva: [you can create yourself as Vajrasattva] with the complete evocation, or with the procedure of the four branches [of service and practice], either gradually or instantaneously; and you also can understand that from other [sources] as well.[511]

[Regarding the vessel for holding the votary cake—] of the three [ways] the votary-cake rite can be practiced by that one: in the extensive [way], the vessel for [holding] the votary cake which is transformed into nectar is said by *The Kiss* to be "a lotus vessel," [which means] a skull-bowl vessel;[512] and the *Clusters of Instructions* {431b} says that a vessel such as a wooden platter, etc., also is suitable; and the *Red Enemy [of Death] Tantra* explains further that this can be a tray or copper vessel;[513]

---

510 These are, respectively, the 29th, 8th and 10th days of the lunar month.

511 TL and ZH read *gdam nga can du gsungs*, and MS reads *b̲dam nga can su gsungs*. The spelling (and root verb) for *gdam nga* is somewhat confused: it varies from source to source whether the root is *'dem* or *'dems* (Gold 583, 605), or *'dam* or *'doms* (Das 679; RY). In any case, Gold (584) says *gdam nga* = "optional, left to one's choice/selection," and Das (679) says that *'dam ka = 'dam ga = 'dam nga = vikalā* = "choice, option."

512 The *Hevajra Tantra* (II, 3, 58; Farrow & Menon, p. 201) indicates that it is part of the Tantric code language (*sandhyābhāṣa*) that *padmabhājana* (a lotus vessel) means *kapāla* (a skull-bowl).

513 *khyogs sam zangs gzhong gi snod*—the meaning of this is unclear. All sources say *gzhong* = "trough, platter, ..." and *zangs* = "copper" (though *zangs* alone can also mean a copper *pot*). The real mystery word here is *khyogs*. All sources say this means "palanquin; bier; tray (RY); a vehicle or conveyance; (Skt. *duli*, *dolā*, *dolaka*, etc.)"; also, RY says that *'khyog* (note different spelling) can = "pot."

but [Abhaya's *Vajra*] *Rosary* explains that you can give [a votary cake] in a clay cup and even in the cupped hands; thus whatever it is will work.

Regarding the substance of the votary cake—[Abhaya's *Vajra*] *Rosary* and *Clusters of Instructions* explain that [you should use] flour, beans,[514] meat, fish, barley soup,[515] pastry,[516] beer, water, onion, white garlic, and milk, etc.; or if you cannot obtain [these], then even just flour and water, etc., are suitable.

Regarding the way of preparing a votary cake and the offering substances—*The Kiss* states:[517]

> The honoring [substances] such as drinking water,
> offerings, etc., and
> The foods such as fish and meat, etc., and
> Also the delights[518] [such as] beer and intoxicants
> —Everything that one needs on the left,
>
> And the water vessels on the right, and
> The vessels of offering substances in front
> —All of these substances
> Should be purified with the five nectars.

Regarding the third line, the *Commentary* [the *Clusters of Instructions*] says:

> Beer [means] desirables that cause joy,...

---

514 *sran ma*—acc. Das (1287) this can apparently refer to a wide variety of peas and/or beans.

515 *chan* = "sop, mash, pulp" (Das 409), or "boiled corn, barley" (RY). *thug (pa)* means "soup."

516 *'khur ba*. Das (187) says that as a sbst. this means "pastry." RY agrees, and adds that *khur ba* (the spelling at ZH 372b) is "pf. of *'khur ba*: 1) cookie, pastry, bread; 2) syn. *thug pa*; 3) vegetables."

517 Tsong Khapa's citation of the second pada of the second verse reads *mdun du* ("in front") which which fits better with the theme of directional placements than the Lhasa edition's *mngon du* ("manifestly"). Otherwise both are the same.

518 *spro ba*. Das (813) says that as a substantive this is *utsāha*, *autsukya* = "joy, energy, cheerfulness." Since the previous pādas ended in substantives, this would seem to be a substantive as well.

If you have two votary cakes, [one] made of meat and [one made of] fish, etc., it is said that you place them to your right and left; and regarding the purification by the five nectars—the *Clusters of Instructions* states that you purify through using a nectar-pill or else through meditation.

Regarding the method of creating the votary cake—the explanation in [Abhaya's *Vajra*] *Rosary* is the intention of *The Kiss*, and it also is elucidated in the *Clusters of Instructions*; and {432a} [Abhaya's *Vajra*] *Rosary* says that that very method of creating it is the same in *The Esoteric Community*, *[Supreme] Bliss*, and *Hevajra*. Namely, from *YAṀ* there arises [a blue bow shaped] wind [mandala] upon which is *RAṀ* from which is produced [a red triangular shaped] fire [mandala] upon which is an *AḤ* from which is produced a white skull-bowl which sits upon [a tripod of] three heads which are produced from the three seed [syllables *OṀ AḤ HŪṀ*]; in that [skull-bowl] the ten seed [syllables] such as *HŪṀ*, etc., produce the five nectars and the five meats which are blessed by—that is, marked by—those ten seed syllables.

The seed [syllables] are:

> *HŪṀ*, *BRUṀ*, *ĀṀḤ*, *HRĪḤ*, *KHAṀ*, and *BRUṀ*, *HŪṀ*, *HRĪḤ*, *TRAṀ [MO]*.[519]

In both [Abhaya's *Vajra*] *Rosary* and *Clusters of Instructions* it is not clear as to what is produced in which of the cardinal and intermediate directions, and there is also nothing clearly written in *The Kiss*, *The Four Seats*, or the *Arisal of Saṁvara [Tantra]*. The *Red Enemy [of Death] Tantra* explains that the five meats which are named *GO*, *KU*, *DA*, *HA*, *NA*

---

519 There are many evident problems here. This is not the expected list of ten; there appears to be a list of nine syllables here, followed by the closing verb/syllable *mo* (in TL & MS) or *ngo* (in ZH). The nine are not the syllables expected in this context, and some (notably *ĀṀḤ*) have seemingly impossible spellings (though this appears again about a page later, near the end of 432b). Either all three *NRC* editions are very corrupt in this one location, or perhaps what Tsong Khapa says in the next sentence about certain texts being "unclear" (*mi gsal zhing… gsal bar ma 'byung*) refers to this list. That is, perhaps this corruption has been copied over from those texts and Tsong Khapa is politely pointing out the corruption by calling it "unclear." In any event, the syllables that are discussed in subsequent sentences are what one would expect for the seed syllables of the nectars and the meats, etc. But then later (mid 432b) he discusses a set of five and a set of four *which is really five* since it shares one member in common (great meat, not a syllable) with the first set of five.

[after the first syllables of their Sanskrit names] are made respectively to have the nature of Vairochana, etc., and are set out respectively from the east [clockwise around] to the center; and [these five buddhas then] arise from the syllables *BRUṀ*, *AṀ*, *JRIṀ*, *KHAṀ*, and *HŪṀ*.[520] The five nectars which are named *VI*, *RA*, *SHU*, *MA*, *MU* [after the first syllbales of their Sanskrit names] [are made] respectively [to] have the nature of Locanā, etc., and are set out respectively beginning from the fire [direction, that is, south-east, going clockwise around] to the center; and [these five consort-buddhas then] arise from the syllables *LAṀ*, *MAṀ*, *PAṀ*, *TAṀ*, and *BAṀ*, and they are marked by them.[521]

Now in [Abhaya's *Vajra*] *Rosary* and *Clusters of Instructions* these appear in the order "the five nectars and the five lamps"; as the *Clusters of Instructions* says:

> The visualizations of the natures of such intuitions as being the actual five transcendent buddhas {432b} are the five lamps and the five iron hooks.[522]

---

[520] Beyer (158) explains in a commentary to a sādhana by Padma dkar po: GO = "cow," KUkkura = "dog," DAmya = "horse," HAstin = "elephant," and NAra = "human." Note that in that sādhana it says "these transform into the five fleshes," so there it is clear that these are the actual seed syllbales from which the meats arise. It might appear from the Tibetan here in the *NRC* that Tsong Khapa is saying that the five meats are *named* by those five syllables, but that the five meats/buddhas then *arise* from *BRUṀ*, *AṀ*, etc. However, it seems that the Tibetan here can be read in such a way as to follow Padma dkar po.

We also can cite here a passage from the *Hevajra Tantra* (1.2.2; p. 25 in Farrow & Menon's edition): *tathāgatānāṁ bījaṁ / buṁ aṁ jrīṁ khaṁ hūṁ //* "The seed-syllables of the five Buddhas are: buṁ, aṁ, jrīṁ, khaṁ, and hūṁ." This supports my reading above (that these five syllables are in fact the direct seed syllables of the five transcendent buddhas, not [directly, at least] of the five meats). Note also here that Sanskrit of this text clearly has *BUṀ* (not *BHRŪṀ*). Many sādhanas have *BHRŪṀ* in this context. Note that throughout this section in the *NRC* (in all editions) we have *BRUṀ,* a spelling half-way between *BUṀ* and *BHRŪṀ*. If the *Hevajra* text is correct, we may see here an intermediate stage in the process of this "corruption" (or evolution).

[521] I am following the same logic here to arrive at the same syntax as in the previous sentence (see previous footnote). Again, Padma dkar po's sādhana explains (*The Cult of Tārā*, p. 158): VIṭ = "excrement," RAkta = "blood," ŚUkra = "semen," MAṁsa (actually MĀṁsa) = "flesh," and MUtra = "urine."

[522] "The visualizations" (*mos pa rnams*) is the subject, and the grammar is "The visualizations of *A* as *B* are *X* and *Y*." I am simplifying *rnam pa de lta bu'i ye shes* (part of *A* here) from the literal, awkward "intiution which is like that form" to the simpler "such intuiton" in order to make this awkward sentence somewhat inteligible.

So the five lamps and the five iron hooks are explained to be the five transcendent buddhas, and since Akṣhobhya, Vairochana, Ratnasambhava, Amitābha, and Amoghasiddhi, "the five iron hooks," also arise in that sequence, it is clear that from the first five syllables the five meats are produced—thus, going from the center and proceeding clockwise through the four directions, from *HŪṀ*, etc.,[523] the great meat, etc., is produced, marked by those [same] letters; and proceeding from the fire [direction, that is, south-east, going clockwise around] to the powerful [direction, that is, north-east], from *BRUṀ*, etc.,[524] excrement, etc., is produced, marked by those [same] letters; [and here] since the great meat is common [to both sets] no more than four are mentioned.

There is also a way of explaining the [five] nectars as the five transcendent buddhas—the *Drop of Mahāmudrā [Tantra]* says:

> Ratnasambhava is explained to be 'blood,'
> Amitābha is expressed as seminal essence,
> Amoghasiddhi is great meat,
> Akṣhobhya is urine,
> Vairochana is explained to be excrement
> —These are the five supreme nectars.

Doing it like that is also what is explained in Ghaṇṭāpa's *Five Deity Supreme Bliss Sādhana*.[525]

> *HŪṀ*, *OṀ*, *KHAṀ*, *ĀṀḤ*, *TRĀṀ*—
> Urine, excrement, great meat,
> Spirit of enlightenment [seminal essence], self-originated
> flower [blood].[526]

---

523 He now seems to refer to the first list above: *HŪṀ*, *BRUṀ*, *ĀṀḤ*, *HRĪḤ*, *KHAṀ*.

524 Again, he seems to be referring to the original list above (which makes sense, since we were puzzled that the second half had four members and not five): *BRUṀ*, *HŪṀ*, *HRĪḤ*, *TRAṀ*.

525 In none of Ghaṇṭāpa's *Supreme Bliss* texts (Tōh. 1431–1439) could I find the passage from the *Drop of Mahāmudrā [Tantra]* (Tōh. 420) cited just above, or anything like that passage. However the next passage (*HŪṀ*, *OṀ*, *KHAṀ*,...) does appear in his *Five Deity Supreme Bliss Sādhana* (Tōh. 1437, at 236a.5).

526 "Spirit of enlightenment" (*bodhicitta*, *byang chub sems*) is well-known to mean "seminal essence" in a Tantric context. What seems less well-known is that "self-originated flower" (*svayaṁbhūkusuma*, *rang [']byung me tog*—cf. LC for this equivalence) means

(cont'd)

> *LAṀ, MAṀ, PAṀ, TAṀ*—
> Cow, dog, elephant,
> Horse—all of the lamps have a seed [syllable].

—so [Ghaṇṭāpa's *Sādhana*] explains. Lavapa also states it similarly, [using a Mother Tantra] system in which one goes counter-clockwise around the main directions and {433a} clockwise around the intermediate directions.[527]

Moreover, regarding the colors of the seed [syllables] *The Further [Tantra of The Esoteric Community]* explains that the center and four main directions are blue, white, yellow, red, and green, and that the colors of the four intermediate directions are white, blue, red, and green; and it is explained that the wind mandala is decorated with banners and the fire mandala with flames, and that the one-piece [white] skull-bowl is red on the inside. Those two [authors][528] align the nectars with the transcendent buddhas and the meats with the mothers, as one can tell from the seed [syllables].

In the Indian treatises most of the rites for creating votary cakes have many [instances] wherein the seed [syllables] of the five clans and the [five] mothers produce the ten substances. Moreover, the creation of each of those ten substances from the first letter of their [Sanskrit] names is explained by [Ratnākarashānti's] *The Jewel Lamp: A Commentary on the Black Enemy [of Death Tantra]*, and by the *Commentary* on Lūipa['s *Evocation*] written by Atīsha, and by Jayasena['s texts];[529] and *The Further [Tantra of The Esoteric Community]* says that going from the southeast and proceeding clockwise around to the center are *GO, KU, DA, HA, NA*, which are white, blue, red, green, and blue, from which [are produced] the meats of cow, dog, elephant, horse, and human, [each] marked by those [same seed syllables], and that going from the east and proceed-

"blood" (or female sexual essence). For example, this appears in the *Hevajra Tanatra* (II, 3, 48); the Sanskrit and translation by Farrow & Menon (p. 198) for the first two pādas are: *svayaṁbhūkusumaṁ prāpya padmabhāṇde niveśayet/* "Obtaining menstrual blood he must place it in a skull-cup ..."

527 This is normal in the Mother Tantras.

528 Presumably the two explanations by Ghaṇṭāpa and Lavapa.

529 Jayasena is cited as the author of eight texts: Tōh. 1516–19, 1521–22, and 1588–89.

ing counter-clockwise around to the center are *VI*, *MU*, *MA*, *RA*, *AḤ*, which are white, green, red, yellow, and white, from which [are produced] excrement, urine, great meat, blood, and seminal essence, [each] marked by those [same seed syllables]. In the two previous ones the seed [syllables] of the five clans are placed upon them—[but] the system of producing each from its own name-letter is good.

In short, the votary-cake[-holding] vessel is created as a skull-bowl, and the votary cake substances {433b} are created as the ten substances. And when you analyze those from the perspective of the seed [syllables] there are two ways: [1] creation from the seed [syllables] of the five clans and the [five] mothers, and [2] creation from the first letter of each one's name. And when you analyze from the perspective of where they are created, then according to the explanation in *The Jewel Lamp: A Commentary on the Black Enemy [of Death Tantra]* there are [again] two ways: [1] placing the seed [syllables] of the ten substances and the five clans in the center and the four main directions—just those five [places]—or [2] doing it in both the main and the intermediate directions. In *The Further [Tantra of The Esoteric Community]* there are [again] two ways: [1] creation of the meats in the center and the four main directions and the nectars in four intermediate directions, and [2] creation [of these things] in the opposite way; and there are [again] two ways: [1] making the meats the male transcendent [buddhas] and the nectars the female transcendent [buddhas], and [2] making [these] in the opposite way—but principally it uses the system wherein Akṣhobhya is in the center.

Regarding the five nectars, four—excrement, urine, and the white and red elements [that is, seminal essence and blood]—are [always explained] the same [way], but there are many explanations regarding the fifth: Nāropa and Vitapāda, etc., explain that it is the great meat; Bhavabhadra in his *Commentary on The Four Seats [Tantra]* explains that it is dried phlegm[530] and mucous; but the *Arisal of Saṁvara [Tantra]* explains three possibilities, a worst, middling, and best: [1] fat produced from

[530] Das (1216): *lud* = "manure"; *lud pa* = "phlegm, mucus." *lud* usually means the former, but given the context (followed by *ngar snabs* = mucous/snot), I am choosing the latter.

meat, [2] marrow and spinal fluid produced from the cavities [of bones],[531] and [3] brains produced from the head.

Moreover, the five meats are called "the five iron hooks and the five lamps" because they attract siddhis and illuminate. Then, having imagined that *HA*, *HOḤ*, *HRĪḤ* within the votary cake sequentially clear away ordinary color, scent, and potency, {434a} you imagine a perfect color, etc. In [Abhaya's] *Clusters of Instructions* and [*Vajra*] *Rosary* it is not explained that in the practice of creating the votary cake there is creation of three deities; but *The Kiss* and *The Four Seats* state that you meditate that from *HA* [comes] Amitābha, from *HOḤ* [comes] Vairochana, and from *HRĪḤ* [comes] Akṣhobhya. If you do that, the *Commentary on The Four Seats* explains that having recited *HA*, *HOḤ*, *HRĪḤ* three times you transform the three—color, scent, and taste, which are cleansed of faults—into the three deities.

Whipped up by the wind, the fire blazes causing an intense heat that melts the letters, etc., which then look like [a pool of] frothy semen with the color of the rising sun.[532] Imagine that the steam [rising] from that transforms into a syllable *HŪṀ* from which is produced a vajra-marked khaṭvāṅga staff. It melts and falls there [on the pool] three times,[533] transforming [it] into nectar. On the surface [of the nectar] is an *OṀ*, from which arises a moon, upon which are the syllables *OṀ*, *ĀḤ*, *HŪṀ* standing one upon the other.[534] They emit light rays which attract

---

531 These are odd words. *sbubs* usually means a hollow, etc. But given the context (*mar* always simply means "marrow"), it must refer to bone-hollows. *gzhung* (no final *s*) normally just means "middle, center," but *klad gzhung* means spinal marrow (Das 1081). Also, Gold (997) has many entries for *gzhung*, but only two *with* our final *s* (*gzhungs*): *gzhungs brgyangs* = "spinal cord," and *gzhungs rings* = "spinal column."

532 *nyi ma 'char kha'i mdog can gyi khu ba'i lbu ba can du blta'o*—Some trivial spelling issues: *kha mdog* is indeed a variant spelling for *kha dog* ("color," Das 135), but I could not find *kha'i mdog*. More likely this breaks differently, after the *kha* (which should be a *ka* or a *ga*): *'char ga* means "appearance" (Das 442), and according to RY, *nyi ma 'char ka* means "the rising sun." Then *mdog* by itself can still mean color, the genitive at the end of *nyi ma 'char kha'i* [read *ga'i* or *ka'i*] makes sense, and the whole translation stands as is anyway ("having the color of the rising sun").

533 Perhaps this means that the khaṭvāṅga staff falls down upon the pool and stirs it around three times.

534 Although Tsong Khapa does not specify it here, usually the *OṀ* is on the bottom of this stack, the *ĀḤ* is in the middle, and the *HŪṀ* is on the top.

the nectars of the spirit of enlightenment of the buddhas dwelling in the ten directions and the nectars abiding in the oceans, etc., which [nectars then] enter into the three syllables and into the moon; that is, they dissolve there into the three syllables together with the moon. Then, reciting the three syllables three times, bless it [the nectar] to have the brilliant nature of mercury. [This whole process] is explained like that in [Abhaya's *Vajra*] *Rosary*; but in the *Clusters of Instructions* it is explained that the [Sanskrit] vowels and consonants [are first arrayed on the moon, and then they] transform into the three seed [syllables]; {434b} and statements by Lavapa and Ghaṇṭāpa similar to the foregoing are the intention of the *Arisal of Saṁvara [Tantra]*.

Moreover, since Lavapa and Ghaṇṭāpa, etc., explain thus the procedure for tasting the nectar, they create it accordingly. However, [Bhavabhadra's] *Commentary on The Four Seats [Tantra]* explains that you imagine that on the tongues of the deities there is a *HŪṀ* from which is produced a white vajra [straw] just [the thickness of] a barley grain,[535] and that you imagine that by drawing up [the nectar] through a light-ray hole in that [vajra] they drink[536] the nectar and are satisfied, and that you offer [the nectar] by sprinkling with the ring finger[537]—that is, you sprinkle it on [your] three places: the tip of the tongue, between the eyebrows, and on the crown.

[II.B.2.c.ii.C'3'c'ii'B''4''a''ii''A°3°b° – The procedure for creating the guests and offering (the votary cake to them)]

Second, regarding the statement in the set of three Tantras such as *The Kiss*, etc., that you should make the triangle white on the outside and

---

535 *lha rnams kyi ljags la h'um las skyes pa'i rdo rje dkar po nas 'bru tsam*—Since *nas* can also mean "barley," I am translating *nas 'bru tsam* as one unit, "a mere barley grain," that is, "merely the thickness of a barley grain," and I am taking the vajra itself to be the straw.

536 Though *gsol ba* usually means "to offer," RY points out that *zhal du gsol ba* means "eating, drinking" [lit. "offering to the mouth"].

537 *mtheb srin gyi 'thor mas dbul*. ZH: *mtheb srin gyis 'thor bas dbul*. One could take this to mean "the thumb and third finger," noting that the thumb is the ocean and the third finger in Mt. Meru. This is of course what is going on here, but *mtheb srin* by itself just means "ring finger"; "thumb" is *the bo* or *mthe bo*. Also, I prefer the ZH reading of *'thor bas* this time, but I suppose *'thor mas* could mean "the scattering."

red on the inside, one cubit[538] [per side]: the commentaries state that you should make the inside red using saffron and red sandalwood, and thus you also should use white sandalwood, etc., on the outside; or else, alternately you can use colored sand—you should make it like that. In the center of that you lay down four lines such that there are then nine sections.[539]

In the central section you create whichever host of deities of the mandala in an instant. Moreover, in [Abhaya's *Vajra*] *Rosary* there is the statement that in the votary-cake rite of *The Esoteric Community [Tantra]* you should make a scent mandala, and thus that is what you should do in *The Esoteric Community [Tantra]*. In the eight other sections the *Clusters of Instructions* explains that [you create] the direction-protectors with their retinue of ogresses, but here we will [only] explain the direction-protectors: in the east from *JUṀ* is yellow Indra with a thousand eyes, {435a} riding his white elephant,[540] holding a vajra; in the south from *KAṀ* is black Yama standing on a buffalo seat with his right leg extended, fierce with hair blazing upwards, holding a club and a [noose with a] threatening gesture;[541] in the west from *VAṀ*[542] is white Varuṇa, with a

---

538 *khru gang ba*. Das has an entry for *khru* [no *gang*] = one cubit. Gold (152) has *khru gang* = "one cubit." RY has *khru gang* = "one cubit (15 inches); approx. 18" from elbow to tip of middle finger; one cubit, (twenty-four finger spans)." Tsong Khapa is probably referring to the following verse from *The Kiss*: *gtor ma'i las chog ji lta bar, ,rdo rje gtso bo rgyal po nyon, ,khru gang tsam gyi tsad du ni, ,dmar po'i dri yis dkyil 'khor bya, ,dkar pos phyi rol gru gsum bya,* (Lhasa 396 [ga]: 471b).

539 That is, you use four lines to create a tic-tac-toe pattern with nine sub-divisions. *le'u* is of course a part/division, but *le'u* tshe does not appear in dictionaries. However, Gold (1130) does say that *le'u* tshan = *le tshan* = "section, chapter, part." Since *tshe* and *tshan* sound very similar, this is most likely two ways of writing the same thing (one or the other being a conventional variant or a common misspelling).

540 *sa srung*—not in Das or Gold. LC (1996) says *sa srung* = *airāvaṇa*. MW (234) says *Airāvaṇa* = "(fr. *irā-van*), N. of Indra's elephant." Then (168) he says *irā* = "any drinkable fluid; ... food, refreshment; comfort, enjoyment...," and *irā-vat* = "possessing food, full of food; granting drink or refreshment, satiating, giving enjoyment...." I am not clear etymologically how the Tibetans translated this name as *sa srung* ('earth protector').

541 The threatening gesture has the forefinger and little finger extended. He is usually also holding a noose in that hand.

542 Text has *BAṀ*, as *BA* and *VA* tend to be confused in Tibetan transliterations of Sanskrit letters.

seven-hooded [dragon for a mount], holding a snake-noose; in the north from *BHAI* is yellow Kubera, sitting on a human, bulky, holding a mongoose and a citrus fruit;[543] in the fire [south-east direction], from *RAṀ* is red Agni, his brow, hairdo, and beard blazing, agitated, very fat,[544] sitting on a goat, [his four hands] sporting a refuge-granting [gesture], a rosary, a cookie,[545] and a small rod; in the Nairṛitya [south-west direction], from *YUṀ* is black Nairṛita[546] seated on a zombie, naked, adorned with human bones, grinding his fangs, holding a chopper-knife and a skull-bowl; in the wind [north-west direction], from *YAṀ* is green Vāyudeva, riding a yellow deer,[547] holding a wind-sock; in the Īshāna [north-east direction], from *ĀḤ* is a white Shiva,[548] sitting on the supreme bull [Nandi], with a top-knot of dreadlocks, and with bone ornaments, holding a khaṭvāṅga staff and a *cang te'u* hand-drum;[549] to the right of Shiva [in the east]

---

543 *bi dza p'u ra*—LC (1246) has an entry under *b'i dza p'u ra* = *bījapūra* (note long *ī* here). MW (732) says that *bīja-pūra* (or *-pūraka*, *-pūrī*, *-pūrṇa*) means "'seed-filled,' a citron, Citrus Medica."

544 *'khrugs pa shin tu tsho ba*—*'khrugs pa* means "disturbed," etc., and *tsho ba* means "fat."

545 *ril ba* = *kuṇḍikā*, *varttanikā* = "a round globular object, such as a round lump of butter, etc." (Das 1185).

546 *bden 'bral* = *nairṛta* ("untrue"). MW (570) says *nairṛta* = "belonging to ... Nirṛti, ... south-western...," so *nairṛta* is the name for the S.W. intermediate direction, and the name for the goddess who rules there is properly Nirṛiti (cf. MW [554] for a description and background of the goddess Nirṛiti). However, MW then also adds that *nairṛta* itself can be a "N. of one of the Loka-pālas (the ruler of the south-west quarter...)." Since we probably want a male deity here, I am assuming the name of this deity is *Nairṛta*. Note that in *YGST* (243) Wayman (quoting Nāgārjuna) mentions the intermediate direction names based on deity's names, giving *nairṛta* for the S.W.

547 The Tibetan here transliterates as Sanskrit *eṇaya*, but in MW (231) only *eṇa* appears: "a species of deer or antelope (described as being of a black colour with beautiful eyes and short legs)...."

548 *dbang ldan* = Indra, and *dbang ldan gyi phyogs* = *Indrakoṇa* = the north-east quarter (Das 907). However, LC (1309) has *īśa* and *īśāna* for *dbang ldan*, and MW (171) says that *īśa* is "...ruler, master, lord,... N. of Śiva as regent of the north-east quarter...," and that *īśāna* is "...ruler, master, one of the older names of Śiva-Rudra...." Wayman (*YGST*, 243) gives *Īśāna* as the name for the north-eastern direction.

549 Das (379) says this is just a *ḍamaru*, a small hand drum. However, this is specifically a thicker *ḍamaru* (wider between the two faces), which produces a bigger sound.

from *HŪṀ* is black Upendra-Viṣhṇu[550] sitting on a garuḍa, [his four hands] holding a wheel, rod, conch, and kaustubha jewel;[551] to the right of Kubera [in the north] from *SHAU* is white Gaṇapati, with an elephant face, sitting on a rat, [his four hands] holding a radish, rod, cookie,[552] and a rosary; {435b} up above from *ĀḤ* is red Sūrya, sitting on a chariot, with dazzling light-rays, holding a lotus; to his left from *AṀ* is white Chandra, sitting on a wheel, holding a moon-lily and a rosary, and from *OṀ* is yellow Brahma sitting on a goose, [his four hands] sporting a lotus, refuge-giving [gesture], a rosary, and a rod; below from *PAṀ* is the black [titan] Vemacitrin,[553] sitting on a chariot, holding a sword, and from *LAṀ* is yellow Pṛithvīdevī, sitting on a lotus, holding a lotus; except for the detatiled explanations of their ornaments, etc., they all have jewelled crowns and a charming expression.

Indra [E], Varuṇa [W], Vāyudeva [NW], Gaṇapati [N], Rakṣhasa [=Nairṛita] [SW], Chandra [UL], Brahma [UL], and Pṛithvīdevī [below] are on moon seats, and the rest are on sun seats. Brahma and Pṛithvīdevī are of the body clan [Vairochana]; Sūrya is of the jewel clan [Ratnasambhava]; Kubera, Shīva, and Varuṇa are of the speech clan [Amitābha]; Vāyudeva is of the Amoghasiddhi clan; and the remainder are of the Akṣhobhya clan. All [of the male deities] such as Indra, etc., have wisdom [female consorts] similar to themselves, and Pṛithvīdevī has art [male consort] similar to herself—each created from their various hand-symbols. Around them you imagine [crowds of] dragon [nāga] lords, etc., and all sentient beings.

Then you should invite the [appropriate] host of guests for each occasion, both the transcendent {436a} and mundane [deities], and unite

---

550 *nye dbang khyab 'jug*.

551 The Tibetan has *kau stu pa*. MW (318) says *kaustubha* = "N. of a celebrated jewel (obtained with thirteen other precious things at the churning of the ocean and suspended on the breast of Kṛishṇa or Vishṇu)...." However this could be a kind of club.

552 *la du*. Das (1201) says this comes from the Sanskrit *lāḍu* or *modaka* and is "a kind of pastry made in Tibet; a medicinal food in which radish preponderates." MW has nothing under *lāḍu*, *laḍu*, *lādu*, or *ladu*.

553 *thags bzang ris*. Das has nothing under this spelling, but he says (567) *thag bzang ris* = "an epithet of the lord of the *Asura* or *lha min* demi-gods." LC (827) has *thags bzang ris* = *Vemacitrin*, citing *Hevajra* II.5.37 (cf. Farrow & Menon, p. 251).

them with the [appropriate] devotee hero.[554] Then you sincerely make offerings, beginning with drinking water, foot-washing water, etc.; and after having offered the votary cake, in order to please the mandala residents, to eradicate faults of omission or excess, and to achieve all objectives, you first should ring your bell and then recite the one-hundred syllable mantra. Then you please them with the lotus-wheel gesture—[or] if you abbreviate the gesture, do it in the manner of an embrace[555]—and then placing your left hand in a vajra-fist at your heart, and placing your outstretched right hand on the ground of the checkered-diagram, then by visualizing that you are holding the feet of the deities, together with the retinue of intuition beings who strive to accomplish the objectives, you recite *OṀ Ātma-tiṣhṭha HŪṀ SVĀHĀ!* [*OṀ! Stay in me! HŪṀ SVĀHĀ!*] and request them to arise from the checkered-diagram.[556] With the [in-]breath that follows that [mantra, the rising deities then] enter into yourself—that is, they become of one taste with yourself—and you then should offer to them. Then, with the gesture of embrace, you should snap your fingers three times, and reciting *OṀ Sarva-duṣhṭa gṛihāṇa gṛihāṇa*[557] *gaccha HŪṀ PHAṬ!* [*OṀ Seize! Seize all evil! Go! HŪṀ PHAṬ!*] you request that the direction-protectors, etc., go [back] to wherever they abide. That is the extensive votary-cake [rite].

Inviting the intuition beings without creating the devotee beings in the checkered-diagram, and then offering as before—that is the middling [votary-cake rite]. And visualizing the direction-protectors, etc., in the form of your own deity,[558] and then offering them the votary cake of your own chosen {436b} deity in the place where they normally abide—that is

---

[554] You visualize that the detities all are transformed into the form of the central deity of the mandala; thus, in the case of the *Esoteric Community* mandala, they all become forms of Buddha Akshobhya, etc.

[555] *phyag rgya sdud pa na 'khyud pa'i tshul byas te*

[556] The grammar is a bit strange in this long, run-on sentence. It seems unclear who is staying and who is going.

[557] Although the Tibetan transliterated Sanskrit stack would seem to be *gṛhṇa*, the more common imperative form for √grah is *gṛhāṇa*.

[558] For example, if you are practicing Hevajra you would visualize that all the deities such as Shiva, Varuṇa, etc., come and enter the checkered-diagram in the bodily form of Hevajra.

the condensed [votary-cake rite]; at that time you do not need the mandala of the triangle, etc., the creation of the devotee being, and the attracting of the intuition being, etc.

That is the votary-cake rite of the creation stage. Now in the perfection stage, with a mind which does not waver from wisdom and art, you merely imagine that you offer a votary cake—indistinguishable from the taste of intuition—to Indra and company, [transformed into forms of] your own chosen deity, invited thus as the actuality of wisdom and art.

Shāntipa explains that after the votary cake, or at the end of offering and praising, you should offer prayers such as *The Deeds of Samantabhadra*, etc.; and many wise persons explain that at the end of the session you should recite the one-hundred [syllable] mantra; that is how you should perform [the rite] at the time of the first session [of practice]. Concerning that, many Tantras—such as *Hevajra* and *The Latter [Tantra of] Clear Expression*—and many treatises—such as [Nāgārjuna's] *Integration of the Scripture [with the Sādhana]*—state that you should do it in [all] four sessions. Regarding 'the four sessions,' according to Jālandharipa's explanation [in his *Hevajra Sādhana, "A Vajra Lamp"*?]:

> What are called "the stages of blessing in the four sessions" are the stages of meditation at pre-dawn, midday, evening, and night.

Vitapāda also explains it like this. Thus, that is the way you should do it in [all] four sessions.

You may wonder: If in the first session, the pre-dawn session, one has practiced as explained above, then does it matter whether or not one does the other three sessions extensively or briefly?

According to Lavapa, having gone through all the procedures in the first session, then in the midday and evening sessions and breaks {437a} you clearly visualize that your own self, having become light, transforms into a *HŪṂ*, and that from a thorough transformation of that, [there arises] the habitat and inhabitant mandalas;[559] and then after the conferral of the initiations you do everything completely. Then in the

[559] So in the middle two sessions (2 and 3) you skip all the preliminary prayers (lineage prayers, refuge and bodhicitta prayers, etc.) and all of the other preliminary rites (defense perimeter, etc.).

final session you perform all of the procedures. Ghaṇṭāpa explains it like that as well. According to the explanation in *The Pearl Rosary [: A Commentary on the Difficult Points of the Hevajra]* [by Ratnākarashānti], in the other [latter three] sessions[560] you meditate your own self as Nairātmyā, emit and set in place the fourteen-goddess retinue from the seed [syllable] at your heart, and then—after the symbolism[-recollection], the blessing of body, speech, and mind, and the conferral of the initiations—you do everything completely. Kṛishṇāchārya and Samayavajra also explain [in the *Hevajra Commentary, "The Jewel Rosary of Yoga"*][561] that in the other [latter three] sessions you radiate and set in place the retinue from the seed [syllable] at your heart, and then after the entry of the intuition being and the conferral of the initiations you do everything completely. So according to their assertions, you have been staying [all day] without having withdrawn the measureless mansion, and thus leaving out the procedure of creating that [mansion] and the defense perimeter and the accumulating of the stores, you completely recall the preliminary union and then do just the radiation of the supreme mandala triumph from your heart.

Moreover, [Shāntipa's] the *Commentary on [Dīpaṅkarabhadra's] The Four Hundred and Fifty [Verses]* states:

> "Also, in the breaks between sessions..."—this means that at midday, day's end, and midnight [breaks] you instantaneously manifest the thoroughly complete mandala, and then having done the offering and praise, etc., again as before, you should sleep at the time of sleep.

{437b} *The Esoteric Community [Tantra]* also says that you should do it like that, that is, like before. The twelfth cluster [of Abhayākaragupta's *Clusters of Instructions*] states:

> When you are busy, the [full] rites [from the first session are carried over] into the other sessions as [more] briefly

---

560 Since the framing question regarded what one is to do in the sessions after the first, here *thun gzhan* presumably refers to all three of the "other sessions," that is, the second, third, and fourth.

561 Cf. note 496 above.

> practiced.[562] If you have the opportunity, you practice everything [again].

He explains that if you take your time in the first session, then if you are busy, the procedures of the other sessions can be abbreviated. And Vitapāda states that if you are busy, then having completely meditated in the first session, in the other sessions you [can just] remain with divine pride on your own seat, and then having radiated the deities of the mandala with the three syllables you should receive initiation, offer, praise, and taste nectar, and then staying within whatever subtle [mandala] lines there are, you should repeat [mantras]. [Thus,] having abbreviated [the full rites], you should do them as before—which according to [Kṛiṣhṇa-]Samayavajra's explanation [in the *Hevajra Commentary, "The Jewel Rosary of Yoga"*][563] means that it is necessary to bring in the intuition being.

That being the case, there is one system in which both the first and last sessions are extensive and the middle two are abbreviated, and [there is another system in which] the first [session] is extensive but the other three are abbreviated—these are not [extensive or abbreviated] due to degree of your leisure or busyness, but both are systems of continuous practice. Even when you are busy you do the first extensively and the final three in an abbreviated way; and depending on whether you either have the time or are busy, you also can do the first session either extensively or in an abbreviated way, but the other three are done in an abbreviated way. From among [these] systems in the *Clusters of Instructions* you should do whatever works; but if you have the time, then if you practice according to the system of Lavapa, etc., there is a great difference in how long you do the meditation on the deity; and moreover, it seems that you will not lose the key points of the creation stage which involve purifying the basis of purification.

---

562 *rjes su bsgrub bo* [**anusiddha* ?]—this must be an idiom for "quickly practice." Indeed, Tsong Khapa's subsequent explanation utilizes the verb *bsdus pa bya ba* ("do abbreviatedly"). MW (41) says that *anusiddha* means "gradually effected or realized."

563 Cf. note 496 above.

[II.B.2.c.ii.C'3'c'ii'B''4''a''ii''B° – The yoga in between sessions]

Second[564]—thus, also in the periods during the breaks, when you have left a previous session {438a} and have not yet begun[565] the next [session], you must spend your time doing virtuous activities. So the way of [doing] that is [to do] the yoga of thoroughly purifying your enjoyments: having recollected the pride of whichever is your principal [deity], when your sense faculties are engaged with objects you see the objects as having the nature of deities, and you visualize that they are making offerings [to your senses visualized as deities].

Moreover, in terms of purification in general, you should view everything as having the form of Vajradhara who has the nature of the intuition of nonduality. Regarding specific purifications, you view [visual] forms as Vairochana, sounds as Akṣhobhya, scents as Ratnasambhava, tastes as Amitābha, and tangibles as Amoghasiddhi—that is the art-purification. In terms of the wisdom-purification, you view the five objects as the five goddesses such as Rūpavajrā [Matter Vajra], etc., and then you should offer [them].

Moreover, conjoining [all activities] with the wisdom that does not objectify the three sectors [of an action][566]—and cultivating mindfulness of this at all times—is the art that easily perfects the two stores [of merit and intuition]; as *The Samantabhadra Sādhana* states:

> By abandoning wrong notions
> All activities should be perfected.
> The complete offering of the muni-chakra[567]
> Is totally supreme.

Having understood things that way, whatever you enjoy, and also whatever you give to others, etc., should be done from that perspective.

Regarding the yoga of purifying evolutionary action—{438b} when you vividly recollect yourself as the principal [deity], having relied on

---

[564] This is the second of three subsections mentioned back on 403a.

[565] *ma zug pa*. Acc. Das (1054), *zug pa* can be a variant of *'dzugs pa*, which can mean "to begin" (among many similar meanings).

[566] The three sectors (*'khor*) of an action are: the doer, the act of doing, and the thing done.

[567] For "muni-chakra," see above, note 281.

that each time, all performances of physical actions such as going, sitting, moving about, etc., and verbal actions such as speaking are the [way of] accumulating the stores of mudrā and mantra; as *The Samantabhadra Sādhana* states:

> All of these and those actions of body, etc.,
> Always should be realized while well concentrated;[568]
> Having a mind like that, [you purify]
> Whichever physical, verbal, or mental actions
> Into the forms of mudrās and mantras—
> That is what all the perfect buddhas state.

And *The Ornament of the Vajra Essence Tantra* states:

> If you remain in the state of equanimity
> Then any movement of the body and
> All kinds of manifestations of words[569]
> Are all mantras and mūdras.

Moreover, all physical and verbal conduct which is initially [ethically] indeterminate can be made virtuous, and then as you gradually strengthen that, even things which would be nonvirtuous for others become methods for increasing great stores [of merit and intuition].

Regarding the yoga for purification [to be used] if your commitments are broken, *The Samantabhadra Sādhana* states:

> When a commitment is broken, then on your heart center
> moon
> Visualize a vajra-cross as the essence,
> And with the yoga of Shrī Samayavajra,
> Visualize that all states of life are naturally pure;
>
> In the center of the petals of a multi-colored lotus
> Thoroughly receive initiation by the above process. **{439a}**

---

568 *rtag tu legs par mnyam par gzhag rtogs bya*. Literally, "always should be well-concentratedly realized." The Derge reads *rtag tu legs par mnyam par gzhag <u>ste</u> bya,* which changes the meaning to "always should be done with good absorption."

569 *tshig tu rab tu 'phro ba'i rnams* (Lhasa: *'gro ba'i rnams*). This instance of a plural marker (*rnams*) after a genitive seems strange, but all editions of the *NRC* and both the Derge and Lhasa editions of *The Ornament of the Vajra Essence Tantra* arrest this.

As for what this means, Shrī Phalavajra states [in the *Commentary on (*Jñānapāda*'s) Samantabhadra Sādhana*]:[570]

> You should meditate that upon a mandala of great power at your own heart center is a variegated lotus upon which there rests a moon, at the center of which is a *HŪṀ* from which there arises a vajra-cross seat, upon which is a *KHAṀ* from which [there arises] a sword that completely transforms into Amoghasiddhi, the nature of art and wisdom.... Then, contemplating that all things are pure by nature,...visualize that the light rays of the seed syllable at the heart of the intuition hero invoke the transcendent buddhas who dwell in space, and that from their light rays arise the goddesses such as Locanā, etc., holding in their hands vessels filled with nectar with which they moisten your own subtle atoms and confer initiation. This—the activities of Secret Mantra stated in the Tantras, such as first meditating the deity and then relying on the five nectars, etc.—is the remedy for the breaking of your commitments which you should keep.

Thus setting forth his own system, he rejects the others' systems, which claim that "You melt yourself, then arise in the form of the devotee being as Amoghasiddhi, and then receive initiation." [On the other hand, Dīpaṅkarabhadra's *The Mandala Rite of the Glorious Esoteric Community*,] *The Four Hundred and Fifty [Verses]* states:

> Having broken[571] your commitments, to take them [again]:
> [You, possessing] the excellent wheel of Amoghavajra,
> Imagine an action-vajra [with a] *KHAṀ* at your heart
> And consecrate [it] with universal purity.[572]

---

570 The following is not a direct quote; rather, Tsong Khapa here is paraphrasing Shrī Phalavajra's statements in these lines, often citing exact phrases or sentences, but just as often leaving out certain phrases or adding in explanatory glosses.

571 Derge reads *dag* ("purify"; or a plural marker) instead of *nyams* ("damage"), which seems odd.

572 "[You, possessing] the excellent wheel of Amoghavajra" (*don yod rdo rje'i 'khor lo bzang*; here the Skt. *amoghavajrasaccakrī* clarifies that this is the agent, "the one [you]

(cont'd)

And Shāntipa's *Commentary* on this states that {439b} you create yourself as Amoghasiddhi—as the lord of the mandala—and that in your heart you visualize a syllable *KHAṀ* upon a vajra-cross, and that you then confer the intitiation yourself. Thus, you can do whichever of those two [methods] you want [either visualizing Amoghasiddhi at your heart, or visualizing that you youself arise as Amoghasiddhi]; what is of foremost importance is that you cleanse any faults such as despising the mentor, etc.

Regarding food yoga—when you nourish yourself with provisions such as drink, etc., moroever, you should recollect yourself as the deity, bless your food to be nectar, and imagining that you are offering it to the deity, you should enjoy it.

Regarding washing yoga—[washing yourself] should be done as if it were an initiation [i.e., washing away taints with nectar].

Regarding sleep yoga—you should imaginatively orient yourself toward the nature of clear light in the actuality of orgasmic joy, [which has] the nature of emptiness, and then with the nature of wisdom and art you should lie down. There are a very great many explanations that accord with these statements from the *Clusters of Instructions*, so that is how you should do these things.

Regarding arising yoga—you should arise [after sleep] having been aroused by the resounding of the ḍamaru drum or the songs of the goddesses.

[**II.B.2.c.ii.C'3'c'ii'B''4''a''ii''C°** – The way of making those yogas magnificent]

Third:[573] When, having increased familiarity with engaging the thatness of awareness itself, you extinguish all misknowledges; and when, having reversed erroneous perceptions of body-mind systems such as matter, etc.—which have the quality of the thatness of the mind—you transform into the body of a buddha; then that body which had the quality

who possesses..."); this phrase means that you adopt the identity of Amoghavajra. An action-vajra (*karmavajra*) is a crossed-vajra. I am uncertain what specifically is meant by "universal purity" (*sarvaśuddhi*).

[573] This is the third of three subsections mentioned back on 403a.

of being ordinary [is revealed to have] had the quality of being an incidental erroneous deception, while the buddha body {440a} [is known to] have the quality of something impossible to lose, since it abides as long as space endures.[574] Moreover, a passage from the *Intuition Vajra Compendium [Tantra]* as quoted in [Vitapāda's] *Commentary on [Jñānapāda's] Direct Speech [of Mañjushrī]* states:

> Lord of Secrets! That which is [perceived to be] a snake in a rope does not exist. However, through hallucination it is perceived as such. When a given person abandons —that is, critically investigates—[such] an hallucination, he sees it as a rope, no other thing [really] existing. Lord of Secrets! Like that, that which is mistaken to be matter, etc., in the eternal [buddha-reality of Vairochana], etc., does not [really] exist. However, because of the instinct for conceiving such things as matter, etc., [they are perceived as such]. When a given person devotes himself to the definitively taught path, he overcomes that imagined [reality of matter, etc.], and he sees the eternal [buddha-reality of Vairochana], etc., no other thing [really] existing.

—"the eternal" is a synonym for Vairochana.[575] Moreover, the *Drop of Liberation* states:

> One who abandons hallucinations
> Will not find anything else in the rope.
> Likewise, one who abandons [mental] elaborations
> Will not find a bit of saṁsāra in the mandala.
> Thus through the profound and vivid mandala
> I am eternally in nirvana.

Therefore, the ordinary body-mind systems have the quality of the thatness of the mind—only through the deception of misknowledge do

[574] That is, the extraordinary buddha body and identity cultivated in the creation stage becomes more real to the adept than the previously experienced ordinary body and ordinary ego-identity.

[575] Vairochana is the buddha of the matter body-mind system.

they exist [as ordinary body-mind systems]. Thus, when they become the object of the intuition of nonduality that is engaged at all times with the thatness of the mind, then the body's ordinariness is entirely overcome, {440b} and as it is no longer a suitable support for that [ordinariness], [the body] serves as a support for the [extraordinary buddha] body with the signs and marks. Therefore, that which has the quality of not being deceived by misknowledge are the bodies of Vairochana, etc.; and thus when the mind that determines all things to be emptiness—having meditated on the meaning of the mantra [*OṀ*] *Svabhāva* [*shuddha sarva-dharma*...]—arises in the form of a body, it arises as the body of Vairochana, etc.

Thus, maintaining accurately the way [of nondually reconciling] the experience of [ultimate] reality with the experience of [the ordinary] things that have the quality of non-deception [as being deity/emptiness indivisible], the mantrin also focuses on the magnificence of that very circle of deities that he is meditating as the path. As [Dīpaṅkarabhadra's *The Mandala Rite of the Glorious Esoteric Community*,] *The Four Hundred and Fifty [Verses]* states:

> Even though you may not perceive the gift, etc.,[576]
> Giving, etc., still has an ordinary nature;
> [Though] selflessness [alone] does not overcome the
> ordinary,
> In the supreme circle [of deities], [ordinariness] is no more.

And the *Commentary* on that by Shāntipa states:

> Even though you may no longer perceive the gift, etc., those things such as the giving, etc., have an ordinary nature because of your [still] determining aspects of place and time; selflessness does not overcome dimensionality; ...[577]

[576] The "three sectors" of the object, agent, and action (*bya byed las gsum*), in this case the gift, giver, and act of giving.

[577] That is, the perception of the three sectors is still something measured or delimited. The text is making an interesting connection between being ordinary and being limited—these are being set up as synonyms.

And:

> That which is not determined with respect to direction and time is great, and thus is magnificent. But that which has the nature of being determinate about its own place and time is itself paltry, and thus is called "ordinary."

This says that although the Transcendence Vehicle has the profund, which is the realization of selflessness, {441a} it lacks the [magnificent] circle of deities, which is the counter-agent to the perception of ordinariness, and thus it is [comparatively] paltry in extent; whereas, since the Mantra [Vehicle] does have that [circle], it is magnificent.

Well then, you may wonder, what is the meaning of saying that according to whether something is or is not measured in terms of place and time it is magnificent or paltry?

When you meditate deity yoga in terms of its being of one taste with the thatness of things and [in terms of the deity circle] having just that [nondual] nondeceptive quality, you are meditating in terms of its totality —without determining from a limited perspective the extent of the excellences, places, and times of the form bodies, etc., of all the transcendent buddhas—and thus it is magnificent. But if you lack that kind of deity yoga, then although you may have the profound yoga of being nondifferentiated from the suchness of all things, you are not meditating without discriminating a [particular] extent, in terms of [ordinary] qualities, and thus it is paltry. Therefore, Shāntipa says [in his *Commentary on [Dīpaṅkarabhadra's] The Four Hundred and Fifty [Verses]*:

> On the strength of your meditation on the stage of the extreme purity of the manifestations of [your ultimate] nature and on their [nondually] having a transcendent [empty] nature, you completely perfect in every mental instant your own transcendences, etc., through the transcendences, etc., of all the buddhas; and even when making offerings to yourself or to others you make offerings to all the buddhas; and you even can make a superlative offering out of inferior things. Thus it is easy to reach enlightenment, and this therefore {441b} comes to be the nature of the path to enlightenment.

> Therefore, by such expressions, it is shown how there is a special distinction [in the Mantra Vehicle] of causing the attainment of enlightenment exclusively with extreme speed—as [Vajradhara] said:
>
> > Oh yogins, by only this very [path],
> > You will achieve buddhahood swiftly!

* * *

And so, as explained above, the way of purifying the bases of purification, and meditating after visualizing the actuality of the infinite qualities of a buddha, are the means for developing the roots of virtue which give rise to the entire the stage of perfection. Therefore, although the three lower classes of Tantra also have meditations on emptiness and on a mere deity body, it [the Unexcelled Yoga creation stage methodology being described here] is extremely distinctive, and thus it is different from those [lower three]. From this perspective, the superlative magnificence brings us to the occasion of the perfection stage.

Although the Transcendence Vehicle has meditation on a path which accords with the truth body, it lacks meditation on a path which accords with the form body, which is the counter-agent to the perception of an ordinary body; therefore, [in this Vehicle] it takes an extremely long time to complete the stores which are the cause of the form body. Since the Mantra Vehicle does have these, it is said that it easily completes the stores; thus, in terms of the nondeceptive quality and qualified [magnificent things],[578] if you understand well the system of how to proceed to meditate on the meaning of the nonduality of the profound and the vivid, then in each and every mental instant you immeasurably perfect [both] the stores, etc. And thus [I have] given the explanations [above]. **{442a}**

* * *

---

[578] *chos dang chos can* (*dharma* and *dharmin*). Here "quality" can mean emptiness (ultimate reality) and "qualified" can mean perceptions (relative reality).

Following taintless scriptures and reasonings,
Not seduced by made-up opinions, I have explained very
clearly
How to purify the bases of purification by the creation stage,
And the stages of [such] creation in one's continuum,
Which is the supreme skill in the art of completely perfecting,
With [relatively] little effort, the causes of the form body,
Which [normally] must be perfected through other vehicles
With huge energies of stores of merit during countless aeons!

This was the twelfth chapter—the teaching on the stage of creation—from *The Critical Elucidation of the Key Instructions in All the Secret Stages of the Path of the Great Vajradhara*.

APPENDIXES, GLOSSARY, BIBLIOGRAPHIES, AND INDEXES

APPENDIX I

English Topical Outline (sa bcad) of Chapters XI–XII of Tsong Khapa's Great Treatise on the Stages of Mantra

Topical Outline of Chapters XI–XI of Tsong Khapa's Great Stages of Mantra **Structure: I A 1 a i A' 1' a' i' A'' 1'' a'' i'' A° 1° a° i° A°° 1°° a°° i°° A* 1* a***	***TL*: Where Introduced**	***TL*: Where Discussed**
CHAPTER V: [Beginning of the Sections on Unexcelled Yoga Tantra]		
C' The three sections on the stages of the path of Unexcelled Yoga	42a.6–42b.1	117a.5–512a
1' An explanation of the general divisions into which the path is collected	117a.6	117a.6–119b.4
2' An explanation of the structure of the path	117a.6	119b.4–121b.5
3' An explanation of the path itself which has [that] structure	117a.6	121b.6–512a.6
a' That one should become a suitable vessel for meditating the path	121b.6	121b.6–348b.3
…	…	…
CHAPTER XI: The Need to Accomplish Enlightenment Through the Integration of the Two Stages		
[**b°** The rite of consecrating the deity in the initiation]	[253b.2]	[348a.4–348b.3]
[**2''** The rites of the components of inititation]	[136a.6]	[348a.4–348b.3]

Topical Outline of Chapters XI–XI of Tsong Khapa's Great Stages of Mantra **Structure: I A 1 a i A' 1' a' i' A'' 1'' a'' i'' A° 1° a° i° A°° 1°° a°° i°° A* 1* a***	***TL*: Where Introduced**	***TL*: Where Discussed**
b' Having become a suitable vessel, how to purify the commitments and vows	121b.6	348b.3–351a.2
c' Grounded in the commitments, how to experientially cultivate the path	121b.6	351a.2–504b.1
i' That you first should understand the path by learning about it and contemplating it	351a.2	351a.3–352b.6
ii' Experiential cultivation [of the path] by meditating on the import of what you have understood	351a.2 -3	352b.6–504b.1
A'' Rejection of the claim that one can attain buddhahood by experientially cultivating either one of the two stages alone	352b.6–353a.1	353a.2–368b.2
1'' Rejection of the claim that one can attain buddhahood by the creation stage without the perfection stage	353a.2	353a.3–355a.6
a'' Expression of the claim	353a.3	353a.3–354a.4
b'' Its refutation	353a.3	354a.4–355a.6
2'' Rejection of the claim that one can attain buddhahood by the perfection stage without the creation stage	353a.2-3	355a.6–368b.2
a'' Expression of the claim	355a.6	355a.6–357a.6
b'' Its refutation	355a.6	357a.6–368b.2

Topical Outline of Chapters XI–XI of Tsong Khapa's Great Stages of Mantra **Structure: I A 1 a i A' 1' a' i' A'' 1'' a'' i'' A° 1° a° i° A°° 1°° a°° i°° A* 1* a***	***TL*: Where Introduced**	***TL*: Where Discussed**
i'' The actual refutation	357a.6	357a.6–362a.5
ii'' Rebuttal of objections to the refutation	357a.6	362a.5–368b.2
B'' The way of experientially cultivating the two stages in an inseparable way	353a.1	368b.2–498b.4
1'' The verbal meaning of the two stages	368b.2	368b.3–372a.3
2'' The determination of the number of the two stages	368b.2	372a.3–372b.5
3'' The determination of the proper sequence of the two stages	368b.2	372b.5–375a.1
CHAPTER XII: The Creation Stage		
4'' The way of learning each of the two stages	368b.2-3	375a.1–498b.4
a'' The way of learning the creation stage	375a.1	375a.1–442a.3
i'' A general presentation of the creation stage	375a.2	375a.2–402b.6
A° That for which the creation stage is created as an antidote	375a.2	375a.2–391a.5
1° Showing how to identify and get rid of what is to be abandoned	375a.3	375a.3–377a.2

Topical Outline of Chapters XI–XI of Tsong Khapa's Great Stages of Mantra **Structure: I A 1 a i A' 1' a' i' A'' 1'' a'' i'' A° 1° a° i° A°° 1°° a°° i°° A* 1* a***	***TL*: Where Introduced**	***TL*: Where Discussed**
2° Showing how to establish vivid perception and stability	375a.3	377a.2–391a.5
a° Meditating on whatever is clearly realized	377a.2	377a.2–381b.2
b° How to bring about vivid perception	377a.2	381b.2–385a.1
c° How to achieve stability	377a.2	385a.1–391a.5
i° The way of meditating on the subtle drop in the first two phases	385a.1	385a.2–389a.6
ii° The way of meditating on the subtle drop in the third phase	385a.1-2	389a.6–391a.5
B° The division of things to be created in the creation stage	375a.2	391a.5–398b.1
1° The segmentation into the four branches and the four yogas	391a.6	391a.6–395a.4
2° The segmentation into the six branches and the three samādhis	391a.6	395a.4–398b.1
C° How to meditate emptiness in that context	375a.3	398b.1–402b.6

Topical Outline of Chapters XI–XI of Tsong Khapa's Great Stages of Mantra **Structure: I A 1 a i A' 1' a' i' A'' 1'' a'' i'' A° 1° a° i° A°° 1°° a°° i°° A* 1* a***	***TL*: Where Introduced**	***TL*: Where Discussed**
ii'' An explanation of the stages of evocation	375a.2	402b.6–442a.3
A° The yoga of the actuality of the session	402b.6	403a.1–437b.6
1° The preliminaries to the actual yoga	403a.1	403a.2–410a.4
a° The accumulation of the stores [of merit and intuition], which establish the favorable conditions [for the practice of yoga]	403a.2	403a.2–408b.5
b° The defense perimeter which clears away adverse conditions	403a.2	408b.5–410a.4
2° The actual yoga with its components	403a.1	410a.4–430a.4
a° Creation of the measureless mansion habitat	410a.4	410a.4–412a.2
b° Creation of the deity inhabitants	410a.4	412a.2–421b.6
i° The actual way of creating the deities	412a.3	412a.3–416b.1
A°° The way of creating [the deities] by the five manifest enlightenments	412a.3	412a.3–415a.5

Topical Outline of Chapters XI–XI of Tsong Khapa's Great Stages of Mantra **Structure: I A 1 a i A' 1' a' i' A'' 1'' a'' i'' A° 1° a° i° A°° 1°° a°° i°° A* 1* a***	***TL*: Where Introduced**	***TL*: Where Discussed**
B°° The way of creating [the deities], the melted [deity] having been exhorted with song	412a.3	415a.5–416b.1
ii° The bases of purification, and homologies with the paths	412a.3	416b.1–420a.2
iii° A summary of the essential points	412a.3	420a.2–421b.6
c° The components which complete it [the actual yoga]	410a.4	421b.6–430a.4
i° The entering of the intuition being and the sealing, then the making of offerings and praises	421b.6	422a.1–425a.4
ii° Tasting nectar, meditating, and repeating [mantras]	421b.6–422a.1	425a.4–430a.4
3° The follow-up [to those yogas]	403a.2	430a.4–437b.6
a° The procedure for fortifying the body and creating the votary cake	430a.4-5	430a.5–434b.3

Topical Outline of Chapters XI–XI of Tsong Khapa's Great Stages of Mantra **Structure: I A 1 a i A' 1' a' i' A'' 1'' a'' i'' A° 1° a° i° A°° 1°° a°° i°° A* 1* a***	***TL*: Where Introduced**	***TL*: Where Discussed**
b° The procedure for creating the guests and offering [the votary cake to them]	430a.5	434b.3–437b.6
B° The yoga in between sessions	402b.6–403a.1	437b.6–439b.5
C° The way of making those yogas magnificent	403a.1	439b.5–442a.3
CHAPTER XIII: General Presentation of the Perfection Stage		
b'' The way of learning the perfection stage	375a.1	442a.3–498b.4
...	...	...
CHAPTER XIV: The Perfection Stage which is Meditated in the Beginning, Together with its Practices; and the Result of the Path		
...	...	...
C'' The [radical] practices that are the method for bringing out the impact of those two [stages]	353a.1	498b.4–499b.4
D'' The way that those [two stages] serve as the path for the three [types of] persons	353a.2	499b.4–504b.1
d' The way of manifesting the result of experiential cultivation	121b.6	504b.1–512a.6

Appendix II

Tibetan Topical Outline (sa bcad) of Chapters XI–XII of Tsong Khapa's Great Treatise on the Stages of Mantra

Topical Outline of Chapters XI–XI of Tsong Khapa's Great Stages of Mantra **Structure: I A 1 a i A' 1' a' i' A'' 1'' a'' i'' A° 1° a° i° A°° 1°° a°° i°° A* 1* a***	***TL*: Where Introduced**	***TL*: Where Discussed**
Chapter V: [Beginning of sections on rnal 'byor bla med kyi rgyud]		
C' rnal 'byor bla med kyi rgyud kyi lam gyi rim pa	42a.6–42b.1	117a.5–512a
1' lam sdud pa'i spyi'i chings bshad pa	117a.6	117a.6–119b.4
2' lam gyi go rims bshad pa	117a.6	119b.4–121b.5
3' go rims can gyi lam nyid bshad pa	117a.6	121b.6–512a.6
a' lam sgom pa'i snod rung du bya ba	121b.6	121b.6–348b.3
…	…	…
Chapter XI: rim gnyis zung 'brel gyis byang chub sgrub dgos par bstan pa ste le'u bcu gcig pa		
[**b°** lha la dbang bskur ba rab gnas kyi cho ga]	[253b.2]	[348a.4–348b.3]
[**2''** dbang gi yan lag tu gyur pa'i cho ga]	[136a.6]	[348a.4–348b.3]

Topical Outline of Chapters XI–XI of Tsong Khapa's Great Stages of Mantra **Structure: I A 1 a i A' 1' a' i' A'' 1'' a'' i'' A° 1° a° i° A°° 1°° a°° i°° A* 1* a***	***TL*: Where Introduced**	***TL*: Where Discussed**
b' snod du gyur nas dam tshig dang sdom pa dag par bya ba	121b.6	348b.3–351a.2
c' dam tshig la gnas nas lam ji ltar nyams su blang ba	121b.6	351a.2–504b.1
i' dang por thos bsam gyis lam shes par bya ba	351a.2	351a.3–352b.6
ii' shes pa'i don bsgom pas nyams su blang ba	351a.2 -3	352b.6–504b.1
A'' rim gnyis phyogs re ba nyams su blangs pas 'tshang rgya bar 'dod pa dgag pa	352b.6–353a.1	353a.2–368b.2
1'' rdzogs rim dang bral ba'i bskyed rim gyis 'tshang rgya bar 'dod pa dgag pa	353a.2	353a.3–355a.6
a'' 'dod pa brjod pa	353a.3	353a.3–354a.4
b'' de dgag pa	353a.3	354a.4–355a.6
2'' bskyed rim dang bral ba'i rdzogs rim gyis 'tshang rgya bar 'dod pa dgag pa	353a.2-3	355a.6–368b.2
a'' 'dod pa brjod pa	355a.6	355a.6–357a.6
b'' de dgag pa	355a.6	357a.6–368b.2
i'' dgag pa dngos	357a.6	357a.6–362a.5
ii'' bkag pa la rtsod pa spang ba	357a.6	362a.5–368b.2
B'' rim gnyis ya ma bral bar nyams su blang ba'i tshul	353a.1	368b.2–498b.4

Topical Outline of Chapters XI–XI of Tsong Khapa's Great Stages of Mantra **Structure: I A 1 a i A' 1' a' i' A'' 1'' a'' i'' A° 1° a° i° A°° 1°° a°° i°° A* 1* a***	***TL*: Where Introduced**	***TL*: Where Discussed**
1'' rim pa gnyis kyi sgra'i don	368b.2	368b.3–372a.3
2'' rim pa gnyis kyi grangs nges pa	368b.2	372a.3–372b.5
3'' rim pa gnyis kyi go rims nges pa	368b.2	372b.5–375a.1
CHAPTER XII: bskyed pa'i rim pa bstan pa ste le'u bcu gnyis pa		
4'' rim gnyis so so'i bslab tshul	368b.2-3	375a.1–498b.4
a'' bskyed rim la bslab tshul	375a.1	375a.1–442a.3
i'' bskyed rim spyi'i rnam gzhag	375a.2	375a.2–402b.6
A° gang gi gnyen por bskyed rim skyed pa'i tshul	375a.2	375a.2–391a.5
1° spang bya ngos gzung zhing de 'gog tshul bstan pa	375a.3	375a.3–377a.2
2° gsal snang dang gnas pa sgrub lugs bstan pa	375a.3	377a.2–391a.5
a° mngon rtogs ci tsam zhig bsgom par bya ba	377a.2	377a.2–381b.2
b° gsal snang 'don tshul	377a.2	381b.2–385a.1

Topical Outline of Chapters XI–XI of Tsong Khapa's Great Stages of Mantra **Structure: I A 1 a i A' 1' a' i' A'' 1'' a'' i'' A° 1° a° i° A°° 1°° a°° i°° A* 1* a***	***TL*: Where Introduced**	***TL*: Where Discussed**
c° gnas pa sgrub lugs	377a.2	385a.1–391a.5
i° gnas skabs dang po gnyis su phra thig sgom tshul	385a.1	385a.2–389a.6
ii° gnas skabs gsum par phra thig sgom tshul	385a.1-2	389a.6–391a.5
B° bskyed par bya ba bskyed rim gyi rnam dbye	375a.2	391a.5–398b.1
1° yan lag bzhi dang rnal 'byor bzhi'i chings	391a.6	391a.6–395a.4
2° yan lag drug dang ting nge 'dzin gsum gyi chings bstan pa	391a.6	395a.4–398b.1
C° de'i skabs su stong nyid ji ltar bsgom pa	375a.3	398b.1–402b.6
ii'' mngon par rtogs pa'i rim pa bshad pa	375a.2	402b.6–442a.3
A° thun gyi ngo bo'i rnal 'byor	402b.6	403a.1–437b.6
1° rnal 'byor dngos kyi sngon 'gro	403a.1	403a.2–410a.4
a° mthun rkyen sgrub pa tshogs bsag pa	403a.2	403a.2–408b.5
b° 'gal rkyen sal ba bsrung ba'i 'khor lo	403a.2	408b.5–410a.4

Topical Outline of Chapters XI–XI of Tsong Khapa's Great Stages of Mantra **Structure: I A 1 a i A' 1' a' i' A'' 1'' a'' i'' A° 1° a° i° A°° 1°° a°° i°° A* 1* a***	***TL*: Where Introduced**	***TL*: Where Discussed**
2° rnal 'byor dngos gzhi yan lag dang bcas pa	403a.1	410a.4–430a.4
a° rten gzhal yas khang bskyed pa	410a.4	410a.4–412a.2
b° brten pa lha bskyed pa	410a.4	412a.2–421b.6
i° hla skyed pa'i tshul dngos	412a.3	412a.3–416b.1
A°° mngon byang lngas skyed tshul	412a.3	412a.3–415a.5
B°° zhu ba glus bskul nas skyed tshul	412a.3	415a.5–416b.1
ii° sbyang gzhi dang lam la sbyar ba	412a.3	416b.1–420a.2
iii° don gyi gnad bsdu ba	412a.3	420a.2–421b.6
c° rdzogs par byed pa'i yan lag	410a.4	421b.6–430a.4
i° ye shes pa gzhug cing rgyas btab nas mchod cing bstod pa	421b.6	422a.1–425a.4
ii° bdud rtsi myang zhing bsgom bzlas bya ba	421b.6–422a.1	425a.4–430a.4

Topical Outline of Chapters XI–XI of Tsong Khapa's Great Stages of Mantra **Structure: I A 1 a i A' 1' a' i' A'' 1'' a'' i'' A° 1° a° i° A°° 1°° a°° i°° A* 1* a***	***TL*: Where Introduced**	***TL*: Where Discussed**
3° mjug gi bya ba	403a.2	430a.4–437b.6
a° lus brtas zhing gtor ma skyed pa'i cho ga	430a.4-5	430a.5–434b.3
b° mgron bskyed cing dbul ba'i cho ga	430a.5	434b.3–437b.6
B° thun mtshams kyi rnal 'byor	402b.6–403a.1	437b.6–439b.5
C° rnal 'byor de dag rgya che bar 'jog lugs	403a.1	439b.5–442a.3
CHAPTER XIII: rdzogs rim spyi'i rnam gzhag bstan pa ste le'u bcu gsum pa		
b'' rdzogs rim la bslab tshul	375a.1	442a.3–498b.4
…	…	…
CHAPTER XIV: thog mar sgom pa'i rdzogs rim spyod pa dang bcas pa dang lam gyi 'bras bu bstan pa'i rim pa ste le'u bcu bzhi pa		
…	…	…
C'' de gnyis la bogs 'byin pa'i thabs spyod pa	353a.1	498b.4–499b.4
D'' de dag gang zag gsum gyi lam du ji ltar 'gro ba'i tshul	353a.2	499b.4–504b.1
d' nyams su blangs pa'i 'bras bu mngon du byed tshul	121b.6	504b.1–512a.6

APPENDIX III

Analysis of the Tantric Section of the Derge Kangyur Correlated to Derge Tengyur Exegesis[1]

TANTRA CLASS, CATEGORY, OR NAME	*KANGYUR* (TŌH. #)	*TENGYUR* (TŌH. #)
A. ANUTTARAYOGA TANTRA		
1. Neither Father nor Mother[2]		
Mañjuśrī-nāma-saṁgīti (*Cf.* also under Yoga Tantra)[3]	360	1395–1400, 2090–2121
Kālacakra	361–365	1346–1394
2. Mother Tantras (Under seven groupings)		
a. All Buddhas ("Ston pa" = *Deśaka)		
Sarvabuddha-samāyoga	366–367	1659–1682
b. Akṣobhya ("Heruka") in five classes		
(1) *Saṁvara*	368–415[4]	1401–1606[5]

[1] This table was adapted from Alex Wayman's *The Buddhist Tantras: Light on Indo-Tibetan Esotericism*, pp. 233–239. Wayman's analysis of the Kangyur *rgyud 'bum* was based on the *Thob yig gsal ba'i me long* by Dzaya-paṇḍita Blo bzang 'phrin las (b. 1642). I found the information in his table to be very useful—however, its layout was so confusing that it was often very difficult to tell what was a sub-category of what, etc. Consequently, I reworked the layout in a standard outline format with progressively nested indents (and occasionally somewhat altered outline numbering). In addition to my own footnotes, I have incorporated many of Wayman's notes (identified as such, but in a considerably paraphrased form). I also changed some of his terminology to conform to my own.

[2] Wayman note paraphrase: A "Nondual" class was not accepted by Tsong Khapa. He classified the *Kālachakra* as a Mother Tantra. The *Mañjuśrī-nāma-saṁgīti* is trickier—see note 3.

[3] Wayman note paraphrase: The *Mañjuśrī-nāma-saṁgīti* has both Anuttarayoga Tantra and Yoga Tantra commentaries. Moreover, whereas Tengyur commentaries 1395–1400 would be in the Anuttara Nondual or Mother class, commentaries 2090–2121 would appear to be (due to their placement) in the Anuttara Father Vairocana class.

[4] Cf. below, note 9, for no. 416.

TANTRA CLASS, CATEGORY, OR NAME	*KANGYUR* (TŌH. #)	*TENGYUR* (TŌH. #)
(2) *Hevajra*	417–423	1180–1345[6]
(3) *Buddhakapāla*	424	1652–1657
(4) *Mahāmāyā*	425	1622–1648
(5) *Ārali*	426–427	1658
c. Vairocana		
Catuḥpīṭha	428–430	1607–1621
Caṇḍamahāroṣaṇa, Krodharāja, Acala	431–434	1782–1783
d. Ratnasambhava ("Rdo rje nyi ma" = Vajraprabhā)		
Vajrāmṛta	435	1649–1651
e. Amitābha ("Padma gar dbang" = Padmanarteśvara)		
Lokanātha	436	1750–1751
Tārā–Kurukullā	437	—
f. Amoghasiddhi ("Rta mchog" = Paramāśva)		
Namastāre Ekaviṁśati[7]	438	1683–1744[8]
Vajrakīlaya	439	—
Mahākāla	440[9]	1752–1781
g. Vajradhara		
Yathālabdhakhasama	441	—
3. Father Tantras (Under six groupings)		

[5] Wayman note paraphrase: 1401–1540 "roughly corresponds" to Cordier's *yab skor* [Father Tantra division], and 1541–1606 to his *yum skor* [Mother Tantra division].

[6] Wayman note paraphrase: 1180–1304 = *yab skor*; 1305–1320 = *yum skor*; 1321–1330 = *gur skor*; 1331–1345 = *thig skor*.

[7] Wayman note paraphrase: The *Namastāre Ekaviṁśati* [Praise of the Twenty-one Tārās] is an extract from the 3rd chapter of a Krīya Tantra, no. 726 (within **D.2.c** below).

[8] Wayman note paraphrase: Most of these are probably on one or another of the 21 Tārās. However, some may be on *Tārā-Kurukullā* (under **A.2.e**). Moreover, 1745–1749 are "general works," placed here perhaps because they contain "generalities pertaining" to Tārā.

[9] Wayman note: And possibly also no. 416.

Tantra Class, Category, or Name	*Kangyur* (Tōh. #)	*Tengyur* (Tōh. #)
a. Akṣobhya		
Guhyasamāja	442–451[10]	1784–1917
Vajrapāṇi	454–464[11]	2147–2216
[*Māyājāla*][12]	[466]	[2513–2514]
b. Vairocana		
Yamāri	467–475, 478	1918–2089
c. Ratnasambhava ("Ratna-kula")—Lacking	—	—
d. Amitābha ("Padma-kula")		
Bhagavadekajaṭā	476	2122–2146
e. Amoghasiddhi ("Karma-kula")—Lacking	—	—
f. Vajradhara		
Candraguhyatilaka	477	—
Tengyur commentaries on generalities of Anuttarayoga Tantra; **Dohas** of Mahāsiddhas.		2217–2500
B. Yoga Tantra		
1. The root Tantra (*mūla*)		
Tattvasaṁgraha (in 4 sections)[13] – chiefly *upāya*	479	
2. The explanatory Tantras (*ākhya*)		
Vajraśekhara – chiefly *upāya*	480	

[10] Wayman note: And possibly also nos. 452–453.

[11] Wayman note: And possibly also no. 465 [*Vajrasukhakrodha-tantrarāja*].

[12] By its number (466) the *Māyājāla* it would seem to be placed wthin the Father Anuttarayoga class. However, I do not know which kula it would fall under. Cf. note 16 below.

[13] Wayman note paraphrase: The *Tattvasaṁgraha* is divided into four sections (*dum bu*), each representing a Buddha-kula. See **B.3** commentaries below.

Tantra Class, Category, or Name		Kangyur (Tōh. #)	Tengyur (Tōh. #)
Paramādya (also a *Cha mthun*)	– chiefly *prajñā*	487–488[14]	
Vajramaṇḍalālaṁkāra	– chiefly *prajñā*	490	
Guhyālaṁkāravyūha	– chiefly *prajñā*	492	
Guhyamaṇitilaka	– chiefly *prajñā*	493	
Tengyur commentaries on the *mūla* and *ākhya* Tantras.			2501–2531[15]
[*Māyājāla*]—the *commentaries* of which are considered Yoga Tantra commentaries[16]		[466]	[2513–2514]
Mañjuśrī-nāma-saṁgīti, as a Yoga Tantra *ākhya* Tantra (*Cf.* also under Anuttarayoga Tantra)[17]		360	2532–2622
3. Concordant explanatory Tantras (*Cha mthun*)[18]			
Sarvarahasya – on 1st section (Tathāgata-kula)	– chiefly *upāya*	481	
Trailokyavijaya – on 2nd section (Vajra-kula)	– chiefly *upāya*	482	
Others	– chiefly *upāya*	483–486	
Prajñāpāramitā-naya-śatapañcaśatikā	– chiefly *prajñā*	489	

[14] Wayman paraphrase (p. 237): These two could also be classified below under **B.3**, "Concordant Explanatory Tantras (*Cha mthun*)" (for the meaning of "*Cha mthun,*" cf. note 18 below). Thus, 488 can be considered a *Cha mthun* explanatory Tantra for 487, and 487 in turn can be considered a *Cha mthun* explanatory Tantra for the *mūlatantra* (479).

[15] Note the nos. 2501–2531 include the *Māyājāla* commentaries (2513–2514).

[16] Wayman note: "The *Māyājāla* was not included by the Dzaya-paṇḍita under the Yoga-Tantra, but its commentaries (nos. 2513–2514) are among the commentaries on the [Yoga-Tantra] *mūla* and explanatory Tantras. The work itself is locatd among the Anuttara-yoga-Tantras in the Derge Kanjur [no. 466], suggesting that its status was a matter of dispute among the Lamas."

[17] Cf. note 3 above.

[18] Wayman note paraphrase: *Cha mthun* explanatory Tantras follow (are in accordance with) the sectional divisions of their *mūla* Tantra. Non-*Cha mthun* explanatory Tantras are topical in structure.

TANTRA CLASS, CATEGORY, OR NAME	*KANGYUR* (TŌH. #)	*TENGYUR* (TŌH. #)
Pañcaviṁśatikā-prajñāpāramitā-mukha – chiefly *prajñā*	491[19]	
[*Paramādya*][20] – chiefly *prajñā*	[487–488]	
Tengyur commentaries on the *Cha mthun* or *'phros pa* Tantras		2623–2661
C. CARYĀ TANTRA		
1. Tathāgata-kula		
Mahāvairocana	494	
Acala-kalpa	495	
Tengyur commentaries on the Tathāgata-kula Tantras		2662–2669[21]
2. Padma-kula—Lacking[22]	—	—
3. Vajra-kula		
Vajrapāny-abhiṣeka	496	—
Aṣṭadevī-dhāraṇī	497	—
Others	498–501	—

[19] Wayman note: "In particular, no. 491 goes with no. 490."

[20] Cf. note 14 above.

[21] Tōh. 2662 is Buddhaguhya's commentary, the *Vairocanābhisambhodi-tantra-piṇḍārtha*, favored by Tsong Khapa (cf. "Destiny Fulfilled," p. 44, in *Life & Teachings of Tsong Khapa*).

[22] According to Panchen Sonam Dragpa (*Yoga of Tibet*, p. 247), an example of a Performance Tantra of the Lotus family is the *Extensive Tantra of Hayagriva* (Sanskrit title not given). However, this was not translated into Tibetan and so does not appear in the Kangyur.

TANTRA CLASS, CATEGORY, OR NAME	*KANGYUR* (TŌH. #)	*TENGYUR* (TŌH. #)
		(2670–3139)
D. KRIYĀ TANTRA[23]		
1. Tathāgata-kula (*lokottara*)		
a. Tantras of the Lord (*gtso bo*)	502–542	2694–2697, 3130–3139
b. Tantras of the Master (*bdag po*)	543–552	2674, 2701–2719
c. Tantras of the Mother (*yum*)		
Prajñāpāramitā (the *Aṣṭaśataka* and *Kauśika*)	553–554	—
Suvarṇaprabhāsottama	555–557	—
Pañcarakṣā	558–563	2690–2693, 3117–3129
Mārīcī	564–566	—
Others	567–589	—
d. Tantras of the Uṣṇīṣa	590–603	2688–2689, 3068–3116
e. Tantras of Fierce Deities (*khro bo*)		
Tantras of Male Fierce Deities (*khro bo*)	604–611	3052 ?
Tantras of Female Fierce Deities (*khro mo*)	612–613	—
f. Tantras of Messengers (*pho nya*)	614–630	
Tantras of the Male and Female Servants (*bka' nyan pho mo*) of the Messengers	631–633	3059–3065

[23] Wayman note: "As in the Caryā-Tantra there are three *lokottara* [transcendent] families, Tathāgata, Padma, and Vajra. In addition there are three *laukika* [mundane, worldly] families, Maṇi, Pañcaka, and Laukika. Included among the Kriyā-Tantra are works of a general character (nos. 805–808) which give basic material that can be used by the higher Tantras (Caryā, etc.) as well. Finally, there is a division, often extracts from other works, of Pariṇāma [Dedications, nos. 809–810] and Praṇidhāna [Prayers, nos. 811–827]."

Given the organization given here by Wayman, it would seem that the three *laukika* families *should* be on the same outline level as the three *lokottara* families. However, after numbering the three *lokottara* families as **1**, **2**, **3**, Wayman (or Dzaya Paṇḍita?) includes the three *laukika* families as *sub*-categories **a**, **b**, and **c** under outline number **4** ("Worldly Families"). I have changed this to what I think is a more logical numbering scheme: The three *lokottara* are still **1**, **2**, **3**, but then the three *laukika* are **4**, **5**, **6**.

TANTRA CLASS, CATEGORY, OR NAME	*KANGYUR* (TŌH. #)	*TENGYUR* (TŌH. #)
g. Bodhisattvas belonging to the family [?]	634–644	—
h. Gods, etc. of the Pure Abode	645–673	—
2. Padma-kula (*lokottara*)		
a. Tantras of the Lord (*gtso bo*)	674–680	2698–2700
b. Tantras of the Master (*bdag po*)	681–723	2720–2864
c. Tantras of the Mother (*yum*)	724–732	—[24]
d. Tantras of Male and Female Fierce Deities (*khro bo*)	733–736	3053–3058
e. Tantras of the Male and Female Servants (*bka' nyan pho mo*)	737–742	—
3. Vajra-kula (*lokottara*)		
a. Tantras of the Lord (*gtso bo*)	743	—
b. Tantras of the Master (*bdag po*)	744, 756 746–751	2675–2687, 2865–3049
c. Tantras of the Mother (*yum*)	752	—
d. Tantras of Male and Female Fierce Deities (*khro bo*)	753–755	—
e. Tantras of the Male and Female Messengers (*pho nya*) and Servants (*bka' nyan pho mo*)	757–763	3050–3051
4. Maṇi-kula (*nor can*) (*laukika*)	764–771	—
5. Pañcaka-kula (*lngas rtsen*) (*laukika*)	772	—
6. Laukika-kula (*'jig rten pa*) (*laukika*)	773–804	—
General Kriyā Tantra		
Subāhuparipṛcchā	805	2671–2673
Sāmānyavidhīnām guhya-tantra	806	—
Susiddhi	807	3066
Dhyānottarapaṭalakrama	808	2670[25]

[24] Wayman note: "...the Sādhana collection nos. 3645–3704 includes a large block of Tārā commentaries (nos. 3666–3696) which are probably Kriyā-Tantra works for the most part. Certainly the ones by Candragomin are Kriyā-Tantra."

[25] Tōh. 2670 is Buddhaguhya's commentary, the *Dhyānottarapaṭalaṭīkā*. Much used by by Tsong Khapa (cf. "Destiny Fulfilled," p. 44, in *Life & Teachings of Tsong Khapa*, and Hopkins' comment in *Yoga of Tibet*, p. 213).

TANTRA CLASS, CATEGORY, OR NAME	*KANGYUR* (TŌH. #)	*TENGYUR* (TŌH. #)
Dedications and Prayers		
Dedications (*pariṇāma, yongs su bsngo*)	809–810	—
Prayers (*praṇidhāna, smon lam*)	811–827	—
E. OTHER TENGYUR TEXTS PERTAINING TO ALL 4 TANTRAS[26]		
1. General on all four Tantras		
Abhayākaragupta's *Vajrāvali*, *Niṣpannayogāvali*, and *Jyotirmañjarī*		3140–3142
2. Sādhana Collections		
a. *Pa-tshab sgrub thabs brgya rtsa*		3143–3304
b. *Ba-ri sgrub thabs brgya rtsa*		3306–3399
c. *Sgrub thabs rgya mtsho*		3400–3644
d. *Lha so so sna tshogs kyi sgrub thabs*		3645–3704
3. Preparation of Mandala		3705–3706
4. Distinctions among the 3 Yānas and 4 Tantras		3707–3720
5. Commitments and vows (*samaya* and *saṁvara*)		3721–3729
Incl. Aśvaghoṣa's *Gurupañcāśikā* (no. 3721)		[3721]
6. Cycle of Dharmapāla, Vasudeva, etc.		3730–3755
7. Miscellaneous, rites (*cho ga*), etc.		3756–3785
8. Later Translations[27]		[3305]

[26] My numbering for this section again varies from Wayman's.

[27] Wayman note paraphrase: All later translations were incorporated into earlier Tengyur sections, with the exception of no. 3305 (on the Vajrācārya's responsibilities), which was placed by itself between **E.2.a** and **E.2.b**.

GLOSSARY

English-Tibetan-Sanskrit Glossary

English	Tibetan	Sanskrit
absorption	mnyam (par) gzhag/ bzhag (pa)	samāpatti
affective obscuration	nyon mongs pa'i sgrib pa	kleśāvaraṇa
analytic meditation	dpyod pa'i sgom pa, dpyad sgom	savicārabhāvanā
art (method)	thabs	upāya
attract, summon	'gugs, bkug, dgug	
body-mind system(s)	phung po	skandha
channel, nerve-channel	rtsa	nāḍī
channel wheel	'khor lo	cakra
clear light	'od gsal	prabhāsvara
clear realization (also evocation)	mngon (par) rtogs (pa)	abhisamaya
cognitive obscuration	shes bya'i sgrib pa	jñeyāvaraṇa
commitment, devotion	dam tshig	samaya
conception of ordinariness	tha mal pa'i zhen pa, tha mal pa'i rnam (par) rtog (pa), tha mal pa'i kun (tu) rtog (pa)	
conceptual adherence	mngon par zhen pa	abhiniveśa
conceptual yoga	brtags pa'i rnal 'byor	
concentration	ting nge 'dzin	samādhi
conduct	spyod	caryā, caraṇa
conformative practice	nye bar grub pa	upasādhana
conformative yoga	rjes kyi rnal 'byor, rjes su rnal 'byor	anuyoga
contemplation	bsam gtan	dhyāna

English	Tibetan	Sanskrit
conviction, confidence, imagination	mos pa	adhimukti
creation stage	bskyed rim	utpattikrama
deity host	tshogs zhing	
deity yoga	lha'i rnal 'byor	devatāyoga
destructive actions	mngon spyod	abhicāra
devotee being	dam tshig pa	samayasattva
devotee hero	dam tshig sems dpa'	samayasattva
direct perception	mngon sum	pratyakṣa
direct realization	mngon sum du rtogs pa, ...du bya	
directly manifest	mngon sum du byed, ...du gyur	
directly see	mngon sum du mthong	
distinctive relative circumstance, distinctive relativity	rten 'brel khyad par can	
distraction [elation]	rgod pa	
divine pride	lha'i nga rgyal	devamāna
drop, neural drop	thig le	bindu
dullness [depression]	bying ba	
elaboration(s) (mental)	spros pa	prapañca
emptiness	stong pa nyid	śūnyatā
equanimity, concentration	mnyam gzhag	samāpatti
evocation (also clear realization)	mngon (par) rtogs (pa)	abhisamaya
evolutionary action	las	karma
excellence (good quality)	yon tan	guṇa
exhort (agitate, arouse, invoke)	(b)skul ba	
extreme yoga	shin tu rnal 'byor	atiyoga

English	**Tibetan**	**Sanskrit**
fabrication (fabricated, fabricative)	bcos (ma)	kṛtaka, kṛtima
fabricative meditation	bcos ma'i sgom pa	
firm realization	rtogs pa brtan po	
firm samādhi [concentration]	ting nge 'dzin brtan po	
firm serenity	zhi gnas brtan po	
firm stability	brtan por gnas pa	
firmness, stability	brtan pa/po	
form, matter	gzugs	rūpa
form (pattern, aspect, appearance, piece, feature, event)	rnam pa	ākāra
great practice	sgrub pa chen po	mahāsādhana
great yoga	rnal 'byor chen po	mahāyoga
habitat and inhabitants	rten dang brten	ādhāra, ādheya
hero	dpa' bo	vīra
illusion body	sgyu ma'i sku, sgyu lus	māyādeha
imminence	nyer thob	[āloka-]upalabdhi, [snang ba]
incidental contrary conditions	glo bur ba'i 'gal rkyen	
indestructible drop	mi shigs pa'i thig le	akṣarabindu
insight [meditation]	lhag mthong	vipaśyanā
instantaneous creation	(d)krong skyed	
instantaneous manifestation	yud tsam gyis [/res] mngon du byed pa	
instantaneous(ly)	yud tsam (gyis)	muhūrta
instinct(s) (80)	rang bzhin	prakṛti
instinct (predisposition)	bag chags	vāsanā
instinctual wrong notions	lhan skyes kyi log rtog	
instruction	gdams	

English	Tibetan	Sanskrit
intellectual wrong notions	kun brtags kyi log rtog	
intense conviction, strong orientation, imaginative orientation, aspiration	lhag par mos pa	adhimukti
intuition	ye shes	jñāna
intuition being	ye shes pa	jñānasattva
intuition hero	yes shes sems dpa'	jñānasattva
invite	spyan drangs	
learning, education, instruction, precept	bslab bya	śikṣā
luminance	snang ba	āloka
luminance-intuition	snang ba ye shes	āloka-jñāna
manifest [verb]	mngon (par) byas	
manifest enlightenment	mngon (par) byang (chub)	abhisaṁbodhi
measureless mansion	gzhal yas khang	vimāna, kūṭāgāra
meditation	bsgoms pa	bhāvanā
mental firmness/ stability	sems brtan po	
mentally imprint	yid la byed pa	manasikāra
mentor	bla ma	guru
natural	rnal (ma)	
nonconceptual yoga	ma brtags pa'i rnal 'byor	
obscuration	sgrib pa	āvaraṇa, nivaraṇa
orgasmic, innate, natural, spontaneous	lhan cig skyes pa, lhan skyes	sahaja
ovum, ovum essence, female sexual essence	rdul	
pattern (form, aspect)	rnam pa	ākāra

English	Tibetan	Sanskrit
perception of ordinariness	tha mal pa'i snang ba	
perception side	snang phyogs	
perfection stage	rdzogs rim	niṣpannakrama
practical instruction	gdams ngag	
practice	sgrub pa	sādhana
preliminary union	dang po sbyor ba	prathama-prayoga
private instruction	man ngag	upadeśa, āmnāya
procedure, rite	cho ga	vidhi
psychic heat	gtum mo	caṇḍa
quality	chos	dharma
quality, good (excellence)	yon tan	guṇa
radiance	[snang ba] gsal ba/ mched pa	[āloka-]ābhāsa
reality	de nyid, de kho na nyid, bden pa, rang bzhin, rang gi ngo bo nyid	tattva, satya, svabhāva, svarūpa
reality realm	chos kyi dbyings	dharmadhātu
reality-source	chos kyi 'byung gnas	dharmodaya
realization	rtogs pa	adhigama
resistance(s), counter-tendencies	mi mthun phyogs	vipakṣa
rite of service	bsnyen po'i cho ga	sevā
rite, procedure	cho ga	vidhi
samādhi [meditative concentration]	ting nge 'dzin	samādhi
savior	mgon po	nātha
science consort	rig ma	vidyā
self-habit	bdag 'dzin	ātmagrāha
seminal essence, semen	khu ba	śukra
serenity [meditation]	zhi gnas	śamatha
service	bsnyen pa/po	sevā

English	Tibetan	Sanskrit
session breaks, in between sessions; sessions and breaks	thun mtshams	
siddhi [spiritual power]	dngos grub	siddhi
slight mastery of intuition	ye shes [la] cung zad dbang [ba],	
	ye shes dbang ba cung zad	
slightly settled intuition	ye shes cung zad babs [pa]	
spirit of enlightenment	byang chub kyi sems	bodhicitta
stability	gnas pa	
static meditation	'jog pa'i sgom pa	
suchness	de bzhin nyid	tathatā
summon, attract	'gugs, bkug, dgug	
supreme action triumph	las rgyal mchog	karmarājāgrī (karma-vijaya)
supreme mandala triumph	dkyil 'khor rgyal mchog	maṇḍala-rājāgrī (vijaya-maṇḍala)
teaching	bka'	vacana
thatness	de kho na nyid	tattva
transcendent buddha	de bzhin gzhegs pa	tathāgata
true mastery of intuition	ye shes la yang dag par dbang [ba],	
	yang dag ye shes dbang [ba]	
visualize, visualization	gsal 'debs/btab/gdab;	
	gsal bar byed pa;	
	gsal ba; dmigs pa	
vitality control; vitality and exertion	srog (dang) rtsol ba	prāṇa-āyāma
vivid perception	gsal snang	
votary cake	gtor ma	bāli
vow	sdom pa	saṁvara

English	Tibetan	Sanskrit
weariness; tiredness; fatigue	skyo ba; ngal ba, ngal bso; dub	kheda; śrama; klamatha
wind	rlung	vāyu, vāta
wind-energy	rlung	prāṇa
wisdom	shes rab	prajñā
withdrawal, retraction	(sor) sdud; bsdu ba	pratyāhāra
wrong notion	log rtog	mithyā-saṁkalpa
yoga	rnal 'byor	yoga
yoga with signs	mtshan bcas kyi rnal 'byor	sanimitta-yoga
yoga without signs	mtshan med kyi rnal 'byor	animitta-yoga

SELECTED BIBLIOGRAPHIES

Canonical Tibetan Texts (Kangyur and Tengyur) Sorted by English Title (Full Citations)

Note: See also cross-reference list sorted by Tōh. number on p. 340.

Abbreviated Practice

Also cited as: *Abbreviated [Practice]*
Sanskrit: *Piṇḍīkṛtasādhana*
Tibetan: *sgrub pa'i thabs mdor byas pa*
Tibetan cited as: *mdor byas pa (Piṇḍīkṛta)*
Author: Nāgārjuna
Tōhoku no.: 1796
Derge location: rgyud, ngi, 1b–11a

Accumulations for Enlightenment

Sanskrit: **Bodhisaṁbhāra[ka]*
Tibetan: *byang chub kyi tshogs*
Chinese: *pú tí zī liáng lùn*
Tibetan cited as: *byang chub kyi tshogs*
Author: Nāgārjuna
Taisho no.: 1660
Taisho location: vol. 32, 517b–541b
Comments: Extant only in Chinese (not in Tibetan Tengyur). See p. 205n371

Activities [of the Yoginīs]

Sanskrit: *Yoginīsañcārya*
Tibetan: *rnal 'byor ma'i kun tu spyod pa*
Tibetan cited as: *kun spyod (Sañcārya)*
Author: Kangyur
Tōhoku no.: 375
Derge location: rgyud, ga, 34a–44b. Lhasa: 394 (ga)

Analysis of [Lūipa's] Evocation

Sanskrit: *Abhisamayavibhaṅga-nāma*
Tibetan: *mngon par rtogs rnam par 'byed pa zhes bya ba*
Tibetan cited as: *l'u a'i pa'i mngon rtogs kyi 'grel pa; l'u a'i pa'i 'grel pa*
Author: Dīpaṅkaraśrījñāna (Atīśa)
Tōhoku no.: 1490
Derge location: rgyud, ṣa, 186a–202b
Comments: According to the Dharma Index (pp. 211, 246), this most likely is a commentary on *Lūipa's Evocation* (Tōh. 1427).

Arisal of Saṁvara Tantra

Sanskrit: *Śrī-Mahāsaṁvarodaya-tantrarāja-nāma*

Tibetan: *dpal bde mchog 'byung ba zhes bya ba'i rgyud kyi rgyal po chen po [Peking: sdom pa 'byung ba'i rgyud]*

Tibetan cited as: *sdom 'byung (Saṁvarodaya)*

Author: Kangyur

Tōhoku no.: 373

Derge location: rgyud, kha, 265a–311a. Lhasa: 389 (ga)

Comments: This is an explanatory Tantra of *Supreme Bliss* (*Chakrasaṁvara*).

Auto-commentary to the Commentary to Lūipa's Evocation

Sanskrit: *Lūyipābhisamaya-vṛtti-ṭīkā-viśeṣa-dyota-nāma*

Tibetan: *Lū yi pa'i mngon par rtogs pa'i 'grel pa'i Ti' ka' khyad par gsal byed ces bya ba*

Tibetan cited as: ---

Author: Thatāgatavajra

Tōhoku no.: 1510

Derge location: rgyud, ṣa, 285a–308b

Comments: This is Tathāgatavajra's auto-commentary on his *Lūhipādābhisamaya-vṛtti-saṁvarodaya-nāma* (Tōh. 1509), which in turn is his commentary on *Lūipa's Evocation* (*Śrī-Bhagavadabhisamaya*, Tōh. 1427).

Black Enemy [of Death] Tantra

Sanskrit: *Sarvatathāgata-kāyavākcitta-kṛṣṇayamāri-nāma-tantra*

Tibetan: *de bzhin gshegs pa thams cad kyi sku gsung thugs gshin rje gshed nag po zhes bya ba'i rgyud*

Tibetan cited as: *dgra nag gi rgyud*

Author: Kangyur

Tōhoku no.: 467

Derge location: rgyud, ja, 134b–151b. Lhasa: 432 (ca)

Blazing Jewels Sādhana

Sanskrit: *Ratnajvalasādhana-nāma*

Tibetan: *rin chen 'bar ba zhes bya ba'i sgrub pa'i thabs*

Tibetan cited as: *rin chen 'bar ba*

Author: Prajñendraruci

Tōhoku no.: 1251

Derge location: rgyud, nya, 214a–241b

Blossoming Kumudā Flower: A Sādhana of the Black Enemy of Death

Sanskrit: *Kṛṣṇayamāri-sādhana-protphulla-kumudā-nāma*

Tibetan: *gzhin rje'i dgra nag po'i sgrub pa'i thabs ku mu da kha bye ba zhes bya ba*

Tibetan cited as: *dgra nag gi sgrub thabs ku mu ta kha bye ba; dgra nag gi sgrub thabs; dgra nag gi mngon rtogs ?*

Author: Śāntipa / Ratnākaraśānti (rin chen 'byung gnas zhi ba)

Tōhoku no.: 1935

Derge location: rgyud, mi, 58b–64b

Buddha-Skullbowl Tantra
Also cited as: *The Skullbowl*
Sanskrit: *Śrī-Buddhakapāla-nāma-yoginītantrarāja*
Tibetan: *dpal sangs rgyas thod pa zhes bya ba rnal 'byor ma'i rgyud kyi rgyal po*
Tibetan cited as: *thod pa (Kapāla)*
Author: Kangyur
Tōhoku no.: 424
Derge location: rgyud, nga, 143a–167a. Lhasa: 400 (nga)

Clear Meaning: A Commentary on the Difficult Points of [Nāgārjuna's] Five Stages
Sanskrit: *Pañcakrama-pañjikā-prabhāsārtha-nāma*
Tibetan: *rim pa lnga pa'i dka' 'grel don gsal ba zhes bya ba*
Tibetan cited as: *rim lnga'i dka' 'grel don gsal*
Author: Vīryabhadra (brtson 'grus bzang po)
Tōhoku no.: 1830
Derge location: rgyud, ci, 142b–180b

Clusters of Instructions
Sanskrit: *Śrī-saṁpuṭa-tantrarāja-ṭikā-amnāyamañjarī-nāma*
Tibetan: *dpal yang dag par sbyor ba'i rgyud kyi rgyal po'i rgya cher 'grel pa man ngag gi snye ma zhes bya ba*
Tibetan cited as: *man snye*
Author: Abhayākaragupta / Abhayā / Abhya ('jigs med 'byung gnas sras pa)
Tōhoku no.: 1198
Derge location: rgyud, cha, 1b–316a

Commentary on [Dīpaṅkarabhadra's] The Four Hundred and Fifty [Verses]
Sanskrit: *Śrī-Guhyasamāja-maṇḍala-vidhi-ṭīkā*
Tibetan: *dpal gsang ba 'dus pa'i dkyil 'khor gyi cho ga'i 'grel pa*
Tibetan cited as: *bzhi brgya lnga bcu pa'i 'grel pa*
Author: Śāntipa / Ratnākaraśānti (dKon-mchog / Rin-chen 'byung gnas zhi ba)
Tōhoku no.: 1871
Derge location: rgyud, ni, 59a–130a

Commentary on [Jñānapāda's] Direct Speech [of Mañjushrī]
Sanskrit: *Sukusuma-nāma-dvikrama-tattvabhāvanā-mukhāgama-vṛtti*
Tibetan: *mdzes pa'i me tog ces bya ba rim pa gnyis pa'i de kho na nyid bsgom pa zhal gyi lung gi 'grel pa*
Tibetan cited as: *zhal gyi lung gi 'grel pa (Mukhāgama-vṛtti)*
Author: Vitapāda
Tōhoku no.: 1866
Derge location: rgyud, di, 87a–139b

Commentary on [Jñānapāda's] The Four-Branched Samantabhadrī Sādhana
Sanskrit: *Caturaṅga-sādhana-samantabhadrī-nāma-ṭīkā*
Tibetan: *yan lag bzhi pa'i sgrub thabs kun tu bzang mo zhes bya ba'i rnam par bshad pa*
Tibetan cited as: ---
Author: Vitapāda
Tōhoku no.: 1872
Derge location: rgyud, ni, 130b–178b

Commentary on [Jñānapāda's] The Four-Branched [Samantabhadrī] Sādhana, "A Bouquet of Quintessences"
Sanskrit: *Caturaṅga-sādhana-ṭīkā-sāramañjarī-nāma*
Tibetan: *yan lag bzhi pa'i sgrub thabs kyi rgya cher bshad pa snying po snye ma zhes bya ba*
Tibetan cited as: ---
Author: Samantabhadra
Tōhoku no.: 1869
Derge location: rgyud, ni, 1b–45b

Commentary on [Jñānapāda's] The Samantabhadra Sādhana
Also cited as: *Samantabhadra Sādhana Root-Commentary (?) (NRC* 430b)
Sanskrit: *Samantabhadra-sādhana-vṛtti*
Tibetan: *kun tu bzang po'i sgrub pa'i thabs kyi 'grel pa*
Tibetan cited as: ---; *sgrub thabs kun bzang rtsa 'grel ? (NRC* 430b)
Author: Śrī Phalavajra
Tōhoku no.: 1867
Derge location: rgyud, di, 139b–187b

Commentary on [Jñānapāda's] The Samantabhadra Sādhana
Sanskrit: *Śrī-samantabhadra-sādhana-vṛtti*
Tibetan: *dpal kun tu bzang po'i sgrub pa'i thabs kyi 'grel pa*
Tibetan cited as: *'grel pa (vṛtti)*
Author: Thagana
Tōhoku no.: 1868
Derge location: rgyud, di, 187b–231a

Commentary on The Arisal of Saṁvara [Tantra]
Sanskrit: *Śrīsaṁvarodaya-mahātantrarāja-padminī-nāma-pañjikā*
Tibetan: *dpal sdom pa 'byung ba'i rgyud kyi rgyal po chen po'i dka' 'grel padma can shes bya ba*
Tibetan cited as: *sdom 'byung 'grel pa*
Author: Ratnarakṣita
Tōhoku no.: 1420
Derge location: rgyud, wa, 1b–101b

Commentary on The [Buddha-]Skullbowl [Tantra]
Sanskrit: *Śrī-Buddhakapāla-tantra-pañjikā-jñāna-vatī-nāma*
Tibetan: *dpal sangs rgyas thod pa'i rgyud kyi dka' 'grel ye shes ldan pa zhes bya ba*
Tibetan cited as: *thod pa'i 'grel pa*
Author: Saraha
Tōhoku no.: 1652
Derge location: rgyud, ra (#4), 104b–150a

Commentary on The Contemplation Addendum [Tantra]
Sanskrit: *Dhyānottara-paṭala-ṭīkā*
Tibetan: *bsam gtan phyi ma rim pr phye ba rgya cher bshad pa*
Tibetan cited as: *bsam gtan phyi ma'i 'grel pa*
Author: Buddhaguhya
Tōhoku no.: 2670
Derge location: rgyud, thu, 1b–38a

Commentary on The Four Seats [Tantra]
Sanskrit: *Śrī-caturpīṭha-tantrarāja-smṛtinibandha-nāma-ṭīkā*
Tibetan: *rgyud kyi rgyal po dpal gdan bzhi pa'i 'grel pa dran pa'i rgyu mtshan zhes bya ba*
Tibetan cited as: *gdan bzhi'i 'grel pa*
Author: Bhavabhadra
Tōhoku no.: 1607
Derge location: rgyud, 'a, 137b–264a

Commentary on The [Vajra] Pavilion [Tantra]
Sanskrit: *Ḍākinī-vajrapañjara-mahātantrarāja-prathamapaṭala-mukhabandha-nāma-pañjikā*
Tibetan: *rgyud kyi rgyal po mkha 'gro ma rdo rje gur gyi dka' 'grel zhal nas brgyud pa zhes bya ba*
Tibetan cited as: *gur 'grel*
Author: Indrabhūti
Tōhoku no.: 1194
Derge location: rgyud, ca, 43b–49a

Compendium of Reality [Tantra]

Sanskrit: *Sarvatathāgata-tattvasaṁgraha-nāma-mahāyāna-sūtra*

Tibetan: *de bzhin gshegs pa thams cad kyi de kho na nyid bsdus pa zhes bya ba theg pa chen po'i mdo*

Tibetan cited as: *de nyid bsdus pa'i rgyud; de nyid bsdus pa (Tattvasaṁgraha)*

Author: Kangyur

Tōhoku no.: 479

Derge location: rgyud, nya, 1b–142a. Lhasa: 447 (cha)

Compendium of Transcendences

Sanskrit: *Pāramitāsamāsa-nāma*

Tibetan: *pha rol tu phyin pa bsdus pa zhes bya ba*

Tibetan cited as: *phar phyin bsdus pa*

Author: Āryaśūra

Tōhoku no.: 3944

Derge location: dbu ma, khi, 217b–235a

Deciphering the Seven Ornaments

Sanskrit: **Vajrajñānasamuccaya-tantrodbhava-saptālaṁkāra-vimocana*

Tibetan: *ye shes rdo rje kun las btus pa'i rgyud las 'byung ba'i rgyan bdun rnam par dgrol ba*

Tibetan cited as: *rgyan bdun dgrol ba*

Author: Śraddhākaravarman

Tōhoku no.: 1789

Derge location: rgyud, A, 8b–10a

Comments: Sanskrit title not attested in Tōhoku. Wayman (*YGST*, 114, 369) restored Sanskrit title from Peking

Direct Speech [of Mañjushrī]

Sanskrit: *Dvikramatattvabhāvanā-nāma-mukhāgama*

Tibetan: *rim pa gnyis pa'i de kho na nyid bsgom pa zhes bya ba'i zhal gyi lung*

Tibetan cited as: ---

Author: Buddhaśrījñāna (Jñānapāda)

Tōhoku no.: 1853

Derge location: rgyud, di, 1b–17b

Direct Speech [of Mañjushrī]

Sanskrit: *Mukhāgama*

Tibetan: *zhal gyi lung*

Tibetan cited as: ---

Author: Buddhaśrījñāna (Jñānapāda)

Tōhoku no.: 1854

Derge location: rgyud, di, 17b–28b

Dispelling the Two Extremes [of the Vajra Vehicle]
Sanskrit: *Vajrayāna-koṭidvayāpoha-nāma*
Tibetan: *rdo rje theg pa'i mtha' gnyis sel ba*
Tibetan cited as: *mtha' gnyis sel ba*
Author: Jñānaśrī
Tōhoku no.: 3714
Derge location: rgyud, tsu, 115a–120a

Distinguishing the Center and Extremes
Also cited as: *Center and Extremes*
Sanskrit: *Madhyāntavibhaṅgakārikā*
Tibetan: *dbus dang mtha' rnam par 'byed pa'i tshig le'ur byas pa*
Tibetan cited as: *dbus mtha' (Madhyānta)*
Author: Maitreya
Tōhoku no.: 4021
Derge location: sems tsam, phi, 40b–45a

Drop of Liberation
Sanskrit: *Muktitilaka-nāma*
Tibetan: *grol ba'i thig le zhes bya ba*
Tibetan cited as: *grol ba'i thig le*
Author: Buddhaśrījñāna (Jñānapāda)
Tōhoku no.: 1859
Derge location: rgyud, di, 47a–52a

Drop of Mahāmudrā Tantra
Sanskrit: *Śrī-Mahāmudrātilaka-nāma-mahāyoginī-tantrarājādhipati*
Tibetan: *dpal phyag rgya chen po'i thig le zhes bya ba rnal 'byor ma chen mo'i rgyud kyi rgyal po'i mnga' bdag*
Tibetan cited as: *phyag chen thig le (Mahāmudrātilaka)*
Author: Kangyur
Tōhoku no.: 420
Derge location: rgyud, nga, 66a–90b. Lhasa: 380 (ka)

Drop of Spring
Sanskrit: *Vasantatilaka-nāma*
Tibetan: *dpyid kyi thig le zhes bya ba*
Tibetan cited as: *dpyid kyi thig le*
Author: Kṛṣṇācārya (Nag po spyod pa ba)
Tōhoku no.: 1448
Derge location: rgyud, wa, 298b–306b

Engaging in the Bodhisattvas' Way of Life
Sanskrit: *Bodhisattvacāryāvatāra*
Tibetan: *byang chub sems dpa'i spyod pa la 'jug pa*
Tibetan cited as: *spyod 'jug*
Author: Śāntideva
Tōhoku no.: 3871
Derge location: dbu ma, la, 1b–40a

Esoteric Community Tantra

Also cited as: *The Community*

Sanskrit: *Sarvatathāgata-kāyavākcitta-rahasya-guhyasamāja-nāma-mahākalpa-rāja*

Tibetan: *de bzhin gshegs pa thams cad kyi sku gsung thugs kyi gsang chen gsang ba 'dus pa zhes bya ba brtag pa'i rgyal po chen po*

Tibetan cited as: *gsang ba 'dus pa; 'dus pa (Guhyasamāja; Samāja)*

Author: Kangyur

Tōhoku no.: 442

Derge location: rgyud, ca, 90a–148a. Lhasa: 416a (nga)

Fifty Verses on the Mentor

Sanskrit: *Gurupañcāśikā*

Tibetan: *bla ma lnga bcu pa*

Tibetan cited as: ---

Author: Aśvaghoṣa

Tōhoku no.: 3721

Derge location: rgyud, Tshu, 10a–12a

Five Commitments

Sanskrit: *Samayapañca*

Tibetan: *dam tshig lnga pa*

Tibetan cited as: *dam tshig lnga pa*

Author: Padmākara (padma 'byung gnas)

Tōhoku no.: 1224

Derge location: rgyud, nya, 26b–28b

Five Deity Supreme Bliss Sādhana

Sanskrit: *Śrī-Bhagavāccakrasaṁvara-sādhana-ratna-cintāmaṇi-nāma*

Tibetan: *bcom ldan 'das 'khor lo bde mchog sgrub pa'i thabs rin po che yid bzhin gyi nor bu zhes bya ba*

Tibetan cited as: *bde mchog lha lnga'i sgrub thabs*

Author: Vajra-Ghaṇṭa (rDo rje dril bu)

Tōhoku no.: 1437

Derge location: rgyud, wa, 233b–237b

Five Stages

Sanskrit: *Pañcakrama*

Tibetan: *rim pa lnga pa*

Tibetan cited as: *rim lnga (Pañcakrama)*

Author: Nāgārjuna

Tōhoku no.: 1802

Derge location: rgyud, ngi, 45a–57a

Four Seats Tantra

Sanskrit: *Śrī-catuḥ-pīṭha-vikhyāta-tantrarāja-nāma*
Tibetan: *dpal gdan bzhi pa'i rnam par bshad pa'i rgyud kyi rgyal po zhes bya ba*
Tibetan cited as: *gdan bzhi (Catuḥ-pīṭha)*
Author: Kangyur
Tōhoku no.: 430
Derge location: rgyud, nga, 260a–304a. Lhasa: 406 (nga)

Fourteen Root Downfalls

Sanskrit: *Vajrayāna-mūlāpatti-ṭīkā*
Tibetan: *rdo rje theg pa'i rtsa ba'i ltung ba'i rgya cher bshad pa*
Tibetan cited as: *rtsa ltung bcu bzhi pa*
Author: Mañjuśrīkīrti
Tōhoku no.: 2488
Derge location: rgyud, zi, 197b–231b

Further Tantra [of the Esoteric Community]

Also cited as: *The Further Tantra; The Further*
Sanskrit: *Uttaratantra*
Tibetan: *rgyud phyi ma*
Tibetan cited as: *rgyud phyi ma; phyi ma*
Author: Kangyur
Tōhoku no.: 443
Derge location: rgyud, ca, 148a–157b. Lhasa: 416b (nga)
Comments: The eighteenth chapter of the *Esoteric Community Tantra* (*Guhyasamāja*, Tōh. 442), but considered a separate *vyākhyā* Tantra

Glorious Evocation: A Commentary [on Lūipa's Supreme Bliss Sādhana]

Sanskrit: *Śrī-abhisamaya-nāma-pañjikā*
Tibetan: *dpal mngon par rtog pa zhes bya ba'i dka' 'grel*
Tibetan cited as: ---
Author: Prajñārakṣita
Tōhoku no.: 1465
Derge location: rgyud, ṣa, 34a–45b
Comments: The Dharma Index states that various indexes cite this as a "commentary on the bDe-mchog-gi sgrub-thabs by Lūyipa" (Tōh. 1454)

Graded Presentation of the Esoteric Community Practice

Also cited as: *Graded Presentation*
Sanskrit: *Samājasādhana-vyavasthāli-nāma*
Tibetan: *'dus pa'i sgrub pa'i thabs rnam par gzhag pa'i rim pa zhes bya ba*
Tibetan cited as: *rnam gzhag rim pa*
Author: Nāgabuddhi (klu'i blo)
Tōhoku no.: 1809
Derge location: rgyud, ngi, 121a–131a
Comments: Peking (P2674, Vol. 61–62) cites this as follows: *Samaja-sadhana-vyavasthana-nama ('dus pa'i sgrub thabs rnam par bzhag pa'i rim pa zhes bya wa)*, by Nāgabuddhi (as cited in *Paths and Grounds of Guhyasamaja*, LTWA, 1995; *YGST* [200] cites the Peking text as having the same name as the Derge/Tōhoku edition). This also is referred to as the *Vyavasthānakramā*,

by Nāgabodhi (klu'i byang chub). Thus, this work appears to be cited with different Sanskrit titles. Perhaps after the original Sanskrit text was lost the Tibetan title *rnam gzhag rim pa* was translated *back* into Sanskrit in different ways. In particular, *gzhag* is variously rendered as *stāli* and *sthāna*. However, for *this* text I have never found *rim pa* translated back as *kramā*; rather, it would appear that the prefixes *vi-* and *ava-* gave the sense of "graded" that the Tibetans rendered as *rim pa*. Regarding the author's name, *The Blue Annals* (982–83) states: "Also one and the same person was sometimes called Nāgabodhi, meaning 'The Enlightenment of a Nāga' (kLu'i byaṅ-chub), and sometimes called Nāgabuddhi, which means 'Nāga's wisdom' (kLu'i-blo)."

Great Commentary: Immaculate Light

Also cited as: *The Great Commentary; The Immaculate Light*

Sanskrit: *Vimalaprabhā-nāma-mūlatantrānusāriṇī-dvādaśasāhasrikā-laghu-kālacakra-tantra-rāja-ṭīkā*

Tibetan: *bsdus pa'i rgyud kyi rgyal po dus kyi 'khor lo'i 'grel bshad, rtsa ba'i rgyud kyi rjes su 'jug pa stong phrag bcu gnyis pa dri ma med pa'i 'od ces bya ba*

Tibetan cited as: *'grel chen dri med 'od (Vimalaprabhā)*

Author: Puṇḍarīka (Avalokiteśvara)

Tōhoku no.: 1347; 845

Derge location: rgyud, tha, 107b–277a (Lhasa not extant)

Comments: This is a key commentary to the *Kālachakra Tantra*

Hevajra Commentary, "The Jewel Rosary of Yoga"

Sanskrit: *Śrī-hevajra-pañjikā-yogaratnamālā-nāmā*

Tibetan: *dpal dgyes pa'i rdo rje'i dka' 'grel rin po che sbyor ba'i 'phreng ba zhes bya ba*

Tibetan cited as: ---

Author: Samayavajra / Kṛṣṇācārya

Peking no.: 4687 (Dharma Index Supplemental 4601)

Comments: Regarding the author's name: there seems to be some confusion (or conflation, or equivalency) between the names Samayavajra and Kṛiṣhṇa. Peking (and hence the Dharma Index) cite the author of the *Yogaratnamālā* as Samayavajra, and they cite a Kṛiṣhṇa-paṇḍita as the translator. Then, as the Dharma Index points out in their entry to the *Sahajasiddhi* (Peking 4694, Dharma Index Supplementary 4608, one of the three texts by Samayavajra), the Peking edition cites dam tshig rdo rje (Samayavajra) as the author, Kṛiṣhṇa-paṇḍita and Tshul khrims rgyal ba as the translators, but then states that it was "translated by 'the author' and Tshul khrims rgyal ba." This leads the editors of the Dharma Index to note here that "Dam-tshig-rdo-rje [Samaya-vajra] would seem to be another name for Kṛṣṇa paṇḍita." Farrow and Menon simply attribute *Yogaratnamālā* to Kṛiṣhṇāchārya with no mention of this discrepancy. In their index, Dharma Index cites the name as "Samayavajra (Kṛṣṇa-samayavajra)." They also cross-list the *Yogaratnamālā* (4601) under the name Kṛṣṇa-pa.

Hevajra Sādhana

Also cited as: *Sādhana*
Sanskrit: *Śrī-hevajra-sādhana*
Tibetan: *dpal dgyes pa rdo rje'i sgrub thabs*
Tibetan cited as: *grub thabs (Sādhana)*
Author: Saroruha (mTsho skyes)
Tōhoku no.: 1218
Derge location: rgyud, nya, 1b–7a
Comments: The Dharma Index lists the author as Padmavajra, but notes that the indexes of Bu ston, Narthang, and Peking list the author as "mTsho skyes (Saroruha)," and that the Derge colophon lists the author as "Padma." Cf. also p. 198, note 355.

Hevajra Sādhana, "A Vajra Lamp"

Sanskrit: *Hevajra-sādhana-vajrapradīpa-nāma-śuddha-ṭippaṇī*
Tibetan: *kye rdo rje'i sgrub thabs kyi mdor bshad pa dag pa rdo rje sgron ma zhes bya ba*
Tibetan cited as: ---
Author: Jālandharipa
Tōhoku no.: 1237
Derge location: rgyud, nya, 73a–96a

Hevajra Sādhana, "An Elimination of Errors"

Sanskrit: *Bhramahāra-sādhana-nāma*
Tibetan: *'khrul pa spong ba zhes bya ba'i sgrub pa'i thabs*
Tibetan cited as: *'khrul spong*
Author: Śāntipa (Ratnākaraśānti)
Tōhoku no.: 1245
Derge location: rgyud, nya, 189a–194b

Hevajra Sādhana [Sole Hero]

Also cited as: *Hevajra Sādhana*
Sanskrit: *Śrī-ekavīrasādhana-nāma*
Tibetan: *dpal dpa' bo gcig pa zhes bya ba'i sgrub pa'i thabs*
Tibetan cited as: *kyee rdor gyi sgrub thabs*
Author: Vajra-Ghaṇṭāpa (rDo rje dril bu pa)
Tōhoku no.: 1226
Derge location: rgyud, nya, 29b–31a

Hevajra Tantra in Two Sections

Also cited as: *The Two Sections*
Sanskrit: *Hevajra-tantrarāja-nāma*
Tibetan: *kye'i rdo rje zhes bya ba rgyud kyi rgyal po*
Tibetan cited as: *brtag gnyis*
Author: Kangyur
Tōhoku no.: 417
Derge location: rgyud, nga, 1b–13b. Lhasa: 378 (ka)

Illumination of the Lamp

Sanskrit: *Pradīpoddyotana-nāma-ṭīkā*
Tibetan: *sgron ma gsal bar byed pa zhes bya ba'i rgya cher bshad pa*
Tibetan cited as: *sgron gsal*
Author: Candrakīrti
Tōhoku no.: 1785
Derge location: rgyud, ha, 1b–201b
Comments: One of the most important commentaries on the *Guhyasamāja Tantra* (Tōh. 442).

Illumination of the Lamp Commentary

Sanskrit: *Pradīpoddyotanoddyota-nāma-pañjikā*
Tibetan: *sgron ma gsal bar byed pa'i gsal byed ces bya ba'i dka' 'grel*
Tibetan cited as: ---
Author: Karuṇaśrīpāda
Tōhoku no.: 1790
Derge location: rgyud, A, 10b–170a

Illusory Net Tantra

Sanskrit: *Māyājāla-mahātantrarāja-nāma*
Tibetan: *rgyud kyi rgyal po chen po sgyu 'phrul dra ba zhes bya ba*
Tibetan cited as: *sgyu dra (Māyājāla)*
Author: Kangyur
Tōhoku no.: 466
Derge location: rgyud, ja, 94b–134a. Lhasa: 431 (ca)

Instruction on Initiation

Sanskrit: *Sekoddeśa*
Tibetan: *dbang mdor bstan pa*
Tibetan cited as: *mdor bstan*
Author: Kangyur
Tōhoku no.: 361
Derge location: rgyud, ka, 14a–21a. Lhasa: 370 (ka)
Comments: In the Kālachakra section of the Kangyur

Integration of the Scripture [with the Sādhana]

Sanskrit: *Śrī-guhyasamāja-mahāyogatantrotpādakrama-sādhana-sūtra-melāpaka-nāma*
Tibetan: *rnal 'byor chen po'i rgyud dpal gsang ba 'dus pa'i bskyed pa'i rim pa bsgom pa'i thabs mdo dang bsres pa zhes bya ba*
Tibetan cited as: *mdo bsre[s] (Sūtramelāpaka)*
Author: Nāgārjuna
Tōhoku no.: 1797
Derge location: rgyud, ngi, 11a–15b
Comments: Cf. Panchen Sonam Dragpa's *Overview*, 143; and *YGST*, 250

Interpenetrating Union [Tantra]
Sanskrit: *Śrī-sarvabuddha-samāyoga-ḍākinījāla-sambara-nāma-uttaratantra*
Tibetan: *dpal sangs rgyas thams cad dang mnyam par sbyor ba mkha' 'gro ma sgyu ma bde ba'i mchog ces bya ba'i rgyud phyi ma*
Tibetan cited as: *mnyam sbyor (Samāyoga)*
Author: Kangyur
Tōhoku no.: 366
Derge location: rgyud, ka, 151b–193a. Lhasa: 376 (ka)

Intuition Vajra Compendium
Sanskrit: *Śrī-Jñanavajrasamuccaya*
Tibetan: *ye shes rdo rje kun las bsdus pa*
Tibetan cited as: *ye shes rdo rje kun las bsdus*
Author: Kangyur
Tōhoku no.: 450
Derge location: rgyud, cha, 1b–35b. Lhasa: 787 (tsha)
Comments: Not to be confused with Tōh. 447 (cited as *ye shes rdo rje kun las btus*)

Intuition Vajra Compendium Tantra
Sanskrit: *Vajrajñānasamuccaya-nāma-tantra*
Tibetan: *ye shes rdo rje kun las btus pa zhes bya ba'i rgyud*
Tibetan cited as: *ye shes rdo rje kun las btus*
Author: Kangyur
Tōhoku no.: 447
Derge location: rgyud, ca, 282a–286a. Lhasa: 419 (ca)
Comments: Not to be confused with Tōh. 450 (cited as *ye shes rdo rje kun las bsdus*). Dharma Index indicates: "Bu, Nar, Der [colophons state]: Text is the second chapter of a text by the above title."

Jewel Lamp: A Commentary on the Black Enemy [of Death Tantra]
Sanskrit: *Śrī-Kṛṣṇayamāri-mahātantrarāja-pañjikā-ratnapradīpa-nāma*
Tibetan: *dpal gzhin rje dgra nag po'i rgyud kyi rgyal po chen po'i dka' 'grel rin po che'i sgron ma zhes bya ba*
Tibetan cited as: *dgra nag gi 'grel pa rin chen sgron me*
Author: Śāntipa / Ratnākaraśānti
Tōhoku no.: 1919
Derge location: rgyud, bi, 124a–172b

Kiss Tantra
Sanskrit: *Saṁpuṭa-nāma-mahātantra*
Tibetan: *yang dag par sbyor ba shes bya ba'i rgyud chen po*
Tibetan cited as: *kha sbyor*
Author: Kangyur
Tōhoku no.: 381
Derge location: *rgyud, ga, 73b–158b. Lhasa: 396 (ga)*
Comments: Not to be confused with Tōh. 376 (*Catur-yoginī-saṁpuṭa-tantra; rnal 'byor ma bzhi'i kha sbyor gyi rgyud*). Abhaya's Tōh. 1198 is a commentary on this text.

Lamp that Integrates the Practices
Also cited as: *Practice Integration*
Sanskrit: *Caryāmelāpaka-pradīpa*
Tibetan: *spyod pa bsdus pa'i sgron ma*
Tibetan cited as: *spyod bsdus (Caryāmelāpaka)*
Author: Āryadeva
Tōhoku no.: 1803
Derge location: rgyud, ngi, 57a–106b

Latter [Tantra of] Clear Expression
Sanskrit: *Abhidhāna-uttaratantra-nāma*
Tibetan: *mngon par brjod pa'i rgyud bla ma zhes bya ba*
Tibetan cited as: *mngon brjod bla ma (Abhidhānottara)*
Author: Kangyur
Tōhoku no.: 369
Derge location: rgyud, ka, 247a–370a. Lhasa: 385 (kha)
Comments: This is an explanatory Tantra of the Saṁvara Tantra. Cf. Martin M. Kalff, *Selected Chapters from the Abhidhānottara-tantra: The Union of Male and Female Deities*. (PhD thesis) Columbia University, 1979. Cf. also discussion of that Tantra in Panchen Sonam Dragpa's *Overview*, pp. 51–54.

Light on Reality
Sanskrit: *Tattvāloka-nāma*
Tibetan: *de kho na nyid kyi snang ba zhes bya ba*
Tibetan cited as: *de nyid snang ba*
Author: Bodhisattva
Tōhoku no.: 1293
Derge location: rgyud, ta, 154a–166a
Comments: This text seems to be of uncertain origin. According to the Dharma Index, the Bu-ston, Narthang, and Peking indexes indicate that "although many paṇḍitas have said this text was written by Bodhisattva, this is questionable"; the Peking colophon indicates that the author is Avalokiteshvara or Lokanātha; and the Derge Index and colophon question whether it was really translated by Somanātha.

Lūipa's Evocation
Sanskrit: *Śrī-Bhagavadabhisamaya-nāma*
Tibetan: *dpal bcom ldan 'das mngon par rtogs pa zhes bya ba*
Tibetan cited as: *mngon rtog (Abhisamaya)*
Author: Lūyipa
Tōhoku no.: 1427
Derge location: rgyud, wa, 186b–193a

Luminous Rosary of the Three Vows
Sanskrit: *Trisaṁvaraprabhāmālā-nāma*
Tibetan: *sdom gsum 'od kyi phreng ba zhes bya ba*
Tibetan cited as: ---
Author: Vibhūticandra
Tōhoku no.: 3727
Derge location: rgyud, tshu, 54b–56b

Mandala Rite of the Glorious Esoteric Community

Also cited as: *Four Hundred and Fifty [Verses]*
Sanskrit: *Śrī-Guhyasamāja-maṇḍala-vidhi-nāma*
Tibetan: *dpal gsang ba 'dus pa'i dkyil 'khor gyi cho ga zhes bya ba*
Tibetan cited as: *dkyil 'khor gyi cho ga [shlo ka] bzhi brgya lnga bcu pa; bzhi brgya lnga bcu pa*
Author: Dīpaṅkarabhadra (Mar me mdzad bzang po)
Tōhoku no.: 1865
Derge location: rgyud, di, 69a–87a

Mañjuvajra Esoteric Community Sādhana

Sanskrit: *Śrī-guhyasamāja-mañjuśrī-sādhana*
Tibetan: *dpal gsang ba 'dus pa'i 'jam dpal gyi sgrub thabs*
Tibetan cited as: --- *('jam rdor)*
Author: Samantabhadra
Tōhoku no.: 1880
Derge location: rgyud, pi, 99a–109b

Nairātmya Sādhana

Sanskrit: *Nairātmyayoginī-sādhana*
Tibetan: *bdag med rnal 'byor ma'i sgrub thabs*
Tibetan cited as: *bdag med ma kyi sgrub thabs*
Author: Ḍombi-heruka
Tōhoku no.: 1305
Derge location: rgyud, ta, 212b–215a

Ornament of the Essence

Sanskrit: *Śrī-sarvaguhya-vidhi-garbhālaṁkāra-nāma*
Tibetan: *dpal gsang ba thams cad kyi spyi'i cho ga'i snying po rgyan zhes bya ba*
Tibetan cited as: *snying po rgyan (Garbhālaṁkāra)*
Author: Ācārya Mañjuśrīkīrti (slob dpon 'jam dpal grags pa)
Tōhoku no.: 2490
Derge location: rgyud, zi, 232b–243b
Comments: Not to be confused with Tōh. 451 (also cited as *[rdo rje] snying po rgyan [gyi rgyud]*)

Ornament of the Vajra Essence Tantra

Sanskrit: *Śrī-vajrahṛdayālaṁkāra-tantra-nāma*
Tibetan: *dpal rdo rje snying po rgyan gyi rgyud ces bya ba*
Tibetan cited as: *rdo rje snying po rgyan gyi rgyud*
Author: Kangyur
Tōhoku no.: 451
Derge location: rgyud, cha, 36a–58b. Lhasa: 788 (tsha)
Comments: Not to be confused with Tōh. 2490 (also cited as *snying po rgyan*). According to Wedemeyer (personal communication), the Tibetan title is mistaken, yeildng an improper Sansrit title reconstruction. The proper Sanskrit title should be: *Śrī-vajramaṇḍalālaṁkāra-tantra-nāma* (almost identical to the title of Tōh. 490).

Ornament of Universal Vehicle Sūtras

Sanskrit: *Mahāyāna-sūtrālaṁkāra-nāmā-kārikā*
Tibetan: *theg pa chen po mdo sde'i rgyan zhes bya ba'i tshig le'ur byas pa*
Tibetan cited as: *mdo sde rgyan (Sūtrālaṁkāra)*
Author: Maitreya
Tōhoku no.: 4020
Derge location: sems tsam, phi, 1b–39a

Pearl Rosary: A Commentary on the Difficult Points of the Hevajra

Also cited as: *The Pearl Rosary*
Sanskrit: *Śrī-Hevajra-pañjikā-nāma-muktikāvalī*
Tibetan: *dpal dgyes pa'i rdo rje'i dka' 'grel mu tig phreng ba zhes bya ba*
Tibetan cited as: *kyee rdor gyi dka' 'grel mu tig phreng ba (Hevajrapañjikā-muktikāvalī)*
Author: Śāntipa (Ratnākaraśānti)
Tōhoku no.: 1189
Derge location: rgyud, ga, 221a–297a

Red Enemy of Death Tantra

Also cited as: *The Red Enemy*
Sanskrit: *Śrī-raktayamāri-tantrarāja-nāma*
Tibetan: *dpal gshin rje'i gshed dmar po zhes bya ba'i rgyud kyi rgyal po*
Tibetan cited as: *gshed dmar*
Author: Kangyur
Tōhoku no.: 474
Derge location: rgyud, ja, 186a–214b. Lhasa: 440 (ca)

Relativity Sūtra

Sanskrit: *Ārya-pratītyasamutpāda-nāma-mahāyānasūtra*
Tibetan: *'phags pa rten cing 'brel bar 'byung ba zhes bya ba theg pa chen po'i mdo*
Tibetan cited as: *rten 'brel gyi mdo*
Author: Kangyur
Tōhoku no.: 212
Derge location: mdo, tsha, 125a–125b. Lhasa: 213 (ma)
Comments: Tōh. 520 and 980 are the same text as Tōh. 212. All three are only one folio long.

Sādhana of the Black Enemy [of Death]

Sanskrit: *Kṛṣṇayamārisādhana-nāma*
Tibetan: *gshin rje gshed nag po'i sgrub thabs zhes bya ba*
Tibetan cited as: *dgra nag sgrub thabs*
Author: Śrīdhara (dpal 'dzin)
Tōhoku no.: 1923
Derge location: rgyud, mi, 1b–8b

Sādhana of the Black Enemy [of Death]

Sanskrit: *Śrī-Kṛṣṇayamāri-sādhana sacakrārtha-vistaravyākhyā*
Tibetan: *dpal gshin rje gshed dgra nag po'i sgrub thabs, 'khor lo'i don rgyas par bshad pa dang bcas pa*
Tibetan cited as: *dgra nag gi sgrub thabs*
Author: Akṣobhyavajra
Tōhoku no.: 1931
Derge location: rgyud, mi, 43a–49b

Samantabhadra Sādhana

Sanskrit: *Samantabhadra-nāma-sādhana*
Tibetan: *kun tu bzang po zhes bya ba'i sgrub pa'i thabs*
Tibetan cited as: *sgrub thabs kun bzang*
Author: Buddhaśrījñāna (Jñānapāda)
Tōhoku no.: 1855
Derge location: rgyud, di, 28b–36a

Samantabhadrī Sādhana

Sanskrit: *Caturaṅgasādhana-samantabhadrī-nāma*
Tibetan: *yan lag bzhi pa'i sgrub thabs kun tu bzang mo zhes bya ba*
Tibetan cited as: ---
Author: Buddhaśrījñāna (Jñānapāda)
Tōhoku no.: 1856
Derge location: rgyud, di, 36a–42b

Secret Treasury Tantra

Sanskrit: *Sarvatathāgata-guhyamahāguhya-kośa-akṣaya-nidhi-dīpa-mahā-pratāpa-sādhana-tantra-jñānāś-caryadyuti-cakra-nāma-mahāyāna-sūtra*
Tibetan: *de bzhin gshegs pa thams cad kyi gsang ba, gsang ba'i mdzod chen po mi zad pa gter gyi sgron ma, brtul zhugs chen po bsgrub pa'i rgyud, ye shes rngam pa glog gi 'khor lo zhes bya ba theg pa schen po'i mdo*
Tibetan cited as: *gsang ba'i mdzod kyi rgyud*
Author: Kangyur
Tōhoku no.: 830
Derge location: rnying rgyud, ka, 290b–358a. Lhasa: 794 (dza)
Comments: One of the 17 Tantras (Tōh. 828–844) within the *rnying rgyud* section of the Tōh. Derge Kangyur

Seven Branches

Sanskrit: *Saptāṅga*
Tibetan: *yan lag bdun pa*
Tibetan cited as: *yan lag bdun ldan*
Author: Vāgīśvarakīrti
Tōhoku no.: 1888
Derge location: rgyud, pi, 190a–203a

Six-Branch Sādhana
Sanskrit: *Ṣadaṅga-sādhana-nāma*
Tibetan: *yan lag drug pa zhes bya ba'i sgrub thabs*
Tibetan cited as: ---
Author: Durjayacandra (mi thub zla ba)
Tōhoku no.: 1239
Derge location: rgyud, nya, 126b–130a

Stages of Meditation I
Sanskrit: *Bhāvanākrama*
Tibetan: *bsgom pa'i rim pa*
Tibetan cited as: *bsgom rim*
Author: Kamalaśīla
Tōhoku no.: 3915
Derge location: dbu ma, Ki (#8), 22a–41b

Stages of Meditation II
Sanskrit: *Bhāvanākrama*
Tibetan: *bsgom pa'i rim pa*
Tibetan cited as: *bsgom rim*
Author: Kamalaśīla
Tōhoku no.: 3916
Derge location: dbu ma, ki, 42a–55b

Stages of Meditation III
Sanskrit: *Bhāvanākrama*
Tibetan: *bsgom pa'i rim pa*
Tibetan cited as: *bsgom rim*
Author: Kamalaśīla
Tōhoku no.: 3917
Derge location: dbu ma, ki, 55b–68b

Stages of the Path of the Universal Vehicle
Sanskrit: *Mahāyāna-patha-krama*
Tibetan: *theg pa chen po'i lam gyi rim pa*
Tibetan cited as: ---
Author: Subhagavajra (skal bzang rdo rje)
Tōhoku no.: 3717
Derge location: rgyud, tsu, 193a–194a

Superb Embrace: A Sādhana of the Mandala Rite
Also cited as: *Hevajra Sādhana; Hevajra Father-Mother Sādhana*
Sanskrit: *Suparigraha-nāma-maṇḍala-vidhi-sādhana*
Tibetan: *dkyil 'khor gyi cho ga'i sgrub thabs bzang po yongs su gzung ba zhes bya ba*
Tibetan cited as: *bzang po yong bzung; kyee rdor gyi sgrub thabs; kyee rdor yab yum gyi sgrub thabs*
Author: Durjayacandra (thub dka' zla ba)
Tōhoku no.: 1240
Derge location: rgyud, nya, 130a–154a

Supreme Bliss Sādhana
Sanskrit: *Bhagavacchrīcakrasambara-sādhana-ratna-cūḍāmaṇi-nāma*
Tibetan: *bcom ldan 'das dpal 'khor lo bde mchog gi sgrub thabs rin po che gtsug gi nor bu zhes bya ba*
Tibetan cited as: *bde mchog sgrub thabs*
Author: Lavapa
Tōhoku no.: 1443
Derge location: rgyud, wa, 243b–251a

Supreme Bliss Sādhana
Sanskrit: *Śrī-vajrasattva-nāma-sādhana*
Tibetan: *dpal rdo rje sems dpa'i sgrub thabs zhes bya ba*
Tibetan cited as:, *bde mchog (gi sgrub thabs)*
Author: Lūyipa
Tōhoku no.: 1454
Derge location: rgyud, ṣa, 1b–3b
Comments: The Dharma Index notes that this also is known as the *Śambara-sādhana* in Sanskrit, and the *bde mchog gi sgrub thabs* in Tibetan.

Supreme Bliss [Tantra]
Sanskrit: *Cakrasamvara-tantra; Śrīherukābhidhāna; Tantrarāja-śrīlaghu-samvara-nāma*
Tibetan: *rgyud kyi rgyal po dpal bde mchog nyung ngu zhes bya ba*
Tibetan cited as: *['khor lo] bde mchog ([Cakra]samvara)*
Author: Kangyur
Tōhoku no.: 368
Derge location: rgyud, ka, 213b–246b. Lhasa: 384 (kha)

Tenfold Thatness
Sanskrit: *Daśatattva*
Tibetan: *de kho na nyid bcu pa*
Tibetan cited as: *de kho na nyid bcu pa*
Author: Ḍombipa
Tōhoku no.: 1229
Derge location: rgyud, nya, 37a–41a

Thousand [Verse] Commentary on the Compendium of Reality [Tantra]
Sanskrit: *Sarvatathāgata-tattvasaṁgraha-mahāyānābhisamaya-tantra-tattvālokakarī-nāma-vyākhyā*
Tibetan: *de bzhin gshegs pa thams cad kyi de kho na nyid bsdus pa theg pa chen po mngon par rtogs pa zhes bya ba'i rgyud kyi bshad pa de kho na nyid snang bar byed pa zhes bya ba*
Tibetan cited as: *de nyid bsdus pa'i stong 'grel*
Author: Ānandagarbha (kun dga' snying po)
Tōhoku no.: 2510
Derge location: rgyud, li, 1b–352a

Twenty Verse Esoteric Community Mandala Rite
Sanskrit: *Śrī-guhyasamāja-maṇḍla-viṁśati-vidhi-nāma*
Tibetan: *dpal gsang ba 'dus pa'i dkyil 'khor gyi cho ga nyi shu pa zhes bya ba*
Tibetan cited as: ---
Author: Nāgabodhi (klu'i byang chub)
Tōhoku no.: 1810
Derge location: rgyud, ngi, 131a–145b

Vajra Pavilion Tantra
Sanskrit: *Ḍākinīvajrapañjaramahātantrarājakalpa*
Tibetan: *mkha' 'gro ma rdo rje gur zhes bya ba'i rgyud kyi gyal po chen po'i brtag pa*
Tibetan cited as: *rdo rje gur (Vajrapañjara)*
Author: Kangyur
Tōhoku no.: 419
Derge location: rgyud, nga, 30a–65b. Lhasa: 379 (ka)

Vajra Peak Tantra
Sanskrit: *Vajraśekhara-mahāguhya-yogatantra*
Tibetan: *gsang ba rnal 'byor chen po'i rgyud rdo rje rtse mo*
Tibetan cited as: *rdo rje rtse mo; rtse mo ([Vajra]śekhara)*
Author: Kangyur
Tōhoku no.: 480
Derge location: rgyud, nya, 142b–274a. Lhasa: 448 (cha)

Varja Rosary
Sanskrit: *Vajrāvali-nāma-maṇḍala-sādhana*
Tibetan: *dkyil 'khor gyi cho ga rdo rje phreng ba zhes bya ba*
Tibetan cited as: *rdo rje phreng ba (Vajrāvali)*
Author: Abhayākaragupta
Tōhoku no.: 3140
Derge location: rgyud, phu, 1b–94b

Vajra Rosary Tantra
Sanskrit: *Śrī-vajramālā-abhidāna-mahāyogatantra-sarvatantra-hṛdaya-rahasya-vibhaṅga-nāma*
Tibetan: *rnal 'byor chen po'i rgyud dpal rdo rje phreng ba mngon par brjod pa rgyud thams cad kyi snying po gsang ba rnam par phye ba zhes bya ba*
Tibetan cited as: *rdo rje phreng ba (Vajramālā)*
Author: Kangyur
Tōhoku no.: 445
Derge location: rgyud, ca, 208a–277b. Lhasa: 417 (ca)

Vajraḍāka Tantra

Sanskrit: *Śrī-vajraḍāka-nāma-mahātantra-rāja*

Tibetan: *rgyud kyi rgyal po chen po dpal rdo rje mkha' 'gro zhes bya ba*

Tibetan cited as: *rdo rje mkha' 'gro lnga bcu pa*

Author: Kangyur

Tōhoku no.: 370

Derge location: rgyud, kha, 1b–125a. Lhasa: 386 (kha)

Comments: This is the fifty-chapter *Vajraḍāka Tantra* which is well over one-hundred folios, and not the two-folio long Tōh. 399 (P44, vol. 3; no Lhasa) entitled *Vajraḍākaguhyatantrarāja (rdo rje mkha' 'gro gsang ba'i rgyud kyi rgyal po)*. See note 131 above.

Vajragarbha's [Hevajra] Commentary

Sanskrit: *Hevajra-piṇḍārtha-ṭīkā*

Tibetan: *kye'i rdo rje bsdus pa'i don gyi rgya cher 'grel pa*

Tibetan cited as: *rdo rje snying 'grel*

Author: Vajragarbha (rdo rje snying po)

Tōhoku no.: 1180

Derge location: rgyud, ka, 1b–126a

Validating Cognition Commentary

Sanskrit: *Pramāṇavārttikakārikā*

Tibetan: *tshad ma rnam 'grel gyi tshig le'ur byas pa*

Tibetan cited as: *tshad ma rnam 'grel (Pramāṇavārttika)*

Author: Dharmakīrti

Tōhoku no.: 4210

Derge location: tshad ma, ce, 94b–161a

Volumes on the Stages

Sanskrit: *Yogacaryābhūmi*

Tibetan: *rnal 'byor spyod pa'i sa*

Tibetan cited as: *sa sde*

Author: Asaṅga

Tōhoku no.: 4035–42

Derge location: sems tsam, tshi, 1b, through 'i, 68b

Comments: Although the *Yogacaryābhūmi* is one large, encyclopedic work, traditionally it is divided up into five texts (*pañca-bhūmi-vastu, sa sde lnga*); the Tōh. catalogue divides it into eight texts.

Canonical Tibetan Texts (Kangyur and Tengyur) Sorted by Tōhoku Number (English Title Only)

Tōh.	**English Title**
212	*Relativity Sūtra*
361	*Instruction on Initiation*
366	*Interpenetrating Union [Tantra]*
368	*Supreme Bliss [Tantra]*
369	*Latter [Tantra of] Clear Expression*
370	*Vajraḍāka Tantra*
373	*Arisal of Saṁvara Tantra*
375	*Activities [of the Yoginīs]*
381	*Kiss Tantra*
417	*Hevajra Tantra in Two Sections*
419	*Vajra Pavilion Tantra*
420	*Drop of Mahāmudrā Tantra*
424	*Buddha-Skullbowl Tantra*
430	*Four Seats Tantra*
442	*Esoteric Community Tantra*
443	*Further Tantra [of the Esoteric Community]*
445	*Vajra Rosary Tantra*
447	*Intuition Vajra Compendium Tantra*
450	*Intuition Vajra Compendium*
451	*Ornament of the Vajra Essence Tantra*
466	*Illusory Net Tantra*
467	*Black Enemy [of Death] Tantra*
474	*Red Enemy of Death Tantra*
479	*Compendium of Reality [Tantra]*
480	*Vajra Peak Tantra*
830	*Secret Treasury Tantra*
1180	*Vajragarbha's [Hevajra] Commentary*
1189	*Pearl Rosary: A Commentary on the Difficult Points of the Hevajra*
1194	*Commentary on The [Vajra] Pavilion [Tantra]*

Tōh.	**English Title**
1198	*Clusters of Instructions*
1218	*Hevajra Sādhana*
1224	*Five Commitments*
1226	*Hevajra Sādhana [Sole Hero]*
1229	*Tenfold Thatness*
1237	*Hevajra Sādhana, "A Vajra Lamp"*
1239	*Six-Branch Sādhana*
1240	*Superb Embrace: A Sādhana of the Mandala Rite*
1245	*Hevajra Sādhana, "An Elimination of Errors"*
1251	*Blazing Jewels Sādhana*
1293	*Light on Reality*
1305	*Nairātmya Sādhana*
1347, 845	*Great Commentary: Immaculate Light*
1420	*Commentary on The Arisal of Saṁvara [Tantra]*
1427	*Lūipa's Evocation*
1437	*Five Deity Supreme Bliss Sādhana*
1443	*Supreme Bliss Sādhana*
1448	*Drop of Spring*
1454	*Supreme Bliss Sādhana*
1465	*Glorious Evocation: A Commentary [on Lūipa's Supreme Bliss Sādhana]*
1490	*Analysis of [Lūipa's] Evocation*
1510	*Auto-commentary to the Commentary to Lūipa's Evocation*
1607	*Commentary on The Four Seats [Tantra]*
1652	*Commentary on The [Buddha-]Skullbowl [Tantra]*
1660 [T]	[Taisho] *Accumulations for Enlightenment*
1785	*Illumination of the Lamp*
1789	*Deciphering the Seven Ornaments*
1790	*Illumination of the Lamp Commentary*
1796	*Abbreviated Practice*
1797	*Integration of the Scripture [with the Sādhana]*
1802	*Five Stages*
1803	*Lamp that Integrates the Practices*
1809	*Graded Presentation of the Esoteric Community Practice*

Tōh.	**English Title**
1810	*Twenty Verse Esoteric Community Mandala Rite*
1830	*Clear Meaning: A Commentary on the Difficult Points of [Nāgārjuna's] Five Stages*
1853	*Direct Speech [of Mañjushrī]*
1854	*Direct Speech [of Mañjushrī]*
1855	*Samantabhadra Sādhana*
1856	*Samantabhadrī Sādhana*
1859	*Drop of Liberation*
1865	*Mandala Rite of the Glorious Esoteric Community*
1866	*Commentary on [Jñānapāda's] Direct Speech [of Mañjushrī]*
1867	*Commentary on [Jñānapāda's] The Samantabhadra Sādhana*
1868	*Commentary on [Jñānapāda's] The Samantabhadra Sādhana*
1869	*Commentary on [Jñānapāda's] The Four-Branched [Samantabhadrī] Sādhana, "A Bouquet of Quintessences"*
1871	*Commentary on [Dīpaṅkarabhadra's] The Four Hundred and Fifty [Verses]*
1872	*Commentary on [Jñānapāda's] The Four-Branched Samantabhadrī Sādhana*
1880	*Mañjuvajra Esoteric Community Sādhana*
1888	*Seven Branches*
1919	*Jewel Lamp: A Commentary on the Black Enemy [of Death Tantra]*
1923	*Sādhana of the Black Enemy [of Death]*
1931	*Sādhana of the Black Enemy [of Death]*
1935	*Blossoming Kumudā Flower: A Sādhana of the Black Enemy of Death*
2488	*Fourteen Root Downfalls*
2490	*Ornament of the Essence*
2510	*Thousand [Verse] Commentary on the Compendium of Reality [Tantra]*
2670	*Commentary on The Contemplation Addendum [Tantra]*

Tōh.	**English Title**
3140	*Varja Rosary*
3714	*Dispelling the Two Extremes [of the Vajra Vehicle]*
3717	*Stages of the Path of the Universal Vehicle*
3721	*Fifty Verses on the Mentor*
3727	*Luminous Rosary of the Three Vows*
3871	*Engaging in the Bodhisattvas' Way of Life*
3915	*Stages of Meditation I*
3916	*Stages of Meditation II*
3917	*Stages of Meditation III*
3944	*Compendium of Transcendences*
4020	*Ornament of Universal Vehicle Sūtras*
4021	*Distinguishing the Center and Extremes*
4035–42	*Volumes on the Stages*
4210	*Validating Cognition Commentary*
4687 [Pk]	[Peking] *Hevajra Commentary, "The Jewel Rosary of Yoga"*

Indigenous Tibetan Texts

Khedrub Jay (mKhas grub rJe)

rgyud sde spyi'i rnam par gzhag pa rgyas par brjod

English: *General Presentation of the Tantra Classes*

Version conslted: edition in Lessing and Wayman (1978)

Yangchen Gaway Lordö (dbyangs can dga' ba'i blos gros, a.k.a. A-kya Yogs-'dzin)

gzhi'i sku gsum gyi rnam gzhag rab gsal sgron me

English: *A Brilliant Lamp: A Presentation of the Three Bodies which are the Basis*

Version consulted: ACIP file S6600

Tsong Khapa

rgyal ba khyab bdag rdo rje 'chang chen po'i lam gyis rim pa gsang ba kun gyi gnad rnam par phye ba zhes bya ba

Abbrev.: *sngags rim chen mo (NRC)*

English: *The Great Treatise on the Stages of Mantra*

Versions consulted:

(1) **TL:** blockprint edition of 1,024 folio sides; from *The Collected Works (gsuṅ 'bum) of Rje Tsoṅ-kha-pa Blo-bzaṅ-grags-pa*, reproduced from an example of the old Bkra-śis-lhun-po redaction from the library of Klu 'khyil Monastery of Ladhakh by Ngawang Gelek Demo. (Vol. 4: 494 folio sides; and vol. 5 [incl. chs. 11–12]: 530 folio sides.) New Delhi: Demo, 1975. Library of Congress classification: BQ7950.T75 1975.

(2) **ZH:** blockprint edition of 883 folio sides; from the 1897 Lhasa "old" Zhol, Dga'-ldan-phun-tshogs-gling blocks. Reprinted New Delhi: Mongolian Lama Gurudeva, 1978–1979 as "The collected works (gsuṅ 'bum) of the incomparable Lord Tsoṅ-kha-pa Blo-bzaṅ-grags-pa." (Vol. 3.)

(3) **MS:** manuscript edition of 732 oversized folio sides contained in the Columbia University library; I-Tib-554 LCCN 76-905625, from the PL480 collection. *Sngags Rim Chen Po*, Dharamsala: n.p., 1969.

(4) **ACIP:** electronic edition input by the Asian Classics Input Project (input from the ZH: Zhol edition). File number S5281E.INC.

drang ba dang nges pa'i don rnam par 'byed pa'i bstan bcos legs bshad snying po
Abbrev.: *legs bshad snying po*
English: *Essence of Eloquence*
Version consulted: ACIP file S5396E.

byang chub lam rim che ba
Abbrev.: *lam rim chen mo (LRC)*
English: *The Great Stages of the Path to Enlightenment*
Version consulted: 1897 Lha-sa "old" Zhol, Dga'-ldan-phun-tshogs-gling blocks. Reprinted New Delhi: Mongolian Lama Gurudeva, 1978–1979 as "The collected works (gsuṅ 'bum) of the incomparable Lord Tsoṅ-kha-pa Blo-bzaṅ-grags-pa."

byang chub lam rim cung ngu
Abbrev.: *lam rim cung ngu (LRC)*
English: *The Middling Stages of the Path to Enlightenment*
Version consulted: ACIP file S5393E.

bla ma lnga bcu pa'i rnam bshad slab pa'i re ba kun skong
Abbrev.: *bla ma lnga bcu pa'i rnam bshad*
English: *Explanation of the Fifty Verses on the Mentor: Fulfilling Students' Every Hope*
Location: *Vol. 1 of gsung 'bum, 321–76*

lam gyi gtso bo rnam gsum rtsa 'grel
Abbrev.: ---
English: *The Three Principles of the Path*
Version consulted: ACIP file S5275P67.

gSang sngags kyi tshul khrims kyi rnam bshad dngos grub kyi snye ma
Abbrev.: *rtsa ltung rnam bshad*
English: *Explanation of the Root [Tantric] Downfalls*
Location: P6188, vol. 160

Dictionaries and Reference Works

Bod rGya Tshig mDzoz Chen mo (The Great Tibetan-Chinese Dictionary) (TTC)

1984 Three Volumes. Lhasa: Mi Rigs dPe sKrun Khang.

A Catalogue-Index of the Tibetan Buddhist Canons (Bkaḥ-ḥgyur and Bstan-ḥgyur) (Tōh.)

1934 Sendai: Tōhoku Imperial University.

Chandra, Lokesh (LC)

1992 Seven Volumes. *Tibetan-Sanskrit Dictionary*. New Delhi: International Academy of Indian Culture, and Aditya Prakashan.

Das, Sarat Chandra (Das)

1979 *A Tibetan-English Dictionary with Sanskrit Synonyms*. Delhi: Motilal Banarsidass.

Eimer, Helmut

1989 *Der Tantra-Katalog des Bu ston im Vergleich mit der Abteilung Tantra des tibetischen Kanjur: Studie, Textausgabe, Konkordanzen und Indices*. Indica et Tibetica, no. 17. Bonn: Indica et Tibetica Verlag.

Goldstein, Melvyn (Gold)

1978 *Tibetan-English Dictionary of Modern Tibetan*. 2nd ed. Kathmandu: Ratna Pustak Bhandar.

Macdonell, Arthur A.

1991 *A Practical Sanskrit Dictionary*. New York: Oxford University Press.

Monier-Williams, Monier (MW)

1988 *A Sanskrit-English Dictionary*. Delhi: Motilal Banarsidass.

The Nyingma Edition of the sDe-dge bKa'-'gyur/bsTan-'gyur Research Catalogue and Bibliography. Sponsored by the Head Lama of the Tibetan Nyingma Meditation Center. Published by Dharma Mudranālaya under the direction of Tarthang Tulku. First printing of 216 copies. (Dharma Index)

n.d. Eight volumes. Oakland: Dharma Publishing.

Rangjung Yeshe Dictionary (Concise Dharma Dictionary) (RY)

1996 Electronic file distributed by Erik Pema Kunsang. Kathmandu: Rangjung Yeshe Translations and Publications.

Tibetan and Himalayan Library Translation Tool (THL)

n.d. Online database of twenty Tibetan-English dictionaries (http://www.thlib.org/reference/dictionaries/tibetan-dictionary/translate.php)

Modern Sources

A-kya Yong-dzin Yang-chan ga-wai lo-dr'o

1980 *A Compendium of Ways of Knowing: A Clear Mirror of What Should be Accepted and Rejected (Blo-rigs-kyi sdom-tshig bland-dor gsal-ba'i me-long)*. Revised 2nd edition. Trans. and ed. by Sherpa Tulku and A. Berzin; Commentary by Geshe Ngawang Dhargyey. Dharamsala: Library of Tibetan Works and Archives.

Bentor, Yael

n.d. "Embodiments of Enlightenment in Tibetan Buddhism." Unpublished manuscript.

n.d. "Developing the Creative Power of the Mind: The Generation Process (*bskyed-rim*) and its Antecedents." Unpublished manuscript.

1996 "Literature on Consecration (*rab gnas*)." In *Tibetan Literature: Studies in Genre*, ed. by José I. Cabezón and Roger R. Jackson, pp. 290–311. Ithaca: Snow Lion.

Beyer, Stephan

1978 *The Cult of Tārā: Magic nd Ritul in Tibet*. Pbk. ed. Berkeley: University of California Press.

Bharati, Agehananda

1993 *Tantric Traditions* [revised and enlarged ed.]. Delhi: Hindustan. [Original edition entitled *The Tantric Tradition*. Rider & Co., 1965.]

Buswell, Robert E.

1990 "Introduction: Prolegomenon to the Study of Buddhist Apocryphal Scriptures." In *Chinese Buddhist Apocrypha*, ed. by Robert E. Buswell, pp. 1–30. Honolulu: University of Hawaii Press.

Cabezón, José I.

1981 "The Concepts of Truth and Meaning in the Buddhist Scriptures." *Journal of the International Association of Buddhist Studies* 4, no. 1: 9–23.

1992 "Vasubandhu's *Vyākhyāyukti* on the Authenticity of the Mahāyāna *Sūtras*." In *Texts in Context: Traditional Hermeneutics in South Asia*, ed. by Jeffrey R. Timm, 221–243. New York: SUNY.

1994 *Buddhism and Language: A Study of Indo-Tibetan Scholasticism*. Albany: SUNY Press.

1998 *Scholasticism: Cross-Cultural and Comparative Perspectives*. Albany: SUNY Press.

Cabezón, José I. and R. Jackson, eds.

1996 *Tibetan Literature: Studies in Genre*. Ithaca: Snow Lion.

Ch'en, Kenneth K.S.

1945–47 "The Tibetan Tripitaka." Harvard Journal of Asiatic Studies 9: 53–62.

Cozort, Daniel

1986 *Highest Yoga Tantra: An Introduction to the Esoteric Buddhism of Tibet*. Ithaca: Snow Lion.

Dalai Lama, H.H. (Tenzin Gyatso)

1997 *Healing Anger: The Power of Patience from a Buddist Perspective*. Ithaca: Snow Lion.

2001 *Stages of Meditation*. Trans Geshe Jordhen, Losang C. Ganchenpa, and Jeremy Russel. [Commentary on Kamalaśīla's *Bhāvanākrama II*.] Ithaca: Snow Lion.

Dalai Lama, H.H. and Alexander Berzin

1997 *The Gelug/Kagyü Tradition of Mahamudra*. Ithaca: Snow Lion.

Davidson, Ronald M.

1990 "An Introduction to the Standards of Scriptural Authenticity in Indian Buddhism." In *Chinese Buddhist Apocrypha*, ed. by Robert E. Buswell, pp. 291–325. Honolulu: University of Hawaii Press.

Dowman, Keith

1985 Masters of Mahamudra: Songs and Histories of the Eighty-Four Buddhist Siddhas. Albany: SUNY Press.

Dreyfus, Georges B.

1997 *Recognizing Reality: Dharmakīrti's Philosophy and its Tibetan Interpretations*. Albany: SUNY Press.

Dutt, Sukumar

1988 *Buddhist Monks and Monasteries of India: Their History and Their Contribution to Indian Culture*. Delhi: Motilal Banarsidass. Reprint of 1962 edition.

Farrow, G.W. and I. Menon, trans. and ed.

1992 *The Concealed Essence of the Hevajra Tantra with the Commentary Yogaratnamālā*. Delhi: Motilal Banarsidass.

Flood, Gavin

1996 *An Introduction to Hinduism*. Cambridge: Cambridge University Press.

Garfield, Jay L. trans.

1995 *The Fundamental Wisdom of the Middle Way: Nāgārjuna's Mūlamadhyamakakārikā*. Oxford: Oxford University Press.

Gombrich, Richard

1978 *On Being Sanskritic: A Plea for Civilized Study and the Study of Civilization*. Oxford: Clarendon Press.

Gyatrul Rinpoche, Ven.

1982 *Generating the Deity*. 2nd ed. Ithaca: Snow Lion.

Gyatso, Geshe Kelsang

1982 *Clear Light of Bliss: Mahamudra in Vajrayana Buddhism*. Boston: Wisdom.

1994 *Tantric Grounds and Paths*. London: Tharpa Publications.

1997a *Essence of Vajrayana: The Highest Yoga Tantra Practice of Heruka Body Mandala*. London: Tharpa Publications.

1997b *Understanding the Mind: The Nature and Power of the Mind*. 2nd ed. Glen Spey, NY: Tharpa Publications.

Gyatso, Janet B.

1986 "Signs, Memory and History: A Tantric Buddhist Theory of Scriptural Transmission." *Journal of the International Association of Buddhist Studies* 9, no. 2: 7–35.

1991 "Genre, Authorship and Transmission in Visionary Buddhism: The Literary Traditions of Tang-stong rGyal-po." In *Tibetan Buddhism: Reason and Revelation*, ed. by Ronald M. Davidson and Steven D. Goodman, pp. 95–106. Albany: State University of New York Press.

1993 "The Logic of Legitimation in the Tibetan Treasure Tradition." *History of Religions* 33, no. 1: 97–134.

1996 "Drawn from the Tibetan Treasury: The *gTer ma* Literature." In *Tibetan Literature: Studies in Genre*, ed. by José I. Cabezón and Roger R. Jackson, pp. 147–169. Ithaca: Snow Lion.

Gyel-tsap

1994 *Yogic Deeds of Bodhisattvas: Gyel-tsap on Āryadeva's Four Hundred*. Comm. by Geshe Sonam Rinchen, trans. and ed. by Ruth Sonam. Ithaca: Snow Lion.

Harrison, Paul

1992 "Meritorious Activity or Waste of Time? Some Remarks on the Editing of Texts in the Tibetan Kanjur." In *Tibetan Studies: Proceedings of the 5th Seminar of the International Association of Tibetan Studies, Narita 1989*, ed. by Ihara Shōren and Yamaguchi Zuihō, pp. 77–93. Narita: Naritasan Shinshoji.

1994 "In Search of the Source of the Tibetan bKa' 'gyur: A Reconnaissance Report." In *Tibetan Studies: Proceedings of the 6th Seminar of the International Association for Tibetan Studies, Fagernes 1992*, vol. 1, ed. by Per Kvaerne, pp. 295–317. Oslo: Institute for Comparative Research in Human Culture.

1996 "A Brief History of the Tibetan bKa' 'gyur." In *Tibetan Literature: Studies in Genre*, ed. by José I. Cabezón and Roger R. Jackson, pp. 70–94. Ithaca: Snow Lion.

Hopkins, Jeffrey

1983 *Meditations on Emptiness*. London: Wisdom.

1984 "Reason as the Prime Principle in Tsong kha pa's Delineation of Deity Yoga as the Demarcation Between Sūtra and Tantra." *Journal of the International Association of Buddhist Studies* 7, no. 2: 95–115.

1985 "The Ultimate Deity in Action Tantra and Jung's Warning Against Identifying with the Deity." In *Buddhist-Christian Studies*, no. 5: 158–172.

1987 *Emptiness Yoga*. Ithaca: Snow Lion.

1990 "Tantric Buddhism, Degeneration or Enhancement: The Viewpoint of a Tibetan Tradition." In *Buddhist-Christian Studies*, no. 10: 87–96.

2008 *Tantric Techniques*. Ithaca: Snow Lion.

Jamgön Kongtrul

1996 *Creation and Completion: Essential Points of Tantric Meditation*. Trans. and ed. by Sarah Harding. Boston: Wisdom.

Jinpa, Thupten

2002 *Self, Reality and Reason in Tibetan Philosophy: Tsongkhapa's Quest for the Middle Way*. London: RoutledgeCurzon.

Kapstein, Mathew

1989 "The Purificatory Gem and Its Cleansing: A Late Tibetan Polemical Discussion of Apocryphal Texts." *History of Religions* 28, no. 3: 217–244.

1996 "*gDams ngag*: Tibetan Technologies of the Self." In *Tibetan Literature: Studies in Genre*, ed. by José I. Cabezón and Roger R. Jackson, pp. 275–289. Ithaca: Snow Lion.

Khedrup Jay

1968 *mKhas grub rJe's Fundamentals of the Buddhist Tantras [rgyud sde spyi'i rnam par gzhag pa rgyas par brjod]*, trans. & ed. by Alex Wayman and Ferdinand D. Lessing. The Hague: Mouton.

Lamotte, Étienne

1947 "La critique d'authenticité dans le bouddhism." In *India Antiqua*, ed. by F.D.K. Bosch et. al., pp. 213-222. Leiden: E.J. Brill.

Lati Rinbochay and Jeffrey Hopkins

1979 *Death, Intermediate State, and Rebirth in Tibetan Buddhism*. Valois: Gabriel/Snow Lion.

Lati Rinbochay and Elizabeth Napper

1980 *Mind in Tibetan Buddhism*. Valois: Gabriel/Snow Lion.

Lessing, F.D. and Alex Wayman, trans. and ed.

1978 *Introduction to the Buddhist Tantric Systems* [mKhas grub rJe's *rgyud sde spyi'i rnam par gzhag pa rgyas par brjod*], 2nd ed. Delhi: Motialal Banarsidass. (First published: the Hague, 1968)

Li, Abbey Petty

1994 "The Gurupañcāśikā in Indian and Tibetan Buddhism." Masters Thesis, University of Washington.

Lopez, Donald S., Jr.

1996 "Polemical Literature (*dGag lan*)." In *Tibetan Literature: Studies in Genre*, ed. by José I. Cabezón and Roger R. Jackson, pp. 217-228. Ithaca: Snow Lion.

Martin, Dan

1996 "Tables of Contents (*dKar chag*)." In *Tibetan Literature: Studies in Genre*, ed. by José I. Cabezón and Roger R. Jackson, pp. 500–514. Ithaca: Snow Lion.

Mayer, Robert

1994 "Scriptural Revelation in India and Tibet: Indian Precursors of the gTer-ma Tradition." In *Tibetan Studies: Proceedings of the 6th Seminar of the International Association for Tibetan Studies, Fagernes 1992*, vol. 2, ed. by Per Kvaerne, pp. 533–544. Oslo: Institute for Comparative Research in Human Culture.

Mullin, Glenn, trans. and ed.

1996 *Tsong Khapa's Six Yogas of Naropa*. Ithaca: Snow Lion.

Mullin, Glenn, trans.

1997 *Reading on the Six Yogas of Naropa*. Ithaca: Snow Lion.

Napper, Elizabeth

1989 *Dependent-Arising and Emptiness: A Tibetan Buddhist Interpretation of Mādhyamika Philosophy Emphasizing the Compatibility of Emptiness and Conventional Phenomena*. Boston: Wisdom.

1995 "Styles and Principles of Translation." In *Buddhist Translations: Problems and Perspectives*, edited by Lama Doboom Tulku, 35–42. New Delhi: Manohar.

Obermiller, E., trans.

1986 *The History of Buddhism in India and Tibet by Bu-ston*. 2nd ed. Delhi: Sri Satguru.

1987 *The Jewelry of Scripture by Bu-ston*. 2nd ed. Delhi: Sri Satguru.

Panchen Sonam Dragpa

1996 *Overview of Buddhist Tantra: General Presentation of the Classes of Tantra, Captivating the Minds of the Fortunate Ones. [rgyud sde spy'i rnam par bzhag pa skal bzang gi yid 'phrog ces bya ba bzhugs so]*. Trans. by Martin Boord and Losang Norbu Tsonowa. Dharamsala: Library of Tibetan Works and Archives.

Powers, John

1996 "History, Politics, and the Interpretation of Tantric Texts: The Case of the *Great Exposition of Secret Mantra*." Unpublished essay delivered at the 1996 annual conference of the American Academy of Religion.

Ray, R.A.

1985 "Buddhism: Sacred Text Written and Realized." In The Holy Book in Comparative Perspective, ed. by F.M. Denny and R.L. Taylor, pp. 148–180. Columbia, South Carolina: University of South Carolina Press.

Rhoton, Jared D.

1985 "A Study of the sDom gSum of Sapan." Doctoral Dissertation, Columbia University.

Roerich, George (trans.)

1976 *The Blue Annals*. Second edition. Delhi: Motilal Banarsidass. [1995 printing]

Ruegg, David S.

1966 *The Life of Bu ston Rin po che*. Rome: Instituto Italiano per il Medio ed Estremo Oriente.

1978 "The Study of Tibetan Philosophy and Its Indian Sources: Notes on Its History and Method." In *Proceedings of the 1976 Csoma de Körös Symposium*, ed. L. Ligeti, Biblioteca Orientalia Hungarica, no.23, pp. 377–91. Budapest.

1981 *Literature of the Madhyamaka School of Philosophy in India*. A History of Indian Literature, editor Jan Gonda, Vol. 7, Fasc. 1. Wiesbaden: Otto Harrassowitz.

1989 *Buddha-nature, Mind and the Problem of Gradualism in a Comparative Perspective*. London: School of Oriental and African Studies.

1995b "On Translating Tibetan Philosophical Texts." In *Buddhist Translations: Problems and Perspectives*, edited by Lama Doboom Tulku, 75–86. New Delhi: Manohar.

Samten, Jampa, translated with Jeremy Russell

1987 "Notes on the Lithang Edition of the Tibetan bKa'-'gyur." Tibet Journal 12, no. 3: 17–40.

1987b "Origins of the Tibetan Canon with Special Reference to the Tshal-pa Kanjur." In *Buddhism and Science*, pp. 763-781. Seoul: Tongguk University.

Skilling, Peter

1994 "Kanjur Titles and Colophons." In *Tibetan Studies: Proceedings of the 6th Seminar of the International Association for Tibetan Studies, Fagernes 1992*, vol. 2, ed. by Per Kvaerne, pp. 768–780. Oslo: Institute for Comparative Research in Human Culture.

Skorupski, Tadeusz

1996 "The Canonical *Tantras* of the New Schools." In *Tibetan Literature: Studies in Genre*, ed. by José I. Cabezón and Roger R. Jackson, pp. 95–110. Ithaca: Snow Lion.

Snellgrove, David L.

1987 *Indo-Tibetan Buddhism: Indian Buddhists and Their Tibetan Successors*. London: Serindia.

Tāranātha

1981 *Tāranātha's History of Buddhism in India*. Ed. by D. Chattopadhyaya, trans. by Lama Chimpa and Alaka Chattopadhyaya. Highlands, N.J.: Humanities Press.

Thurman, Robert A. F., ed.

1982 *Life & Teachings of Tsong Khapa*. Dharamsala: Library of Tibetan Works and Archives.

Thurman, Robert A. F.

n.d. "The Practice of Unexcelled Yoga Tantra." Unpublished essay.

1981 "Confrontation and Interior Realization in Indo-Tibetan Buddhist Traditions." In *The Other Side of God: A Polarity in World Religions*. Ed. by Peter Berger. Garden City: Anchor Press/Doubleday.

1988 "Vajra Hermeneutics." In *Buddhist Hermeneutics*, ed. by Donald Lopez, 119–148. Honolulu: University of Hawaii Press, 1988.

1989 *The Speech of Gold*. Delhi: Motilal Banarsidass. [Translation and study of Tsong Khapa's *Essence of Eloquence*. Reprint of *The Central Philosophy of Tibet*. Princeton: Princeton University Press, 1984.]

1991 "Tibetan Psychology: Sophisticated Software for the Human Brain." In *Mind Science: An East-West Dialogue*. Ed. by Daniel Goleman and Robert Thurman. Boston: Wisdom.

1994 *The Tibetan Book of the Dead: Liberation Through Understanding in the Between*. New York: Bantam.

1995 *Essential Tibetan Buddhism*. San Francisco: Harper Collins.

Tsong-ka-pa (or Tsong Khapa, or Tsongkhapa)

1977 *Tantra in Tibet: The Great Exposition of Secret Mantra Vol. 1*, intro. by H.H. Tenzin Gyatso, the Fourteenth Dalai Lama, trans. & ed. by Jeffery Hopkins. London: George Allen & Unwin.

1981 *Yoga of Tibet: The Great Exposition of Secret Mantra Vol. 2 and 3*, intro. by H.H. Tenzin Gyatso, the Fourteenth Dalai Lama, trans. & ed. by Jeffery Hopkins. London: George Allen & Unwin.

1999 *The Fulfillment of All Hopes: Guru Devotion in Tibetan Buddhism (A Commentary on Aśvaghoṣa's Gurupañcāśikā... by Tsongkhapa)*. Translated and introduced by Gareth Sparham. Boston: Wisdom Publications.

2000 *The Great Treatise on the Stages of the Path to Enlightenment*. Vol. I. Trans. by the Lamrim Chenmo Translation Committee with Joshua Culter as editor-in-chief. Ithaca: Snow Lion.

2002 *The Great Treatise on the Stages of the Path to Enlightenment*. Vol. III. Trans. by the Lamrim Chenmo Translation Committee with Joshua Culter as editor-in-chief. Ithaca: Snow Lion.

2004 *The Great Treatise on the Stages of the Path to Enlightenment*. Vol. II. Trans. by the Lamrim Chenmo Translation Committee with Joshua Culter as editor-in-chief. Ithaca: Snow Lion.

2005 *Yoga Tantra: Paths to Magical Feats* [book 3 of the *Great Exposition of Secret Mantra* series], intro. by H.H. Tenzin Gyatso, the Fourteenth Dalai Lama; trans. & ed. by Jeffery Hopkins. Ithaca: Snow Lion.

2005 *Tantric Ethics: An Explanation of the Precepts for Buddhist Vajrayāna Practice* [Study and translation of Tsong Khapa's *Explanation of the Root (Tantric) Downfalls*]. Translated and introduced by Gareth Sparham. Boston: Wisdom Publications.

2010 *Brilliant Illumination of the Lamp of the Five Stages (rim lnga rab tu gsal ba'i sgron me)*. Introduction and Translation by Robert A.F. Thurman. Edited by Thomas F. Yarnall. New York: American Institute of Buddhist Studies.

Tucci, Giuseppe

1958 *Minor Buddhist Texts*. Part II. Serie Orientale Roma, IX, 2. [Kamalaśīla's *Bhāvanākrama I*]. Roma: Instituto Italiano per il Medio ed Estremo Oriente.

1971 *Minor Buddhist Texts*. Part III Serie Orientale Roma, XLIII. [Kamalaśīla's *Bhāvanākrama III*]. Roma: Instituto Italiano per il Medio ed Estremo Oriente.

Varela, Francisco, ed.

1997 *Sleeping, Dreaming, and Dying: An Exploration of Consciousness with The Dalai Lama*. Boston: Wisdom.

Wayman, Alex

1991 *Yoga of the Guhyasamājatantra: The Arcane Lore of Forty Verses*. Delhi: Motilal Banarsidass. [First ed. 1977]

1993 *The Buddhist Tantras: Light on Indo-Tibetan Esotericism*. Delhi: Motilal Banarsidass. [First ed. 1973]

1997 *Calming the Mind and Discerning the Real: Buddhist Meditation and the Middle View, from the Lam rim chen mo of Tsoṅ-kha-pa*, 2nd revised edition. Delhi: Motilal Banarsidass. [First ed. New York: Columbia University Press, 1978]

Wedemeyer, Christian K.

1993 "Orientalism is a Humanism?! Materials and Methods for an History and Ideological Critique of Buddhist Studies." Masters Thesis, Columbia University.

1999 "Vajrayāna and its Doubles: A Critical Historiography, Exposition, and Translation of the Tantric Works of Āryadeva." Doctoral Dissertation, Columbia University.

2007 *Āryadeva's Lamp that Integrates the Practices (Caryāmelāpakapradīpa): The Gradual Path of Vajrayāna Buddhism According to the Esoteric Community Noble Tradition*. New York: American Institute of Buddhist Studies.

2013 *Making Sense of Tantric Buddhism: History, Semiology, & Transgression in the Indian Traditions*. New York: Columbia University Press.

Wittgenstein, Ludwig

1958 *Philosophical Investigations*. Third edition. New York: Macmillan.

1969 *On Certainty*. Third edition. New York: Harper.

Yangchen Gawai Lodoe

1995 *Paths and Grounds of Guhyasamaja According to Arya Nagarjuna*. Trans. by Tenzin Dorjee and Jeremy Russel, ed. by David R. Komito and Andrew Fagan. Dharamsala: Library of Tibetan Works and Archives.

INDEXES

Index of Canonical Texts Cited

Index of Canonical Authors Cited

General Index

A

absorption, 144, 251, 278
action clan, 183
Action Tantra. *See* Tantras (types/categories)
action triumph. *See* supreme action triumph
action(s)
evolutionary. *See* evolutionary action
fabricative. *See* fabricative action(s)
four types (peaceful, prospering, dominating, destructive), 72, 187, 247, 248, 250, 256, 257
making fit for, 41, 130, 144
miraculous, 183
of body, speech, and mind, 277, 278
ritual, 77, 97, 105, 187
three sectors of, 73, 277, 282
action-vajra, 279, 280
activities. *See* action(s)
adept, xiv, 22, 111, 114, 148, 180, 196, 208, 281
Akṣhobhya, 97, 142, 149, 158, 175, 180, 183, 243, 244, 245, 265, 267, 268, 272, 277
alienated individual, 109
Amitābha, 72, 180, 183, 244, 245, 265, 268, 272, 277
Amoghasiddhi, 183, 244, 245, 265, 272, 277, 279, 280
analytic meditation, 13, 15, 17, 93, 103, 104, 156, 158, 160, 163, 207, 208
anger/hatred, 38, 80, 175, 245, 246
art(s), 8, 29, 86, 126, 188, 272
and sciences, xiv, xv, 8, 9
and wisdom, 99, 124, 178, 184, 221–223, 233, 274, 279, 280
as the cause of a buddha's form body, 29, 31, 57, 99, 238, 285
as the distinguishing feature of Mantra, 29, 31
for perfecting the stores, 277
for purifying the bases, 36, 277, 284, 285, *See also* bases of purification.
for stabilizing vivid perception, 59
artificial. *See also* fabrication; fabricative.
forms, 42
imagination, 102
methods/yogas, 6, 41, 43
nature of the creation stage, 54, 55
attracting, summoning, 123, 141, 168, 187, 199, 212, 249, 251, 259, 268, 274, *See also* inviting (deities, etc.).

B

bases of purification, 53, 58, 71, 125, 127, 185, *See also* art(s), for purifying the bases.
creation stage as indispensible for purifying, 4, 28, 43, 44, 54, 56, 70, 71, 131, 157, 187, 239, 241, 276, 284, 285
gross, subtle, and extremely subtle levels of, 35–39, 41, 55, 67, 228
homologies with paths and fruits, 66–70, 217, 228, 234, 238, *See also* homology, between base, path, and fruit *(cont'd…)*

C

D

E

intuition body. *See* body(ies) of a buddha, intuition
intuition hero/being, 58, 62, 66, 71, 123, 150, 162–164, 177, 178, 182, 186, 239–242, 250, 257, 273, 275, 276, 279
intuition(s), 142, 172, 196, 203, 205, 206, 241, 264, 274
  aftermath, 102
  body of. *See* body(ies) of a buddha, intuition
  five, 206, 218, 225, 243
    all-accomplishing, 206, 218, 225
    equalizing, 206, 218, 225
    individuating, 206, 207, 218, 225
    mirror-like, 192, 206, 218, 225
    ultimate reality, 178, 206, 218, 225
  luminance-. *See* luminance-intuition
  nectar of, 164, 242
  nonconceptual. *See* nonconceptual, intuition/realization
  nondual, xiv, 95, 96, 99, 120, 122, 209, 240
  of emptiness, 29, 133, 203, 206
  of nonduality, 277, 282
  orgasmic, 136
  pure mundane, 209
  slight mastery of. *See* slight mastery of intuition
  slightly settled. *See* slightly settled intuition
  store of. *See* stores of merit/intuition
  true mastery of. *See* true mastery of intuition
  vajra, 175
inviting (deities, etc.), 71, 164, 178, 199–201, 234, 272–274, *See also* attracting, summoning.

K

khaṭvāṅga staff, 77, 268, 271

L

luminance, 38, 42, 130, 234
luminance-intuition, 27, 28, 36, 38
lust. *See* desire/lust

M

Maitreya (Buddha), 249, *See also* entry under Author Index.
mandala triumph. *See* supreme mandala triumph
manifest enlightenment(s), 44, 58, 62, 66, 67, 174, 178, 182, 215–218, 225–227, 232, 235, 237, 238
Mañjushrī, xiv, xv, 244, 249, 281
mantra, 58, 62, 65, 66, 72, 73, 79, 96, 97, 120, 122, 132, 136, 157, 158, 160, 165, 172, 173, 175, 187, 201–207, 209, 212, 239, 246, 248–257, 276, 278, 282
  one-hundred syllable, 198, 201, 273, 274
Mantra Vehicle. *See* Vehicle, Mantra
measureless mansion, 58, 62, 66, 123, 142, 148, 165, 173, 180, 181, 213–216, 236, 275
mentor(s), 83, 86, 87, 109, 171
  as the deity host, 200
  as the root of all siddhis, 82
  commitments with respect to, 80, 82, 83, 85, 200, 280 *(cont'd...)*

N

O

S

T

U

V

W

Y